DATA PROTECTION, MIGRATION AND BORDER CONTROL

This book assesses data protection rules that are applicable to the processing of personal data in a law enforcement context. It offers the first extensive analysis of the LED and Regulation (EU) 2018/1725. It illustrates the challenges arising from the unclear delineation between the different data protection instruments at both national and EU level. Taking a practical approach, it exemplifies situations where the application of data protection instruments could give rise to a lowering of data protection standards where the data protection rules applicable in the law enforcement context are interpreted broadly. Given the scope of data protection instruments applied by law enforcement authorities, processing for border control, migration management and asylum, could all be impacted due to this unclear delineation between the different data protection instruments.

Volume 17 in the series Hart Studies in European Criminal Law

Hart Studies in European Criminal Law

Series Editors: Professor Katalin Ligeti, University of Luxembourg; Professor Valsamis Mitsilegas, Queen Mary University of London; Professor Anne Weyembergh, Brussels Free University

Since the Lisbon Treaty, European criminal law has become an increasingly important field of research and debate. Working with the European Criminal Law Academic Network (ECLAN), the series will publish works of the highest intellectual rigour and cutting edge scholarship which will be required reading for all European criminal lawyers.

The series is happy to consider both edited and single authored titles. The series defines 'European' and 'criminal law' in the broadest sense, so books on European criminal law, justice and policy will be considered. The series also welcomes books which offer different methodological approaches.

Volume 1: *EU Criminal Law after Lisbon: Rights, Trust and the Transformation of Justice in Europe*
Valsamis Mitsilegas

Volume 2: *Challenges in the Field of Economic and Financial Crime in Europe and the US*
Edited by Vanessa Franssen and Katalin Ligeti

Volume 3: *Chasing Criminal Money: Challenges and Perspectives On Asset Recovery in the EU*
Edited by Katalin Ligeti and Michele Simonato

Volume 4: *Limits to EU Powers: A Case Study of EU Regulatory Criminal Law*
Jacob Öberg

Volume 5: *The Needed Balances in EU Criminal Law: Past, Present and Future*
Edited by Chloé Brière and Anne Weyembergh

Volume 6: *Redefining Organised Crime: A Challenge for the European Union?*
Edited by Stefania Carnevale, Serena Forlati and Orsetta Giolo

Volume 7: *White Collar Crime: A Comparative Perspective*
Edited by Katalin Ligeti and Stanislaw Tosza

Volume 8: *Criminal Liability of Managers in Europe: Punishing Excessive Risk*
Stanisław Tosza

Volume 9: *The European Union and Deprivation of Liberty: A Legislative and Judicial Analysis from the Perspective of the Individual*
Leandro Mancano

Volume 10: *The Legitimacy of EU Criminal Law*
Irene Wieczorek

Volume 11: *The Fight Against Impunity in EU Law*
Edited by Luisa Marin and Stefano Montaldo

Volume 12: *Controlling Immigration Through Criminal Law: European and Comparative Perspectives on 'Crimmigration'*
Edited by Gian Luigi Gatta, Valsamis Mitsilegas, and Stefano Zirulia

Volume 13: *The Principle of Mutual Trust in EU Criminal Law*
Auke Willems

Volume 14: *Surveillance and Privacy in the Digital Age: European, Transatlantic and Global Perspectives*
Edited by Valsamis Mitsilegas and Niovi Vavoula

Volume 15: *The External Dimension of the EU's Policy against Trafficking in Human Beings*
Chloé Brière

Volume 16: *Criminal and Quasi-criminal Enforcement Mechanisms in Europe: Origins, Concepts, Future*
Edited by Vanessa Franssen and Christopher Harding

Volume 17: *Data protection, Migration and Border Control: The GDPR, the Law Enforcement Directive and Beyond*
Teresa Quintel

Data Protection, Migration and Border Control

The GDPR, the Law Enforcement Directive and Beyond

Teresa Quintel

•HART•

OXFORD • LONDON • NEW YORK • NEW DELHI • SYDNEY

HART PUBLISHING

Bloomsbury Publishing Plc

Kemp House, Chawley Park, Cumnor Hill, Oxford, OX2 9PH, UK

1385 Broadway, New York, NY 10018, USA

29 Earlsfort Terrace, Dublin 2, Ireland

First published in Great Britain 2022

A catalogue record for this book is available from the British Library.

A catalogue record for this book is available from the Library of Congress.

ISBN: HB: 978-1-50995-963-1
ePDF: 978-1-50995-965-5
ePub: 978-1-50995-964-8

Typeset by Compuscript Ltd, Shannon

To my husband Juraj

PREFACE

In the aftermath of increased migration flows coming to Europe in 2015, the so-called *migration crisis*, irregular migration and related crimes such as migrant smuggling and human trafficking became a hotly debated topic at the European Union (EU) level. The results of those discussions were the fortification of the EU's external borders, the strengthening of the mandate of the relevant EU Agencies and the establishment of new databases in the Area of Freedom, Security and Justice (AFSJ). As a final step, the European Commission was tasked with examining the possibility of establishing a legal framework to enable the sharing of information among the different databases. The long-term objective was rendering all existing and anticipated AFSJ databases interoperable in order to create more comprehensive profiles of third-country nationals (TCNs) with all the available data. Migration management, border control and asylum had become a relevant element in the debate of internal security within the EU with a strong focus on the processing of personal data in that context.

In May 2018, the EU Data Protection Reform entered into force and introduced, besides a Regulation covering personal data processing of general nature (the General Data Protection Regulation (GDPR)) and a Directive applicable to the processing of personal data carried out in the context of police and criminal justice (the Law Enforcement Directive (LED)). The Reform had become both necessary and possible after the entry into force of the Lisbon Treaty and the Charter of Fundamental Rights of the European Union becoming legally binding. In addition, under Article 16 of the Treaty on the Functioning of the European Union, the European Parliament as new co-legislator obtained a robust mandate to adopt, together with the Council, solid data protection rules, also in the former Third Pillar. While the GDPR emphasises the principle of transparency, in the law enforcement context many processing operations may be carried out in secrecy and without involving the individual whose personal data are processed.

Where migration and related crimes are increasingly treated as security concerns, the scope of the LED may be widened to include processing of personal data of TCNs in the area of border control. Hence, while data protection rules should apply to everyone in the EU irrespective of their nationality, in the context of border control, migration management and asylum, where personal data are needed for the assessment of TCNs, the rights of those individuals are seemingly of a secondary nature compared to those of EU citizens.

Taking into account the difference made between general processing and processing for law enforcement purposes under EU data protection law, and a potential division between certain groups of persons (in this case EU citizens and TCNs), the following questions will be answered: how are TCNs affected by the unclear delineation between different data protection laws and what solutions could clarify this delineation?

While answering these questions, this volume demonstrates that, in the area of migration, border control and asylum, EU data protection law potentially allows for a lowering of data protection rights of TCNs. The assessment emphasises the way in which legislative texts inherently criminalise migrants, for instance, by streamlining law enforcement access to personal data of TCNs stored in non-law enforcement AFSJ databases. The analysis identifies situations in which data protection rules originally determined for the law enforcement context may be applied in the area of migration. Further, potential risks for TCNs as data subjects at both the national and EU levels are exemplified. The concluding remarks propose several amendments to existing data protection laws in the law enforcement area that could contribute to a clearer delineation between general rules and law enforcement rules, and thereby prevent the latter from being applied to processing in a non-law enforcement context.

ACKNOWLEDGEMENTS

I would like to thank my supervisors for their support, both work-related and privately, for believing in my research topic and for always standing behind my decisions: *Professor Mark D Cole*, who accepted me as his PhD candidate and supported all my projects without questioning my abilities. *Professor Maria Bergström* who could not have been more supportive from the moment I sent her my first email.

I would also like to thank the members of my defence jury: *Professor Stefan Braum*, *Professor Eleni Kosta*, *Professor Anna-Sara Lind*, *Professor Vagelis Papakonstantinou* and *Professor Wojciech Wiewiórowski*.

Thanks are due to my parents and my brother, who always backed me up in my decisions and helped me whenever they could, especially during the last months before submitting my dissertation.

Special thanks to my colleagues *Carsten Ullrich*, *Julia Sinnig* and *Fabio Guiffrida*, not only for their very helpful comments, but also for many nice moments spent together, and to *Justin Jütte*, who helped me with my PhD application and without whom I would not be where I am today. Special thanks also to *Cosimo Monda* and the ECPC team for their support.

Of course, I would like to thank *Anna Moscibroda* and *Diana Alonso Blas* for their very insightful comments and for having taken the time to provide them, as well as *Niovi Vavoula*, *Nora Buol*, *James Galand-Jones*, *Gavin Robinson* and *Rebecca Thorburn Stern* for reading respective sections of my dissertation.

Finally, I would like to thank *Olof Klingström* for encouraging me to start this PhD, *John Stanley Hunter* for standing by my side whenever needed and my colleagues *Desarah Dushi*, *Emma Salemme*, *Simona Demková*, *Maxime Lassalle*, *Erdal Demir*, *Ioannis Asimakopoulos* and *Angelica Maria Ahumada Fernandez* for their moral support. Most importantly, my children, who showed me that there is something much more important in life than work.

CONTENTS

ABBREVIATIONS

AFSJ	Area of Freedom, Security and Justice
AI	Artificial Intelligence
API	Advanced Passenger Information
BMS	Biometric Matching Service
CEAS	Common European Asylum System
CIR	Common Identity Repository
CISA	Convention Implementing the Schengen Agreement
CJEU	Court of Justice of the European Union
CoE	Council of Europe
CSDP	Common Security and Defence Policy
DG	Directorate-General
DPA	Data Protection Authority
DPO	Data Protection Officer
DPFD	Data Protection Framework Decision
DPIA	Data Protection Impact Assessment
EASO	European Asylum Support Office
EBCGA	European Border and Coast Guard Agency
ECHR	European Convention on Human Rights
ECRIS	European Criminal Records Information System
ECRIS-TCN	European Criminal Records Information System for Third-Country Nationals and Stateless Persons
ECtHR	European Court of Human Rights
EDPB	European Data Protection Board
EDPS	European Data Protection Supervisor
EDU	European Drugs Unit

EEAS	European External Action Service
EES	Entry/Exit System
EMN	European Migration Network
EMSC	European Migrant Smuggling Centre
EPPO	European Public Prosecutor's Office
ESP	European Search Portal
ESTA	Electronic System for Travel Authorization
ETA	Electronic Travel Authorization
ETIAS	European Travel Information and Authorization System
EU	European Union
EU Charter	European Union Charter of Fundamental Rights
EUAA	European Union Agency for Asylum
eu-LISA	European Union Agency for the Operational Management of Large-Scale IT Systems in the Area of Freedom, Security and Justice
Eurodac	European Dactyloscopy
Eurojust	European Union Agency for Criminal Justice Cooperation
EUROSUR	European Border Surveillance System
FADO	False and Authentic Documents Online
FRA	European Union Agency for Fundamental Rights
FRONTEX	European Border and Coast Guard Agency
FSC	Frontex Situation Centre
GDPR	General Data Protection Regulation
IFC	Information Fusion Centre
IOM	International Organization for Migration
JHA	Justice and Home Affairs
JIT	Joint Investigation Team
JSA	Joint Supervisory Authority
JSB	Joint Supervisory Body
LEA	Law Enforcement Authority

LED	Law Enforcement Directive
MEP	Member of Parliament
MID	Multiple Identity Detector
OLAF	European Anti-Fraud Office
PNR	Passenger Name Record
RABIT	Rapid Border Intervention Teams
RTP	Registered Traveller Programme
SCC	Standard Contractual Clause
SIRENE	Supplementary Information Request at the National Entries
SIS I	First Generation Schengen Information System
SIS II	Second Generation Schengen Information System
SIS III	Third Generation Schengen Information System
SLTD	Stolen and Lost Travel Documents database
TCN	Third-Country National
TDAWN	Travel Documents Associated with Notices database
TEU	Treaty on European Union
TFEU	Treaty on the Functioning of the European Union
VIS	Visa Information System

CASES AND LEGISLATION

Case Law

Court of Justice of the European Union

European Court of Human Rights

Supranational and Intergovernmental Legislation

Proposals for EU Legislation

Introduction

The Emergence of Multiple Function Creeps

In a world where more and more data are available and used to generate unprecedented insights into behaviour, governments progressively seek to exploit data analytics for law enforcement and national security purposes, as well as in the field of migration and border control. Data analytics are not only valuable for retroactively restoring facts related to a crime or for forecasting criminal behaviour, but may also be used for immigration monitoring and in taking decisions to grant international protection, or to prevent illegal entry into a territory.[1]

In recent years, migration has become a crucial element in the debate on internal security within the European Union (EU) and its Member States. In many EU Member States, this security debate reached new dimensions during the aftermath of the arrival of great numbers of individuals seeking asylum in the EU in 2015. The belief that many of those coming to the EU might be infiltrated by radicals and could commit terrorist acts in the receiving Member States led to calls for increased security measures.[2] The latter certainly affected and still affect asylum seekers and other third-country nationals (TCNs),[3] whether on justified grounds or not.

[1] See Tal Zarsky, 'Incompatible: The GDPR in the Age of Big Data' (2017) 47 No 4(2) *Seton Hall Law Review* 995–1020; Tal Z Zarsky, 'Transparent Predictions' (2013) 2013(4) *University of Illinois Law Review* 1503–1570; and Douwe Korff, 'New Challenges to Data Protection Study – Working Paper No. 2: Data Protection Laws in the EU: The Difficulties in Meeting the Challenges Posed by Global Social and Technical Developments' (January 15, 2010). European Commission DG Justice, Freedom and Security Report, Available at SSRN: https://ssrn.com/abstract=1638949 or http://dx.doi.org/10.2139/ssrn.1638949.

[2] European Commission, 'Preventing the Risk of Radicalisation of Asylum Seekers and Refugees, and Far-Right Mobilisation against Asylum Seekers, Refugees and Immigrants, December 2019' (17 January 2020), https://ec.europa.eu/home-affairs/pages/page/preventing-risk-radicalisation-asylum-seekers-and-refugees-and-far-right-mobilisation-against-asylum_en.

[3] 'Third-country national' means a person who is not a citizen of the EU within the meaning of art 20(1) of the Treaty on the Functioning of the European Union (TFEU), or who is a stateless person or a person whose nationality is unknown. 'Other TCNs' means, for instance, visa applicants or migrants in an irregular situation. The latter shall be understood as defined by the International Organization for Migration (IOM) as: 'Movement that takes place outside the regulatory norms of the sending, transit and receiving countries. From the perspective of destination countries, it is entry, stay or work in a country without the necessary authorization or documents required under immigration regulations.'

With the European Agendas on Security[4] and on Migration,[5] as well as the EU Security Union Strategy[6] and the New Pact on Asylum and Migration,[7] the EU set the direction to address the parallel challenges of migration management and the fight against terrorism and organised crime. The call for an increased use of large-scale databases set up at the EU level in order to improve the management of migration flows by facilitating information exchanges between law enforcement authorities (LEAs) emanated in particular from the Member States.[8] These large-scale databases had been set up at different times in order to better manage visa applications,[9] register the country of first entry of an asylum seeker,[10] and enable competent authorities to enter and consult alerts on persons or objects.[11]

In recent years, the European Commission (hereinafter 'the Commission') has proposed changes on the expansion of the main operational databases in order to enable the storage of additional information and to widen access to data by LEAs.[12] In addition, proposals issued by the Commission on the establishment of new systems that should close the alleged information gap by covering those TCNs' personal data that had not been stored in the existing databases were approved in the trilogues. As a final step, the Commission was tasked with examining the possibility of establishing a legal framework to enable the sharing of information

[4] European Commission, 'Communication from the Commission to the European Parliament, the Council, the European Economic and Social Committee and the Committee of the Regions. The European Agenda on Security' COM (2015) 185 final, Strasbourg, 28 April 2015.

[5] European Commission, 'Communication from the Commission to the European Parliament, the Council, the European Economic and Social Committee and the Committee of the Regions. The European Agenda on Migration' COM (2015) 240 final, Brussels, 13 May 2015.

[6] European Commission, 'Communication from the Commission to the European Parliament, the European Council, the Council, the European Economic and Social Committee and the Committee of the Regions on the EU Security Union Strategy' COM (2020) 605 final, Brussels, 24 July 2020.

[7] European Commission, 'Communication from the Commission to the European Parliament, the Council, the European Economic and Social Committee and the Committee of the Regions on a New Pact on Migration and Asylum' COM (2020) 609 final, Brussels, 23 September 2020.

[8] Alyna C Smith and Michele LeVoy, 'Mo'databases, Mo'problems? The EU's New Interoperability Systems and Enhanced Policing of Third Country Nationals – Migration Policy Centre – MPC', https://migrationpolicycentre.eu/databases-eu-new-interoperability-systems.

[9] European Commission, 'Visa Information System (VIS)' (6 December 2016), https://ec.europa.eu/home-affairs/what-we-do/policies/borders-and-visas/visa-information-system_en; Hartmut Aden, 'Interoperability between EU Policing and Migration Databases: Risks for Privacy' (2020) 26 *European Public Law* 93; 'Statewatch | Databases for Deportations', https://www.statewatch.org/deportation-union-rights-accountability-and-the-eu-s-push-to-increase-forced-removals/deportations-at-the-heart-of-eu-migration-policy/databases-for-deportations.

[10] European Commission, 'Identification of Applicants (EURODAC)' (6 December 2016), https://ec.europa.eu/home-affairs/what-we-do/policies/asylum/identification-of-applicants_en.

[11] European Commission, 'Schengen Information System' (6 December 2016), https://ec.europa.eu/home-affairs/what-we-do/policies/borders-and-visas/schengen-information-system_en.

[12] Niovi Vavoula, 'Interoperability of European Centralised Databases: Another Nail in the Coffin of Third-Country Nationals' Privacy? – EU Immigration and Asylum Law and Policy', https://eumigrationlawblog.eu/interoperability-of-european-centralised-databases-another-nail-in-the-coffin-of-third-country-nationals-privacy.

among the different databases.[13] The long-term objective of rendering all existing and anticipated EU databases interoperable in order to create more comprehensive profiles of TCNs, with all data available in the underlying systems, materialised at the end of 2017. Two proposals for an interoperable framework between EU databases were issued by the Commission in December 2017[14] and adopted by the co-legislators in April 2019.[15] The Interoperability Regulations introduced considerable changes to those databases (the underlying databases) that would feed the interoperable system with information and personal data,[16] as well as to the competences of both national and EU authorities and agencies. The interoperability initiative was followed by a proposal for a so-called Screening Regulation,[17] which would put forward changes to one of the Interoperability Regulations by introducing a pre-entry screening procedure allowing national authorities at external borders to channel irregular TCNs.[18]

At the same time, national legislation in the Member States was amended in order to respond to the *migration crisis*.[19] In many instances, asylum laws became

[13] European Commission, 'Communication from the Commission to the European Parliament and to Council Stronger and Smarter Information Systems for Borders and Security' COM (2016) 205 final, Brussels, 6 April 2016.

[14] 'Proposal for a Regulation of the European Parliament and of the Council on establishing a framework for interoperability between EU information systems (police and judicial cooperation, asylum and migration)' COM (2017) 794 final, Brussels, 12 December 2017; and 'Proposal for a Regulation of the European Parliament and of the Council on establishing a framework for interoperability between EU information systems (borders and visa) and amending Council Decision 2004/512/EC, Regulation (EC) No 767/2008, Council Decision 2008/633/JHA, Regulation (EU) 2016/399 and Regulation (EU) 2017/2226' COM (2017) 793 final, Strasbourg, 12 December 2017.

[15] Regulation (EU) 2019/817 of the European Parliament and of the Council of 20 May 2019 on establishing a framework for interoperability between EU information systems in the field of borders and visa and amending Regulations (EC) No 767/2008, (EU) 2016/399, (EU) 2017/2226, (EU) 2018/1240, (EU) 2018/1726 and (EU) 2018/1861 of the European Parliament and of the Council and Council Decisions 2004/512/EC and 2008/633/JHA [2019] OJ L135/27; Regulation (EU) 2019/818 of the European Parliament and of the Council of 20 May 2019 on establishing a framework for interoperability between EU information systems in the field of police and judicial cooperation, asylum and migration and amending Regulations (EU) 2018/1726, (EU) 2018/1862 and (EU) 2019/816 [2019] OJ L135/85; Regulation (EU) 2019/818 of the European Parliament and of the Council on establishing a framework for interoperability between EU information systems in the field of police and judicial cooperation, asylum and migration and amending Regulations (EU) 2018/1726, (EU) 2018/1862 and (EU) 2019/816 [2019] OJ L135/85.

[16] See the European Travel Information and Authorization System (ETIAS) consequential amendments: Regulation (EU) 2021/1150 of the European Parliament and of the Council of 7 July 2021 amending Regulations (EU) 2018/1862 and (EU) 2019/818 as regards the establishment of the conditions for accessing other EU information systems for the purposes of the European Travel Information and Authorisation System [2021] OJ L249/1; and Regulation (EU) 2021/1151 of the European Parliament and of the Council amending Regulations (EU) 2019/816 and (EU) 2019/818 as regards the establishment of the conditions for accessing other EU information systems for the purposes of the European Travel Information and Authorisation System [2021] OJ L249/7.

[17] 'Proposal for a Regulation of the European Parliament and of the Council introducing a screening of third country nationals at the external borders and amending Regulations (EC) No 767/2008, (EU) 2017/2226, (EU) 2018/1240 and (EU) 2019/817' COM (2020) 612 final, Brussels, 23 September 2020.

[18] European Parliament, 'Legislative Train Schedule: Screening of Third Country Nationals at the External Borders', https://www.europarl.europa.eu/legislative-train.

[19] The term 'migration crisis' is given in italics throughout to emphasise that it is used in a colloquial sense without implying that the author qualifies this phenomenon as a crisis. See European Parliament,

stricter and often required the collection of additional personal data of TCNs.[20] At the EU level, the role of EU Agencies was strengthened, for instance, with the entry into force of a new European Border and Coast Guard Agency (EBCGA, formerly called Frontex) Regulation[21] and a recast Europol Regulation.[22] Already before the changes to their founding acts, those EU Agencies were attributed a greater operational role in the processing of personal data, including (or particularly) those of TCNs.[23]

Personal data, and the protection thereof, had been the pivotal motif of a legislative reform that was adopted in May 2016. Hence, only one year before the above-mentioned legislative developments took place, the rights of individuals in the area of data protection were significantly strengthened with the so-called EU Data Protection Reform, which entered into force in May 2018.[24] The EU Data Protection Reform consisted of two instruments: the General Data Protection Regulation (GDPR)[25] and a Directive[26] that should apply where personal data would be processed by competent LEAs for law enforcement purposes. In 2018, these two laws were complemented by a Regulation[27] that introduced amendments to the data protection rules applicable at the EU level.[28]

'Europe's Migration Crisis' (30 June 2017), https://www.europarl.europa.eu/news/en/headlines/society/20170629STO78631/europe-s-migration-crisis.

[20] See, for instance, §15a of the German Asylum Law (AsylG), 'Auswertung von Datenträgern' (analysis of data mediums).

[21] Regulation (EU) 2019/1896 of the European Parliament and of the Council of 13 November 2019 on the European Border and Coast Guard and repealing Regulations (EU) No 1052/2013 and (EU) 2016/1624 [2019] OJ L295/1.

[22] 'Proposal for a Regulation of the European Parliament and of the Council amending Regulation (EU) 2016/794, as regards Europol's cooperation with private parties, the processing of personal data by Europol in support of criminal investigations, and Europol's role on research and innovation' COM (2020) 796 final, Brussels, 9 December 2020.

[23] In that regard, see David Fernandez-Rojo, 'Regulation 2019/1896 on the European Border and Coast Guard Agency (FRONTEX)' (*Caught You Red-Handed*, 14 November 2019), https://caughtredhanded.ideasoneurope.eu/2019/11/14/regulation-2019-1896-on-the-european-border-and-coast-guard-agency-frontex.

[24] European Commission, 'Reform of EU Data Protection Rules', https://ec.europa.eu/info/law/law-topic/data-protection/reform_en.

[25] Regulation (EU) 2016/679 of the European Parliament and of the Council of 27 April 2016 on the protection of natural persons with regard to the processing of personal data and on the free movement of such data, and repealing Directive 95/46/EC (General Data Protection Regulation) [2016] OJ L119/1.

[26] Directive (EU) 2016/680 of the European Parliament and of the Council of 27 April 2016 on the protection of natural persons with regard to the processing of personal data by competent authorities for the purposes of the prevention, investigation, detection or prosecution of criminal offences or the execution of criminal penalties, and on the free movement of such data, and repealing Council Framework Decision 2008/977/JHA [2016] OJ L119/89.

[27] Regulation (EU) 2018/1725 of the European Parliament and of the Council of 23 October 2018 on the protection of natural persons with regard to the processing of personal data by the Union institutions, bodies, offices and agencies and on the free movement of such data, and repealing Regulation (EC) No 45/2001 and Decision No 1247/2002/EC [2018] OJ L295/39.

[28] These rules do not apply to the European Public Prosecutor's Office (EPPO), which would only apply Regulation (EU) 2018/1725 to the processing of administrative personal data.

The EU Data Protection Reform had become both necessary and possible with the entry into force of the Lisbon Treaty and the Charter of Fundamental Rights of the European Union (hereinafter 'the EU Charter') obtaining full legal effect. Similarly, since the entry into force of the Lisbon Treaty, the Court of Justice of the European Union (CJEU) had progressively bolstered the rights of data subjects through its case law,[29] relying on Articles 7 and 8 of the EU Charter.

Both the provisions that form part of the EU Data Protection Reform and the rights under Articles 7 and 8 of the EU Charter apply to everyone in the EU, irrespective of nationality. Yet, in the context of border control and migration management, where personal data are needed for the assessment of TCNs, the rights of those individuals are seemingly of a secondary nature.

In the area of migration, border control and asylum, EU data protection law potentially allows for a lowering of the data protection rights of TCNs. The assessment specifically considers the way in which the personal data of TCNs are accessed and processed by competent (law enforcement) authorities at both the national and EU levels. In certain situations, data protection rules originally determined for the law enforcement context may be applied in the area of migration. On the one hand, the interoperable framework of EU databases adds to the trend to progressively increase the use of TCNs' personal data by various authorities and agencies. On the other hand, the handling of certain groups of individuals 'as security threats' affects the privacy and data protection rights of all TCNs who wish to come to the EU. In other words, where TCNs would be seen as security threats, competent authorities could revert to the less robust data protection rules under the Directive instead of those under the GDPR.

In this context, it is of particular importance which specific data protection instrument applies. In EU data protection law, the purpose of the processing and the authority processing the data determine the applicability of different sets of rules. Hence, whereas EU data protection law (theoretically) grants strong rights to individuals in the field of border control, migration and asylum, in a security-related context and in the area of criminal justice, competent authorities need to be able to apply the data protection rules more flexibly and are granted more leeway to restrict the data subject rights of individuals.

However, the delineation between those rules may prove difficult, as the events that occurred in recent years and in the aftermath of the *migration crisis* have not

[29] For cases concerning data retention and mass surveillance, see: CJEU, Case C-301/06, *Ireland v European Parliament and Council*, ECLI:EU:C:2009:68, 10 February 2009; CJEU, Joined Cases C-293/12 and C-594/12, *Digital Rights Ireland Ltd* (C-293/12) and *Seitlinger* (C-594/12), ECLI:EU:C:2014:238, 8 April 2014; CJEU, Case C-362/14, *Maximillian Schrems v Data Protection Commissioner*, ECLI:EU:C:2015:650, 6 October 2015; CJEU, Joined Cases C-203/15 and C-698/15, *Tele2 Sverige AB* (C-203/15) and *Watson* (C-698/15), ECLI:EU:C:2016:970, 21 December 2016; CJEU, *Opinion 1/15* on the Draft PNR Agreement between the EU and the US, ECLI:EU:C:2017:592, 26 July 2017; CJEU, Case C-311/18, *Data Protection Commissioner v Facebook Ireland Ltd and Maximillian Schrems*, ECLI:EU:C:2020:559, 16 July 2020; CJEU, Joined Cases C-511/18, C-512/18 and C-520/18, *La Quadrature du Net*, ECLI:EU:C:2020:791, 6 October 2020.

only led to the above-mentioned revision of many legal instruments in that area, but have also blurred the line between migration and security, migration law and criminal law.

The reform of the EU data protection framework, which was proposed in 2012,[30] was agreed during the 2015 Luxembourg Presidency[31] and was eventually adopted in April 2016,[32] contributed to an increased public awareness regarding data protection rules. In particular, the GDPR, which replaced Directive 95/46/EC[33] from 1995 (hereinafter the '95 Data Protection Directive'), attracted attention. As mentioned above, alongside the GDPR, the EU Data Protection Reform encompassed Directive (EU) 2016/680 (the Law Enforcement Directive, hereinafter LED or 'the Directive'), which established rules for the protection of individuals with regard to the processing of personal data by competent authorities for law enforcement purposes. The Directive was to be transposed into the national laws of the EU Member States by 6 May 2018[34] and put forward new rules in an area that had previously not been substantially regulated by EU law.[35]

The negotiations on both legal instruments – the GDPR and the LED – took place during the 'peak' of the *migration crisis*, which had triggered a debate on the shortcomings of the Common European Asylum System (CEAS), including the Dublin framework,[36] according to which the first country of entry in the EU is responsible for examining an asylum application.[37] The lack of coordination among the Member States regarding the registration and distribution of those

[30] 'Proposal for a Regulation of the European Parliament and of the Council on the protection of individuals with regard to the processing of personal data and on the free movement of such data (General Data Protection Regulation)' COM (2012)11 final, Brussels, 25 January 2012; and 'Proposal for a Directive of the European Parliament and of the Council on the protection of individuals with regard to the processing of personal data by competent authorities for the purposes of prevention, investigation, detection or prosecution of criminal offences or the execution of criminal penalties, and the free movement of such data' COM (2012) 10 final, Brussels, 25 January 2012.

[31] Luxembourg Presidency, 'Luxembourg Presents the Achievements of its Presidency of the Council of the European Union', www.eu2015lu.eu//en/actualites/communiques/2015/12/31-bilan/index.html.

[32] European Commission, 'Joint Statement on the Final Adoption of the New EU Rules for Personal Data Protection', https://ec.europa.eu/commission/presscorner/detail/en/STATEMENT_16_1403.

[33] Directive 95/46/EC of the European Parliament and of the Council of 24 October 1995 on the protection of individuals with regard to the processing of personal data and on the free movement of such data [1995] OJ L281/31.

[34] Teresa Quintel, 'Follow the Money, If You Can – Possible Solutions for Enhanced FIU Cooperation under Improved Data Protection Rules' (31 January 2019), http://dx.doi.org/10.2139/ssrn.3318299.

[35] Juraj Sajfert and Teresa Quintel, 'Data Protection Directive (EU) 2016/680 for Police and Criminal Justice Authorities' (1 December 2017_, https://papers.ssrn.com/sol3/papers.cfm?abstract_id=3285873.

[36] Anja Radjenovic, 'Reform of the Dublin System', European Parliamentary Research Service (2019), https://www.europarl.europa.eu/RegData/etudes/BRIE/2016/586639/EPRS_BRI(2016)586639_EN.pdf. On 23 September 2020, the European Commission presented a new proposal for a regulation on asylum and migration management, in which it indicated that the present proposal would be formally withdrawn.

[37] European Commission, 'Country Responsible for Asylum Application (Dublin)' (6 December 2016), https://ec.europa.eu/home-affairs/what-we-do/policies/asylum/examination-of-applicants_en.

who came or desired to come to the EU evolved into an ardently debated topic. The acknowledgement that large numbers of individuals had not been registered by the authorities in the first country of entry and were able to cross the entire EU without being stopped further intensified the criticism towards the (lack of) external border controls, and incentivised calls to 'regain control over the national borders'.[38]

Against the background of these migratory challenges, the Luxembourg Presidency (which ran from 1 July 2015 to 31 December 2015) identified priority actions such as the strengthening of border controls at the external borders of the EU, improving the exchange of information among the authorities of the Member States and making more systematic use of EU databases.[39] The Commission sought to counter a rising nationalism and the lack of information sharing by issuing several proposals on the reform of existing (and the creation of new) databases, or by strengthening the mandate of those EU Agencies that were involved in the management of the external borders.

TCNs such as visa applicants, (irregular) migrants and asylum seekers are subject to certain types of profiling measures when they apply for a visa in the EU or are in the process of being registered in the receiving countries.[40] In order to determine whether an individual may be granted a visa, the personal details of the applicant are examined by the respective visa authorities. In the case of asylum applications, information regarding the route via which the person applying for international protection arrived in the recipient state is thoroughly scrutinised.

Such administrative processing for the determination of visa eligibility or refugee status falls within the scope of the GDPR. On the other hand, for processing that is carried out for the prevention, investigation, detection or prosecution of criminal offences, the LED applies. Hence, where national competent authorities such as the police, prosecutors or criminal judges process personal data for preventative and investigatory purposes, or to prosecute perpetrators, such processing falls within the scope of the Directive. However, due to differences between national orders in the field of criminal law and the heterogeneous definitions in the criminal codes of the Member States, no coherent definition of *crime* exists in the EU. Although some legislative instruments (such as the European Arrest Warrant and the Europol Regulation) provide a list of serious crime, outside those

[38] This debate is nothing new. See Randall Hansen and Demetrios G Papademetriou, 'Securing Borders: The Intended, Unintended, and Perverse Consequences (January 2014)' [2014] *Migration Policy Institute* 21.

[39] Luxembourg Presidency, 'On Behalf of the Presidency of the Council, Luxembourg Minister Nicolas Schmit Presented the Renewed EU Internal Security Strategy to the European Parliament in Plenary Session', www.eu2015lu.eu//en/actualites/articles-actualite/2015/07/pe-schmit-strategie-securite/index.html.

[40] Jans Jeroen, 'Profiling of Asylum Seekers' (2010), https://www.unhcr.org/uk/50aa05599.pdf.

rules, Member States have more or less full autonomy to define what constitutes a criminal offence under their national laws.[41]

Taking a look at the list of serious crimes pursuant to EU law, many of the offences referred to in the relevant EU provisions[42] may be attributable to (irregular) migration and, irrespective of whether TCNs are perpetrators or victims, the link to such criminal offences may lead to the inclusion of their personal data in relevant EU databases. In addition, several EU Member States criminalise irregular entry and stay under national law.[43] Thus, it may seem logical to assume that irregular migrants, asylum seekers and other TCNs are likely to become subject to additional processing measures carried out by competent LEAs. Whether TCNs arrive in the EU with the assistance of human traffickers, are under suspicion of being terrorists or have used forged travel documents to enter the EU, all scenarios would be valid grounds to process their personal data with a view to detecting, preventing, investigating or prosecuting crime.

Being able to generate in-depth knowledge about migration routes and improving the identification of individuals enhances the control over TCNs who come to the EU and creates opportunities to better monitor immigration. The collection and analysis of TCNs' personal data not only takes place in the event of (suspected) crime, but also generally commences with the storage of their data in large-scale databases before, and as soon as, they enter the territory of an EU Member State. At the EU level, large-scale IT systems store the personal data of visa applicants, asylum seekers, missing persons and criminals, and are supposed to store the data of visa-exempted travellers, rejected asylum seekers and so-called overstayers, as well as data relating to criminal records of TCNs in the near future.[44]

Under the previous founding acts of the underlying databases, LEAs were, in specific cases, authorised to access TCNs' personal data that are stored in purely

[41] The list of crimes in the European Arrest Warrant Framework Decision or the Europol Regulation may lack relevance, as it is indeed a list without any definition whatsoever. What instead may have to be acknowledged is the fact that there are several EU Directives that expressly harmonise some crimes (terrorism, fraud against the EU budget, euro counterfeiting etc). It is true that, being Directives, it is for the Member States to eventually implement them, yet it is also true that, with regard to these forms of crime, more consistency now exists throughout the EU.

[42] Listing, for instance, terrorism, forgery of administrative documents, trafficking in human beings, facilitating unauthorised entry and residence, or arson as serious crimes. See, for example, art 2(2) of Framework Decision 2002/584/JHA of 13 June 2002 on the European Arrest Warrant and the Surrender Procedures between Member States [2002] OJ L190/1; arts 1–4 of Council Framework Decision 2002/475/JHA of 13 June 2002 on combating terrorism [2002] OJ L164/3; Annex II of Directive 2016/681 of the European Parliament and of the Council of 27 April 2016 on the use of passenger name record (PNR) data for the prevention, detection, investigation and prosecution of terrorist offences and serious crime [2016] OJ L199/132.

[43] See, for instance, European Union Agency for Fundamental Rights (FRA), 'Criminalisation of Migrants in an Irregular Situation and of Persons Engaging with Them' (27 March 2014), https://fra.europa.eu/en/publication/2014/criminalisation-migrants-irregular-situation-and-persons-engaging-them.

[44] Teresa Quintel, 'Connecting Personal Data of Third Country Nationals: Interoperability of EU Databases in the Light of the CJEU's Case Law on Data Retention' (2018), https://papers.ssrn.com/sol3/papers.cfm?abstract_id=3132506.

immigration-related databases such as the Visa Information System (VIS),[45] which retains the personal data of individuals who have applied for short-term Schengen visas.[46] Similar law enforcement access opportunities[47] exist for the Eurodac database,[48] which stores the personal data of asylum seekers who have applied for international protection in (ideally) the country of first entry. Conditions for access by LEAs are, inter alia, reasonable grounds that access to the VIS will contribute to the prevention, detection or investigation of serious crime, verification by the designated authorities and limited access to certain categories of personal data.[49] These requirements are very similar regarding access to the Eurodac database.

It is foreseen that law enforcement access to both the VIS and the Eurodac database will be facilitated in the future.[50] In addition, more personal data of TCNs will be stored in additional databases and further access opportunities will be provided to more authorities.[51] On the one hand, new databases will be established

[45] Regulation (EC) 767/2008 of the European Parliament and of the Council concerning the Visa Information System (VIS) and the exchange of data between Member States on short-stay visas (VIS Regulation) [2008] OJ L218/60. The VIS Regulation is currently being amended – see 'Proposal for a Regulation of the European Parliament and the Council amending Regulation (EC) No 767/2008, Regulation (EC) No 810/2009, Regulation (EU) 2017/2226, Regulation (EU) 2016/399, Regulation XX/2018 [Interoperability Regulation], and Decision 2004/512/EC and repealing Council Decision 2008/633/JHA' COM (2018) 302 final, Brussels, 16 May 2018.

[46] Article 3(1) of Regulation (EC) No 767/2008.

[47] Article 5 of Regulation (EU) No 603/2013 of the European Parliament and of the Council of 26 June 2013 on the establishment of 'Eurodac' for the comparison of fingerprints for the effective application of Regulation (EU) No 604/2013 establishing the criteria and mechanisms for determining the Member State responsible for examining an application for international protection lodged in one of the Member States by a third-country national or a stateless person and on requests for the comparison with Eurodac data by Member States' law enforcement authorities and Europol for law enforcement purposes, and amending Regulation (EU) No 1077/2011 establishing a European Agency for the operational management of large-scale IT systems in the area of freedom, security and justice [2013] OJ L180/1 (hereinafter 'the Eurodac Regulation').

[48] Regulation (EU) No 603/2013. The Eurodac Regulation is currently being amended – see 'Proposal for a Regulation of the European Parliament and the Council on the establishment of "Eurodac" for the comparison of fingerprints for the effective application of [Regulation (EU) No 604/2013 establishing the criteria and mechanisms for determining the Member State responsible for examining an application for international protection lodged in one of the Member States by a third-country national or a stateless person], for identifying an illegally staying third-country national or stateless person and on requests for the comparison with Eurodac data by Member States' law enforcement authorities and Europol for law enforcement purposes (recast)' COM (2016) 272 final, Brussels, 4 May 2016; and 'Amended proposal for a Regulation of the European Parliament and the Council on the establishment of "Eurodac" for the comparison of biometric data for the effective application of Regulation (EU) XXX/XXX [Regulation on Asylum and Migration Management] and of Regulation (EU) XXX/XXX [Resettlement Regulation], for identifying an illegally staying third-country national or stateless person and on requests for the comparison with Eurodac data by Member States' law enforcement authorities and Europol for law enforcement purposes and amending Regulations (EU) 2018/1240 and (EU) 2019/818' COM (2020) 614 final, Brussels, 23 September 2020.

[49] Articles 4(1) and 5(2) of Council Decision 2008/633/JHA concerning access for consultation of the Visa Information System (VIS) by designated authorities of Member States and by Europol for the purposes of the prevention, detection and investigation of terrorist offences and of other serious criminal offences [2008] OJ L218/129.

[50] See, for instance, COM (2020) 614 final or COM (2018) 302 final.

[51] See, for instance, COM (2017) 793 and 794 final.

to store the personal data of visa-exempted TCNs and holders of long-term visas. On the other hand, making both existing and planned EU databases interoperable will contribute to a higher level of security within the EU by streamlining the conditions for access by designated authorities to ensure the correct identification of persons.[52]

While the EU Agency eu-LISA[53] provides the technical and operational framework for EU databases that support external border control, police and judicial cooperation, or the exchange of visa data, and is responsible for the management of the Area of Freedom, Security and Justice (AFSJ) databases,[54] national authorities act as controllers when processing personal data obtained from the databases. As mentioned above, data gathered for immigration purposes are to be processed under the GDPR, which applies to all processing of an administrative nature. Thus, whenever data are stored in EU immigration databases for identification and registration purposes, competent authorities such as embassies, border guards, immigration agencies or asylum authorities must process these data within the scope of the GDPR. Only when data in such databases are accessed and further processed by LEAs for law enforcement purposes does the LED apply.

The widening of law enforcement access to personal data is a phenomenon that is observable in many other aspects of society.[55] However, in the area of migration, such use of personal data is particularly visible and even encouraged. This raises the question, on the one hand, as to whether TCNs enjoy the same level of data protection as EU citizens and, on the other hand, to what extent it is legitimate to limit data protection rights, – for instance, when this is deemed necessary for the prevention, investigation, detection or prosecution of criminal offences. While it is not guaranteed that non-citizens should have the same rights as citizens of a country (or, in this case, territory), the EU, not only through Articles 7 and 8 of the EU Charter, but also through secondary data protection legislation, pledged itself to also confer those rights to non-EU citizens. Thereby, the right to data protection

[52] Article 2(1)(c) and 2(2)(f) of Regulation (EU) 2019/817; and Regulation (EU) 2019/818.

[53] Regulation (EU) 2018/1726 of the European Parliament and of the Council of 14 November 2018 on the European Union Agency for the Operational Management of Large-Scale IT Systems in the Area of Freedom, Security and Justice (eu-LISA), and amending Regulation (EC) No 1987/2006 and Council Decision 2007/533/JHA and repealing Regulation (EU) [2018] OJ L295/99.

[54] Within the scope of Regulation (EU) 2018/1725.

[55] For instance, with regard to passenger name record (PNR) data, Advanced Passenger Information (API) data or financial data. See, for instance, Directive (EU) 2016/681 of the European Parliament and of the Council of 27 April 2016 on the use of passenger name record (PNR) data for the prevention, detection, investigation and prosecution of terrorist offences and serious crime [2016] OJ L119/132; Study on Advance Passenger Information (API) – Evaluation of Council Directive 2004/82/EC on the obligation of carriers to communicate passenger data, final report (February 2020); Commission Staff Working Document Evaluation of the Council Directive 2004/82/EC on the obligation of carriers to communicate passenger data (API Directive), SWD(2020)174, 8 September 2020; and European Commission, 'Anti-money Laundering and Countering the Financing of Terrorism Legislative Package' (20 July 2021), https://ec.europa.eu/info/publications/210720-anti-money-laundering-countering-financing-terrorism_en.

is a very far-reaching right, not only because it applies to TCNs, but also because it could be argued that it applies extraterritorially in certain situations.[56]

Concerns may arise during different stages in which the personal data of TCNs may be processed by competent (law enforcement) authorities in the EU. Issues concerning law enforcement access to databases that were primarily set up for border control, asylum and immigration purposes are addressed against the background that there might be a justified interest on the part of LEAs in analysing personal data for investigative purposes.

As indicated above, the unclear delineation between security and migration purposes is decisive for the determination of the legal instrument applicable to the processing of personal data and thus has an impact on the way in which data may be processed. Consequently, this generates imbalances between the EU's objective to provide the highest data protection standards possible and legislation that is being proposed in the area of migration, asylum and border control (seemingly) circumventing key data protection principles.

[56] See, for instance, Dan Jerker B Svantesson, 'Extraterritoriality and Targeting in EU Data Privacy Law: The Weak Spot Undermining the Regulation' (2015) 5 *International Data Privacy Law* 226; Brendan van Alsenoy, 'Reconciling the (Extra)Territorial Reach of the GDPR with Public International Law', in Gert Vermeulen and Eva Lievens (eds) *Data Protection and Privacy under Pressure* (Maklu, 2021) 77–98.

1

The Developments Towards the Area of Freedom, Security and Justice and the Right to the Protection of Personal Data

Under EU law, the protection of natural persons in relation to the processing of personal data is a fundamental right and is stipulated in EU primary legislation.[1] The right to the protection of personal data is enshrined in Article 8 of the EU Charter and Article 16 TFEU.[2] Both state that everyone has the right to the protection of their personal data, irrespective of their nationality.[3]

The right to the protection of personal data is closely linked to the right to human dignity,[4] which in itself constitutes the basis for other fundamental rights.[5] However, unlike the right to human dignity, the right to data protection is not an absolute right and needs to be balanced against other fundamental rights and values, as well as public and private interests.[6] The conditions according to which fundamental rights may be limited in EU law are laid down under Article 52 of the EU Charter. Paragraph 1 of that provision is inspired by the case law of both the ECtHR and the CJEU,[7] and clarifies the prerequisites that must be satisfied to allow for the restriction of the rights enshrined in the EU Charter. Any limitation on EU Charter rights may be imposed if it is laid down by law, respects the essence of the rights and freedoms of the EU Charter, and if it is necessary and meets the objectives of a general interest recognised by the EU.[8]

[1] Recital 1 of Regulation (EU) 2016/679.

[2] Consolidated versions of the Treaty on European Union and the Treaty on the Functioning of the European Union (TFEU) [2016] OJ C202/1.

[3] Recital 2 of Regulation (EU) 2016/679.

[4] Article 1 of the EU Charter stipulates that human dignity is inviolable. It must be respected and protected. Council of the European Union, Charter of Fundamental Rights of the European Union [2007] OJ C303/1.

[5] 'Article 1 – Human Dignity' (25 April 2015), https://fra.europa.eu/en/charterpedia/article/1-human-dignity.

[6] European Data Protection Supervisor (EDPS), 'Data Protection' (11 November 2016), https://edps.europa.eu/data-protection/data-protection_en.

[7] See CJEU, Case C-292/97, *Kjell Karlsson and Others*, ECLI:EU:C:2000:202, 13 April 2000.

[8] Paragraph 3 of art 52 clarifies that the meaning and scope of the Charter rights shall be the same as those laid down by the European Convention on Human Rights (ECHR).

Those general interests recognised by the EU cover interests protected by specific provisions[9] of the EU Treaties and, in particular, the objectives stated under Article 3 of the Treaty on European Union (TEU).[10,11] Paragraph 2 of that Article constitutes the legal basis for the AFSJ, which was created to ensure the free movement of persons and to offer a high level of security and justice to its citizens.[12] This area without internal frontiers shall be ensured in conjunction with appropriate measures on external border controls, asylum, immigration, and the prevention and combating of crime. In that regard, Articles 67–89 under Title V TFEU on the AFSJ contain specific chapters concerning policies on border checks, asylum and immigration, judicial cooperation in civil and in criminal matters, as well as police cooperation.[13] Hence, those provisions concern areas that are traditionally core functions of national states and in which the EU Member States are generally reluctant to transfer competences and thus sovereignty to the EU.[14]

With regard to the right to the protection of personal data in the AFSJ, particular interest was devoted to the balance between privacy and security in the broader sense. When, in 1985, the Schengen Agreement[15] on the gradual abolition of the internal borders was signed by five out of the then ten European Economic Community members and, in 1990, the adoption of the Convention Implementing the Schengen Agreement (CISA)[16] followed, it could hardly be imagined that the abolition of the internal borders and the free movement of people would become one of the most important, yet controversial, achievements of the EU.

However, as indicated above, the free movement of persons is but one part of the Schengen project, the other one being security.[17] While previously, security-related measures had been regarded as merely compensatory for the

[9] Article 4(1) TEU.

[10] Consolidated Version of the Treaty on European Union [2008] OJ C115/13.

[11] 'Article 52 – Scope and Interpretation' (25 April 2015), https://fra.europa.eu/en/charterpedia/article/52-scope-and-interpretation-rights-and-principles.

[12] EUR-lex, 'Justice, Freedom and Security – EUR-Lex' <https://eur-lex.europa.eu/summary/chapter/justice_freedom_security.html?root_default=SUM_1_CODED%3D23 accessed 26 May 2020.

[13] European Parliament, 'An Area of Freedom, Security and Justice: General Aspects | Fact Sheets on the European Union', https://www.europarl.europa.eu/factsheets/en/sheet/150/an-area-of-freedom-security-and-justice-general-aspects.

[14] Florian Trauner and Ariadna Ripoll Servent, 'The Communitarization of the Area of Freedom, Security and Justice: Why Institutional Change Does Not Translate into Policy Change' (2016) 54 *JCMS: Journal of Common Market Studies* 1417.

[15] The Schengen acquis – Agreement between the Governments of the States of the Benelux Economic Union, the Federal Republic of Germany and the French Republic on the gradual abolition of checks at their common border [2000] OJ L239/13.

[16] Convention Implementing the Schengen Agreement of 14 June 1985 between the Governments of the States of the Benelux Economic Union, the Federal Republic of Germany and the French Republic, on the Gradual Abolition of Checks at their Common Borders ('Schengen Implementation Agreement') [1990] OJ L239.

[17] Markéta Votoupalová, 'Schengen Cooperation: What Scholars Make of it' (2020) 35 *Journal of Borderlands Studies* 403.

abolition of the internal borders,[18] since the 1990s, the focus progressively shifted towards Schengen cooperation. The latter included the strengthening of external border controls, information exchange between relevant Member State authorities and a general increase in security checks within the Schengen Area itself.[19] The Schengen Information System (SIS),[20] a database for the exchange of information considered relevant for cross-border investigations, became one of the most powerful tools for police cooperation in the Schengen Area. In addition to security-related provisions, the key objectives of the 1990 Dublin Convention[21] and the CISA, such as the prevention of irregular migration and the establishment of a Community-wide mechanism to deal with asylum applications, became priorities.[22]

While the Maastricht Treaty[23] still differentiated between the Second and the Third Pillars, in 1997, the Treaty of Amsterdam,[24] alongside the ambitious objective to create the AFSJ, incorporated borders, visa, immigration and asylum policies as former Third Pillar matters into the Community method. In 1999, the Tampere Conclusions[25] of the European Council marked a rather ambitious programme in that context: to fully *communitarise* more areas in the framework of establishing the AFSJ.

Besides political guidelines in the field of immigration, police and justice cooperation and the fight against crime,[26] the Member States declared their desire to develop the CEAS.[27] The latter should include common standards for a fair

[18] Emilio de Capitani, 'Progress and Failure in the Area of Freedom, Security, and Justice' in Francesca Bignami (ed), *EU Law in Populist Times: Crises and Prospects* (Cambridge University Press, 2020).

[19] Elspeth Guild, 'Moving the Borders of Europe: The Inaugural Lecture Delivered on the Occasion of the Assumption of the Professorship of the CPO Wisselleerstoel at the University of Nijmegen on 30 May, 2001', http://cmr.jur.ru.nl/cmr/docs/oratie.eg.pdf; Simone Paoli, 'Migration in European Integration: Themes and Debates' (2016) 22 *Journal of European Integration History* 279, 279–96.

[20] Constituted by three legal instruments: Regulation (EC) No 1987/2006 of the European Parliament and of the Council of 20 December 2006 on the establishment, operation and use of the second generation Schengen Information System (SIS II) [2006] OJ L381/4 on border control cooperation; Regulation (EC) No 1986/2006 of the European Parliament and of the Council of 20 December 2006 regarding access to the Second Generation Schengen Information System (SIS II) by the services in the Member States responsible for issuing vehicle registration certificates [2006] OJ L381/1 on cooperation on vehicle registration; and Council Decision 2007/533/JHA of 12 June 2007 on the establishment, operation and use of the second generation Schengen Information System (SIS II) [2007] OJ L205/63 on law enforcement cooperation.

[21] Convention Determining the State Responsible for Examining Applications for Asylum Lodged in One of the Member States of the European Communities ('Dublin Convention'), 15 June 1990, OJ C254/19.

[22] De Capitani (n 18).

[23] Treaty on European Union (Consolidated Version), Treaty of Maastricht [1992] OJ C325/5, 7 February 1992.

[24] Treaty of Amsterdam [1997] OJ C340, 10 November 1997 (entered into force 1 May 1999).

[25] Council of the European Union, Presidency Conclusions, Tampere European Council, 15–16 October 1999.

[26] European Commission, 'Tampere Council Conclusions 1999' (21 October 2013), https://ec.europa.eu/anti-trafficking/eu-policy/tampere-council-conclusions-1999_en.

[27] European Council, Presidency Conclusions of the Tampere European Council, 15–16 October 1999, Bulletin of the European Union 10/1999.

and efficient asylum procedure, common minimum conditions for the reception of asylum seekers and a mechanism for the determination of the Member State responsible for the examination of an asylum application.[28] These plans were quite ambitious considering that the Amsterdam Treaty had merely anticipated minimum harmonisation with regard to the standards of certain aspects of the national asylum systems.[29]

Compared to the Treaty of Amsterdam and the Tampere Programme, both the 2002 Nice Treaty[30] and the 2004 Hague Programme[31] introduced only limited changes and were less visionary than their predecessors. However, in the meantime, the 9/11 terrorist attacks marked a decisive turning point for the security strategy not only in the US, but also in Europe.[32] The focus was put on more police and security cooperation, and on facilitated access to (personal) data in order to ensure 'the security of the European Union and its Member States'.[33]

With the Hague Programme, and in the context of the anti-terrorist fight against Al-Qaida, the 'principle of availability'[34] became more prominent.[35] In addition, that time marked the beginning of a move towards an integrated management of the external borders of the EU Member States[36] for the fight against terrorism, illegal immigration networks and the trafficking in human beings.[37] The control

[28] 'European Parliament, 'Tampere European Council 15–16.10.1999: Conclusions of the Presidency,' https://www.europarl.europa.eu/summits/tam_en.htm#a, 1.

[29] Christian Kaunert and Sarah Léonard, 'The European Union Asylum Policy after the Treaty of Lisbon and the Stockholm Programme: Towards Supranational Governance in a Common Area of Protection?' (2012) 31 *Refugee Survey Quarterly* 1.

[30] European Union, Treaty of Nice, Amending the Treaty on European Union, the Treaties Establishing the European Communities and Certain Related Acts [2000] OJ C80, 10 March 2001.

[31] The Hague Programme: Strengthening Freedom, Security and Justice in the European Union [2004] OJ C53/01.

[32] De Capitani (n 18) 111.

[33] For a critical assessment of the framing of security and liberty in the Hague Programme, see Didier Bigo, 'Liberty, Whose Liberty? The Hague Programme and the Concept of Freedom' in Sergio Carrera and Balzacq (eds), *Security versus Freedom? A Challenge for Europe's Future* (Ashgate, 2006).

[34] The principle of availability of information is based on mutual recognition rather than uniformisation or harmonisation. It presupposes an agreement between the relevant parties on what information should be exchanged and how it should be used. In addition, it seeks to abolish external checks and controls over the exchange of information between LEAs. *cf* Didier Bigo, 'The Principle of Availability of Information, Briefing Paper PE: 378272 for Directorate-General Internal Policies Policy Unit C: Citizens' Rights and Constitutional Affairs, European Parliament' (2006), https://www.europarl.europa.eu/RegData/etudes/note/join/2006/378272/IPOL-LIBE_NT(2006)378272_EN.pdf.

[35] European Parliament, 'Briefing Paper – The Principle of Availability of Information', PE: 378272 (2006).

[36] European Commission, 'Communication from the Commission to the Council and the European Parliament, towards Integrated Management of the External Borders of the Member States of the European Union' COM (2002) 233 final, Brussels, 7 May 2002'.

[37] European Commission, 'Communication from the Commission to the Council and the European Parliament, towards Integrated Management of the External Borders of the Member States of the European Union' COM (2002) 233 final, Brussels, 7 May 2002', https://eur-lex.europa.eu/LexUriServ/LexUriServ.do?uri=COM:2002:0233:FIN:EN:PDF, 2.

of the external borders to better manage migration flows and to contribute to the prevention of terrorism[38] led to a general rise in security measures, such as increased efforts to enhance mutual legal assistance,[39] the introduction of biometric passports[40] and the adoption of the so-called 2006 Data Retention Directive,[41] which was later annulled by the CJEU in its landmark judgment in *Digital Rights Ireland*.[42]

From the 1980s and until the entry into force of the Lisbon Treaty in 2009, both cooperation on asylum and migration matters and police and judicial cooperation developed gradually, initially outside the framework of the then European Community and, with the adoption of the Treaty of Maastricht and Amsterdam, became more and more *communitarised*.[43] After the entry into force of the Treaty of Amsterdam and the creation of the First Pillar,[44] the EU developed an emergent common policy on migration, borders and asylum, despite the persistent division between the First and Third Pillars.[45]

The gradual abolition of the internal borders and the introduction of the Schengen rules considerably changed the perception of borders and the nature of border controls. The removal of border checks at the internal borders was, alongside the strengthening of external border controls and other forms of checks inside the territory of the EU Member States, to be compensated by alternative measures. The issuance of Schengen visas, the imposition of sanctions on carriers,[46] the establishment of large-scale AFSJ databases and the engagement of EU Agencies to assist Member States at the external Schengen borders were examples of such measures. In addition, border control was 'externalised', in particular to North African countries, which should serve as 'buffer zones' to prevent people

[38] In this context, the Madrid and London bombings in 2004 and 2005 respectively.

[39] Council Act of 16 October 2001 establishing, in accordance with Article 34 of the Treaty on European Union, the Protocol to the Convention on Mutual Assistance in Criminal Matters between the Member States of the European Union; see European Criminal Law Academic Network (ECLAN), 'Convention of 29 May 2000 on Mutual Assistance in Criminal Matters between the Member States of the European Union', https://eclan.eu/en/eu-legislatory/convention-of-29-may-2000-on-mutual-assistance-in-criminal-matters-between-the-member-states-of-the-european-union, 29.

[40] Council Regulation (EC) No 2252/2004 of 13 December 2004 on standards for security features and biometrics in passports and travel documents issued by Member States [2004] OJ L358/1.

[41] Directive 2006/24/EC of the European Parliament and of the Council of 15 March 2006 on the retention of data generated or processed in connection with the provision of publicly available electronic communications services or of public communications networks and amending Directive 2002/58/EC [2006] OJ L105/54.

[42] CJEU, *Digital Rights Ireland* (C-293/12) and *Seitlinger* (C-594/12), ECLI:EU:C:2014:238, 8 April 2014; *cf* Mark D Cole and Franziska Boehm, 'Data Retention after the Judgement of the Court of Justice of the European Union' (30 June 2014), https://www.zar.kit.edu/DATA/veroeffentlichungen/237_237_Boehm_Cole-Data_Retention_Study-June_2014_1a1c2f6_9906a8c.pdf.

[43] Kaunert and Léonard (n 29).

[44] Title IV of the EC Treaty on Visas, Asylum, Immigration and Other Policies Related to Free Movement of Persons, arts 61–69.

[45] Elspeth Guild and Paul Minderhoud, *The First Decade of EU Migration and Asylum Law: First Decade of EU Migration and Asylum Law* (Brill, 2011).

[46] Article 4 of Council Directive 2004/82/EC of 29 April 2004 on the obligation of carriers to communicate passenger data [2004] OJ L262/24.

transiting via Western Balkan countries such as Albania, Montenegro, Serbia, Bosnia and Herzegovina, and North Macedonia,[47] or from different parts of the African continent to continue their journey to Europe.[48]

I. Processing of Personal Data in the Law Enforcement Context

The coming into force of the Lisbon Treaty in 2009 brought, besides the considerable changes in terms of institutional setting of the Union, amendments to the legislative process and enhanced the powers for both the CJEU and the European Parliament, important novelties regarding the right to the protection of personal data. As mentioned above, the EU Charter as primary EU law provided for the right to privacy and the right to data protection under its Articles 7 and 8. In addition, Article 16 TFEU served as a strong legal basis for the Union to legislate on matters concerning data protection.[49]

With the abolition of the Pillar structure, the Union not only obtained the right of initiative for former Third Pillar matters, but also the competence to legislate by way of Regulations and Directives in that area. In particular, Framework Decisions were no longer mentioned under Article 288 TFEU, which exhaustively enumerates all forms of EU legislative acts.[50] This meant that Conventions and Framework Decisions in the area of criminal justice were to be replaced, which also made the revision of the LED's predecessor, a 2008 Data Protection Framework Decision (DPFD), necessary.[51] However, while some assumed that the DPFD would be included under a revised version of the 95 Data Protection Directive,[52] the EU legislator decided to devote a separate legal instrument to data processing carried out in the area of judicial and police cooperation.

While the 95 Data Protection Directive was repealed by the GDPR, the processing of personal data in the law enforcement context would be regulated under the LED, replacing the DPFD. On the one hand, this separation between

[47] See also Statewatch, 'Briefing: External Action: Frontex Operations outside the EU', https://www.statewatch.org/analyses/2021/briefing-external-action-frontex-operations-outside-the-eu.

[48] Violeta Moreno Lax et al, 'Border-Induced Displacement: The Ethical and Legal Implications of Distance-Creation through Externalization' (*QIL QDI*, 28 February 2019), www.qil-qdi.org/border-induced-displacement-the-ethical-and-legal-implications-of-distance-creation-through-externalization.

[49] *cf* Hielke Hijmans, *The European Union as Guardian of Internet Privacy: The Story of Art 16 TFEU* (Springer, 2016).

[50] Helmut Satzger, 'Legal Effects of Directives Amending or Repealing Pre-Lisbon Framework Decisions' (2015) 6 *New Journal of European Criminal Law* 528.

[51] Council Framework Decision 2008/977/JHA of 27 November 2008 on the protection of personal data processed in the framework of police and judicial cooperation in criminal matters [2008] OJ L350/60.

[52] Joseph A Cannataci and Mireille M Caruana, 'Report: Recommendation R (87) 15 – Twenty-Five Years down the Line' (Council of Europe, 2013).

rules for 'general' processing and specific rules on the protection of personal data in the fields of judicial cooperation in criminal matters and police cooperation had been acknowledged in Declaration 21,[53] which is attached to the Lisbon Treaty. On the other hand, Member States were not willing to regulate the processing of personal data in that area by way of a Regulation and instead opted for a minimum harmonisation instrument, the LED. Eventually, two laws in the form of a Regulation and a Directive were adopted instead of one all-encompassing directly applicable legal instrument covering all data-processing activities and incorporating special rules for law enforcement processing.[54]

A. The EU Data Protection Reform

In 2012, the European Commission presented a legislative package to reform the outdated data protection framework that was primarily based on the 95 Data Protection Directive, which dated from a time when the internet was in its infancy.[55] Technological developments in the years after the adoption of the 95 Directive called for a modernised data protection regime that would be capable of ensuring a high level of data protection, while coping with new challenges in the digital age.[56] At the same time, the enormous increase in data-processing activities and of cross-border data flows demanded a coherent legal framework that would further facilitate the free flow of personal data within the Union, as well as to third countries and international organisations.

The broad scope of Article 16 TFEU, which the Lisbon Treaty materialised as solid legal basis to legislate in the area of data protection, was particularly important for the legislative progression of the EU Data Protection Reform and, in particular, the updated data protection rules applicable in the law enforcement area. Article 16 TFEU conferred a strong mandate on the European Parliament and on the Council, granting the EU-wide powers to act in the domain of privacy and data protection.[57] In addition, the EU Charter became primary law and consequently, whenever legislation would be based on Article 16 TFEU, Member States acting within the scope of EU law were automatically bound by the Charter.

[53] 'The Conference acknowledges that specific rules on the protection of personal data and the free movement of such data in the fields of judicial cooperation in criminal matters and police cooperation based on Article 16 of the Treaty on the Functioning of the European Union may prove necessary because of the specific nature of these fields.'

[54] Juraj Sajfert and Teresa Quintel, 'Data Protection Directive (EU) 2016/680 for Police and Criminal Justice Authorities', 1 December 2017, https://ssrn.Com/Abstract=3285873.

[55] EDPS, 'The History of the General Data Protection Regulation', https://edps.europa.eu/data-protection/data-protection/legislation/history-general-data-protection-regulation_en.

[56] European Commission, 'Data Protection in the EU: The General Data Protection Regulation (GDPR), the Data Protection Law Enforcement Directive and Other Rules Concerning the Protection of Personal Data', https://ec.europa.eu/info/law/law-topic/data-protection/data-protection-eu_en.

[57] Hijmans (n 49).

As previously mentioned, the EU Data Protection Reform comprised two legislative instruments, the GDPR and the LED, which were applicable for the police and criminal justice sector. The introduction of a Directive that would cover data processing in the area of law enforcement was a novelty, as data protection legislation at the EU level governed by such instruments had mainly been concerned with commercial data processing, while law enforcement processing was subject to weaker instruments.[58] As the first piece of comprehensive data protection legislation that would be legally binding in all EU Member States, the Directive was specifically designed to ensure high standards in the protection of personal data in the law enforcement context, while enabling the competent authorities to process and exchange personal data in the digital age.[59]

When the Luxembourg Presidency started in July 2015, the negotiations on the EU Data Protection Reform package had already been taking place since January 2012, when the Commission put forward the proposals.[60] On 15 December 2015, the Luxembourg Presidency and the European Parliament were able to reach an agreement on the reform package. The agreement was approved on 17 December by a vote of the Committee on Civil Liberties, Justice and Home Affairs (LIBE Committee) of the European Parliament and, at the level of the Council of the EU, during a Committee of Permanent Representatives (COREPER) meeting on 18 December 2015.[61]

Technological developments and the increased need for LEAs to exchange personal data, thereby ensuring high data protection standards via a comprehensive legal framework, was one of the most relevant incentives to reform the EU data protection regime in the area of police and judicial cooperation.[62] Together with the GDPR, the LED came into force in April 2016 and had to be transposed by the Member States until May 2018. Both instruments seek to guarantee high data protection standards for individuals while providing sufficient room for technological innovation and smooth data exchanges. However, while the GDPR as a Regulation is directly applicable in all 27 Member States, the effectiveness of the Directive depends on its correct transposition and consistent application at

[58] Such as Framework Decisions. *cf* Gloria Gonzàlez Fuster, 'Fighting for Your Right to What Exactly: The Convoluted Case Law of the EU Court of Justice on Privacy and/or Personal Data Protection' (2014) 2 *Birkbeck Law Review* 263.

[59] An increasing number of crimes are committed on the internet and perpetrators leave digital traces that can assist LEAs in their tasks of carrying out crime prevention, detection, investigation and prosecution. Therefore, LEAs were *obliged* to utilise new investigative techniques, including big data analytics; see Sajfert and Quintel (n 54).

[60] COM (2012) 10 final and COM (2012) 11 final.

[61] 'Félix Braz Presented the Achievements of the Luxembourg Presidency in the Field of Justice and Data Protection to the LIBE Committee of the European Parliament', http://www.eu2015lu.eu/fr/actualites/articles-actualite/2015/12/21-pe-libe-braz/index.html.

[62] Petra Beckerhoff, 'Reform des europäischen Datenschutzrechts: Ein Überblick unter besonderer Berücksichtigung des Datenaustausches zwischen Polizei-, Strafjustiz- und Geheimdienstbehörden' [2017] *Eucrim* 88.

the national level. In that regard, the Directive seeks to increase the level of data protection afforded to individuals by expanding the limited scope of its predecessor, the 2008 DPFD.[63]

In order to achieve harmonisation, numerous provisions in the LED require a coherent interpretation at a national level, particularly regarding the delineation between the scope of the GDPR and that of the Directive. Only if those provisions are applied in a coherent manner can situations where some authorities in one Member State apply the GDPR while the national authorities in other Member States apply the LED be averted.

B. Directive (EU) 2016/680

In the performance of their tasks, competent LEAs are required to process personal data both for preventative and repressive purposes.[64] Hence, the work of those authorities is determined by the collection, analysis and usage of personal data in more general terms. Consequently, the activities of competent LEAs, namely the gathering of evidence for crime investigation and prosecution, but also in order to prevent criminal offences and/or to maintain public order, have consequences for the legal protection of the individuals whose personal data are processed. The protection of personal data of potential perpetrators, but also of witnesses and victims, is thus of the utmost importance. The processing of personal data by competent authorities for the purposes of the prevention, investigation, detection or prosecution of criminal offences or the execution of criminal penalties is excluded from the material scope of the GDPR. Instead, such processing is regulated under an additional instrument: the LED.

Like the GDPR, the LED was adopted in May 2016 as the first legally binding horizontal instrument to set out rules for both the domestic and cross-border processing of personal data in the field of law enforcement, with the aim of establishing a comprehensive EU data protection regime.[65] As mentioned above, the Directive succeeded a Framework Decision from 2008,[66] which had a much

[63] Paul de Hert and Vagelis Papakonstantinou, 'The Data Protection Framework Decision of 27 November 2008 Regarding Police and Judicial Cooperation in Criminal Matters – A Modest Achievement However Not the Improvement Some Have Hoped for' (2009) 25 *Computer Law & Security Review* 403.

[64] On preventative policing, *cf* Jan Dirk Roggenkamp, '§ 21 Datenschutz und präventive Tätigkeit der Polizei' in Louisa Specht and Reto Mantz (eds), *Handbuch Europäisches und deutsches Datenschutzrecht* (CH Beck, 2019).

[65] See Thomas Marquenie, 'The Police and Criminal Justice Authorities Directive: Data Protection Standards and Impact on the Legal Framework' (2017) 33 *Computer Law & Security Review* 324.

[66] Council Framework Decision 2008/977/JHA of 27 November 2008 on the protection of personal data processed in the framework of police and judicial cooperation in criminal matters [2008] OJ L350/60.

more limited territorial scope and applied solely to cross-border data processing between the Member States.[67]

The rules under the Directive had to be transposed into the national laws of all the then 28 Member States, as well as Norway, Iceland, Switzerland and Lichtenstein[68] by 6 May 2018. As the second part of the data protection reform package that had been under discussion for four years, the Directive received less attention than the GDPR when comparing the contributions of the Directive to the number of academic writings that exist on the GDPR.[69] Nevertheless, the collection of personal data and the exchange thereof progressively grew in importance for successful police work. In addition, with perpetrators moving their activities to the online domain, LEAs were obliged to follow such trends and to turn to new investigative techniques, including the use of electronically processed datasets and more sophisticated analyses carried out by way of new technologies.[70]

The processing activities covered by the LED include processing carried out by national police authorities and other LEAs related to criminal activities, but also to threats that may lead to a criminal offence, while administrative processing (ie, the processing of HR, asylum or border control data) is not covered by the Directive and (should) instead fall within the scope of the GDPR.[71] And yet, delineating between the GDPR and the LED is not an easy exercise. On the one hand, EU law does not provide for a harmonised notion of criminal offence, and some Member States' national systems recognise minor offences as a branch of criminal law.[72] On the other hand, essential definitions in the Directive leave much room for interpretation as to the situations in which the LED may apply.

First, the Directive applies to processing carried out for the *prevention* of criminal offences, which means that there is no clear line as to the point of time when an LEA may switch from applying the GDPR to the LED for the processing of personal data. This is particularly the case where national systems recognise minor offences as criminal offences. Second, national authorities that qualify as competent authorities and are therefore eligible to apply the LED differ from Member State to Member State. While in some Member States, only the national police, the prosecutor and criminal courts qualify as competent authorities, in other Member States, border and coast guards[73] fall within the personal scope of the

[67] Sajfert and Quintel (n 54). On the shortcomings of Framework Decision 2008/977/JHA, *cf* Paul de Hert and Vagelis Papakonstantinou, 'The New Police and Criminal Justice Data Protection Directive: A First Analysis' (2016) 7 *New Journal of European Criminal Law*, 7.

[68] The Directive is a development of provisions of the Schengen *acquis*. See Recitals 101, 102 and 103.

[69] Sajfert and Quintel (n 54).

[70] See Andrew Guthrie Ferguson, *The Rise of Big Data Policing* (NYU Press, 2017) 272.

[71] Commission expert group on Regulation (EU) 2016/679 and Directive (EU) 2016/680 (E03461), 'Minutes of the Third Meeting of the Commission Expert Group on the Regulation (EU) 2016/679 and Directive (EU) 2016/680' (7 November 2016).

[72] For instance, in Germany, administrative offences – so-called Ordnungswidrigkeiten – may be processed within the scope of the Directive.

[73] In Germany, the federal police (Bundespolizei) are competent for border protection; in Sweden, both the Swedish Coast Guard and the Swedish police carry out border protection tasks.

Directive. In addition, in many Member States, activities relating to immigration and border control, such as irregular entry or stay, are criminalised. Against that background, it becomes challenging for LEAs to draw a clear line between the scope of application of the GDPR and that of the LED, which create considerable leeway for competent authorities to apply the Directive to their processing activities.

The two main objectives of the Directive are considered the most relevant in the context of this chapter: first, the strengthened protection of fundamental rights in the area of police and criminal justice that the LED is supposed to promote;[74] and, second, the fact that the Directive seeks to ensure an enhanced sharing of personal data between the LEAs of the Member States, as they may rely on uniform data protection rules.[75]

With regard to the first objective, it is argued that the promotion of fundamental rights should include the notion of fair processing in the sense that the Directive should solely apply when this is justified in accordance with the strict purposes of processing. Hence, the processing of personal data should only fall within the scope of the LED if it is carried out in relation to those criminal offences that are classified as such under national law in accordance with certain uniform criteria. With regard to the second objective, it is important to acknowledge the potential of the Directive in terms of providing more flexibility to competent authorities when processing is carried out for the prevention, investigation, detection and prosecution of criminal offences. This means that competent authorities, when processing personal data within the scope of the LED, are subject to less strict transparency obligations, may limit data subject rights more flexibly and are less restricted when exchanging information with their counterparts that are subject to similar rules. This is an important factor to consider where processing takes place for the performance of police and other law enforcement tasks. For those processing activities, controllers evidently need more flexibility in order not to jeopardise ongoing investigations, which means that transparency cannot be guaranteed in the same way as under the GDPR.

However, whenever the first objective, including the criterion of fair processing, is not complied with and the Directive is applied in unjustified situations, this signifies repercussions in terms of data subject rights and obligations that have to be fulfilled by controllers that are bound by the LED. The wide margin of appreciation with regard to the Directive's scope, and the fact that in many Member States authorities responsible for migration, border control and asylum are also

All three authorities qualify as a 'competent authority' within the personal scope of the LED under national legislation. Whereas the Bundespolizei may process migration-related matters within the scope of the Directive, the Swedish Coast Guard may apply the Directive in a similar way, as long as processing is carried out for the purpose of the prevention, investigation, detection or prosecution of criminal offences.

[74] Article 1(2)(a) of Directive (EU) 2016/680.

[75] ibid art 1(2)(b).

competent authorities within the personal scope of the LED, may lead to such unjustified situations for TCNs.

II. The Growth of Powers of the EU Agencies

For the sake of the overall topical framework, three EU Agencies are of particular interest and assessed in more detail concerning the development of their mandate and tasks in relation to border control and migration management, as well as the data protection rules to which they are subject. These Agencies are the European Union Agency for Law Enforcement Cooperation (Europol) as an EU law enforcement agency; Frontex, the European Border and Coast Guard Agency, including the European Border Surveillance System (EUROSUR); and Eurojust, the European Union Agency for Criminal Justice Cooperation.

Europol was established as a European police organisation to promote and strengthen cooperation among the LEAs of the EU Member States.[76] Since its establishment following the adoption of the Europol Convention[77] in 1995, Europol has been subject to several developments and has undergone dynamic legislative changes.[78] In 1999, it became fully operational and since then has experienced massive modifications in terms of its status, mandate and competences.[79] This mandate comprises an increased engagement of Europol in migration-related activities, including the processing of personal data.[80]

Frontex, as the European Agency for the Management of Operational Cooperation at the External Borders of the Member States of the EU, was established on 26 October 2004[81] and is today one of the fastest-growing EU Agencies.[82]

[76] Emma Disley, 'Evaluating the Implementation of the Europol Council Decision' (Rand Report 2012), https://www.rand.org/pubs/technical_reports/TR1264.html, XV.

[77] Convention on the Establishment of a European Police Office, based on Article K3 of the Treaty on European Union (TEU Maastricht) ('Europol Convention') [1995] OJ C316/2.

[78] Agathe Piquet, 'Supranational Activism as an Assertion Process? The Case of Europol' (2017) 13 *Journal of Contemporary European Research*, https://jcer.net/index.php/jcer/article/view/773.

[79] Europol's predecessor, the European Drugs Unit (EDU), had already become operational in the early 1990s. For further information, see Francis Monaco, 'Europol: The Culmination of the European Union's International Police Cooperation Efforts' (1995) 19 *Fordham International Law Journal* 247, 282.

[80] Teresa Quintel, 'The Impact of Interoperability on the Processing of (Biometric) Data of Third Country Nationals by Europol' (2018) 101 *Kritische Vierteljahresschrift für Gesetzgebung und Rechtswissenschaft* 332.

[81] Council Regulation (EC) No 2007/2004 of 26 October 2004 establishing a European Agency for the Management of Operational Cooperation at the External Borders of the Member States of the European Union [2004] OJ L349/1.

[82] *cf* Arne Niemann and Johanna Speyer, 'A Neofunctionalist Perspective on the "European Refugee Crisis": The Case of the European Border and Coast Guard' (2018) 56 *Journal of Common Market Studies* 23; Francesca Ferraro and Emilio de Capitani, 'The New European Border and Coast Guard: Yet Another "Half Way" EU Reform?' (2016) 17 *ERA Forum* 385; Jorrit Rijpma, 'The Proposal for a European Border and Coast Guard: Evolution or Revolution in External Border Management? Study for the LIBE Committee' (2016), https://www.europarl.europa.eu/RegData/etudes/STUD/2016/556934/IPOL_STU(2016)556934_EN.pdf Philippe de Bruycker, 'The European Border and Coast Guard: A New Model Built on an Old Logic' (2016) 1 *European Papers* 559.

Both Europol and the EBCGA are crucial in the context of border management, migration, asylum and police cooperation. Europol, as an EU law enforcement agency, plays an increasingly important role in the context of security checks on migrants, whereas the EBCGA, an agency that previously only *assisted* Member States in the area of migration, turned, within a relatively short timeframe, into a powerful information hub with a mandate to carry out law enforcement tasks. This includes the processing of so-called operational data, ie, personal data processed for law enforcement purposes.

Compared to Europol and the EBCGA, Eurojust is more restricted when it comes to the processing of personal data, as it still very much depends on the national authorities in the Member States to open investigations and to transmit personal data to it. Moreover, it neither actively engages its staff in on-site activities, nor does it have access to AFSJ databases in a similar manner to Europol or the EBCGA. However, Eurojust's caseload has increased rapidly in recent years.[83] More importantly in the context of the subject matter of this book, it has become more involved in cases relating to migration, for instance, when it comes to migrant smuggling.[84] In addition, Eurojust is supposed to gradually increase the inter-agency exchanges of personal data with Europol and the EBCGA. Although Eurojust remains a secondary actor regarding the processing of personal data of TCNs, it is important to include it with respect to its future involvement in such processing.

As previously mentioned, and in a broader sense, the EU Data Protection Reform could be said to include the revision of the data protection rules applicable to EU Agencies in order to harmonise and make the rules that apply to EU institutions, bodies and agencies more coherent with those at the national level. On the one hand, this was necessary because the rules applicable to EU institutions, bodies and agencies originated from a Regulation from 2001 and were outdated. On the other hand, stand-alone instruments applicable to specific agencies led to a fragmentation of data protection rules at the EU level. With increased exchanges of personal data between the national and EU levels, such fragmentation led to variations in terms of safeguards, obligations and supervision.

Since December 2019, the EBCGA and Eurojust have been subject to Regulation (EU) 2018/1725, which to a great extent reflects the rules at the national level under the LED. However, Europol maintained its own data protection regime under the 2016 Europol Regulation, which was only supposed to be reviewed in 2022. Prior to that date, in December 2020, the Commission proposed amendments to the

[83] Eurojust, 'Casework at Eurojust', https://www.eurojust.europa.eu/crime-types-and-cases/casework.

[84] Eurojust, 'Report on Eurojust's Casework in the Field of Migrant Smuggling' (2018), www.eurojust.europa.eu/doclibrary/Eurojust-framework/Casework/Report%20on%20Eurojust%20casework%20in%20the%20field%20of%20migrant%20smuggling%20(Redacted)%20-%20April%202018/2018-04_Migrant-smuggling-report_Redacted_EN.pdf.

2016 Europol Regulation, including with regard to the rules on the protection of personal data. After considerable changes during the negotiations, the recast Europol Regulation was adopted in February 2022.

III. The Case of EU Databases

With the establishment of the AFSJ and the gradual abolition of internal border controls, the latter were to be replaced by alternative measures both with regard to police cooperation in criminal matters and concerning policies on border checks, asylum and immigration. On the one hand, police cooperation was to be established, inter alia, by the collection, storage, processing, analysis and exchange of relevant information between the competent law enforcement authorities of the Member States to prevent and combat crime.[85] On the other hand, in the absence of any internal border controls, a common visa and asylum policy for the carrying out of checks on persons to ensure an efficient monitoring of the crossing of the external borders, a gradual introduction of an integrated management system for external borders was to be developed.[86]

In order to allow for an efficient exchange of information between the competent authorities of the Member States, three large-scale information-sharing systems (AFSJ databases) were developed to preserve the EU's internal security and to enable the storage of information about those individuals who would no longer be checked at internal border crossings. The three databases that are currently operational are the SIS, the Eurodac database and the VIS. All three systems allow competent LEAs and additional authorities as well as EU Agencies to enter and consult data. The SIS, Eurodac and VIS pursue the objectives of facilitating the preservation of the EU's internal security in the absence of internal border controls,[87] to determine responsibility for examining an asylum application[88] and to assess visa applications to support the implementation of the common EU visa policy.[89] From 2016, three additional databases were adopted in order to complement the existing systems, in particular with regard to those categories of TCNs that had previously not been registered in either of the three operational databases. The following text will provide, as part of the developments in the AFSJ, a short overview of the three operational and the three anticipated databases.

[85] Article 87(1)(a) TFEU.

[86] ibid art 77(1)(b).

[87] European Commission, 'Schengen Information System' (6 December 2016), https://ec.europa.eu/home-affairs/policies/schengen-borders-and-visa/schengen-information-system_en.

[88] European Commission, 'Identification of Applicants (EURODAC)' (6 December 2016), https://ec.europa.eu/home-affairs/what-we-do/policies/asylum/identification-of-applicants_en.

[89] European Commission, 'Visa Information System (VIS)' (6 December 2016), https://ec.europa.eu/home-affairs/what-we-do/policies/borders-and-visas/visa-information-system_en.

A. Operational Databases

i. The Schengen Information System

This first generation of the SIS (SIS I) became operational in 1995[90] and has, since then, been updated[91] into a second (SIS II)[92] and a third (SIS III)[93] generation, which is currently used by 26 of the EU Member States (and four Schengen Associated Countries – Switzerland, Norway, Liechtenstein and Iceland).[94] The SIS I[95] was established in 1990 as the 'crown jewel' of Schengen cooperation,[96] with the overarching aim to maintain public order and public security, including state security, and to apply the provisions of the CISA relating to the movement of persons by using information transmitted via the system.[97] Since SIS I became operational in 1995, it was progressively expanded in terms of participating Member States, and hence users, and data records. In 2001, the SIS I was expanded to the SIS I+ in order to include five Nordic countries,[98] and in 2007, it was updated to SISone4all to accommodate the countries that formed part of the

[90] At that time, the system was used by seven Member States: Belgium, the Netherlands, Luxembourg, France, Spain, Portugal and Germany.

[91] Inter alia, due to the 9/11 terrorist attacks.

[92] On 31 May 2005, the Commission presented proposals for three legislative instruments governing the SIS II, which were adopted on 12 June 2007: two Regulations (Regulation (EC) 1987/2006 of the European Parliament and of the Council on the development, operation and use of the second generation Schengen Information System (SIS II), [2006] OJ L381/4 (hereinafter 'the SIS II Regulation') and Regulation (EC) 1986/2006 of the European Parliament and of the Council of 20 December 2006 regarding access to the Second Generation Schengen Information System (SIS II) by the services in the Member States responsible for issuing vehicle registration certificates [2006] OJ L381/1) and on 12 June 2007 a Council Decision (Council Decision 2007/533/JHA of 12 June 2007 on the establishment, operation and use of the second generation Schengen Information System (SIS II) [2007] OJ L205/63 (hereinafter 'the SIS II Decision')).

[93] Regulation (EU) 2018/1860 (on the use of the Schengen Information System for the return of illegally staying third-country nationals); Regulation (EU) 2018/1861 (on the establishment, operation and use of the Schengen Information System (SIS) in the field of border checks); and Regulation (EU) 2018/1862 (on the establishment, operation and use of the Schengen Information System (SIS) in the field of police cooperation and judicial cooperation in criminal matters).

[94] The second-generation SIS extended its users and allowed for new functions. In addition, it included non-EU Member States. There are Member States with special arrangements – for instance, Bulgaria, Romania and Croatia are not yet part of the area without internal border checks. However, since August 2018, Bulgaria and Romania started fully using the SIS. Ireland operates the SIS, but as it has chosen not to join the Schengen Area, it cannot issue or access Schengen-wide alerts for refusing entry and stay into the Schengen Area. Cyprus is not yet connected to the SIS as it has a temporary derogation from joining the Schengen Area.

[95] Set up pursuant to the provisions of Title IV of the Convention of 19 June 1990 implementing the Schengen Agreement of 14 June 1985 between the governments of the States of the Benelux Economic Union, the Federal Republic of Germany and the French Republic on the gradual abolition of checks at their common borders (the Schengen Convention, CISA); see Recital 1 of Council Decision 2007/533/JHA.

[96] European Parliament, 'Security: Improving the Schengen Information System' (17 October 2018), https://www.europarl.europa.eu/news/en/headlines/security/20181011STO15882/security-improving-the-schengen-information-system.

[97] Article 93 of the CISA.

[98] Denmark, Sweden, Finland, Norway and Iceland.

Eastern enlargement.[99] The current form of the system, the SIS II, was adopted in 2006 and became operational in 2013.[100] Today, the SIS II[101] is the most widely used information system within the EU.[102]

The system enables competent authorities such as the national border guards, police, customs, judicial, visa and vehicle registration authorities to enter alerts into the system and to consult the stored data where relevant for the performance of their tasks.[103] With regard to law enforcement access to stored data, the SIS differs from the other AFSJ databases, as instead of LEAs accessing data that were stored for purposes other than for the prevention, investigation and prosecution of crime, LEAs are the ones creating the alerts in the SIS.[104] A SIS alert permits the accessing authorities to identify a person via alphanumeric and/or biometric data, and provides additional information on whether that person is armed, violent, or has absconded or escaped.[105]

The system is twinned with so-called national SIRENE[106] Bureaux, auxiliary systems responsible for any supplementary information exchange and the coordination of activities related to SIS alerts at a national level.[107] Such exchanges may take place for different purposes – for instance, to allow LEAs in the Member States to consult or inform each other whilst entering an alert or to communicate in order to allow appropriate action to be taken after a hit was discovered.

SIRENE Bureaux are mainly concerned with exchanges of information amongst their counterparts in other EU Member States. Furthermore, they receive additional details on information exchanges relating to police cooperation in the EU. In that vein, they should be informed about information exchanges between national authorities and Europol, and should act as national contact points for

[99] Connecting the Czech Republic, Estonia, Hungary, Latvia, Lithuania, Malta, Poland, Slovakia and Slovenia; see Joanna Parkin, 'The Difficult Road to the Schengen Information System II: The Legacy of "Laboratories" and the Cost for Fundamental Rights and the Rule of Law' (*CEPS Paper in Liberty and Security in Europe*, 2011), http://aei.pitt.edu/31282/1/SIS_II_paper_liberty_security_formatted1[1].pdf.

[100] European Commission (n 87).

[101] The rapid growth of the Schengen group, even outside the EU through association agreements with Norway, Iceland and Switzerland, and the prospect of further enlargement of the EU led to the decision to develop a second generation of the system as early as December 1996. *cf* Paul de Hert, 'Trends in de Europese politiële en justitiële informatiesamenwerking' (2004) 25 *Panopticon* 26.

[102] European Commission (n 87).

[103] Franziska Boehm, *Information Sharing and Data Protection in the Area of Freedom, Security and Justice: Towards Harmonised Data Protection Principles for EU Internal Information Exchange* (Springer, 2012).

[104] The system registers alerts on wanted or missing persons and objects, alerts on persons sought in relation to criminal activity, and on those who do not have the right to enter the Schengen Area.

[105] See, for instance, art 20(3) and, concerning additional information, art 30(3)(h) of the SIS II Decision or art 20(2)(j)(i), (ii), (iii), (iv), (v), (vi) of Regulation (EU) 2018/1862.

[106] Supplementary information request at national entry (additional data exchange possibility within the framework of the SIS II).

[107] European Commission, 'SIRENE Cooperation' (6 December 2016), https://ec.europa.eu/home-affairs/what-we-do/policies/borders-and-visas/schengen-information-system/sirene-cooperation_en.

members of Eurojust.[108] The SIRENE Bureaux also cooperate with each other in order to determine the priority of alerts and in situations where a required action cannot be taken. In those latter cases, they may add flags in the SIS. In addition, they are responsible for assessing the quality of SIS data, for instance, with regard to outgoing alerts and the verification of incoming alerts.[109] Finally, they may have to deal with data subject access requests.[110]

In 2016, after the SIS II had been in operation for three years, the Commission conducted an overall evaluation of the database and, as a result, issued a legislative package to update the SIS II. The legislative package was composed of three draft SIS III Regulations on police and judicial cooperation,[111] border checks[112] and the return of illegally staying TCNs.[113] The three Regulations were to contribute to a more consistent, coherent and comprehensive legal framework by legally *de-pillarising* the database with their entry into force in 2021.[114] Adopted in November 2018,[115] the general purposes of the first generation of the SIS and of the SIS II were maintained under the new SIS III Regulations, yet, with a specific reference to Chapter 2 (border checks, asylum and migration) of Title V of Part Three TFEU.

The main changes under the three new SIS III Regulations are the storage of new types of biometrics,[116] additional data on so-called preventive alerts,[117] as well

[108] Points 1.5 and 1.7 of the SIRENE Manual, Commission Implementing Decision (EU) 2015/219 of 29 January 2015 replacing the Annex to Implementing Decision 2013/115/EU on the SIRENE Manual and other implementing measures for the second generation Schengen Information System (SIS II) [2015] OJ L44/75.

[109] If this is provided for by national law. See ibid point 1.1(f).

[110] Commission Implementing Decision (EU) 2015/219 (n 109).

[111] 'Proposal for a Regulation of the European Parliament and of the Council on the establishment, operation and use of the Schengen Information System (SIS) in the field of police cooperation and judicial cooperation in criminal matters, amending Regulation (EU) No 515/2014 and repealing Regulation (EC) No 1986/2006, Council Decision 2007/533/JHA and Commission Decision 2010/261/EU' COM (2016) 883 final, Brussels, 21 December 2016.

[112] 'Proposal for a Regulation of the European Parliament and of the Council on the establishment, operation and use of the Schengen Information System (SIS) in the field of border checks, amending Regulation (EU) No 515/2014 and repealing Regulation (EC) No 1987/2006' COM (2016) 882 final, Brussels, 21 December 2016.

[113] 'Proposal for a Regulation of the European Parliament and of the Council on the use of the Schengen Information System for the return of illegally staying third country nationals' COM (2016) 881 final, Brussels, 21 December 2016.

[114] EDPS, 'Summary of the Opinion of the European Data Protection Supervisor on the New Legal Basis of the Schengen Information System' (2 May 2017), https://edps.europa.eu/sites/edp/files/publication/17-05-02_sis_ii_opinion_en.pdf.

[115] European Parliament, 'Security Union: political agreement on strengthened Schengen Information System' (12 June 2018), https://www.europarl.europa.eu/news/en/press-room/20180612IPR05604/security-union-political-agreement-on-strengthened-schengen-information-system.

[116] SIS III stores palm prints (art 40 of Regulation (EU) 2018/1862 regarding alerts on unknown wanted persons for the purposes of identification under national law), fingerprints (art 20(3)(y) of Regulation (EU) 2018/1862), facial images (art 20(3)(w) of Regulation (EU) 2018/1862) and DNA. The latter may only be used for missing persons to confirm their identity. See arts 20(3)(x), 32(1)(a) and 42(3) of Regulation (EU) 2018/1862.

[117] These alerts are supposed to protect certain categories of vulnerable persons (missing persons, children at risk of abduction or potential victims of trafficking in human beings or gender-based violence).

as return decisions[118] and entry bans.[119] The reformed SIS III systems encourage a better enforcement of entry bans and return decisions by making it mandatory to enter alerts in cases where such an order has been issued against an illegally or irregularly staying TCN.[120] This illustrates that the SIS is no longer a purely criminal database, but adds elements of migration management to its objectives. Apart from the creation of crime- and terrorism-related alerts, the SIS is used for the purpose of effective migration law enforcement. The end-users of SIS alerts relating to migration management are border guards, customs and police authorities, consular offices and embassies responsible for the assessment of Schengen Visa applications. In some countries, direct access to the SIS is also granted to the asylum authorities.[121] At the EU level, Europol obtained access to all alert categories that are entered in the SIS III while the EBCGA operational teams are now granted access to the system for the purpose of performing their tasks in the hotspots.[122]

The SIS III Regulations seek to align the retention periods of the system with those of other AFSJ databases.[123] Nevertheless, national retention periods that apply with regard to certain SIS alerts have to be taken into account. Alerts on persons stored in accordance with the SIS III Regulation applicable in the field of police cooperation and judicial cooperation in criminal matters shall be retained for the period required to achieve the purpose for which they were entered into the SIS or for a maximum period of five years, except if specific provisions in national law provide for a longer retention period.[124] Under the SIS III Regulation applicable in the field of border checks, alerts for refusal of entry and stay shall be deleted when the decision on the basis of which the alert was entered has been withdrawn or annulled by the competent authority.[125] Likewise, under the SIS III Regulation

[118] See art 4 of Regulation (EU) 2018/1860.

[119] Article 4(1)(z) of Regulation (EU) 2018/1860 and art 20(2)(q)(iv) of Regulation (EU) 2018/1861.

[120] Adding an obligation to create a SIS alert for return decisions and alerts on a wider range of stolen and falsified goods and documents. See art 3(1) and 4 of Regulation (EU) 2018/1860. See European Commission, 'Security Union: Technical and Operational Updates of the Schengen Information System – Questions & Answers', https://ec.europa.eu/commission/presscorner/detail/en/MEMO_16_4427.

[121] Rocco Bellanova and Georgios Glouftsios, 'Controlling the Schengen Information System (SIS II): The Infrastructural Politics of Fragility and Maintenance' (2022) 27 *Geopolitics* 160.

[122] European Commission, 'Schengen Information System (SIS III)' (6 December 2016), https://ec.europa.eu/home-affairs/what-we-do/policies/borders-and-visas/schengen-information-system_en.

[123] 'Proposal for a Regulation of the European Parliament and of the Council on the establishment, operation and use of the Schengen Information System (SIS) in the field of police cooperation and judicial cooperation in criminal matters, amending Regulation (EU) No 515/2014 and repealing Regulation (EC) No 1986/2006, Council Decision 2007/533/JHA and Commission Decision 2010/261/EU' COM (2016) 883 final, Brussels, 21 December 2016, 20.

[124] See, for instance, art 53 of Regulation (EU) 2018/1862. The retention period depends on the type of alert issued. For instance, in accordance with art 53(2), (3) and (4) of Regulation (EU) 2018/1862, the storage of information about persons it is one, three or five years, with the possibility to extend. This retention period may change for alerts on objects.

[125] Article 40(1) of Regulation 2018/1861. An alert shall also be deleted where the person in question acquired citizenship of a Member State or of any state whose nationals are beneficiaries of the right of free movement under EU law in accordance with art 40(3) of Regulation (EU) 2018/1861. For alerts for discreet inquiries or specific checks, the retention period remains one year.

on the return of illegally staying TCNs, alerts on return shall be deleted when the decision on the basis of which the alert was entered has been withdrawn or annulled by the competent authority.[126] Alerts on return shall also be deleted when the TCN concerned can demonstrate that he or she has left the territory of the Member States in compliance with the respective return decision.[127]

As mentioned above, Europol and the EBCGA will be granted access to the SIS III for the performance of their tasks.[128] This means that, besides storing new types of personal data and further categories of data subjects, the SIS III will grant access to more authorities for additional purposes. Particularly with regard to the EBCGA, its new right to access a law enforcement database is somewhat interesting. Under Article 50 of the SIS III Regulation on police cooperation and judicial cooperation in criminal matters and Article 36 of the SIS III Regulation on border checks, EBCGA teams, teams of staff involved in return-related tasks, and members of the migration management support teams may access data in the SIS III. Such access shall take place within the mandate of the respective EBCGA teams, provided that those teams have received the necessary training and access is required by the operational plan for a specific operation.[129]

Access under the two SIS III Regulations may *generally*[130] be granted for the purposes of border control,[131] police and customs checks,[132] for the prevention, detection, investigation or prosecution of terrorist offences or other serious criminal offences or for the execution of criminal penalties,[133] for examining the conditions and taking decisions relating to the entry and stay of TCNs,[134] for security checks on TCNs who apply for international protection[135] or for the examination of visa applications.[136] EBCGA teams may within these purposes be granted access to the SIS III, provided that the above requirements are fulfilled. Theoretically, EBCGA teams would not only be allowed to access a law enforcement database, but also to subsequently process the personal data from that database for law enforcement purposes.

[126] Article 14(1) of Regulation (EU) 2018/1860.

[127] ibid. In addition, under art 14(2) of Regulation (EU) 2018/1860, alerts on return concerning a person who has acquired citizenship of a Member State or of any state whose nationals are beneficiaries of the right of free movement under EU law shall be deleted as soon as the issuing Member State becomes aware of this.

[128] Article 36 of Regulation (EU) 2018/1861, art 50 of Regulation 2018/1862 and art 17(3) of Regulation (EU) 2018/1860.

[129] Article 36(1) of Regulation (EU) 2018/1861 and art 50(1) of Regulation (EU) 2018/1862.

[130] Article 34(1) of Regulation 2018/1861 and art 44(1) of Regulation (EU) 2018/1862 on purposes of access to the SIS III by national competent authorities do not specifically refer to purposes of EBCGA access.

[131] Article 34(1)(a) of Regulation (EU) 2018/1861 and art 44(1)(a) of Regulation (EU) 2018/1862.

[132] Article 34(1)(b) of Regulation (EU) 2018/1861 and art 44(1)(b) of Regulation (EU) 2018/1862.

[133] Article 34(1)(c) of Regulation (EU) 2018/1861 and art 44(1)(c) of Regulation (EU) 2018/1862.

[134] Article 34(1)(d) of Regulation (EU) 2018/1861 and art 44(1)(d) of Regulation (EU) 2018/1862.

[135] Article 34(1)(e) of Regulation (EU) 2018/1861 and art 44(1)(e) of Regulation (EU) 2018/1862.

[136] Article 34(1)(f) of Regulation (EU) 2018/1861.

Under Article 17(2) of the SIS III Regulation for the return of illegally staying TCNs, Europol may access the database for the purpose of supporting and strengthening action by the competent authorities of the Member States and their mutual cooperation in preventing and combating migrant smuggling and facilitation of irregular migration. In addition, it may access information contained in the SIS III in the field of border checks where necessary for the performance of its tasks.[137] For those purposes, it may process supplementary information provided to it by Member States in order to compare this with its own databases and operational analysis projects. This is supposed to help Europol identifying connections or other relevant links for its strategic and operational analyses.[138] Consequently, it may access the border control and migration management components of SIS III, receive additional information by national authorities and cross-check those data against any analyses that it has carried out in its own data environment in order to find links between these datasets.

ii. Eurodac

Since its establishment in 2003, the purpose of the Eurodac database[139] is the determination of the Member State responsible for processing an asylum application by checking in the system whether a person has previously applied for international protection in another EU Member State.[140] Eurodac thereby assists the implementation of the Dublin system in order to ensure that an individual applies for asylum in the first country of entry and to prevent 'asylum shopping' in different Member States.

[137] ibid art 35.

[138] ibid art 35(3).

[139] Regulation (EU) No 603/2013 of the European Parliament and of the Council of 26 June 2013 on the establishment of 'Eurodac' for the comparison of fingerprints for the effective application of Regulation (EU) No 604/2013 establishing the criteria and mechanisms for determining the Member State responsible for examining an application for international protection lodged in one of the Member States by a third-country national or a stateless person and on requests for the comparison with Eurodac data by Member States' law enforcement authorities and Europol for law enforcement purposes, and amending Regulation (EU) No 1077/2011 establishing a European Agency for the operational management of large-scale IT systems in the area of freedom, security and justice [2013] OJ L180/1, 29 June 2013. In September 2020, the Commission issued an amended 'Proposal for a Regulation of the European Parliament and of the Council on the establishment of 'Eurodac' for the comparison of biometric data for the effective application of Regulation (EU) XXX/XXX [Regulation on Asylum and Migration Management] and of Regulation (EU) XXX/XXX [Resettlement Regulation], for identifying an illegally staying third-country national or stateless person and on requests for the comparison with Eurodac data by Member States' law enforcement authorities and Europol for law enforcement purposes and amending Regulations (EU) 2018/1240 and (EU) 2019/818' COM (2020) 614 final, Brussels, 23 September 2020. This proposal is not being taken into account at present. The Eurodac database shall only be assessed in terms of general functionalities.

[140] Teresa Quintel, 'Connecting Personal Data of Third Country Nationals: Interoperability of EU Databases in the Light of the CJEU's Case Law on Data Retention' (2018), https://papers.ssrn.com/sol3/papers.cfm?abstract_id=3132506.

In the future, the Eurodac database is supposed to hold data from irregular migrants and persons illegally staying in the territory of an EU Member State for the purpose of expulsion.[141] A Commission proposal[142] from May 2016 on the reform of Eurodac aimed at expanding the system's scope to wider objectives of immigration control, such as the monitoring of illegal migration and secondary movements[143] of irregular migrants within the EU.[144] This shall, inter alia, be achieved through storing the personal data of TCNs for longer periods in order to investigate travel routes and to identify unauthorised stays. Retention periods under the proposal range from five years for personal data of illegally staying TCNs who do not claim asylum[145] to ten years for data of applications for international protection.[146]

Following judicial or administrative authorisation, Eurodac allows for access by national LEAs and Europol where there is a substantiated suspicion that the data of a suspect or perpetrator of a terrorist offence and other serious crime, or the data of a potential victim is stored in Eurodac.[147] However, at the time of writing, due to the current deadlock on the CEAS, the proposal from 2016 has not been adopted.

Instead, on 23 September 2020, the Commission proposed a new Eurodac Regulation[148] amending the 2016 proposal for a recast Eurodac Regulation, inter alia, to allow Eurodac to function within the interoperability framework between AFSJ databases, which will be discussed below.[149] The 2020 Eurodac proposal

[141] ibid.

[142] 'Proposal for a Regulation of the European Parliament and of the Council on the establishment of 'Eurodac' for the comparison of fingerprints for the effective application of [Regulation (EU) No 604/2013 establishing the criteria and mechanisms for determining the Member State responsible for examining an application for international protection lodged in one of the Member States by a third-country national or a stateless person], for identifying an illegally staying third-country national or stateless person and on requests for the comparison with Eurodac data by Member States' law enforcement authorities and Europol for law enforcement purposes (recast)' COM (2016) 272 final, Brussels, 4 May 2016, 12.

[143] In this context, secondary movements occur when refugees or asylum seekers move from the Member State in which they first arrived to seek asylum in another Member State.

[144] The legal basis for the proposed Eurodac Regulation is art 79(2)(c) TFEU; whereas the legal basis of Regulation 603/2013 was art 78(2)(e), the wider purpose remains immigration.

[145] The retention period for data of irregular migrants was extended from 18 months to five years in order to monitor secondary movements within the EU, particularly where an irregular migrant makes efforts to remain undetected. See Quintel (n 140).

[146] ibid.

[147] And if there are reasonable grounds to consider that the comparison will substantially contribute to the prevention, detection or investigation of any of the criminal offences in question. Article 21 of the 2016 Eurodac Proposal. See ibid.

[148] 'Proposal for a Regulation of the European Parliament and of the Council on the establishment of 'Eurodac' for the comparison of biometric data for the effective application of Regulation (EU) XXX/XXX [Regulation on Asylum and Migration Management] and of Regulation (EU) XXX/XXX [Resettlement Regulation], for identifying an illegally staying third-country national or stateless person and on requests for the comparison with Eurodac data by Member States' law enforcement authorities and Europol for law enforcement purposes and amending Regulations (EU) 2018/1240 and (EU) 2019/818' COM (2020) 614 final, Brussels, 23 September 2020.

[149] COM (2020) 614 final, 2.

builds on the provisional agreement between the Parliament and the Council on the 2016 proposal and seeks, with additional changes, to transform Eurodac into a common European database in order to support EU policies on asylum, resettlement and irregular migration.[150] Hence, with the new Eurodac proposal, the initial purpose of the databases is being completely overhauled in order to accommodate all amended, adopted and newly proposed databases and procedures, such as those put in place with the proposal for a Screening Regulation. Thereby, the Eurodac database extends its functionalities in order to establish a link between all stages of the pre-entry procedure with those relating to the return of TCNs.[151]

This intended change of the Eurodac database is already visible in the title of the proposal, which includes requests for the comparison with Eurodac data by Member States' LEAs and Europol for law enforcement purposes. Europol will have a single access point to query data in the system to gain access to both alphanumeric and biometric data. As will be shown in Chapter 4, which the recast Europol Regulation from 2022,[152] this possibility is worrying, as Europol will be able to cross-match both types of data against its entire data environment without having to establish the existence of a link to a criminal activity. In addition, with regard to biometric data, Europol may process these personal data without putting in place additional safeguards, despite the fact that these data are of a particular intrusive nature.[153]

iii. The Visa Information System

The first generation of the SIS served as a model for the VIS,[154] a large-scale IT system, seeking to facilitate the administration, issuance and checks of short-stay visas[155] to the Schengen Area by enabling the exchange of visa information and the matching of biometric data to verify the authenticity of a visa.[156] Further objectives of the VIS are to prevent 'visa shopping' in different Member States and to impede individuals from 'overstaying', as a legal stay in the EU may easily turn into an illegal one when a person does not leave the Union after the period of an authorised stay expired.[157] The VIS allows for both the verification of visas and

[150] ibid.

[151] ibid.

[152] The final text on the provisional agreement between the Council Presidency and the European Parliament on the Agency's new mandate was agreed on 1 February 2022. See Annex of Dossier interinstitutionnel: 2020/0349 (COD), Brussels, 9 February 2022 (hereinafter 'recast Europol Regulation').

[153] Teresa Quintel, 'The EDPS on Europol's Big Data Challenge in Light of the Recast Europol Regulation' (2022) 8 *European Data Protection Law Review* 90.

[154] Regulation (EC) No 767/2008 of 9 July 2008 concerning the Visa Information System (VIS) and the exchange of data between Member States on short-stay visas (VIS Regulation) [2008] OJ L218/60.

[155] For short-stay visas in the Schengen Area, this period is normally 90 days within six months (multiple-entry visas).

[156] European Commission (n 89). See also Quintel (n 140).

[157] Quintel (n 140).

the identification of persons. During the verification process, the visa holders' fingerprints are compared with those stores in his or her visa file at the border crossing before entry. For identification purposes, competent border authorities may compare the fingerprints of a visa holder against the entire VIS database. In accordance with Article 23 of the VIS Regulation, visa application files shall be retained for a maximum period of five years, starting from the expiry date of the respective visa.[158]

The VIS was originally established by a Council Decision[159] and a Regulation,[160] which was supplemented by rules regarding Europol and law enforcement access to the system.[161] A new legal basis for the VIS was presented in May 2018 to amend the old rules and to extend the system's functionalities. Two new Regulations[162] – one to establish the VIS and one to allow access to other AFSJ databases for VIS purposes – were formally adopted on 7 July 2021[163] and introduced numerous amendments to the remaining AFSJ databases as well as the Interoperability Regulations.

The new VIS Regulation establishes default interoperability with the remaining AFSJ databases, Europol data environment as well as two INTERPOL databases: the Stolen and Lost Travel Document database (SLTD) and the Travel Documents Associated with Notices database (TDAWN). As a consequence, any newly created VIS application file will be compared against the data stored in those systems.[164] The cross-checking between those systems shall serve the purposes of assessing whether a visa applicant presents a risk of illegal immigration, a risk to the security of the Member States or a risk of overstaying,[165]

[158] In cases where the applicant withdrew the application or the visa was not granted, the period starts from date of withdrawal or the date of refusal respectively. See ibid.

[159] Council Decision 2004/512/EC of 8 June 2004 establishing the Visa Information System (VIS) [2004] OJ L213/5.

[160] Regulation (EC) No 767/2008 of the European Parliament and of the Council of 9 July 2008 concerning the Visa Information System (VIS) and the exchange of data between Member States on short-stay visas (VIS Regulation) [2008] OJ L218/60.

[161] Council Decision 2008/633/JHA of 23 June 2008 concerning access for consultation of the Visa Information System (VIS) by designated authorities of Member States and by Europol for the purposes of the prevention, detection and investigation of terrorist offences and of other serious criminal offences [2008] OJ L218/129.

[162] Regulation (EU) 2021/1134 of the European Parliament and of the Council of 7 July 2021 amending Regulations (EC) No 767/2008, (EC) No 810/2009, (EU) 2016/399, (EU) 2017/2226, (EU) 2018/1240, (EU) 2018/1860, (EU) 2018/1861, (EU) 2019/817 and (EU) 2019/1896 of the European Parliament and of the Council and repealing Council Decisions 2004/512/EC and 2008/633/JHA, for the purpose of reforming the Visa Information System [2021] OJ L11 and Regulation (EU) 2021/1133 of the European Parliament and of the Council of 7 July 2021 amending Regulations (EU) No 603/2013, (EU) 2016/794, (EU) 2018/1862, (EU) 2019/816 and (EU) 2019/818 as regards the establishment of the conditions for accessing other EU information systems for the purposes of the Visa Information System [2021] OJ L248/1.

[163] 'Key Documents and Legislation on VIS', https://ec.europa.eu/home-affairs/policies/schengen-borders-and-visa/visa-information-system/key-documents-and-legislation-vis_en.

[164] Article 9a of Regulation (EU) 2021/1134.

[165] Article 21(1) of Regulation (EC) No 810/2009 of the European Parliament and of the Council of 13 July 2009 establishing a Community Code on Visas (Visa Code) [2009] OJ L243/1.

to verify whether the applicant fulfils the entry conditions[166] and that his or her travel document is not false, counterfeit or forged.[167] In addition, it shall be cross-checked whether a SIS entry ban alert exists on the applicant[168] and whether the applicant is considered to be a threat to public policy, internal security or public health.[169]

Under the revised VIS framework, access for law enforcement purposes by national LEAs, Europol[170] and the EBCGA[171] may be granted. The conditions to access the SIS III/VIS for the identification of a TCN by the police within the territory of a Member State differ from those that allow access to facilitate return, whereas the requirements that apply to police checks are different from those that apply to custom checks, which in turn impose other conditions than for border checks. However, those different forms of access may coincide, which could then lead to a *mélange* of purposes and a less strict separation between access provided for migration purposes and access provided for law enforcement purposes. This, in turn, could diminish the boundaries between criminal and migration law and, eventually, have an impact on the applicable data protection instrument used for any subsequent processing of personal data.

Under Article 22m of the 2021 VIS Regulation, Europol shall designate one of its operating units as a 'Europol designated authority', which shall be authorised to request access to VIS through a central access point. The latter shall act independently when performing its tasks and shall not receive instructions from the Europol designated authority.[172] In addition, the accompanying Regulation on access to the VIS introduces amendments to the 2016 Europol Regulation in order to allow designated national authorities as well as the EBCGA to search Europol data on a hit/no hit basis.[173]

Interestingly enough, the accompanying Regulation on access to other databases for the purpose of reforming the VIS creates new possibilities for the EBCGA to access Europol data. Such access may be granted for the purposes of contributing to a high level of security, the prevention of illegal immigration, the protection of public health, the prevention, detection and investigation of terrorist offences or of other serious criminal offences, to support the objectives of the SIS and to enhance the effectiveness of border checks.[174] In addition, EBCGA teams may, pursuant to their tasks and powers under the 2019 EBCGA Regulation, for

[166] ibid art 21(3).
[167] ibid art 21(3)(a).
[168] ibid art 21(3) (c).
[169] ibid art 21(3)(d).
[170] Chapter IIIB of Regulation (EU) 2021/1134.
[171] ibid art 45e.
[172] Article 22m(2) of Regulation (EU) 2021/1134.
[173] Article 2 of Regulation (EU) 2021/1133.
[174] Namely, the objectives under art 4 (a), (b), (c), (d) and (f) of Regulation (EU) 2018/1240 (hereinafter 'the ETIAS Regulation').

border control and return purposes[175] and to fulfil operational aims on border surveillance,[176] access the VIS.

B. Adopted Databases

i. *The Entry/Exit System*

The first steps towards the Entry/Exit System (EES)[177] had already been put forward in 2001, in the form of suggested amendments to the CISA,[178] to register entries and exits to and from the Schengen Area and to replace the manual stamps in passports.[179] In 2004, the Hague Programme called for security measures that would effectively link visa application procedures with entry and exit procedures at external border crossings.[180] In 2005,[181] the Commission's Stockholm Programme Action Plan[182] incorporated an intention to issue a legislative proposal in order to set up an EES by 2011.[183] Following the unsuccessful negotiations on the 2013 'Smart Borders'[184]

[175] Article 82(1) of Regulation 2019/1896 (hereinafter 'the EBCGA Regulation').

[176] Article 82(10) of Regulation 2019/1896.

[177] Regulation (EU) 2017/2226 of the European Parliament and of the Council of 30 November 2017 establishing an Entry/Exit System (EES) to register entry and exit data and refusal of entry data of third-country nationals crossing the external borders of the Member States and determining the conditions for access to the EES for law enforcement purposes, and amending the Convention implementing the Schengen Agreement and Regulations (EC) No 767/2008 and (EU) No 1077/2011 [2017] OJ L327/20.

[178] To extend art 96 CISA alerts.

[179] Council Document 12813/01 (15 October 2001), 3.

[180] The Hague Programme: Strengthening Freedom, Security and Justice in the European Union [2005] OJ C53/01 3 March 2005, 7 point 1.7.2.

[181] See European Commission, 'Communication on improved effectiveness, enhanced interoperability and synergies among European databases in the area of Justice and Home Affairs' COM (2005) 597 final, Brussels, 24 November 2005, 6; and Commission, 'Communication on policy priorities in the fight against illegal immigration of third-country nationals' COM (2006) 402 final, Brussels, 19 July 2006.

[182] The Entry/Exit System and a Registered Traveller Programme were suggested by the Council in the Stockholm Programme, requiring the Commission to propose legislation on that matter; see European Commission, 'Communication, 'Overview of information management in the area of freedom, security and justice' COM (2010) 385 final, Brussels, 20 July 2010, 19; Commission, 'The Stockholm Programme – An open and secure Europe serving and protecting citizens' COM (2010) 171, 20 April 2010 (hereinafter 'Stockholm Programme Action Plan').

[183] COM (2010) 171, 44.

[184] Already in February 2013, the Commission presented three legislative proposals forming the so-called 'Smart Borders' package, including a proposal to establish the Entry/Exit System ('Proposal for a Regulation of the European Parliament and of the Council establishing an Entry/Exit System (EES) to register entry and exit data of third country nationals crossing the external borders of the Member States of the European Union' COM (2013) 95 final, Brussels, 28 February 2013), a proposal to set up a Registered Traveller Programme (RTP) ('Proposal for a Regulation of the European Parliament and of the Council establishing a Registered Traveller Programme' COM (2013) 97 final, Brussels, 28 February 2013 (hereinafter 'RTP proposal')) and a proposal on the amendments to the Schengen Borders Code (SBC) (Regulation (EU) 2016/399 of the European Parliament and of the Council of 9 March 2016 on a Union Code on the rules governing the movement of persons across borders (Schengen Borders Code) [2016] OJ L77/1).

package, the 2016 EES proposal[185] was, subject to changes, eventually adopted in November 2017.[186]

The EES is supposed to improve the management of the external Schengen borders, prevent irregular immigration and facilitate the administration of migration flows.[187] The main objectives of the EES are manifold and are laid down under Article 6(1)(a)–(i) of the EES Regulation. As a secondary objective, the EES grants law enforcement access to stored data in order to contribute to the prevention, detection and investigation of terrorist offences or of other serious criminal offences.[188] In addition, it shall enable the aggregation of information for investigations relating to terrorist offences or other serious criminal offences, including the identification of perpetrators, suspects and victims who have crossed external EU borders.[189]

Both national LEAs and Europol may be granted access to the EES, and thus to all entries and exits of short-term visa holders and visa-exempted travellers to and from the Schengen Area.[190] The system thereby functions like a 'tracking tool' and will first be interoperable with the VIS and Eurodac to complement the information stored on visa applications, rejected visas and data about asylum applicants.[191] This is the first logical step towards facilitating the exchange of information between the individual systems and achieving full interoperability between all remaining AFSJ databases. Retention periods for entry/exit records and refusals of entry were set to a maximum period of five years in the initial proposal, but were ultimately shortened to three years in the final EES Regulation.[192]

[185] 'Proposal for a Regulation of the European Parliament and of the Council establishing an Entry/Exit System (EES) to register entry and exit data and refusal of entry data of third country nationals crossing the external borders of the Member States of the European Union and determining the conditions for access to the EES for law enforcement purposes and amending Regulation (EC) No 767/2008 and Regulation (EU) No 1077/2011' COM (2016) 194 final, Brussels, 6 April 2016. This was accompanied by a proposal concerning changes to the SBC: 'Proposal for a Regulation of the European Parliament and of the Council amending Regulation (EU) 2016/399 as regards the use of the Entry/Exit System' COM (2016) 196 final, Brussels, 6 April 2016.

[186] Council of the European Union, 'Entry-Exit System: Final Adoption by the Council', www.consilium.europa.eu/en/press/press-releases/2017/11/20/entry-exit-system-final-adoption-by-the-council.

[187] European Commission, 'Security Union: Commission Welcomes Adoption of Entry/Exit System for Stronger and Smarter EU Borders' (25 October 2017), https://ec.europa.eu/home-affairs/news/security-union-commission-welcomes-adoption-entryexit-system-stronger-and-smarter-eu-borders_en. For an analysis of the EES, see D Cole Mark and Teresa Quintel, 'Data Retention under the Proposal for an EU Entry/Exit System (EES): Analysis of the Impact on and Limitations for the EES by Opinion 1/15 on the EU/Canada PNR Agreement of the Court of Justice of the European Union' (2017), https://www.greens-efa.eu/files/assets/docs/data_retention_under_the_proposal_for_an_eu_entry_exit_system__ees_.PDF.

[188] Article 6(2)(a) of Regulation (EU) 2017/2226.

[189] ibid art 6(2)(b).

[190] Quintel (n 140).

[191] Article 8 of Regulation (EU) 2017/2226.

[192] ibid art 34(1) and (2).

Whether and how the EES will, after detecting that a TCN overstayed his or her visa, allow the identification and detection of that TCN and enable the competent national authorities of the Member States to take appropriate measures[193] is questionable. Although detecting a person who overstayed might lead the responsible Member State to issue a return decision and/or an entry ban, which would also be included in the SIS III, it might not be possible to locate that person and enforce the return decision/entry ban. Hence, the EES may be able to detect overstayers, but not tackle any of the underlying causes and, taken on its own, has no means to reduce the number of overstayers.[194]

ii. The European Travel Information and Authorisation System

In 2008, the Commission issued a plan to establish an Electronic System of Travel Authorisation, which was finally proposed as the European Travel Information and Authorisation System (ETIAS) in 2016.[195] The ETIAS, which will apply to visa-exempt persons[196] travelling to the EU, was adopted in September 2018. According to the ETIAS Regulation, the ETIAS will be an automated system used to determine the eligibility of TCNs to cross the external borders of the EU.[197] Like the American ESTA, or the Canadian and Australian eTA, travellers will have to submit an online travel authorisation request prior to their arrival at the external border of a Schengen country.[198] Border guards would, however, still have the final say as to whether or not entry to the Schengen Area will be granted.

To remedy the lack of information available to border guards concerning a person entering the EU and to reinforce the internal security of the Union, the ETIAS shall identify persons who pose a security risk before they arrive at the Schengen external border. As secondary objective, the ETIAS shall make information from the system available to national LEAs and Europol for law enforcement purposes relating to serious crime and terrorism.[199] In addition, ETIAS applications will be cross-checked against an ETIAS watch-list and against the so-called ETIAS screening rules, an algorithm enabling profiling through

[193] ibid art 6(1)(c).

[194] This had already been pointed out by the Article 29 Data Protection Working Party (WP29) in 2014. See WP29, 'Opinion 01/2014 on the Application of Necessity and Proportionality Concepts and Data Protection within the Law Enforcement Sector' (2014). For the assessment of the 2013, see: WP29, 'Opinion 05/2013 on Smart Borders, Adopted on 6 June 2013' (2013).

[195] 'Proposal for a Regulation of the European Parliament and of the Council establishing a European Travel Information and Authorisation System (ETIAS) and amending Regulations (EU) No 515/2014, (EU) 2016/399, (EU) 2016/794 and (EU) 2016/1624' COM (2016) 731 final, Brussels, 16 November 2016.

[196] Currently, nationals of around 60 countries worldwide do not need a visa to enter the EU.

[197] European Commission, Directorate-General for Migration and Home Affairs, and PricewaterhouseCoopers, *Feasibility Study for a European Travel Information and Authorisation System (ETIAS): Final Report* (2016), http://dx.publications.europa.eu/10.2837/36503.

[198] Not having been granted a travel authorisation would always result in a refusal of entry.

[199] Articles 43 and 44 of Regulation (EU) 2018/1240.

the comparison of data recorded in an ETIAS application file with specific risk indicators. These risk indicators will be established by the ETIAS Central Unit and indicate any security, illegal immigration or high epidemic risks.[200] Furthermore, ETIAS data will be matched against the other AFSJ databases as well as Europol data, the Interpol Stolen and Lost Travel Documents database (SLTD) and the Interpol Travel Documents Associated with Notices database (TDAWN). The ETIAS travel authorisation is valid for three years, but may be revoked or annulled prior to that expiry date.[201] Finally, Europol is supposed to enter data into an ETIAS watch-list and to connect information that might not be available to individual Member States. This shall enable ETIAS authorities to receive information necessary to assess potential risks concerning individuals travelling to the EU.

Arguably, the ETIAS is the most complex system and includes some of the most dispersed purposes in comparison to the other AFSJ databases. This complexity is exacerbated by the numerous implementing acts that lay down the specific procedures applicable, for instance, with regard to the refusal, annulment or revocation of ETIAS travel authorisations,[202] or to accessing, amending, erasing and advance erasing of data in the ETIAS Central System.[203] The so-called ETIAS Consequential Amendments[204] that establish interoperability between the ETIAS and the other AFSJ databases render understanding the system practically impossible.

In addition, many provisions in the Regulation itself remain unclear, which makes it difficult to separate between law enforcement and migration purposes and to draw a line between criminal law enforcement and migration law enforcement processing of personal data. Where additional functionalities are being added to the database and blur the line between border control and security objectives, it becomes more difficult to differentiate and strictly define the purposes of processing. Moreover, the roles of actors involved in the

[200] ibid art 33(1).

[201] European Commission, 'Security Union: A European Travel Information and Authorisation System – Questions & Answers', https://europa.eu/rapid/press-release_MEMO-18-4362_en.htm.

[202] Commission Implementing Decision (EU) 2022/102 of 25 January 2022 laying down forms for refusal, annulment or revocation of a travel authorisation [2022] OJ L17/59.

[203] Commission Implementing Decision (EU) 2021/1028 of 21 June 2021 adopting measures for the application of Regulation (EU) 2018/1240 of the European Parliament and of the Council as regards accessing, amending, erasing and advance erasing of data in the ETIAS Central System [2021] OJ L224/13.

[204] Regulation (EU) 2021/1150 of the European Parliament and of the Council amending Regulations (EU) 2018/1862 and (EU) 2019/818 as regards the establishment of the conditions for accessing other EU information systems for the purposes of the European Travel Information and Authorisation System [2021] OJ L249/2; and Regulation (EU) 2021/1151 of the European Parliament and of the Council amending Regulations (EU) 2019/816 and (EU) 2019/818 as regards the establishment of the conditions for accessing other EU information systems for the purposes of the European Travel Information and Authorisation System [2021] OJ L249/7.

processing of personal data in the ETIAS are often unclear. For instance, Europol may request to consult data stored in the ETIAS and submit a request to consult specific sets of data stored in the ETIAS to the ETIAS Central Unit.[205] The latter will be established within the EBCGA and be responsible, inter alia, for verifying hits in the system, defining risk indicators and communicating with national ETIAS Units[206] and Europol. The EBCGA will be the controller in relation to the processing of personal data in the ETIAS Central System[207] while eu-LISA is to be considered a controller in relation to information security management of the ETIAS Central System,[208] while in relation to the processing of personal data in the ETIAS Central System by a national authority,[209] the ETIAS National Unit is to be considered a controller.[210] With regard to the ETIAS watch-list and the ETIAS screening rules, data protection concerns are by no means reduced.

iii. The European Criminal Records Information System for Third Country Nationals

In June 2017, the Commission proposed the establishment of a European Criminal Records Information System for Third Country Nationals and stateless persons (ECRIS-TCN).[211] As the name indicates, the ECRIS-TCN is a centralised system that enables the exchange of criminal records of convicted TCNs and stateless persons in the EU.[212] It was adopted in April 2019 and will complement the current ECRIS system that enables the exchange of criminal records of EU citizens.[213]

[205] Article 53 of Regulation (EU) 2018/1240.

[206] In accordance with art 8 of Regulation (EU) 2018/1240, ETIAS National Units are responsible for examining and deciding on applications for travel authorisation where the automated application process has reported a hit and the manual processing of the application has been initiated by the ETIAS Central Unit.

[207] ibid art 57(1).

[208] ibid.

[209] The so-called ETIAS National Units, which examine and decide on applications for travel authorisation where the automated application process has reported a hit and the manual processing of the application has been initiated by the ETIAS Central Unit.

[210] Article 57(2) of Regulation (EU) 2018/1240.

[211] 'Proposal for a Regulation of the European Parliament and of the Council establishing a centralised system for the identification of Member States holding conviction information on third country nationals and stateless persons (TCN) to supplement and support the European Criminal Records Information System (ECRIS-TCN system) and amending Regulation (EU) No 1077/2011' COM (2017)344 final, Brussels, 29 June 2017.

[212] Meijers Committee, standing committee of experts on international immigration, and refugee and criminal law, 'CM1710 Note on the Definition of Third-Country Nationals in the Commission's ECRIS-TCN Proposal' (2 October 2017), https://www.commissie-meijers.nl/sites/all/files/cm1710_note_on_ecris-tcn.pdf.

[213] Council Framework Decision 2009/315/JHA of 26 February 2009 on the organisation and content of the exchange of information extracted from the criminal record between Member States [2009] OJ L93/23.

However, other than the ECRIS, the updated ECRIS-TCN will store the personal data of TCNs on a centralised basis. While with regard to EU citizens, the Member State of nationality would be requested to provide additional information concerning one of its citizens in accordance with the ECRIS Framework Decision, it is difficult to identify the Member State that would 'centralise' the data of convicted TCNs. Arguably this cannot be done for TCNs and thus the ECRIS-TCN centralises the data on convicted TCNs at the EU level.

The ECRIS-TCN is not a law enforcement database per se. Its purpose – the identification of the Member State(s) holding criminal records of TCNs – should not necessarily be regarded as a law enforcement purpose.[214] Only where a criminal record exists will data be transferred by the convicting Member State to the requesting Member State on a bilateral basis. For the procedure of exchanging criminal records, the ECRIS-TCN follows the procedure that was implemented for the current legal instruments governing the ECRIS.

The central ECRIS-TCN system, in which all queries shall be submitted, will contain identity information such as name, nationality or gender and the code of the convicting Member State, but will also store fingerprints and facial images, where those are registered in criminal records by the Member States.[215] How long the data will be retained in the ECRIS-TCN will depend on the retention periods of the criminal records in the national databases.[216]

IV. Conclusion

The above-mentioned AFSJ databases share similar, recurring characteristics. With the exception of the ETIAS, all the operational databases, the amended versions or proposed systems, are increasingly based on biometric data such as fingerprints and facial images. In addition, all databases retain the information for a similar period, from three to five years and longer.[217] Consequently, where data are being retained for comparably similar periods, the competent authorities accessing and processing these data will be able to create very detailed profiles of TCNs, provided they can connect the data from different databases.

In order to use these profiles for investigative purposes, all systems, whether law enforcement or non-law enforcement databases, grant national LEAs and Europol access to stored data for the prevention, detection and investigation of

[214] Information on a criminal record could also be requested where the TCN in question applied for employment in a profession where such record is required. On this, see also CJEU, Case C-439/19, *B v Latvijas Republikas Saeima*, ECLI:EU:C:2021:504, 22 June 2021.

[215] Article 5 of Regulation (EU) 2019/816.

[216] ibid art 8(1).

[217] Quintel (n 140).

terrorist offences and other serious crimes. In addition, other authorities and EU Agencies such as the EBCGA have been provided with a new operational mandate. In particular, the EBCGA will, in the future, play a pivotal role in cooperating with Europol and national competent (law enforcement) authorities. Access to TCNs' personal data has been progressively widened with regard to already-existing databases and has become a standard feature for new systems.

In addition, with the adoption of the EES, the changes that were proposed under the ETIAS consequential amendments, the 2020 Eurodac proposal and the VIS reform, all of the abovementioned AFSJs will become more interoperable in the near future. This will include all of the databases mentioned in the preceding section. Evidently, this will result in a mixing of purposes and allow the competent authorities to process personal data within very broadly defined objectives.

On 12 December 2017, the EU Commission presented two proposals on the establishment of interoperability between EU large-scale databases, which were adopted in May 2019. Interoperability is supposed to enable the interconnectivity of all centralised EU databases for security, border and migration management by 2023.[218]

The new interoperable architecture between AFSJ databases reflects the continuous paradigm shift in the area of border management away from physical and manual operations and towards more and more automated set-ups. In addition, interoperability leads away from the traditional silo-based approach that was an inherent feature of the earlier versions of AFSJ databases.[219] By merging immigration and law enforcement databases and both blurring and multiplying immigration and law enforcement purposes, interoperability has grave privacy and data protection repercussions.[220] In particular, coherent retention periods and similar conditions for law enforcement access will pave the way for streamlined access conditions and a dilution of migration and security purposes.[221]

The Interoperability Regulations could be seen as a final stage in the evolutionary development of AFSJ databases, transforming into an overarching system, which abandons the initial compartmentalisation of the AFSJ databases. However, this final system is by no means intended to be static or finalised; rather, interoperability should be perceived as an expandable toolbox that may be extended

[218] Katrien Luyten and Sofia Voronova, 'Briefing: Legislation in Progress, Interoperability between EU Border and Security Information Systems' (2019), https://www.europarl.europa.eu/thinktank/en/document/EPRS_BRI(2018)628267.

[219] Working Party on Frontiers/Mixed Committee, 'Beyond the Technical Implementation of the Future IT Systems for Border Management: Re-engineering of Business Processes, Brussels, 15 February 2021', https://docplayer.net/206639003-6138-21-mdl-cr-1-jai-1-limite-en.html.

[220] Niovi Vavoula, 'Databases for Non-EU Nationals and the Right to Private Life' in Francesca Bignami (ed), *EU Law in Populist Times: Crises and Prospects* (Cambridge University Press, 2020) 265.

[221] Quintel (n 140).

with additional functionalities, access possibilities and databases. The latest initiatives, such as the proposed Police Cooperation Code,[222] consisting of a proposal for a Prüm II Regulation,[223] a proposed Recommendation on operational police cooperation[224] and new rules on information exchange between law enforcement authorities of Member States,[225] may be seen as such extensions that are supposed to be included within the interoperable framework.

[222] Commission, 'Police Cooperation Code: Boosting Police Cooperation', https://ec.europa.eu/commission/presscorner/detail/en/ip_21_6645.

[223] 'Proposal for a Regulation of the European Parliament and of the Council on automated data exchange for police cooperation ("Prüm II"), amending Council Decisions 2008/615/JHA and 2008/616/JHA and Regulations (EU) 2018/1726, 2019/817 and 2019/818 of the European Parliament and of the Council' COM (2021) 784 final, Brussels, 8 December 2021. See also EDPS, 'Opinion 4/2022 on the Proposal for a regulation on automated data exchange for police cooperation ("Prüm II")' (2 March 2022).

[224] 'Proposal for a Council Recommendation on operational police cooperation' COM (2021) 780, Brussels, 8 December 2021.

[225] 'Proposal for a Directive of the European Parliament and of the Council on information exchange between law enforcement authorities of Member States, repealing Council Framework Decision 2006/960/JHA' COM (2021) 782 final, Brussels, 8 December 2021. See also EDPS, 'Opinion 5/2022 on the proposal for a Directive on information exchange between law enforcement authorities of Member States' (7 March 2022).

2

The End of Purpose Limitation

I. Interoperability in a Nutshell

The Interoperability Regulations may, apart from their scope, be regarded as more or less identical 'sister regulations'. This means that most of their provisions are replicated, whereas the remaining parts that differ under the first Regulation should be regarded as being complemented by those under the second and vice versa.

On the one hand, Regulation (EU) 2019/817 covers the area of borders and visa, and comprises the VIS, the EES, the ETIAS and those parts of the SIS III that are applicable in the field of border checks. On the other hand, Regulation (EU) 2019/818 applies in the field of police and judicial cooperation, asylum and migration, and covers the remaining databases, namely Eurodac, the ECRIS-TCN, and both the SIS III Regulation on the return of illegally staying TCNs as well as the SIS II Regulation applicable in the field of police cooperation and judicial cooperation in criminal matters.[1] Consequently, when read together, the two Regulations achieve full interoperability of all underlying AFSJ databases.[2]

The four main novel components that are supposed to be established under the interoperability regime are a European Search Portal (ESP),[3] a shared Biometric Matching Service (BMS),[4] a Common Identity Repository (CIR)[5] and a Multiple Identity Detector (MID).[6] These components will be connected among each other and with the underlying databases,[7] either directly or indirectly,[8] and information

[1] At the time of writing, Eurodac is not included within the scope of Regulation (EU) 2019/818, but is foreseen to be connected once the co-legislators reach political agreement on the proposal for a recast Eurodac Regulation.

[2] Article 1(1) of Regulation (EU) 2019/817 and Regulation (EU) 2019/818.

[3] Article 6 of Regulation (EU) 2019/817 and Regulation (EU) 2019/818.

[4] Article 12 of Regulation (EU) 2019/817 and Regulation (EU) 2019/818.

[5] Article 17 of Regulation (EU) 2019/817 and Regulation (EU) 2019/818.

[6] Article 25 of Regulation (EU) 2019/817 and Regulation (EU) 2019/818; art 1(2) of Regulation (EU) 2019/817 and Regulation (EU) 2019/818.

[7] In the following, 'underlying databases' shall mean the VIS, the EES, the ETIAS, the ECRIS-TCN and Eurodac.

[8] Personal data contained in the SIS III will not be directly linked to the interoperability components, as the SIS III also includes personal data of EU citizens, while the interoperable system is only supposed to include the personal data of TCNs. Nevertheless, personal data in the SIS III will be searchable via the ESP.

stored in the entire system will be accessible to authorities designated in accordance with national law or the provisions of the Interoperability Regulations and subject to certain conditions.

Whereas the ESP will provide a single search infrastructure, the BMS, the CIR and the MID are central databases that will store the personal data from the underlying AFSJ databases at the EU level. Both the MID and the CIR may be accessed by designated national authorities as well as Europol and the EBCGA, whereas the BMS, in addition to storing the data centrally, will serve as a platform to automatically match the data retrieved from the other two components.

A. The European Search Portal

The ESP, as a central search tool, is supposed to allow the competent authorities the simultaneous querying of the underlying AFSJ databases as well as the Europol and INTERPOL systems.[9] INTERPOL data, according to Article 4(1) of the interoperability Regulations, includes the INTERPOL SLTD database and the INTERPOL TDAWN database,[10] while Europol data theoretically includes all data that it may process for the performance of its tasks.[11] The end-users would in principle use travel or ID document data[12] to launch a query in the underlying databases, the CIR, Europol data and the INTERPOL databases via a direct connection to the ESP. Should a search with the input data lead to a match[13] in the CIR, the MID or the underlying databases, the end-user would be informed in accordance with his or her access rights.

Instead of queries being carried out in eight different databases separately, searches via the ESP will be systematically conducted within all systems in parallel

[9] Article 6(2)(b) of Regulation (EU) 2019/817 and Regulation (EU) 2019/818.

[10] At present, no international agreement with INTERPOL is in place that would allow for the sharing of personal data in the interoperability components with INTERPOL. However, negotiations between the EU and INTERPOL for a cooperation agreement are currently ongoing. This cooperation agreement is supposed to provide the legal basis to authorise the ESP to connect with INTERPOL databases. See European Commission, 'Recommendation for a Council Decision authorising the opening of negotiations for a cooperation agreement between the European Union and the International Criminal Police Organisation (ICPOINTERPOL)' COM (2021) 177 final, Brussels, 14 April 2021, 4. See also EDPS Opinion 8/2021, 'On the Recommendation for a Council Decision authorising the opening of negotiations for a cooperation agreement between the European Union and the INTERPOL' (25 May 2021); and Council of the European Union, 'Council Decision N (EU) authorising the opening of negotiations for a cooperation agreement between the European Union and the International Criminal Police Organization (ICPO-INTERPOL)', 10264/21, Brussels, 13 July 2021; European Parliament, 'Draft report Recommendations on the negotiations for a cooperation agreement between the European Union and the International Criminal Police Organization (ICPO-INTERPOL)', PE732.613v01-00 and PE732.613v02-00 (24 May 2022).

[11] The Interoperability Regulations refer to Europol data as personal data processed by Europol for the purposes referred to in Article 18(2)(a), (b) and (c) of Regulation (EU) 2016/794/the recast Europol Regulation from 2022.

[12] Meaning both biographical or alphanumeric data and biometric data.

[13] Data searched corresponding to data in one of the systems.

using both alphanumeric and biometric data, and the combined results will be displayed on one single screen.[14] The ESP results emanating from the underlying AFSJ databases are supposed to be limited to the information to which the end-user is granted access pursuant to the provisions laying down the conditions according to which Eurodac, the VIS, the EES, the ETIAS, the ECRIS-TCN and the SIS III may be consulted by the designated authorities under national law.

Whenever an end-user queries the ESP, then the AFSJ underlying databases, the Europol data, (potentially) the INTERPOL databases, the CIR and the MID shall provide the data that they hold and indicate in which system the data are stored.[15] Consequently, where the user is not granted access to one or more of the underlying AFSJ databases, Europol or INTERPOL data, the ESP should neither indicate whether a person is stored in those systems nor alter their access conditions.[16] For each category of ESP-user, eu-LISA shall configure a profile based on the purposes of the queries and the end-user's access rights in accordance with EU and national law.[17] In addition, each access to the ESP requires a log, indicating the user, the data requested and time of the query, as well as the EU and INTERPOL database(s) queried[18] in order to ensure monitoring for data protection purposes.[19]

However, it is not entirely clear whether the querying user would be granted access to datasets that will be generated by and stored in the interoperability components. Hence, while the ESP shall reveal no information regarding the underlying AFSJ databases, access conditions to Europol and INTERPOL data, and to personal data that will be stored in the MID and CIR are much less precise and could lead to the circumvention of the stricter rules that are laid down in the founding acts of the underlying databases. Access to both components – the MID and the CIR – is regulated, although at times implicitly. Almost all queries in the interoperability system would require access to the CIR, the BMS and the MID to execute the search, while – hypothetically – users would only have access to one system. Nevertheless, the users are informed of the corresponding data and, hence, implicitly also about information stored in the CIR and the BMS.

B. The Shared Biometric Matching Service

The BMS will establish a common platform that will use the biometric data from the SIS III, Eurodac, the EES, the VIS and the ECRIS-TCN to generate and store so-called biometric templates by replacing those parts of the central systems in

[14] Article 9(1) of Regulation (EU) 2019/817 and Regulation (EU) 2019/818.
[15] Article 9(4) of Regulation (EU) 2019/817 and Regulation (EU) 2019/818.
[16] Article 9(4), third sentence of Regulation (EU) 2019/817 and Regulation (EU) 2019/818.
[17] Article 8(1) of Regulation (EU) 2019/817 and Regulation (EU) 2019/818.
[18] Article 10(1) of Regulation (EU) 2019/817 and Regulation (EU) 2019/818.
[19] Article 10(3) of Regulation (EU) 2019/817 and Regulation (EU) 2019/818.

the underlying databases that store biometrics, such as fingerprint data and facial images.[20] In essence, the BMS would create biometric samples, or templates, while the original biometric data would be stored in the CIR or remain in the national systems of the underlying AFSJ databases.[21] With the use of those templates, the BMS is supposed to substitute the checking of each underlying database in five separate searches.

To achieve its main purpose, the BMS shall facilitate the identification of individuals who are registered in several databases.[22] By simultaneously comparing the biometrics from all connected systems in an automatic manner, the BMS is supposed to make the identification of TCNs not only more reliable but also more cost-effective and faster.[23] The BMS itself would not be directly searchable, but would serve as feeder database for the CIR and the MID, supporting the objectives of the underlying AFSJ databases connected to it.[24]

C. The Multiple Identity Detector

The MID[25] uses the personal data retained in the CIR and the SIS III in order to carry out the detection of multiple identities and to provide searchable results via the ESP.[26] For that purpose, the MID will be interconnected with the CIR and the SIS III in order to check, by automatically cross-matching the data stored in both systems, whether information concerning a person already exists in either the CIR or the SIS III at the time when new data are added in one of the underlying databases.[27] This process of multiple identity detection shall be launched in accordance with Article 27 of the Interoperability Regulations whenever an application file is created or updated in the VIS, the ETIAS, or the EES,[28] when a data record is created or updated in the ECRIS-TCN, or when an alert in the SIS III is created or updated.[29]

[20] The ETIAS will not store biometric data and will therefore not be linked to the shared BMS. In addition, palm print and DNA data that are only stored in the SIS will not be included in the BMS. According to Recital 19, this follows the principles of necessity and proportionality.

[21] According to Recital 19, biometric templates should be obtained from biometric data, but it should not be possible to obtain that same biometric data from the biometric templates.

[22] Recital 18 of Regulation (EU) 2019/817 and Regulation (EU) 2019/818.

[23] COM (2017) 793 and 794 final, 6.

[24] Article 12(1) of Regulation (EU) 2019/817 and Regulation (EU) 2019/818.

[25] Most on the discussion on the MID here is based on the following chapter: Teresa Quintel and Diana Dimitrova, 'Technological Experimentation without Adequate Safeguards? Interoperable EU Databases and Access to the Multiple Identity Detector by SIRENE Bureaux' in Paul de Hert et al (eds), *Data Protection and Privacy Data Protection and Artificial Intelligence* (Bloomsbury, 2020).

[26] Although the Regulations do not clearly state that the ESP would display the results of the multiple identity detection, this seems logical, as the ESP's sole purpose is to search in the other systems (and hence is not a database), while the MID will only store the results of such multiple identity detection.

[27] COM (2017) 793 and 794 final, 7.

[28] It is assumed that the Eurodac databases will be linked once the Asylum Package has been agreed.

[29] Article 27(1)(a), (b), (c), (d) of Regulation (EU) 2019/817 on borders and visa and Article 27(1) (a) and (b) of Regulation (EU) 2019/818 on police and judicial cooperation, asylum and migration.

Hence, where an authorised user, such as a visa, immigration or other designated authority and, in the case of the SIS, the SIRENE staff, would add or update data in the underlying AFSJ databases, this would enable the detection of multiple identities by matching the newly added data against sets of stored biometric and biographical data across the systems. Because all identification data from the central systems in the underlying databases will be stored in the CIR, the BMS and the MID will only need to cross-match CIR data with those stored in SIS III. Where identical data exist in more than one system and can be associated with the same person, the MID will automatically create white or yellow links, which need to be changed into different colours in order to indicate whether the different identities are likely to be lawfully referring to the same person or whether there is a case of identity fraud.[30] While white links refer to either the same/similar identity or multiple lawful identities held by a person, red links indicate identity fraud. Before being turned into red, any MID link that points towards identity fraud needs to be verified by a verifying authority. Where such suspicion turns out to be invalid, MID links will be changed to green.

Pursuant to Article 30 of the Interoperability Regulations, yellow links indicate unsolved matches that are to be verified manually in order to ascertain whether a person was registered either lawfully or unlawfully under multiple identities. The yellow links must be changed into white, red or green links in accordance with the procedure laid down in Article 29 of the Interoperability Regulations. Finally, a green link indicates that the linked data refer to two different persons who do not share biometrics, but have similar identity data.[31] In essence, this means that, theoretically, whenever personal data of an individual would be stored in more than one of the underlying databases and would report some kind of a match, the MID should indicate either a white or a yellow link.[32]

In accordance with Article 29 of the Interoperability Regulations, the authority responsible for the manual verification of MID links is the one that added the data that led to a match in one of the underlying AFSJ databases connected to the CIR. The personal data from the central systems of the underlying AFSJ databases are stored in the CIR, separated according to the underlying database from which they originated. The personal data can only be amended at the national level (in the national systems that will feed the CIR from the national version of each database) and no direct change of data in the CIR is possible. Generally, personal data that was added to Eurodac and led to the creation of a MID link would need to be verified by the authorities competent to assess a request for international protection in the respective Member State, while the national SIRENE Bureaux and the central

[30] COM (2017) 793 and 794 final, 7.

[31] European Union Agency for Fundamental Rights (FRA), 'FRA Opinion – 1/2018, Interoperability and Fundamental Rights Implications Opinion of the European Union Agency for Fundamental Rights' (2018).

[32] According to Recital 39 of Regulation (EU) 2019/817 and Regulation (EU) 2019/818, the MID should only contain links between data on individuals present in more than one of the underlying databases.

authorities of the convicting Member State that inserted alerts or files into the SIS III and the ECRIS-TCN respectively would be responsible for manually verifying MID links concerning those data. With regard to data stored in the EES, manual verification would, in most cases, be carried out by the border authority creating or updating a file, whereas data in the VIS would have to be verified by the authorities competent to issue visas such as migration offices or embassies and consulates. Finally, personal data originally stored in the ETIAS would have to be manually verified by the national ETIAS Units or the ETIAS Central Unit.

In a nutshell, yellow MID links oblige the verifying authority to improve the accuracy of the data in the national systems of the underlying databases and change the colour into white, green or red categories. White and green links would indicate that the authority responsible for the manual verification concluded that the linked identities lawfully belong to the same person or refer to two different persons in a legitimate manner.[33] Consequently, no risk of identity fraud, either from the results of automatic checks or after manual verification, would be detected. In the case of red links, the authority responsible for the manual verification would conclude that identity fraud had occurred.[34] However, the mere existence of a red link will not lead to legal consequences for the individual, but would require follow-up action (concerning identity fraud) in accordance with national or EU law.[35] Where more than one link would be created, the authority responsible for the manual verification of different identities would have to assess each link separately.[36]

Different questions emerge with regard to a national competent authority that concluded that identity fraud exists as well as concerning the follow-up action that would have to be taken in accordance with national or EU law. On the one hand, there is no harmonised procedure to *conclude* on identity fraud, as national competent authorities would probably give preference to the procedure according to their national system. On the other hand, the procedure on how to prosecute identity fraud would depend on each criminal code in the respective Member State, as would the punitive measures. Hence, the provisions on the manual verification of MID links as well as the measures that are supposed to follow when identity fraud is assumed remain rather vague under the Interoperability Regulations.

The information to be stored in the MID is broadly described under Article 25(1) and (2)(a) of the Interoperability Regulations. Pursuant to the first paragraph of that provision, the MID is supposed to store so-called identity confirmation files. In accordance with paragraph 2(a), the MID shall be composed of a central infrastructure storing the different links and references to the underlying databases.

[33] Articles 31 and 33 of Regulation (EU) 2019/817 and Regulation (EU) 2019/818.
[34] Article 32 of Regulation (EU) 2019/817 and Regulation (EU) 2019/818.
[35] Article 32(2) of Regulation (EU) 2019/817 and Regulation (EU) 2019/818.
[36] Article 29(4) of Regulation (EU) 2019/817 and Regulation (EU) 2019/818.

The content of the MID identity confirmation files is laid down in Article 34 of the Interoperability Regulations. According to that provision, a MID identity confirmation file shall denote the authority responsible for the manual verification of different identities,[37] a reference to the AFSJ information systems in which the linked data are held,[38] the date of creation of the link or of any update to it[39] and a single identification number allowing for the retrieval of the linked data from the corresponding AFSJ databases.[40] Red and white MID links would not only be contained in the identity confirmation files, but would also be added to an individual file that would be stored in the CIR and which is supposed to hold an individual set of information of each person whose data are present in the underlying databases.[41]

D. The Common Identity Repository

Connected to the ESP, the BMS and the MID, the CIR could be described as the *crown jewel* of the interoperable system. The CIR will replace parts of the central systems of the EES, Eurodac, the VIS, the ETIAS and the ECRIS-TCN,[42] and will instead store a number of the data from those underlying AFSJ databases in its own repository, thereby serving as a new shared component.[43] In that central repository, the CIR will create one individual file for any person who is registered in the five underlying feeder databases.[44] These individual files that will be generated by the CIR will comprise both biometric and biographical data. In addition, the individual file will include a reference number that will indicate the underlying AFSJ database from which the data were retrieved.[45] In accordance with Article 18(1) of the Interoperability Regulations, all data stored in the CIR shall be logically separated according to the database from which they originate.[46]

Pursuant to Article 18(2) of the Interoperability Regulations, the CIR shall include a reference indicating the underlying databases to which the personal data originally belong. The Interoperability Regulations differentiate in terms of access rights to personal data stored under Article 18(1) and those stored under Article 18(2). This differentiation between access to categories of personal data under Article 18(1) and access to those data stored in accordance with Article 18(2) of the interoperability Regulations is important, as different authorities may obtain access to these categories, which varies in accordance with the

[37] Article 34(d) of Regulation (EU) 2019/817 and Regulation (EU) 2019/818.
[38] Article 34(b) of Regulation (EU) 2019/817 and Regulation (EU) 2019/818.
[39] Article 34(e) of Regulation (EU) 2019/817 and Regulation (EU) 2019/818.
[40] Article 34(c) of Regulation (EU) 2019/817 and Regulation (EU) 2019/818.
[41] Article 19(2) of Regulation (EU) 2019/817 and Regulation (EU) 2019/818.
[42] Article 17(2)(a) of Regulation (EU) 2019/817 and Regulation (EU) 2019/818.
[43] Recital 23 of Regulation (EU) 2019/817 and Regulation (EU) 2019/818.
[44] Article 17(1) of Regulation (EU) 2019/817 and Regulation (EU) 2019/818.
[45] Article 18(2) of Regulation (EU) 2019/817 and Regulation (EU) 2019/818.
[46] Article 18(1) of Regulation (EU) 2019/817 and Regulation (EU) 2019/818.

different purpose(s) of such access. These purposes for access to the CIR are, besides the access rules under of the underlying AFSJ databases, laid down in Articles 20–22 of the Interoperability Regulations and shall be discussed below.

The establishment of the CIR shall serve three main purposes, which are laid down in Article 17(1) of the Interoperability Regulations. First, the CIR shall facilitate and assist in the correct identification within the Schengen Area by the national police authorities of persons (TCNs) registered in the underlying AFSJ databases.[47] The conditions for such identity checks carried out by national police officers are laid down in Article 20 of the Interoperability Regulations.

Furthermore, the CIR shall support the functioning of the MID and the BMS by providing a repository of all identification data. Specifically, the CIR supports the verification of MID links by providing access to data stored in the CIR that are connected by yellow and red MID links. Authorities responsible for the verification of yellow and red MID links may access identity data in the CIR pursuant to the rules laid down in Article 21 of the Interoperability Regulations.

The third purpose of the CIR is to facilitate and streamline access by national LEAs and Europol to the EES, the VIS, the ETIAS and Eurodac for the purposes of preventing, detecting or investigating terrorist offences or other serious criminal offences. The conditions for accessing the CIR for such purposes are stipulated in Article 22 of the Interoperability Regulations.

Generally, the CIR should be queried via the ESP[48] in accordance with the three above-described purposes of the CIR[49] and the access rights under both national law and under the Interoperability Regulations. Depending on the purpose of access, the authority accessing the data may obtain full access to all categories of personal data stored in either the CIR or the underlying AFSJ databases, in accordance with Article 18(1) and (2) and subject to varying rules.

While the authority responsible for verifying yellow and red MID links may obtain access to personal data stored in the CIR under both Article 18(1) and (2) for the sole purpose of verification in accordance with Article 21 of the Interoperability Regulations, access to CIR data by a national police officer under Article 20 of the Interoperability Regulations for the purpose of identifying a TCN is more limited. Only where the query indicates that data on that person are stored in the CIR shall the police authority have access to consult the data referred to in Article 18(1) of the Interoperability Regulations.

Access to the CIR pursuant to Article 22 of the Interoperability Regulations by the designated national authorities and Europol for the purposes of preventing, detecting or investigating terrorist offences or other serious criminal offences follows a similar logic to Article 20 queries. The CIR will be queried by means of

[47] Whereas art 17(1) does not refer to the Schengen Area, Recital 24 of Regulation (EU) 2019/818 and of Regulation (EU) 2019/817 specifies that CIR checks are supposed to achieve the correct identification of persons within the Schengen Area.

[48] Recital 17 of Regulation (EU) 2019/817 and Regulation (EU) 2019/818.

[49] It should be noted that the purpose does not necessarily translate into access rights.

a two-step approach. In a first step, the underlying database(s), which hold data that correspond to the input information, will be displayed to the querying user in the form of a reference, as referred to in Article 18(2) of the Interoperability Regulations. In a second step, the user should request access to each individual system that contains matching data on the person whose personal data were queried.[50] Whether personal data that are stored in the underlying databases may be accessed will remain subject to prior authorisation by a verifying authority. All access conditions will remain the same as is currently the case, alongside the provisions in the legal instruments governing the SIS III, the VIS, Eurodac, the ETIAS, the ECRIS-TCN and the EES.[51]

In that regard, the CIR will complement the purposes of the MID and vice versa. According to the interoperability proposals, the two-step approach to search the CIR would be particularly useful in situations where suspects, perpetrators or victims of a serious crime would be unknown to the querying user.[52] As a result, searches in the CIR would allegedly render the current cascade regime of checking national systems prior to searching the AFSJ databases superfluous.[53] In addition, the CIR shall serve to achieve the objective of facilitating the identification of unknown persons who are unable to identify themselves, or of unidentified human remains in the case of a natural disaster, accident or terrorist attack.[54] The CIR and the SIS III would use the shared BMS to detect possible links on the basis of biometric data, and the ESP to detect possible links on the basis of alphanumeric data.

II. Interoperability as a Logical Step

Back in 2010, the European Commission stated that purpose limitation is a key consideration for most EU-level measures regulating the management of personal information. The Communication added that although a 'single, overarching EU information system with multiple purposes would deliver the highest degree of information sharing', creating such a system would 'constitute a gross and illegitimate restriction of individuals' right to privacy and data protection'. In addition, such a system would 'pose huge challenges in terms of development and operation'.[55]

[50] Teresa Quintel, 'Connecting Personal Data of Third Country Nationals: Interoperability of EU Databases in the Light of the CJEU's Case Law on Data Retention' (2018), https://papers.ssrn.com/sol3/papers.cfm?abstract_id=3132506.

[51] Article 22(2) of Regulation (EU) 2019/817 and Regulation (EU) 2019/818.

[52] COM (2017) 793 and 794 final, 9.

[53] Quintel (n 50).

[54] Article 2(1)(g) of Regulation (EU) 2019/817 and Regulation (EU) 2019/818.

[55] European Commission, 'Communication from the Commission to the European Parliament and the Council: Overview of Information Management in the Area of Freedom, Security and Justice' COM (2010) 385 final, Brussels, 20 July 2010.

Seven years later, the Commission proposed two Regulations on establishing a framework for interoperability between EU large-scale information systems in the AFSJ to close the remaining 'information gaps' between the existing AFSJ databases.[56] The two Interoperability Regulations legally interconnect all large-scale centralised AFSJ databases for security, border and migration management by amending their founding acts and establishing three new centralised databases: the MID, the CIR and the BMS. These interoperability components may be queried via a single search interface: the ESP.

Theoretically, interoperability is supposed to create new possibilities to exchange information, to better manage migration challenges and to enhance the EU's internal security.[57] In practice, interoperability will lead to new processing operations that are not always supported by a valid legal basis, will grant access to personal data of TCNs by additional authorities and will put an end to the purpose limitation principle by mixing migration with law enforcement purposes.

In the past, and particularly post-9/11 and after the Madrid/London terrorist attacks, several more or less unsuccessful attempts were made to build a comprehensive system for the registration of non-EU citizens coming to the Schengen Area.[58] At that time, however, the available technology was not sufficiently advanced to build an ambitious system such as the one envisaged under the interoperability framework. Besides the technological progress, the Paris/Brussels/Berlin terrorist attacks in 2015/16[59] and, in particular, *the refugee and migration crisis*[60] led to the narrative that all of those situations could have been prevented with a more gapless and interconnected landscape of immigration, border control and law enforcement databases.[61]

As illustrated above, the instrumentalisation of migration as a threat to the EU's internal security led to the usage of AFSJ databases, which had been established for asylum or visa purposes, to also serve the prevention and investigation of terrorism and other forms of serious crime by granting law enforcement access to stored personal data, subject to more or less strict conditions. For access by national LEAs, those conditions relied on a cascading system that required, inter alia, prior checks in national databases, necessity in a specific and serious case and prior authorisation by an (independent) body.

[56] European Commission, 'Security Union: Commission Closes Information Gaps to Better Protect EU Citizens', https://ec.europa.eu/commission/presscorner/detail/en/IP_17_5202.

[57] EDPS, 'European Data Protection Supervisor Statement on the Concept of Interoperability in the Field of Migration, Asylum and Security, 8 May 2017'.

[58] Niovi Vavoula, *Immigration and Privacy in the Law of the European Union: The Case of Information Systems* (Brill Nijhoff, 2022).

[59] European Parliament, 'Terrorism in the EU: Terror Attacks, Deaths and Arrests' (25 July 2018), https://www.europarl.europa.eu/news/en/headlines/security/20180703STO07125/terrorism-in-the-eu-terror-attacks-deaths-and-arrests.

[60] United Nations High Commissioner for Refugees, '2015: The Year of Europe's Refugee Crisis' (8 December 2015), https://www.unhcr.org/news/stories/2015/12/56ec1ebde/2015-year-europes-refugee-crisis.html.

[61] European Commission (n 56).

Between 2016 and 2019, updates of all existing operational EU databases were proposed, and three new systems were established. For all pre-existing databases, the revisions added additional categories of personal data to be processed, the purposes of the databases were expanded and law enforcement access to stored information was broadened. Interoperability will not only create new datasets by automatically matching the information retained in the underlying databases, but will further supplement the systems' current purposes and streamline law enforcement access to non-law enforcement databases.

Altogether, the Interoperability Regulations foresee seven purposes that the system shall achieve, ranging from improving the effectiveness of border controls to ensuring the identification of persons, contributing to the prevention and the combating of illegal immigration, but also to the prevention, detection and investigation of terrorist offences and of other serious criminal offences. The term 'streamlining' serves as an innocent word describing the rather problematic aligning and simplifying of the conditions to provide access across various systems. In addition, the Interoperability Regulations attribute more powers to the relevant EU Agencies in terms of connectedness to the system regarding access rights to the stored information, feeding the databases with their own data and even with regard to managing individual components of the interoperable framework.

Whereas for some, interoperability is a logical step to address the remaining information gap[62] between information systems and competent authorities, others see the interoperable framework as 'point of no return'.[63] The fundamental concern that emerges with the interoperable system is the circumvention of the purpose limitation principle, which stipulates that personal data should be collected for specified purposes and should not be used for new, incompatible purposes. That principle is enshrined in Article 8(1) of the EU Charter as well as Article 5 (1)(b) GDPR and Article 4 (1)(b) LED. Whereas the founding acts of the underlying databases and the Interoperability Regulations set out an inherent data protection regime, the GDPR and the Directive are relevant with regard to certain processing operations – for instance, once personal data are accessed by the competent authorities. However, the EU Charter, and therefore Article 8(1), applies horizontally to provisions that are addressed to the institutions, bodies, offices and agencies of the Union when they are implementing Union law.[64] Consequently, the purpose limitation principle must be respected in all EU legislative texts.

[62] Communication from the Commission to the European Parliament, the European Council and the Council, 'Progress report on the implementation of the European Agenda on Migration' COM (2018) 301 final, Brussels, 16 May 2018, 5.

[63] Tony Bunyan, 'Analysis: The "Point of No Return". Interoperability Morphs into the Creation of a Big Brother Centralised EU State Database Including All Existing and Future Justice and Home Affairs Databases (*Statewatch*, May 2018), https://www.statewatch.org/media/documents/analyses/no-332-eu-interop-morphs-into-central-database-revised.pdf, 12.

[64] Article 51(1) of the EU Charter.

Under the Interoperability Regulations, AFSJ databases that were initially established in so-called silos and compartmentalised according to their individual purposes will connect the dots by aggregating information from different sources and generate new data on that basis. Interoperability thereby makes conclusions or observations on relationships between those datasets. As discussed above, beyond the primary purposes of the underlying databases, which is that of border control, asylum, migration and the management of short-term visas, all of these systems are now supposed to contribute to the fight against (serious) crime, the detection of identity fraud and the identification of (unknown) suspects. It is important to note that the variety of new purposes that the Interoperability Regulations introduce explicitly is added on top of the underlying regulations in each AFSJ database. In addition, and as observed above, the list of purposes in the underlying systems was extended when these databases were modernised. None of the pieces within this patchwork is fully meaningful on its own, but interoperability will create an all-encompassing system that will render the boundaries between the different patches more fluid in order to merge their different purposes.

In that vein, the Interoperability Regulations shall streamline law enforcement access to non-law enforcement databases that hold information concerning TCNs. Thus, interoperability changes the initial purpose of the underlying databases more drastically than the previous revisions of their founding acts. The Interoperability Regulations substantially elevate the ancillary objective of the underlying databases (the fight against crime) at a seemingly equal level as the initial purposes and thereby transform immigration into semi-law enforcement databases.

By establishing a system that broadens and even merges originally separated purposes, the interoperability framework makes it more difficult for competent LEAs to distinguish between the actual purposes for access on the one hand and, on the other, facilitates access based on unspecified purposes. Parallel to this widening of the overall purposes that shall be achieved by the interoperable system, the Interoperability Regulations themselves encourage the intertwinement of law enforcement and non-law enforcement purposes by introducing provisions that authorise LEAs to access the system for the performance of different kinds of non-law enforcement tasks, such as the identification of TCNs during random identity checks.

By abolishing the cascading system of mandatory checks in national databases prior to accessing the EU systems, interoperability pushes the repurposing even further. The consequences of such abolition are manifold and will not only lead to new access and processing possibilities for competent authorities, but might also encourage false suspicions against persons whose data are stored in the databases. Where an LEA may be granted access to datasets in the interoperable system that connect migration and law enforcement data, those authorities might be more tempted to suspect certain types of crimes without any prior hint in a national database. While obscuring the purposes for law enforcement access and, in parallel, indirectly increasing the competences of both national and EU LEAs, interoperability may eventually provide fruitful ground for function creeps.

The increased involvement of EU Agencies poses additional data protection concerns, as discrepancies may arise in the context of interoperability where systematic data exchanges take place between actors on different levels that apply dissimilar data protection regimes. On the one hand, the legal gaps include the deficiencies that emerge with regard to the data protection regimes that apply at the national and EU levels. On the other hand, data protection concerns arise regarding the applicable legal framework where competent authorities at the national and EU levels exchange information pursuant to different data protection rules.

The Interoperability Regulations aim at fostering exchanges between competent LEAs at both the national and EU levels, which will make it increasingly difficult to supervise not only the processing authorities, but also the processing activities that will be carried out. Any function creep will make it even more difficult to determine whether a certain processing operation was carried out on justified grounds. It will become more challenging not only to clearly identify the authorities that initially inserted the personal data into the system, but also to follow the data flows where automated matching of information will be involved. Consequently, determining the authority responsible for inserting data will be extremely complicated and difficult to supervise, particularly where different data protection regimes apply and multiple supervisory authorities are responsible for supervision. These issues are aggravated where incorrect data are inserted into the interoperable system and matched against other data, as false positives may be multiplied, which also affects supervision.

Nevertheless, the above concerns need to be considered against the background that there might be a justified interest of LEAs to apply effective measures to analyse personal data for investigative purposes. According to the Impact Assessments to the interoperability proposals, the interoperable system will improve decision-making processes and increase the accuracy of data.[65] Yet, where the underlying databases hold inaccurate or wrong data, which currently is often the case,[66] cross-checking these data will certainly lead to false matches and an increased number of wrongful hits instead of improved decision-making procedures.[67] With interoperability, the number and levels of authorities required to input information into the underlying systems multiply and the possibilities for a straightforward identification of the initial input source will be obscured. Not only would this negatively affect the individual who might be wrongfully accused, but it would also obstruct the work of competent authorities, who might find themselves confronted with an abundance of wrong matches.[68]

[65] COM (2017) 793 and 794 final, 4, 10 and 23. See Quintel (n 50).

[66] 'Inaccurate Data in Schengen System "Threatens Rights"' (*EUobserver*, 8 January 2018), https://euobserver.com/tickers/140468.

[67] Quintel (n 50) 12.

[68] ibid 13.

Both the establishment of the interoperability framework and the streamlined access for LEAs to non-law enforcement databases need to be considered against the principles of necessity and proportionality. According to Article 52(1) of the EU Charter, an interference must genuinely meet the objectives of general interest recognised by the EU or the need to protect the rights and freedoms of others. Hence, the establishment of the interoperable system that will create new processing operations must pass the necessity and proportionality test. In particular, the new access provisions that will allow LEAs to search, consult and retrieve personal data from the system need to be justified in accordance with the necessity and proportionality principles in order to satisfy the requirements laid down in Article 52(1) of the EU Charter.

The CJEU has on several occasions held that the objective of preventing illegal entry to the EU represents an objective of general interest recognised by the Union[69] and has found that the objective of effective management of migratory flows[70] and effective control of immigration[71] may constitute an overriding reason in the public interest. It even accepted that administrative authorities have a wider margin of discretion when determining whether a TCN represents a 'threat to public policy or public security'.[72] However, those objectives are not to be equated or interchangeable with purposes.

Whereas the distinction between objectives and purposes is generally under-researched, in data protection law, such a differentiation is essential in order to enhance the reasonable expectation of data subjects.[73] One could refer to an objective as being of general nature – for instance, referring to an overall aim of a legislative measure when processing is provided for by law. In that case, the law would serve as the legal basis authorising the processing and would need to lay down both objectives and purposes. However, in other instances, the objective of the processing is already provided for, whereas the controller still needs to specify the specific purposes of processing.[74] Hence, while a legal basis only needs to specify the objective, the purposes of processing need to be specific at all times.

However, with regard to access, the Interoperability Regulations use their objectives as purposes in order to allow LEAs to access the CIR and the MID. Consequently, using the objectives of a legal act as the purpose of a processing activity will most probably lead to a broadening of the purpose and run the risk of

[69] CJEU, Case C-291/12, *Michael Schwarz v Stadt Bochum*, ECLI:EU:C:2013:670, 17 October 2013, para 36; and CJEU, Case C-225/12, *C Demir v Staatssecretaris van Justitie*, 7 November 2013, ECLI:EU:C:2013:725, para 41.

[70] CJEU, Case C-652/15, *Furkan Tekdemir v Kreis Bergstraße*, EU:C:2017:2, 29 March 2017, para 39; and CJEU, Case C-123/17, *Nefiye Yön v Landeshauptstadt Stuttgart*, ECLI:EU:C:2018:632, 7 August 2018, para 77.

[71] *Nefiye Yön v Landeshauptstadt Stuttgart* (n 70) para 87.

[72] CJEU, Case C-380/18, *Staatssecretaris van Justitie en Veiligheid v EP*, ECLI:EU:C:2019:1071, 12 December 2019, para 51.

[73] Recital 50 GDPR on further processing of personal data.

[74] For instance, with regard to consent under art 6(1)(a) of Regulation (EU) 2016/679.

being used discretionally by those that process the personal data in question. With regard to law enforcement access under the Interoperability Regulations, such discretionary processing could ultimately lead to discrimination and processing creep, where LEAs are permitted to process personal data for a multitude of broad objectives instead of clearly defined purposes.

III. Law Enforcement Access to the Interoperability Components

Law enforcement access to the underlying databases in the interoperable system for the prevention, investigation, detection and prosecution of serious crime follows a similar pattern as the access conditions that apply regarding the underlying AFSJ databases: in order to gain full access to (the SIS III), the EES, the VIS, the ETIAS, the ECRIS-TCN and Eurodac, the accessing authority must follow the conditions for access that are laid down in the founding act of each database. Consequently, similar concerns to those discussed in the previous part of this chapter concerning law enforcement access to the individual systems arise.

However, the interesting element regarding law enforcement access under interoperability is that the Regulations abandon the previous safeguard of prior searches in national databases, add additional access possibilities for LEAs and simultaneously allow access to further sets of personal data. The ESP will not only indicate whether data are stored in those underlying databases that the respective querying authority has permission to access, but will also display yellow and red MID links. With regard to law enforcement access to the CIR, the Interoperability Regulations even go a step further.

Access by competent law enforcement authorities to the CIR for law enforcement purposes follows the two-step approach, which brings new concerns regarding data subjects' privacy. First, the interoperable system allows national police authorities to access personal data for non-law enforcement purposes. In addition, queries in the CIR for the detection of multiple identities will indicate whether yellow or red MID links about a person exist in the system. Finally, the procedure of verification concerning MID links grants access to the data creating the link by those authorities that added the data, including national LEAs, such as the SIRENE Bureaux.

The following section will begin by briefly assessing the purposes for access to the CIR and the MID, and thereafter will illustrate the new data protection and privacy concerns that may arise regarding the new access possibilities for LEAs to consult CIR data for non-law enforcement purposes under Article 20 of the Interoperability Regulations, as well as law enforcement access to the MID for the purpose of verifying yellow MID links pursuant to Article 29 of the interoperability Regulations.

A. Access to the European Search Portal

Besides being connected to the CIR and the SIS, the ESP shall be linked to the MID via a secure communication infrastructure.[75] When a Member State authority or EU Agency launches a query in the ESP, all underlying databases – the CIR, the MID, as well as the Europol and (probably also in the future) the INTERPOL databases – shall provide the data that they hold in response to that query. It should be noted that the ESP will be configured in a way that only the databases to which the querying authority has access will show results.[76] However, this is only valid for the EES, the VIS, Eurodac, the ETIAS, the ECRIS-TCN, the SIS III, Europol data and the INTERPOL databases, and not those datasets that are generated by the interoperability components themselves. In those cases, the purposes for processing laid down in the Interoperability Regulations apply.

The objectives of the ESP are to facilitate the fast, seamless, efficient, systematic and controlled access of Member State authorities and EU Agencies to the AFSJ information systems, Europol data and the INTERPOL databases.[77] This facilitated access shall be for the performance of the tasks of those authorities and in accordance with their access rights and the objectives and purposes of the underlying databases.[78] Pursuant to Article 7(1) of the Interoperability Regulations, that access shall be governed by each legal instrument that establishes the respective connected system.

The use of the ESP shall be reserved to the Member State authorities and EU agencies having access to at least one of the underlying AFSJ databases. Access to the EES, the VIS, the ETIAS, Eurodac, the SIS III and the ECRIS-TCN will only be granted in accordance with the legal instruments governing these EU information systems. In addition, the ESP may be used by authorities having access to the CIR and the MID in accordance with the Interoperability Regulations. Access to Europol data and to the INTERPOL databases will be granted in accordance with the Europol Regulation and with EU or national law governing such access.[79] Further, use of the ESP and the data provided by it must follow the objectives and purposes laid down in the legal instruments governing the underlying AFSJ databases, in the Europol Regulation and/or in the interoperability Regulations.[80]

[75] Articles 6(2)(2)(c) and 25(2)(b) of Regulation (EU) 2019/817 and Regulation (EU) 2019/818.

[76] Article 9(4) of Regulation (EU) 2019/817 and Regulation (EU) 2019/818.

[77] In accordance with art 9(5) of Regulation (EU) 2019/817 and Regulation (EU) 2019/818, any queries of the INTERPOL databases launched via the ESP shall be performed in such a way that no information shall be revealed to the owner of the INTERPOL alert. The ESP shall only query the INTERPOL databases once the technical arrangements allow compliance with art 9(5). Pursuant to art 68(1), second sentence of Regulation (EU) 2019/817 and Regulation (EU) 2019/818, any impossibility of complying with art 9(5) shall have the result that the ESP does not query the INTERPOL databases, but shall not delay the start of operations of the ESP.

[78] Article 6(1) of Regulation (EU) 2019/817 and Regulation (EU) 2019/818.

[79] Article 7(1), first sentence of Regulation (EU) 2019/817 and Regulation (EU) 2019/818.

[80] Article 7(1), second sentence of Regulation (EU) 2019/817 and Regulation (EU) 2019/818.

The ESP adopts the objectives of the underlying databases, the Europol Regulation,[81] those enshrined in the INTERPOL constitutive acts and the purposes for access to the CIR and the MID laid down in the Interoperability Regulation. As illustrated above, both the CIR and the MID store red and yellow MID links as well as a reference to the underlying AFSJ databases. Hence, access given to datasets that were generated by the interoperable system and are stored in the MID and the CIR follow the objectives and purposes laid down in the Interoperability Regulations. As will be shown below, the Interoperability Regulations adopt the objectives laid down in Article 2(1)(a)–(g) as the purposes of access to the MID and the CIR, and thereby circumvent the purpose limitation principle.

A similar approach was chosen for identity checks that are to be carried out in accordance with Article 20 of the Interoperability Regulations. This provision requires CIR identity checks to be carried out for the sole purpose of identifying a person. Paragraph 5 of that Article stipulates that the national legislative measures implementing Article 20 shall specify the *precise* purposes of the identification within the purposes referred to in Article 2(1)(b) and (c) of the Interoperability Regulations.[82] Consequently, Article 20, just like the provisions on ESP searches, transforms the overall objectives of the Interoperability Regulations into purposes that may justify access to the CIR by LEAs.

Pursuant to Article 25 of the Interoperability Regulations, the MID is supposed to enable the detection of multiple identities in order to serve the dual purpose of facilitating identity checks and combating identity fraud. However, as for the ESP and the CIR, the Interoperability Regulations use their objectives as purposes for access to the MID, while from the wording of the declared MID purposes, those could at most serve as a *means to achieve* the overall objective of fighting illegal immigration and not as a purpose in itself. As previously mentioned, Article 2(1) of the Interoperability Regulations lists seven objectives that interoperability shall fulfil, including improving the effectiveness and efficiency of border checks, combating illegal immigration and ensuring a high level of security in the EU and its Member States. These objectives are broadly phrased and there is a risk of misuse to justify broad types of access to the MID if those objectives are used purposes, which should be specified and explicit.

In addition, Article 2(2)(a) and (b) of the Interoperability Regulations broadly state that in order to achieve these general objectives, the competent authorities shall take measures to combat identity fraud and ensure the correct identification of individuals. Hence, combating identity fraud should be seen solely as

[81] A recast Europol Regulation was adopted in April 2022, which will be further discussed in ch 4. This recast Regulation generates additional doubts as to the way in the which personal data of TCNs may be analysed in the Europol data environment and subsequently matched against data in the interoperability components.

[82] To contribute to the prevention and the combating of illegal immigration and to contribute to a high level of security within the AFSJ of the EU, including the maintenance of public security and public policy and safeguarding security in the territories of the Member States.

a measure to achieve the objective to prevent illegal immigration and not as a clearly specified and explicit purpose to access the CIR or the MID.[83]

Although preventing illegal migration and contributing to a high level of security within the AFSJ can be considered an objective recognised by the EU,[84] in the context of access to the CIR and the MID under the Interoperability Regulations, the use of these objectives as purpose is too broad[85] and implies a direct link between migration and certain forms of crime.

B. Article 20 Searches in the Common Identity Repository

Beyond standardising law enforcement access to the underlying databases and streamlining it under the new interoperable system, the Interoperability Regulations shall authorise national police authorities to access one of the interoperability components – the CIR – for the purpose of identifying a person.

Under Article 20 of the Interoperability Regulations, Member States may adopt national measures permitting national police authorities to query the CIR with both biometric and biographical data in order to establish the identity of a person where that person is unable to identify himself or herself. Such an inability to identify oneself may be established on several grounds. Queries in the CIR for identification may be carried out where a person is not in the possession of a (valid) travel document or another credible identity document,[86] where a person is unable or refuses to cooperate,[87] where there are doubts as to the authenticity of a provided ID or travel document[88] concerning the identity data provided by a person,[89] or where there are doubts as to the identity of the holder of a travel document or of another credible document.[90]

In addition, Member States may empower national police authorities to query the CIR with the biometric data of persons who are unable to identify themselves in the event of a natural disaster, an accident or a terrorist attack. This includes unidentified human remains pursuant to Article 20(4) of the Interoperability Regulations. In accordance with paragraph 3 of that Article, the police authority shall search the CIR with identity data of the person in combination with travel document data, or with the identity data provided by that person in situations where the biometric data of a person cannot be used.

[83] Quintel and Dimitrova (n 25).

[84] See, for instance, *Michael Schwarz v Stadt Bochum* (n 69) para 45.

[85] EDPS, 'Opinion 4/2018 on the Proposals for Two Regulations Establishing a Framework for Interoperability between EU Large-Scale Information Systems' (2018) 4, 13.

[86] Article 20(1)(a) of Regulation (EU) 2019/817 and Regulation (EU) 2019/818.

[87] Article 20(1)(e) of Regulation (EU) 2019/817 and Regulation (EU) 2019/818.

[88] Article 20(1)(c) of Regulation (EU) 2019/817 and Regulation (EU) 2019/818.

[89] Article 20(1)(b) of Regulation (EU) 2019/817 and Regulation (EU) 2019/818.

[90] Article 20(1)(d) of Regulation (EU) 2019/817 and Regulation (EU) 2019/818.

Under Article 17(1) of the interoperability Regulation, the CIR shall create an individual file for each person whose data are stored in the underlying AFSJ databases, logically separated according to the system from which they originated.[91] These individual files will contain the data from the central systems of the underlying databases that will be replaced and stored in the CIR, a reference to the database to which the data belong, as well as white and red links that were generated during the multiple identity detection in the MID.[92]

Where, during an identity check, a search indicates that data on that person are stored in the CIR, the querying police officer may, pursuant to Article 20(3) of the Interoperability Regulations, obtain access to the personal data retained in the central repository. The data replacing the central systems of the underlying databases that will be stored in the CIR shall, besides the names, previous names, pseudonyms, sex, date of birth, place and country of birth, current nationalit(ies), type and number of the travel document(s), a facial image and fingerprints of visa applicants, also include the code of the convicting Member State stored in the ECRIS-TCN where relevant. In addition, red MID links will be added to each individual CIR file, and it may be assumed that those will be shown during Article 20 CIR searches.

While the initial interoperability proposals did not specify whether a queried person must be present during CIR searches, the adopted Interoperability Regulations stipulate that the procedure under Article 20 of the Interoperability Regulations must be initiated in the presence of that person.[93] This was one of the requirements added by the European Parliament during the negotiations of the interoperability proposals.[94] In turn, the possibility to query the CIR with the biometric data of unidentified human remains in case of a natural disaster, accident or terrorist attack was added under paragraph 4 of Article 20.[95]

Besides the mandatory presence of a person during CIR identity searches, two additional safeguards were added under Article 20. First, CIR queries shall not be allowed against minors under the age of 12, unless this would be in the best interests of the child.[96] Second, Member States shall take into account the need to avoid any discrimination against TCNs.[97] How this would be implemented and

[91] Article 18(1) of Regulation (EU) 2019/817 and Regulation (EU) 2019/818.

[92] Articles 33(3) and 32(3) of Regulation (EU) 2019/817 and Regulation (EU) 2019/818.

[93] Article 20(2) of Regulation (EU) 2019/817 and Regulation (EU) 2019/818.

[94] Under art 20 of the amendments from June and October 2018, the European Parliament added that a queried person must be present during identity checks with biometric data. See 'Amended proposal for a Regulation of the European Parliament and of the Council on establishing a framework for interoperability between EU information systems (borders and visa) and amending Council Decision 2004/512/EC, Regulation (EC) No 767/2008, Council Decision 2008/633/JHA, Regulation (EU) 2016/399, Regulation (EU) 2017/2226, Regulation (EU) 2018/XX [the ETIAS Regulation], Regulation (EU) 2018/XX [the Regulation on SIS in the field of border checks] and Regulation (EU) 2018/XX [the eu-LISA Regulation], 2017/0351 (COD)', http://www.statewatch.org/news/2018/oct/eu-trilogue-interoperabilty-bordders-4-column.pdf.

[95] Article 20(4) of Regulation (EU) 2019/817 and Regulation (EU) 2019/818.

[96] Article 20(1), second sentence of Regulation (EU) 2019/817 and Regulation (EU) 2019/818.

[97] Article 20(5) of Regulation (EU) 2019/817 and Regulation (EU) 2019/818.

supervised in practice is mainly left to the national legislators that will implement the specificities related to Article 20, and whether those two requirements can be regarded as genuine safeguards remains questionable.

The national legislative measures that would lay down the legal basis for Article 20 CIR searches would have to specify the precise purposes of the identification within the objectives (Article 20 refers to purposes) referred to in Article 2(1)(b) and (c) of the Interoperability Regulations.[98] The provision thereby turns the objectives under Article 2 of the Interoperability Regulations into purposes. This confusion between overall objectives and specified purposes may negatively impact numerous provisions of the Regulations, as the objectives of interoperability are, as stated above, anything but clearly specified and strictly limited.

With regard to Article 20, a person may be identified in order to contribute to the prevention and the combating of illegal immigration or to contribute to a high level of security within the AFSJ of the EU, including the maintenance of public security and public policy, and safeguarding security in the territories of the Member States. Although one of the objectives of the Interoperability Regulations is to facilitate the identification of unknown persons who are unable to identify themselves, or unidentified human remains in the case of a natural disaster, accident or terrorist attack,[99] and would therefore directly correspond to Article 20 CIR searches, that objective is not referred to under Article 20(5). Why the EU legislator did not make use of the objective under Article 2(1)(g) of the Interoperability Regulations remains a mystery. Instead, Member States are free to allow CIR identity searches by police authorities for unreasonably wide purposes (objectives).

How CIR identity searches will be carried out in practical terms remains to be seen once the interoperable system becomes fully operational and after the Member States have transposed the option under Article 20(5) and (6) of the Interoperability Regulations into national law. However, national law adopted under Article 20 of the Interoperability Regulations could allow national police authorities to randomly stop individuals on the street in order to require them to provide both biometric and identity data within the objectives of Article 2(1)(b) and (c) of the Interoperability Regulations. Hence, anyone who would, purely by his or her physical appearance, seem suspicious to a police officer could become subject to random controls or identity checks within the definition of the national laws implementing Article 20 of the Interoperability Regulations. Accordingly, identity checks under that Article increase the risk of discriminatory or racial profiling and could lead to privacy intrusions based on appearance without a solid justification. Much will therefore depend on the national implementation acts of Article 20, any anti-discrimination clause and its application by police officers

[98] Article 20(5) of Regulation (EU) 2019/817 and Regulation (EU) 2019/818.
[99] Article 20(2)(g) of Regulation (EU) 2019/817 and Regulation (EU) 2019/818.

who would be permitted to search a person via his or her biometric data against the data in the CIR.

In the context of preventing and combating irregular migration, it might be difficult, if not impossible, to 'regulate one's conduct', as required by the ECtHR. Identity checks would presumably be based on the appearance of a person instead of a certain behaviour. Consequently, literally everyone could be queried in the CIR for identity checks under Article 20, without any standard criminal law threshold for reasonable suspicion. In that context, it might very well be that EU citizens could become subject to Article 20 police checks whenever they show certain physical appearances. Here, the question of racial profiling would probably be another issue that would have to be considered in order to carry out random identity checks in a non-discriminatory manner.[100]

C. The Multiple Identity Detector

Serving as legal basis for the MID,[101] Article 25 of the Interoperability Regulations lays down the purposes, architecture and functionalities of the MID, which will store links generated by the connection between the CIR and the SIS III identity data in order to detect multiple identities. The MID pursues the dual purpose of facilitating identity checks and combating identity fraud. As will be discussed below, it is questionable if the fight against identity fraud may be regarded as a genuine purpose, as strictly defined in line with data protection standards, or whether it should rather be seen as a *means* to achieve the general objective of preventing illegal entry to the EU.[102]

As illustrated above, the MID is supposed to create links between sets of personal data that are stored in the CIR and the SIS III in order to indicate any suspicious correlations between these data in connection with document fraud or identity theft to the competent authorities querying the ESP, or the CIR and when creating or updating information in one of the underlying AFSJ databases. Each of these links will be stored in the MID identity confirmation files and will specify the level of likelihood of suspicion in different colours, ranging from white to green, yellow and red links. Theoretically, whenever the personal data of an individual is stored in more than one of the underlying databases and reports some kind of a match,[103] the MID should indicate either a white or a yellow link

[100] Teresa Quintel, 'Interoperability of EU Databases and Access to Personal Data by National Police Authorities under Article 20 of the Commission Proposals' (2018) 4 *European Data Protection Law Review* 470.

[101] This section is based on a draft of the following book chapter: Quintel and Dimitrova (n 25).

[102] In the *Schwarz* case, the CJEU regarded the prevention of illegal entry into the EU as objective: *Schwarz v Stadt Bochum* (n 69) paras 40, 45 and 61.

[103] Article 28(1) of the Interoperability Regulations. In principle, there should always be the match.

to the authority updating or querying the systems.[104] Yellow MID links would have to be manually verified and subsequently turned into either a green, white or red link, and where more than one link is created, the authority responsible for the manual verification of different identities would have to assess each link separately.[105]

Different conditions apply when access is granted to different MID links, depending on the likelihood of identity fraud. Where it is less likely that an individual committed identity fraud and his or her data led to the creation of a white[106] or green[107] link, the access conditions are stricter and access is limited to the actual links, whereas access to red and yellow links is less restrained and allows the competent authorities to consult additional categories of personal data.

Hence, in order to be granted access to green or white links stored in the MID identity confirmation files, Member State authorities or EU Agencies must be authorised to access at least two of the underlying AFSJ databases in accordance with the access conditions laid down in the acts establishing the SIS III, the VIS, Eurodac, the EES, the ETIAS or the ECRIS-TCN.[108] Less strict requirements are to be applied regarding access to red or yellow MID links: in order to be granted access to information stored in the Identity Confirmation Files regarding red links,[109] Member State authorities and EU Agencies only need to be authorised to access *one* of the underlying databases.[110] Access to yellow links is granted to all authorities that create or update the respective files or alerts in the underlying databases.

In terms of the categories of personal data that the authorities responsible for the manual verification of different identities are permitted to consult regarding yellow links, these are broader than data that may be consulted with regard to white, green or red links. The broad access rights granted to the verifying authorities, and in particular the SIRENE offices of the Member States, will be the focus of this section.

[104] Only white and yellow links are created automatically, while green and red links are only created after manual verification has taken place. However, white links may also be created after manual verification, where data were linked between multiple lawful identities.

[105] Article 29(4) of the Interoperability Regulations on police and judicial cooperation, asylum and migration and art 29(5) of the Interoperability Regulations on borders and visa.

[106] It is not certain what data are included in the term 'white links', but in accordance with art 33 of the Interoperability Regulations, these could include all personal data stored in the different underlying systems that created the link when matched against each other. This is supported by a literal interpretation of art 21 of the Interoperability Regulations.

[107] It is not certain what data are included in the term 'green links', but in accordance with art 31 of the Interoperability Regulations, these could include all personal data stored in the different underlying systems that created the link when matched against each other.

[108] Article 26(3) with regard to access to white links and art 26(4) with regard to access to green links.

[109] Data under art 34(a) and (b), which includes the respective links and a reference to the EU information systems in which the linked data are held.

[110] Article 29(2) of Regulation (EU) 2019/817 and of Regulation (EU) 2019/818.

While the procedures regarding access to yellow MID links are laid down in Article 26(1) of the Interoperability Regulations, the authorities responsible for the manual verification of those links concerning identity fraud are listed in Article 29(1)(a)–(d). In accordance with that latter provision, the authority creating or modifying files or alerts in one of the underlying databases shall be the authority responsible for the manual verification of different identities when the creation or modification of those files or alerts led to a match. Pursuant to Article 26(1) of the Interoperability Regulations, the authority creating or updating a file or alert that generated a match will be granted access to data referred to under Article 34 and Article 21.

i. Access to Yellow Multiple Identity Detector Links by SIRENE Bureaux

Whenever the creation or updating of a SIS III alert leads to the generation of a yellow MID link, in the sense that personal data contained in the SIS III alert matches with data in the CIR, the authority responsible for the manual verification of the linked identities is the SIRENE Bureau of the Member State that created the initial SIS III alert.[111] In conjunction with Article 34 of the Interoperability Regulations, that SIRENE Bureau would be granted access to a distinct identity confirmation file that contains certain information concerning both the MID link(s) and the TCN whose personal data were linked during the multiple identity detection. Not only would the SIRENE Bureau obtain access to the MID link(s) and a reference to the underlying AFSJ database(s) in which the linked data concerning that TCN are held,[112] but, in addition, the designated SIRENE staff would be allowed to consult and retrieve the linked data in the corresponding database(s) with an identification number in order to check the sources of the yellow link.[113]

Article 34(c) of the Interoperability Regulations is rather vague, stating that the identity confirmation file would contain a single identification number allowing

[111] In accordance with the Interoperability Regulations, different provisions apply with regard to access, since different databases are covered by the scope of either Regulation (EU) 2019/917 or Regulation (EU) 2019/818. Hence, with regard to the first Interoperability Regulation, art 29(1)(d) of Regulation (EU) 2019/817 lays down that the SIRENE Bureau under Regulation (EU) 2018/1860 and Regulation (EU) 2018/1861 on SIS III for the return of illegally staying TCNs and in the field of border checks shall be the authority responsible for the manual verification of different identities, and art 29(2) of Regulation (EU) 2019/817 regulates that the SIRENE Bureau under Regulation (EU) 2018/1862 on the SIS III in the field of police cooperation and judicial cooperation in criminal matters shall be responsible for the manual verification of yellow MID links. With regard to the second Interoperability Regulation (in the field of police and judicial cooperation, asylum and migration), art 29(1)(a) and (2) of Regulation (EU) 2019/818 stipulate that the SIRENE Bureau with regard to Regulation (EU) 2018/1862 on the SIS III in the field of police cooperation and judicial cooperation in criminal matters shall be the authority responsible for the manual verification of different identities that lead to yellow MID links.

[112] Article 34(a) and (b) of Regulation (EU) 2019/817 and Regulation (EU) 2019/818.

[113] Article 34(c) of Regulation (EU) 2019/817 and Regulation (EU) 2019/818.

the retrieval of the linked data from the corresponding databases. Article 21(1) of the Interoperability Regulations states that the authority responsible for the manual verification of different identities shall have access, solely for the purpose of that verification, to the data referred to in Article 18(1) and (2) stored in the CIR connected by a yellow link. Hence, it is not entirely clear under what conditions the verifying authority would be granted access to the linked data in the underlying systems and whether it would need to follow the access requirements laid down in the respective founding acts. Yet, although access to the linked data for the purpose of verification might be necessary, the SIRENE Bureau will be able to access personal data in the underlying AFSJ databases that were previously not accessible by such authorities.

Furthermore, even if such access is strictly limited to the linked data, informing the SIRENE Bureaux about the database(s) in which the linked data are stored would already reveal additional details about a person. Moreover, Article 29(3) of the Interoperability Regulations states that the authority responsible for the manual verification of different identities shall, in addition to the linked data contained in the relevant identity confirmation file, have access to the identity data linked in the CIR and, where relevant, the SIS III. This would add additional access possibilities to the already problematic rules regarding manual verification under Article 26(1).[114]

Consequently, SIRENE Bureaux would obtain access not only to alerts stored in the SIS III, but also to data held in immigration databases, which LEAs such as SIRENE Bureaux may generally only access for the purpose of fighting *serious* crime and after prior authorisation by an independent body. The use of fraudulent identity or travel documents is not listed as a serious criminal offence in relevant EU legislation,[115] nor do the Interoperability Regulations foresee any prior authorisation of SIRENE access to the underlying databases and the MID Identity Confirmation Files under Article 29.

While the Interoperability Regulations make reference to the access conditions stipulated in the underlying AFSJ databases with regard to queries in the ESP, these conditions do not seem to apply for access to personal data via the MID or the CIR. It could be argued that the degree of intrusion when access is granted to personal data stored in the MID identity confirmation files is lower, since access is limited to the linked data. Yet, the limitations and safeguards applicable for access to MID links, especially by SIRENE Bureaux, are comparatively weak, and hence

[114] In the following, the analysis will make reference only to arts 26 and 29 in order to avoid confusion with regard to the subparagraphs of those provisions.

[115] Article 2(2) of the European Arrest Warrant Framework Decision only includes forgery of administrative documents and trafficking therein in the list of offences that give rise to surrender pursuant to a European Arrest Warrant. In addition, those offences must be punishable in the issuing Member State by a custodial sentence or a detention order for a maximum period of at least three years as defined by the law of the issuing Member State. See Council Framework Decision 2002/584/JHA of 13 June 2002 on the European Arrest Warrant and the surrender procedures between Member States – Statements made by certain Member States on the adoption of the Framework Decision [2002] OJ L190/1.

the Interoperability Regulations facilitate access by authorities that previously only had access to one single system: the SIS III.

While the authorities accessing the MID for the verification of yellow links and in order to take follow-up measures of red links will not be granted access to all data held in the underlying AFSJ databases and are subject to certain limitations, access to the MID is highly problematic. Concerns arise not only with regard to the legal bases of such access. The purpose, necessity, and proportionality of MID access under both Article 26 and Article 29 of the Interoperability Regulations are highly controversial. In addition, adequate safeguards to prevent unauthorised access and the misuse of MID data are either weak, inconsistent with the access requirements set out in the underlying databases or completely non-existent. Finally, mandatory access logs as required under Article 36 of the Interoperability Regulations[116] do not as such prevent unauthorised access, but should rather be regarded as a means to investigate personal data breaches.[117]

Hence, with regard to access and verification to and of yellow MID links, data protection concerns that were already present with regard to the individual AFSJ databases are magnified, particularly concerning the widened access that SIRENE Bureaux will gain under Articles 26 and 29 of the Interoperability Regulations. This widened law enforcement access is in contrast to the legal instruments governing the underlying databases and the SIS III. First, access to the SIS III by SIRENE Bureaux was previously subject to strict security measures such as biometric identification procedures of the staff. Indeed, there are no obligations for the authentication of SIRENE staff under the Interoperability Regulations and hence questions regarding legality and implementation issues arise. Second, SIRENE Bureaux are currently not authorised to access the remaining AFSJ databases and any access by LEAs to those data is, for the time being, strictly regulated and limited to designated units on a need-to-know basis and subject to prior verification by an independent body.

Overall, the access conditions regarding MID links by SIRENE Bureaux indicate serious gaps with regard to key data protection principles and may lead to risks for data subjects. Hence, the unclear formulation of the relevant provisions regarding SIRENE access to the MID seemingly expands the tasks of these national authorities and risks to facilitate abuses and the unauthorised processing of personal data.

Whether the widened access possibilities under the interoperability framework and, in particular, Articles 26 and 29 of the Interoperability Regulations fulfil the requirements that are enshrined in Article 52(1) of the EU Charter will be discussed in the subsequent sections.

[116] Article 36 only applies to the requirement to keep logs with regard to the MID. These requirements equally exist for processing carried out with regard to the ESP (art 10), the BMS (art 26) and the CIR (art 24).

[117] Quintel and Dimitrova (n 25).

IV. Law Enforcement Access in Light of Article 52(1) of the EU Charter

This section analyses the above-mentioned provisions authorising law enforcement access to the ESP, the CIR and the MID in light of the requirements laid down in Article 52(1) of the EU Charter. Both the EU Charter and the ECHR set out a prohibition regarding limitations of absolute rights – ie, the right to human dignity, the right to the integrity of the person, the prohibition of torture and inhuman or degrading treatment or punishment, the prohibition of slavery and forced labour. The right to privacy and data protection are not absolute rights and may be restricted under both the EU Charter and the ECHR.

In accordance with ECtHR and CJEU jurisprudence, law enforcement access to the personal data of identified or identifiable individuals constitutes an interference with Article 8 ECHR and Articles 7 and 8 of the EU Charter.[118] In order to be permissible, such interference is subject to the conditions laid down in the ECHR and the EU Charter as interpreted by the ECtHR and the CJEU. Over the years, the Strasbourg Court established that a measure must be in accordance with the law/prescribed by law,[119] must pursue legitimate aims[120] and must be necessary in a democratic society[121] in order to allow for the interference with the enjoyment of a protected right under the Convention.[122]

With Article 52(1), the EU Charter codified the case law in which the ECtHR[123] adopted the conditions to allow for the restrictions of human rights.

[118] *Big Brother Watch and Others*, App Nos 58170/13, 62322/14 and 24960/15 (ECtHR, 13 September 2018 and 25 May 2021); and CJEU, Case C-207/16, *Ministerio Fiscal*, ECLI:EU:C:2018:788, 2 October 2018.

[119] In *Malone v UK*, App No 8691/79 (ECtHR, 2 August 1984) para 66, the ECtHR established that both formulations are to be read in the same way. See also *Sunday Times v UK (No 1)*, App No 6538/74 (ECtHR, 26 April 1979) para 49, in which the Court added to further criteria for a rule to be 'law' those of being adequately accessible and of precision.

[120] Article 8(2) ECHR lists the legitimate aims which may justify an infringement upon the rights protected in art 8: in the interests of national security, public safety or the economic well-being of the country, for the prevention of disorder or crime, for the protection of health or morals, or for the protection of the rights and freedoms of others. However, the ECtHR has observed that its practice is to be quite succinct when it verifies the existence of a legitimate aim within the meaning of the second paragraphs of arts 8–11 ECHR. See *SAS v France*, App No 43835/11 (ECtHR, 1 July 2014) para 114. See ECtHR, 'Guide on Article 8 of the European Convention on Human Rights Right to Respect for Private and Family Life, Home and Correspondence' (2019), https://www.echr.coe.int/Documents/Guide_Art_8_ENG.pdf.

[121] Although not a case concerning Article 8 ECHR, in *Handyside v UK*, the ECtHR explained the meaning of 'necessity' by noting 'that, while the adjective "necessary" … is not synonymous with "indispensable", neither has it the flexibility of such expressions as "admissible", "ordinary", "useful", "reasonable" or "desirable"'. See *Handyside v UK*, App No 5493/72 (ECtHR 7 December 1976) para 48.

[122] David Harris et al, *Harris, O'Boyle, and Warbrick Law of the European Convention on Human Rights*, 3rd edn (Oxford University Press, 2014) 505–21.

[123] On an assessment of the criteria under the ECHR, see WP29, 'Opinion 01/2014 on the Application of Necessity and Proportionality Concepts and Data Protection within the Law Enforcement Sector' (2014).

In order for an interference with the fundamental rights enshrined in the EU Charter to be justified, it must satisfy all requirements laid down in Article 52 (1). In accordance with that provision, any interference with Charter rights must be provided for by law, respect the essence of the concerned right, be necessary and proportionate, and meet the general interest objectives recognised by the EU, or the need to protect the rights and freedoms of others. Thus, Article 52(1) of the EU Charter expands the criteria established by the ECtHR by adding that any limitation must respect the essence of the rights and freedoms recognised by the Charter.[124]

Whereas Article 52(1) of the EU Charter applies horizontally and could be regarded as general limitation clause,[125] the system allowing for restrictions of the rights under the ECHR is laid down in individual derogation clauses that follow each qualified right[126] enshrined in the Convention.[127] However, despite a different approach regarding the system that allows for limitations, the Charter and the ECHR apply mutatis mutandis regarding the threshold for limiting qualified rights. Against that background, the following discussion will be oriented along the lines of the wording of Article 52(1) of the EU Charter, but must also assume applicability to EU law when referring to ECtHR jurisprudence.

While the question of whether the restrictions that arise with interoperability concern qualitative fundamental rights can be answered in the affirmative, the subsequent sections will analyse the remaining requirements under Article 52(1) of the Charter. This analysis will take into consideration whether the limitations on Articles 7 and 8 Charter rights through the Interoperability Regulations satisfy the quality of law requirement, respect the essence of those two rights, meet the general interest objectives and are both necessary and proportionate.

A. The Quality of Law Requirement

The quality of law prerequisite is inextricably linked to the 'provided for by law requirement', which represents the first condition to allow for a restriction of the rights under both the EU Charter and the ECHR.[128] The ECtHR has ruled on several occasions that a legal provision needs to fulfil several criteria in order to satisfy the quality of law requirement, namely a law should be clear, foreseeable

[124] That term may be found in the constitutions of the Member States. See, for instance, art 19(2) of the German Basic Law, which provides that '[i]n no case may the essence of a basic right be affected'. The ECtHR refers to the 'essence' of a right in its case law. However, it is generally not included in the list of conditions regarding the limitations of human rights under the Convention.

[125] Anne Levade, Fabrice Picod and Laurence Burgorgue-Larsen, *Traité établissant une Constitution pour l'Europe. L'architecture constitutionnelle, Partie II – La Charte des droits fondamentaux de l'Union, Commentaire article par article* (Bruylant, 2005) 658.

[126] These rights that may be subject to limitations.

[127] Koen Lenaerts, 'Exploring the Limits of the EU Charter of Fundamental Rights' (2012) 8 *European Constitutional Law Review* 375, 388.

[128] ibid.

and adequately accessible.[129] Hence, it must be sufficiently foreseeable to enable individuals to act in accordance with the law.[130] The CJEU has endorsed this line of interpretation in its case law.[131]

The law providing for the restriction (the Interoperability Regulations), albeit formulated in a complicated manner,[132] could be regarded as being sufficiently accessible[133] and precisely enough[134] in the sense that it does not, or at least not *directly*, allow for discretion. Nevertheless, it could be argued that the numerous and broadly defined objectives of the Interoperability Regulations are used as purposes to grant access to the interoperable components. Whereas under data protection law, purposes should be strictly defined and explicit, the interoperability Regulations multiply purposes. In addition, the streamlined access rights for competent (law enforcement) authorities serve, all the same, as a point of departure for discretionary processing at the national level. Yet, in order to satisfy the quality of law requirement, the limitations of fundamental rights must be foreseeable,[135] meaning that legal certainty must be established.[136] If the implementing or transposing acts of different national laws that will play a role for the processing of personal data in relation to the interoperable system have been wrongfully implemented, lack certain safeguards or allow for discretion by national authorities, any revision thereof will be lengthy and discretionary processing will be difficult to prove.

B. The Essence of the Right Requirement

The second condition under Article 52(1) of the Charter lays down that a limitation on the exercise of the rights and freedoms recognised by the Charter must respect the essence of those rights and freedoms.[137] In other words, if the essence of a right or freedom is not respected when introducing limitations, Article 52(1) of the Charter is violated, as the essence of a fundamental right cannot be subject to limitations.[138]

[129] See, for instance, *Del Río Prada v Spain*, App. No. 42750/09 (ECHR, 21 October 2013) para 91; *SW v UK*, App No 20166/92 (ECHR, 22 November 1995) para 35; Harris et al (n 122) 507; or *MM v UK*, App No 24029/07 (ECtHR, 13 November 2012).

[130] *Lebois v Bulgaria*, App No 67482/14 (ECHR, 19 October 2017) paras 66–67.

[131] *Opinion 1/15* (EU-Canada PNR Agreement), 26 July 2017, EU:C:2017:592, para 146.

[132] In *Autronic AG v Switzerland*, App No 12726/87 (ECtHR, 22 May 1990) paras 55 and 59, the ECtHR held that the horrendously complicated regime which regulated international broadcasting was sufficiently accessible to those whose activities as broadcasters were regulated by it. See Harris et al (n 121) 507.

[133] Meaning that an individual must be able to have an indication that is adequate in the circumstances of the legal rules applicable to a given case.

[134] *Huvig v France*, App No 11105/84 (ECtHR, 24 April 1990).

[135] *Kruslin v France*, App No 11801/85 (ECtHR, 24 April 1990) para 27.

[136] Lenaerts (n 127) 389.

[137] Hielke Hijmans, *The European Union as Guardian of Internet Privacy: The Story of Art 16 TFEU* (Springer, 2016).

[138] Tuomas Ojanen, 'Making the Essence of Fundamental Rights Real: The Court of Justice of the European Union Clarifies the Structure of Fundamental Rights under the Charter' (2016) 12 *European Constitutional Law Review* 318.

The 'essence of a right requirement' is under-researched, and this section will not attempt to establish a new interpretation of what it means at its core. Rather, this analysis will aim at comparing the intrusions to which interoperability will give rise in terms of interfering with the rights to privacy and data protection with the (sparse) standards that the CJEU used in its case law on Article 7 of the EU Charter,[139] and whether those intrusions are capable of entering the balancing test under Article 52(1), or whether they touch upon the very core (the essence) of the right to privacy and data protection, and as such cannot be subject to any kind of balancing or justification.[140] Hence, this analysis adopts the *absolute* approach that assumes that every fundamental right has an inviolable core, which is positioned outside the scope of application of the principle of proportionality.[141]

There are not many occasions in which the CJEU ruled on the essence of a fundamental right. However, in *Schrems*, it did so in relation to both Article 7 and Article 47 of the EU Charter, and for the first time found a violation of the essence of the right to privacy and the right to effective judicial review at once.[142] The Court held that any legislation allowing for generalised access to the content of electronic communications would compromise the essence of the right to privacy.[143] It further found that 'likewise, legislation not providing for any possibility for an individual to pursue legal remedies in order to have access to personal data relating to him, or to obtain the rectification or erasure of such data, does not respect the essence of the fundamental right to effective judicial protection, as enshrined in Article 47 of the Charter'.[144] In *Schrems*, the CJEU applied the requirement under Article 52(1) of the Charter that any interference with fundamental rights must respect the essence of those rights, for the first time on the level of a concrete court case dealing with privacy and data protection.[145] With that, the CJEU developed the notion of an inviolable core of a respective right that may not be violated under any circumstances, which it had touched upon in earlier case law.[146]

[139] CJEU, Joined Cases C-293/12 and C-594/12, *Digital Rights Ireland Ltd* (C-293/12) and *Seitlinger* (C-594/12), ECLI:EU:C:2014:238, 8 April 2014; CJEU, Case C-362/14, *Maximillian Schrems v Data Protection Commissioner*, ECLI:EU:C:2015:650, 6 October 2015, para 94.

[140] Maja Brkan, 'The Concept of Essence of Fundamental Rights in the EU Legal Order: Peeling the Onion to its Core' (2018) 14 *European Constitutional Law Review* 332.

[141] ibid 866–67. See also Julian Rivers, 'Proportionality and Variable Intensity of Review' (2006) 65 *Cambridge Law Journal* 174, 187; Aharon Barak, *Proportionality: Constitutional Rights and Their Limitations* (Cambridge University Press, 2012).

[142] *Schrems* (n 139) paras 94 and 95.

[143] ibid para 94.

[144] The essence of the fundamental right to effective judicial protection, as enshrined in art 47 of the Charter, is not respected if an individual cannot 'pursue legal remedies in order to have access to personal data relating to him, or to obtain the rectification or erasure of such data': ibid para 95. See Hijmans (n 137) 31.

[145] ibid 322.

[146] Ojanen (n 138) 320–21.

One decisive difference between *Schrems* and comparable judgments[147] in which the Court did not find the essence of the right to private life compromised, albeit holding that there had been a violation of Article 7 and/or 8 of the EU Charter, was the possibility of public authorities to have generalised access to the content of a communication. Whereas generalised access by public authorities to meta-data would, due to its ability to provide very precise conclusions to be drawn concerning the private lives of persons whose data has been retained,[148] be likely to cause individuals to be subject to constant surveillance,[149] such access to content data would indeed touch upon the very core of the right to private life.

Leaving aside the question of whether the interoperable system will become fully operational and in fact achieve the foreseen objectives, the relevant factor is what the Interoperability Regulations as well as the underlying AFSJ databases suggest delivering and whether these functionalities would be capable of touching upon the essence of the rights under Article 7 and 8 of the Charter. Looking at the EES, the system shall register all entries and exits from the EU in order to facilitate the management of migration flows, allow for the identification and detection of overstayers, and enable the competent national authorities of the Member States to take appropriate measures.[150] The ETIAS is supposed to include a watch-list based on specific risk indicators compiled from different information systems, from Europol data and INTERPOL databases,[151] established for the purposes of identifying connections between data in an application file and information relating to persons who are suspected of having committed or having taken part in a serious criminal offence.[152] Connected with the other AFSJ databases, the aggregated information about a person and the cross-checking thereof could easily lead to a feeling of constant surveillance, even of those who did not commit any sort of crime. While the storage of such information in the separated database might be justified for each system that pursues a specific purpose, these individual purposes will no longer be recognisable in the connected system.

Although this alone might not be sufficient to argue that interoperability touches upon the essences of the right to privacy and data protection, additional factors should be taken into account. Whereas the interoperable system will not contain content data per se, the underlying databases are increasingly relying on biometric data, which because of their sensitive nature and their potential to uniquely identify a natural person are being defined as special categories of data under relevant EU legislation.[153] Whereas in *Schwarz* the CJEU regarded

[147] *Digital Rights Ireland* (n 139) para 65; CJEU, Joined Cases C-203/15 and C 698/15, *Tele2 Sverige AB* (C-203/15) and *Watson* (C-698/15), ECLI:EU:C:2016:970, 21 December 2016, para 134.

[148] *Tele2* (n 147) para 99.

[149] *Digital Rights Ireland* (n 139) para 37 and *Tele2* (n 147) para 100.

[150] Recital 15 and Article 6(1)(c) of Regulation (EU) 2017/2226.

[151] Recital 23 of Regulation (EU) 2018/1240.

[152] ibid Recital 28.

[153] See, for instance, art 9 of Regulation (EU) 2016/679 or art 10 of Directive (EU) 2016/680.

the processing of biometrics in passports for the establishment of a reliable link between the genuine holder and the document, and, ultimately, to attain an objective of general interest to be justified, the use of biometric data in the interoperable system goes much further. First, the fingerprints and facial images of TCNs will no longer be stored in separate databases, but centrally and for a very long period of time.[154] Second, biometrics will no longer be used only for the purpose of verification, but also in order to identify a person. Third, those biometric data would be matched against other personal data and information compiled from different sources, principally by automated means.

Beyond those biometrics to be retained in the system, the interoperability framework will retain further personal data that are capable of revealing information about a TCN's private life. Besides information that is stored on a conventional travel document, the underlying databases will process information concerning a person's education, his or her current occupation, past convictions on criminal offences, any travels to war or conflict zones over the past ten years, and information concerning family ties he or she has in the EU.[155] However, this information will not be transferred to the interoperability components, the interoperable system might facilitate access by LEAs to such data.

In addition, and as mentioned above, the interoperable components will cross-match the information from the different systems and merge them into new datasets that are decisive regarding a TCN's ability to enter the EU. Moreover, with the inclusion of data collected by Europol and the EBCGA in the interoperability regime as well as in the underlying AFSJ databases,[156] the source of information that led to a final match not only becomes dispersed, but could also contain personal data that indeed consists of content data. Although processing of personal data about TCNs by Europol and the EBCGA is very relevant in the context of security cross-checks developed under the ETIAS, the new VIS and the proposed Screening Regulation, it will not be used for cross-matching by the BMS and the MID. Yet, both Europol and the EBCGA may use information scraped from publicly available sources,[157] which could indeed also include content data. The EBCGA may process information received from the EUROSUR national coordination centres, compiled from sources that were compiled by national situational pictures.[158] Publicly available information may, when cross-matched with additional data, be assembled to a complete picture

[154] Due to its scale and the nature of the data to be stored in this database, the consequences of any data breach could seriously harm a potentially very large number of individuals. See EDPS (n 85) 2, 3.

[155] See for instance, art 17(2) of Regulation (EU) 2018/1240.

[156] Both Europol and the EBCGA will play a central role in feeding the ETIAS watch-list with information and setting the ETIAS screening rules.

[157] Pursuant to art 17(2) of Regulation (EU) 2016/794, Europol may directly retrieve and process information, including personal data, from publicly available sources, including the internet and public data.

[158] Article 25(2)(l) of Regulation (EU) 2019/1896.

concerning individuals and lead to adverse effects for TCNs who intend to travel to the EU.[159]

Lastly, by connecting information from different authorities and sources that operate in different and originally disconnected fields, interoperability complicates access to judicial redress and the possibility for an individual to challenge a decision adversely affecting him or her before a court will be impeded, as will be demonstrated below.

While the CJEU in a judgment from 2019[160] was not required to consider the compliance of the Interoperability Regulations with Article 52(1) of the Charter, but simply assumed their legality, it will ultimately be for the Court to decide on that matter, in particular with regard to law enforcement access to the CIR and the MID and the applicability of Article 7 and 8 Charter rights also to TCNs. Since the EU legislator adopted the Interoperability Regulations and thereby assumed their compliance with the Charter, it will be left to the CJEU to decide whether the two Interoperability Regulations touch upon the essence of the right to privacy and data protection or if they merely represent an intrusion that is justifiable by a wider margin of appreciation regarding the processing of personal data of TCNs.[161] However, it should be borne in mind that the fact that the essence of right might not be affected does not in itself mean that a measure in question is justified (on any ground); it would merely signify that the measure in question would be *capable* of being justified.

C. The Objectives of General Interest Recognised by the Union Requirement

Generally, a limitation of a Charter right is prohibited unless it is justified and appropriate for ensuring the accomplishment of a legitimate objective pursued[162] and does not go beyond what is necessary and proportionate to attain it.[163]

[159] On some of the problems related to the use of publicly available information for criminal investigations, see Jan-Jaap Oerlemans, 'Investigating Cybercrime' (doctoral thesis, Leiden University, 2017).

[160] CJEU, Case C-70/18, *Staatssecretaris van Justitie en Veiligheid v A, B and P*, ECLI:EU:C:2019:823, 3 October 2019.

[161] See *Staatssecretaris van Justitie en Veiligheid v EP* (n 72) paras 41 and 41, where the Court held that administrative authorities have a wider margin of appreciation with regard to TCNs.

[162] In ECtHR terms, 'in pursuit of a legitimate aim' and 'necessary in a democratic society'; see, for instance, art 8(2) ECHR, referring to the prevention or detection of disorder or crime, and protection of the rights and freedoms of others. See *MM v UK*, App No 24029/07 (ECtHR, 13 November 2012); *Handyside v UK*, App No 5493/72 (ECtHR, 7 December 1976) paras 48–49; *Sunday Times v UK*, App No 6538/74 (ECtHR, 6 November 1980) para 59; *S and Marper v UK*, App Nos 30562/04 and 30566/04 (ECtHR, 4 December 2008) para 101; *Khelili v Switzerland*, App No 16188/07 (ECtHR, 18 October 2011); *Klass and Others v Germany*, App No 5029/71 (6 September 1978); *Leander v Sweden*, App No 9248/81 (ECtHR, 26 March 1987); *Huvig v France*, App No 11105/84 (ECtHR, 24 April 1990); *Z v Finland*, App No 22009/93 (ECtHR, 25 February 1997); *K & T v Finland*, App No 25702/94 (12 July 2001); *Dudgeon v UK*, App No 7525/76 (ECtHR, 22 October 1981).

[163] *Staatssecretaris van Justitie en Veiligheid v A, B and P* (n 160) para 44.

In 2013, the CJEU held that the objective of general interest (preventing illegal entry into the EU) is achieved by way of two specific aims: first, to prevent the falsification of passports; and, second, to prevent fraudulent use thereof.[164] The limitation (taking and storing of fingerprints when issuing passports), through the pursuit of those aims, pursues an objective of a general interest recognised by the EU (illegal entry into the EU).[165] Hence, the taking of fingerprints could be seen as the means to achieve the aim, which in turn would serve as a means to achieve the objective. Both the limitation to achieve the aim and the aim itself must be proportionate when being employed to achieve the overall objective. Hence, in a hierarchy, the overall objective should be situated above the aims that are supposed to achieve the objective.

Whether the objective satisfies the conditions to be validated as one of general interest recognised by the EU depends on different factors. On the one hand, the EU legislator must consider and prove the pursuit of a specific objective to serve a general interest of the EU in order to adopt a law that is built upon that objective. On the other hand, the objective must be *approved* by the CJEU in the event that the Court is being required to decide on that matter.

However, while previously illegal entry was recognised as objective, whereas the prevention/combating of identity fraud was merely a means to achieve such objective, in *Staatssecretaris van Justitie*, the CJEU understood the *objective of preventing illegal entry* into the EU as the *objective of preventing and combating identity and document fraud*.[166] It did so by referring to both *Schwarz* and *Demir*, where it found that preventing unlawful (in the case of *Schwarz* illegal) entry into the EU presents an objective of public interest.

In addition, in *Staatssecretaris van Justitie* the Court simply *presumed* the lawfulness of the rules under the Interoperability Regulations without evaluating any arguments as to whether the provisions might be excessive and disproportionate.[167] Regardless of the question of whether the Interoperability Regulations indeed use the correct objective (to improve the effectiveness and efficiency of border checks at external borders and contributing to the combating of illegal immigration), which shall be achieved by specific means (ensuring the correct identification of persons and contributing to combating identity fraud), the CJEU determined that the objective of preventing and combating identity and document fraud may likewise be treated as objectives of general interest.

[164] *Schwarz* (n 69) para 36. On objectives, see also *C Demir v Staatssecretaris van Justitie* (n 69) para 41.

[165] *Schwarz* (n 69) paras 35–38.

[166] *Staatssecretaris van Justitie en Veiligheid v A, B and P* (n 160) para 49.

[167] Niovi Vavoula, 'Is Processing Biometric Data of Turkish Nationals in a National Database Lawful under the EEC-Turkey Agreement? Reflections on the Judgment in A, B and P (C-70/18) – EU Immigration and Asylum Law and Policy', http://eumigrationlawblog.eu/is-processing-biometric-data-of-turkish-nationals-in-a-national-database-lawful-under-the-eec-turkey-agreement-reflections-on-the-judgment-in-a-b-and-p-c-70-18.

As a result, the CJEU refers to previous case law and the Interoperability Regulations in order to establish a new objective, thereby opening the door for justifying the use of very broadly defined objectives in future legislation. Consequently, the Interoperability Regulations pursue an objective of general interest and could, in accordance with the recent CJEU judgment, have even gone further. However, both the expansion of objectives by the Court and the use of general objectives as purposes are dangerous and risk not only criminalising TCNs on a general level, but also processing their personal data for a multitude of objectives.

D. Necessity and Proportionality of Law Enforcement Access to the Interoperability Components

The principle of proportionality requires that acts of the EU institutions are appropriate for attaining the legitimate objectives pursued by the legislation at issue and do not exceed the limits of what is appropriate and necessary in order to achieve those objectives.[168] In other words, in order to test the necessity and proportionality of an interference enshrined in an EU legal act, it is necessary to look at whether the interference is appropriate for achieving a legitimate objective and whether it is the least intrusive measure in terms of attaining such objective.[169]

As the CJEU established in its case law, access to the personal data of identified or identifiable individuals constitutes an interference with Article 7 and 8 of the EU Charter.[170] In order for this interference to be proportionate, the content and form of an EU action shall not exceed what is necessary to achieve the objectives of the treaties.[171] Proportionality[172] is a general principle of EU law and, as such, encompasses both necessity and appropriateness.[173] In order to assess the proportionality of a measure, the necessity and appropriateness of that measure must be

[168] *Digital Rights Ireland* (n 139) para 46. See also Case C-343/09, *Afton Chemical v Secretary of State for Transport*, EU:C:2010:419, 8 July 2010, para 45; Joined Cases C-92/09 and C-93/09, *Volker und Markus Schecke and Eifert v Land Hessen*, EU:C:2010:662, 9 November 2010, para 74; Cases C-581/10 and C-629/10, *Nelson and Others v Deutsche Lufthansa AG and TUI Travel plc and Others v Civil Aviation Authority*, EU:C:2012:657, 23 October 2012, para 71; Case C-283/11, *Sky Österreich GmbH v Österreichischer Rundfunk*, EU:C:2013:28, 22 January 2013, para 50; and Case C-101/12, *Herbert Schaible v Land Baden-Württemberg*, EU:C:2013:661, 17 October 2013, para 29.

[169] EDPS, 'EDPS Guidelines on Assessing the Proportionality of Measures That Limit the Fundamental Rights to Privacy and to the Protection of Personal Data' (2019).

[170] *Ministerio Fiscal* (n 118) para 51; *Opinion 1/15* (n 131) paras 124 and 126; *Digital Rights Ireland* (n 139) para 35. See also *Staatssecretaris van Justitie en Veiligheid v A, B and P* (n 160).

[171] See the case law above and art 5(4) TEU. See also EDPS (n 169).

[172] On ECtHR case law on proportionality, see, for instance, *Z v Finland* (n 162) and *S and Marper v UK* (n 162).

[173] See also EDPS, 'Assessing the Necessity of Measures That Limit the Fundamental Right to the Protection of Personal Data: A Toolkit' (2017).

fulfilled, which means conversely that there is no need to assess proportionality if necessity is not established beforehand.[174]

First, necessity[175] should be assessed based on facts, meaning that a measure must be effective in order to fulfil a particular objective; second, the measure must be the least intrusive means in order to achieve that objective; and, third, the advantages resulting from the measure should not be outweighed by the disadvantages the measure causes with respect to the exercise of an individual's fundamental rights.[176]

In the context of interoperability, a number of factors need to be taken into account – for instance, whether the processing of special categories is necessary to attain an objective or whether other, less intrusive means of processing or types of personal data could be used instead. In that respect, the ECtHR explicitly distinguished between different types of personal data and different categories of data subjects. In *S and Marper*,[177] the Court highlighted the special nature of fingerprints and held that the processing of biometric data without the consent of the individual concerned was not to be regarded as neutral or insignificant, and thus was capable of affecting his or her private life.[178]

Further, the ECtHR pointed out that 'individuals who [had not been] convicted of any offence and are entitled to the presumption of innocence, are treated in the same way as convicted persons'.[179] Hence, the fact that the Interoperability Regulations strongly rely on the processing of biometric data and connect databases that hold personal data from both immigration and law enforcement databases, which are made accessible for LEAs, should be taken into account in the assessment of necessity and proportionality.

Whilst the objective of preventing unlawful entry and residence to the EU may constitute an overriding reason in the public interest, it is also important that the measure at issue should be suitable for securing the attainment of that objective and that it does not go beyond what is necessary in order to attain it.[180] Whether the connection of all AFSJ databases in one central system is necessary to achieve the objectives under the Interoperability Regulations is highly doubtful, and whether the processing operations that may be carried out by competent authorities are proportionate to those objectives is all the more questionable.

As has been found, the number of TCNs who have been issued with a return decision which has become enforceable but remained within the EU is

[174] The Advocate General Opinion in *Tele2* (n 147) paras 132,172, 247 and 248, stating that the CJEU in *Digital Rights Ireland* did not examine proportionality.

[175] On ECtHR case law on necessity, see, for instance, *Campbell v UK* App No 3578/05 (ECtHR, 27 March 2008).

[176] CJEU, 16 July 2015, Case C-83/14, *CHEZ Razpredelenie Bulgaria AD v Komisia za zashtita ot diskriminatsia*, ECLI:EU:C:2015:480, para 123; see also EDPS (n 169).

[177] *S and Marper v UK* (n 162).

[178] ibid para 84; see also Vavoula (n 167).

[179] *S and Marper v UK* (n 162) para 122.

[180] *C Demir v Staatssecretaris van Justitie* (n 69) para 41.

assumed – albeit on a very tentative basis – at approximately 300,000 migrants per annum.[181] Compared to the potential number of around 500 million TCNs that will be stored in the interoperable system,[182] the endeavour of building and operating the system seems outrageously disproportionate in terms of both privacy intrusion and resources. Although interoperability pursues six additional objectives, the question must be asked as to whether these could not have been achieved by less intrusive means and smaller investment.[183]

In addition, law enforcement access to the interoperable system constitutes a separate limitation to the right to privacy and data protection, which must likewise be assessed against the principle of proportionality and necessity.[184] Other criteria to be taken into consideration for the assessment of the proportionality of a measure and concerning access by LEAs to stored data are, inter alia, the prior review by a court or by an independent administrative authority and the requirement to notify a data subject as soon as notification is not liable to jeopardise investigations.[185] Additional conditions, such as a cascading system to allow for law enforcement access to personal data stored in the interoperable system, should be considered as safeguards, which can contribute to the proportionality of a measure.[186]

However, as mentioned previously, the Interoperability Regulations abandon prior checks in national databases before accessing the interoperable system. On the one hand, the abolition of such mandatory checks prior to accessing the EU systems seems illogical with respect to criminal investigations: the question here would be why should a national law enforcement authority check an AFSJ database such as Eurodac before checking a national police database for the fingerprints of a potential suspect or perpetrator? It seems likely that this reverse procedure would simply lead to additional processing operations, where competent authorities would have to search national databases *after* an unsuccessful query in the EU systems.[187] Moreover, a hit during a search in the AFSJ databases could lead to an inference that could have been clarified with a prior check in the national systems. For instance, a police officer could receive a match to data about the irregular entry

[181] Council of the European Union, 'Presidency Paper on Addressing Challenges Relating to Migrants in a Situation of Prolonged Illegal Stay, 7560/20', www.statewatch.org/news/2020/may/eu-council-unremovable-migrants-7560-20.pdf.

[182] European Commission and Directorate-General for Migration and Home Affairs, 'Feasibility Study of a Common Identity Repository (CIR): Management Summary' (2017), http://dx.publications.europa.eu/10.2837/330396.

[183] The interoperability proposals estimate the costs of interoperability over a period of nine years to be €424.7 million, excluding training of staff. See COM (2017) 793 and 794 final, 80.

[184] On the proportionality of law enforcement access to the underlying databases, and in particular Eurodac, see Vavoula (n 58) 217 ff.

[185] *Tele2* (n 147) paras 120–22.

[186] EDPS (n 169) 34.

[187] Teresa Quintel, 'From Tampere over Stockholm to Luxembourg and Brussels: Where are We Now? The Evolution of AFSJ Databases – Meandering between Security and Data Protection' (2020), https://www.ceps.eu/wp-content/uploads/2020/05/MPC-Tampere-Programme-final.pdf.

of a person, although he or she was supposed to merely register that person in a national asylum database. Such an inference may lead to an unnecessary suspicion against a person and could motivate a police officer to process personal data of that person within a data protection regime that would make it easier to limit that person's rights.

On the other hand, the checking of immigration databases for purposes of criminal investigations might be futile and only lead to additional work for the competent authorities. Comparing the access requests by law enforcement authorities to the SIS and to Eurodac, the difference is striking. While the SIS was accessed a total of 6,185,199,597 times by all Member States in 2018,[188] searches in Eurodac carried out by law enforcement authorities amounted to only 296 by 10 Member States in that year and to 85 in 2020.[189] Certainly, it should be taken into account that while Eurodac's main purpose is related to asylum, while the SIS is a law enforcement database that, obviously, is mainly searched by the competent authorities. However, the above numbers demonstrate that law enforcement authorities do not make use of the access possibilities granted to them regarding Eurodac. Consequently, the necessity of such access rights is not attained.[190]

Depending on the implementation of the provision in the individual Member States, queries in the CIR under Article 20 of the Interoperability Regulations would be far more intrusive than the police checks that were assessed by the CJEU and the ECtHR, and therefore it is questionable whether such queries would be proportionate in the light of the Courts' requirements. Whereas an individual would have to provide his or her identity or travel document(s) during 'conventional' identity checks such as those that were examined in the Courts' judgments, a query in the CIR would reveal far more intrusive personal data and, beyond that, would be carried out on the basis of biometric identifiers, the processing of which requires strict necessity and additional safeguards.[191] Even if Member States would specify the conditions and procedures for Article 20 identity checks regarding limitations to intensity and frequency in their national legislation,[192] it has not been demonstrated that such checks would not be the least intrusive means and therefore would exceed the necessity requirement for establishing the identity of a person. Because of the CIR's features, a query under Article 20 of the Interoperability Regulations could be used disproportionally as an investigative

[188] European Agency for the Operational Management of Large Scale IT Systems in the Area of Freedom, Security and Justice., *SIS II: 2018 Statistics: February 2019* (Publications Office, 2019), https://data.europa.eu/doi/10.2857/29573.

[189] In 2018, Europol performed 10 Category 5 searches, while no number for such searches was indicated for 2020; see European Agency for the Operational Management of Large Scale IT Systems in the Area of Freedom, Security and Justice, *Eurodac: Annual Report 2018: June 2019* (Publications Office, 2019) and *Eurodac 2020 Annual Report: November 2021* (Publications Office, 2021).

[190] Quintel (n 187).

[191] EDPS (n 85) 4, 5 and 6.

[192] CJEU, Case C-278/12 PPU, *Atiqullah Adil v Minister voor Immigratie, Integratie en Asiel*, ECLI:EU:C:2012:508, 19 July 2012, para 88.

tool for police officers, who would receive additional information concerning a person from the underlying AFSJ databases.

With regard to the MID, SIRENE Bureaux and other LEAs would be granted access not only to yellow links and a reference to the underlying database(s) in which the linked data are held; in addition, they would be permitted to retrieve the linked data from the corresponding AFSJ databases in order to check the sources of the yellow link. Consequently, SIRENE Bureaux would have access not only to alerts stored in the SIS III, but also to data held in immigration databases. Both the legality and proportionality of such retrieval from the underlying databases, which normally do not grant access to SIRENE Bureaux without strict access requirements and prior verification, remain questionable.

In addition, it remains rather unclear how far individuals could challenge red links in cases where SIRENE Bureaux deem that notifying the concerned individuals might jeopardise criminal investigations. Pursuant to Article 13(3) LED, such a limitation may be imposed only for as long as there is a real risk that the investigation of criminal offences or the protection of public and national security could be impeded. Hence, as soon as notification no longer jeopardises ongoing investigations, the concerned individual must be notified.[193] However, as will be shown in Chapter 3, the notification requirement under Article 13(3) of the LED has been insufficiently transposed in many Member States and the right to indirect access by a national data protection authority (DPA) under Article 17 of that Directive is rarely evoked.[194]

Whether the intrusions that would be permitted through CIR and MID queries would be proportionate in relation to the objectives pursued by the Interoperability Regulations is highly questionable. Law enforcement access to both components no longer requires prior checks in national databases and fails to make access subject to prior verification by a court or an independent administrative authority as required by CJEU case law. In addition, the systems store biometric data of TCNs and connect personal data from immigration databases with personal data from law enforcement databases to generate links.

Ultimately, the numbers of illegal entries and stays to and in the EU are either insufficiently low in relation to the objectives pursued by the Interoperability Regulations in order to be able to demonstrate proportionality. Yet, as has been mentioned previously with regard to other databases, it is difficult to see how there can be a proper assessment of the potential implications of the interoperable system when its development is to be so flexible that it is unclear what form the system will ultimately take.[195]

[193] See also on notification *Tele2* (n 147) para 121.

[194] 'CPDP 2020: DPAs, Policing and Law Enforcement', *YouTube*, https://www.youtube.com/watch?v=0tJ0WV3sdU0&t=17s.

[195] Schengen JSA, 'Opinion on the Development of the SIS II' (19 May 2004) 3. See also EDPS, 'Schengen Information System', https://edps.europa.eu/data-protection/european-it-systems/schengen-information-system_en.

V. Access to the Interoperability Components by the Relevant EU Agencies

Besides the national authorities having broader access to the interoperable system, EU Agencies will obtain increased access possibilities to the underlying databases as well as to the MID, the CIR and the ESP. In that vein, two EU agencies – Europol and the EBCGA – should be mentioned as being particularly pertinent regarding the processing of personal data in the context of migration management, asylum and border control. In addition, the European Union Agency for Criminal Justice Cooperation (Eurojust) progressively coordinates cross-border cases of organised crime that are related to illegal immigrant smuggling.[196]

As previously mentioned, the Interoperability Regulations could be seen as final step in a sequence of measures that suggest relying on information stored in large-scale AFSJ databases to mitigate security concerns associated with migration. Structural exchanges of personal data between competent authorities on different levels endorse such association and risk blurring the lines between migration management and the safeguarding of public security.[197] Such blurring may also be observed in the context of data exchanges between EU Agencies.

Europol, an EU Agency originally responsible to support national LEAs in the fight against organised crime and terrorism, became increasingly engaged in migration-related investigations such as migrant smuggling or document fraud. Since 2016, Europol has progressively been involved in the processing of personal data not only for police cooperation purposes, but also, in the context of migration management, for the identification and security screening of migrants and in cross-border anti-migrant (smuggling) operations. Europol's engagement in the so-called Hotspots[198] to carry out secondary security checks on TCNs arriving in the EU fostered its involvement in the processing of personal data within that area.[199] The establishment of the European Migrant Smuggling Centre (EMSC) was a further step in deepening the sharing of

[196] Eurojust, 'Report on Eurojust's Casework in the Field of Migrant Smuggling' (2018), www.eurojust.europa.eu/doclibrary/Eurojust-framework/Casework/Report%20on%20Eurojust%20casework%20in%20the%20field%20of%20migrant%20smuggling%20(Redacted)%20-%20April%202018/2018-04_Migrant-smuggling-report_Redacted_EN.pdf. It should be noted that the report refers to the number of migrant smuggling cases referred to Eurojust increasing from 1.7% to 2.7% in the period from 2012 to 2014, which is still marginal.

[197] Teresa Quintel, 'Interoperable Data Exchanges within Different Data Protection Regimes: The Case of Europol and the European Border and Coast Guard Agency' (2020) 26 *European Public Law* 205.

[198] European Commission, 'Hotspot Approach' (6 December 2016), https://ec.europa.eu/home-affairs/what-we-do/networks/european_migration_network/glossary_search/hotspot-approach_en.

[199] Europol, 'Europol Programming Document 2019–2021, Adopted by Europol Management Board on 30.11.2018', https://www.europol.europa.eu/publications-documents/europol-programming-document.

intelligence between Europol and other authorities involved in border control and migration management.[200]

The EBCGA is the central pillar in the EU's integrated border management.[201] Initially established as supranational agency tasked with assisting the Member States with migration management and border control, the EBCGA developed into a powerful coordination hub between Member States and other EU Agencies as well as third countries, progressively gaining operational competences in further areas relating to migration. In that vein, under the new EBCGA Regulation, which was proposed in September 2018[202] and adopted on 15 April 2019,[203] the EBCGA obtained even more competences to cooperate with relevant actors, such as Europol, and exchange information in the fight against organised cross-border crime and terrorism.[204]

Compared to Europol and the EBCGA, Eurojust's role in migration-related cases is (so far) rather marginal, as it is still perceived as a coordinating body that depends primarily on the initiative of the Member States. Hence, while Europol may analyse personal data by way of cross-matching information in different working files, Eurojust is obliged to seek permission from its national desks before merging cases whenever links between files are detected. Nevertheless, in recent years, Eurojust allocated a considerable amount of its resources to the coordination of migrant smuggling cases, albeit only a low number of such cases referred to it by the Member States.[205] In 2017, migrant smuggling cases belonged to the top three types of crimes that triggered the most frequent use of judicial cooperation tools[206] within Eurojust.[207] Beyond Eurojust's increased involvement in migrant smuggling cases, it is predicted that existing cooperation channels with Europol and the EBCGA will be fostered.[208]

[200] Europol/INTERPOL, 'Europol-INTERPOL Report on Migrant Smuggling Networks. Migrant Smuggling Networks. Joint Europol-INTERPOL Report Executive Summary May 2016', https://www.europol.europa.eu/publications-documents/europol-INTERPOL-report-migrant-smuggling-networks.

[201] Anja Radjenovic, 'Protection of EU External Borders', PE 630.316' (2019), https://www.europarl.europa.eu/RegData/etudes/BRIE/2018/630316/EPRS_BRI(2018)630316_EN.pdf.

[202] 'Proposal for a Regulation of the European Parliament and of the Council on the European Border and Coast Guard and repealing Council Joint Action 98/700/JHA, Regulation (EU) 1052/2013 of the European Parliament and of the Council and Regulation (EU) 2016/1624 of the European Parliament and of the Council' COM (2018) 631 final, Brussels, 12 September 2018.

[203] Regulation (EU) 2019/1896 of the European Parliament and of the Council of 13 November 2019 on the European Border and Coast Guard and repealing Regulations (EU) No 1052/2013 and (EU) 2016/1624 [2019] OJ L295/1.

[204] See, for instance, art 10(1)(q) of Regulation (EU) 2019/1896 regarding cooperation with Europol and Eurojust.

[205] Compared to the assumed number of facilitated entries to the EU; see Eurojust (n 196).

[206] The main judicial cooperation tools at Eurojust are coordination meetings (CMs), coordination centres (CCs) and joint investigation teams (JITs).

[207] Eurojust, 'Casework at Eurojust', www.eurojust.europa.eu/Practitioners/operational/casework/Pages/Casework-at-Eurojust.aspx.

[208] See, for instance, Council of the European Union, Final Report Future Group on Travel Intelligence and Border Management, *Annex: Europol and Frontex Final Report* (The Hague/Warsaw, 16 September 2021) EDOC 1182065/Frontex No 9870, Brussels, 3 March 2022.

Europol and the EBCGA in particular will play a key role with regard to the development and operation of the updated AFSJ databases and some of the interoperability components. Whereas Europol's databases will be connected to the interoperable system via the ESP, the EBCGA will be responsible for the ETIAS Central Unit. It goes without saying that both Agencies will feed the databases with information gathered during their missions – for instance, (indirectly) via EUROSUR or (directly) in the ETIAS watch-list.[209] Such information could also include personal data that were obtained during data exchanges with Eurojust. In addition, all three Agencies will be granted access to the systems for the performance of their tasks.[210]

Europol may retrieve personal data from EU databases in order to cross-match these data against information in its own working files. Such cross-matching of personal data in Europol's data environment allows the Agency to deliver tailored analytical products to the competent authorities in the Member States. Its recast Regulation permits Europol to process large datasets in order to provide better insights into specific crime dynamics and to engage in the use of bulk data analysis for a better understanding of patterns. This bears risks not only where Europol processes biometric data in bulk, but also regarding the purpose limitation principle, as any data-driven analysis, by its very nature, raises concerns regarding its compliance with core EU data protection principles.[211]

One of the objectives of interoperability is to facilitate and streamline access by national and EU LEAs to EU databases that were not exclusively established for law enforcement purposes. In addition, all underlying AFSJ databases feature provisions granting Europol access to retained data for the purposes of fighting serious crime and terrorism. Requirements for access by Europol staff are, inter alia, the existence of reasonable grounds to consider that the consultation of data in the systems may substantially contribute to the prevention, detection or investigation of criminal offences, or, if consultation is necessary, to support and strengthen action by Member States within the mandate of Europol.[212]

With regard to Frontex, the Agency's transformation into the EBCGA was finalised in October 2016. Since then, the EBCGA has been in charge of monitoring the EU's external borders and, together with the Member State authorities and Europol, the identification and registration of TCNs, including the assessment

[209] Article 34 of the ETIAS Regulation provides for a new EU watch-list if a person is suspected of having committed or taken part in a terrorist offence or other serious criminal offence. It will also include persons in respect of whom there are factual indications or reasonable grounds for believing that they will commit such offences. In addition to a new watch-list, the ETIAS regulation provides for an algorithm to profile applications against pre-determined risk indicators relating to security, illegal immigration or high epidemic transmission.

[210] Quintel (n 197).

[211] ibid.

[212] Teresa Quintel, 'The Impact of Interoperability on the Processing of (Biometric) Data of Third Country Nationals by Europol' (2018) 101 *Kritische Vierteljahresschrift für Gesetzgebung und Rechtswissenschaft* 332.

of potential security threats. The EBCGA progressively became active in the field of security and gained additional competences to process personal data when consulting AFSJ databases.[213] With the establishment of ETIAS and the interoperability regime, the EBCGA will obtain even more powers in terms of data processing activities. For instance, the ETIAS Central Unit that is supposed to be established within the EBCGA[214] shall be responsible for verifying whether personal data triggering hits during an ETIAS application is present in other information systems, including Europol and INTERPOL databases.[215] In addition, the legislative instruments of other databases and the Interoperability Regulations refer to the strengthened mandate and access rights of the EBCGA.[216]

While Europol became more and more involved in EU border management and migration control, the EBCGA was granted more and more law enforcement-like tasks that are related to its initial area of operation. Both Agencies developed into powerful information hubs with increasing competences to process personal data and to access information in AFSJ large-scale databases.[217]

Eurojust, at least for the time being, plays a less prominent (if not to say negligible) role regarding access to AFSJ databases[218] and interoperability. Nevertheless, it is supposed to become increasingly involved in terms of data exchanges of personal data among EU Agencies that are involved in migration management and border control. Whereas cooperation with Europol is laid down in the founding acts of both Agencies, an updated Memorandum of Understanding between Eurojust and the EBCGA is being pushed at a political level.[219]

Although the growing synergy between the tasks of these three Agencies may be seen as progress towards a more harmonised and integrated EU border management approach, the overlapping purposes for which they may exchange personal data may lead to concerns, as different data protection regimes apply.[220] Against that background, discrepancies may arise in the context of interoperability where systematic data exchanges take place between actors that apply different data protection regimes. While national authorities such as immigration offices, visa authorities, the police or other LEAs such as the SIRENE Bureaux apply the GDPR and the LED to their processing activities, Europol, the EBCGA and

[213] Anja Radjenovic, 'EPRS Briefing: EU Legislation in Progress – European Travel Information and Authorisation System (ETIAS)', PE 599.298 (2018), https://www.europarl.europa.eu/RegData/etudes/BRIE/2017/599298/EPRS_BRI%282017%29599298_EN.pdf.

[214] Article 7(1) of Regulation (EU) 2018/1240.

[215] ibid art 7(2)(a).

[216] Quintel (n 197).

[217] ibid.

[218] For the time being, Eurojust is only granted access to the ECRIS-TCN.

[219] Interview with Eurojust official. The EDPS generally agreed that closer cooperation between Eurojust and the EBCGA, including the exchange and sharing of personal data, could be possible under their new legal frameworks. See letter sent by the EDPS, Wojciech Wiewiórowski, 'Formal Consultation on the Interpretation of the Legal Basis for Exchange of Operational Data between Eurojust and the European Border and Coast Guard (Frontex)', Brussels, 3 March 2020.

[220] Quintel (n 197).

Eurojust process personal data within the scope of Regulation (EU) 2018/1725, which applies to EU institutions, bodies, offices and agencies, the recast Europol Regulation and the Eurojust Regulation.

Although the adoption of Regulation (EU) 2018/1725 represented a first step towards more coherence between the national and EU levels, persisting fragmentation of data protection rules may also lead to problems where personal data are being exchanged between authorities and agencies on different levels. Concerns arise with regard to the supervision of processing operations, as Member State authorities are supervised by national supervisory authorities, while the supervision of EU Agencies falls within the remit of the EDPS. The additional layer of complexity that will be added with interoperability in terms of supervision is the subject of the following section.

VI. Supervision of Processing within the Interoperable System

In a world where more and more data are being used in order to analyse the movement of individuals, connecting information from different sources on a systematic basis may be a logical step to carry out such analyses more effectively. In addition, interoperable databases allow immediate data exchanges intended to facilitate and streamline decision making by digital means.[221] Interoperability is supposed to offer new possibilities to facilitate the exchange of information, to better manage migration and to enhance the EU's internal security in general. Competent authorities shall be provided with relevant information on TCNs, and blind spots in the existing databases shall be eliminated to enable effective and comprehensive cooperation in the area of border control and migration management.[222]

At the same time, it becomes more challenging to trace the data exchanges and sources of information in the interconnected system. In particular, where authorities exchange and further process personal data in order to use them for different purposes at both the national and EU levels, the supervision becomes more intricate. To that end, this section will assess the interoperability of AFSJ databases with regard to the role of national and EU supervisory authorities.

Due to the complex landscape of information exchange channels and the multitude of actors, data processing activities within the AFSJ are opaque, which makes it difficult for data subjects to ascertain who is processing their personal data. Therefore, compliance with the data protection principles to ensure clearly

[221] Interoperability is commonly referred to as 'the ability of different information systems to communicate, exchange data and use the information that has been exchanged'. See EDPS, 'Reflection Paper on the Interoperability of Information Systems in the Area of Freedom, Security and Justice, 17 November 2017'.

[222] COM (2017) 793 and 794.

defined processing activities that are subject to strict supervision are of utmost importance to warrant fundamental rights standards. Independent overview is stipulated by Article 8(3) of the EU Charter and therefore applies horizontally to all areas regulated by EU law. In addition, the GDPR, the LED and Regulation (EU) 2018/1725 regulate independent supervisions in particular sections. Yet, Chapter VI of Regulation (EU) 2018/1725 does not apply to operational personal data, and Chapter IX – the chapter under Regulation (EU) 2018/1725 that governs the processing of operational personal data – is incomplete with regard to supervision by the EDPS.

Hence, there will be situations in which certain processing activities will remain unknown to the data subject. For instance, the national supervisory authority in one Member State has no competence to scrutinise the processing activities of the competent (law enforcement) authorities in another Member State. Yet, where systematic data exchanges between those authorities take place, cooperation between the national supervisory authorities is crucial. However, such cooperation is lengthy and will be even slower in a complex system such as the one that is envisaged with the interoperability of AFSJ databases. Therefore, the rules on coordinated supervision that were adopted by the European Data Protection Board (EDPB),[223] represent a first step to prepare a harmonised approach to ensure the exchange of relevant information on supervision.[224]

With the blurred lines between migration and security leading to the obscuring of different purposes and the dilution of responsibilities between different processors, it is challenging for supervisory authorities to get a concrete picture of processing activities and hence the risks involved for data subjects. In an environment in which data constantly move between different actors, it is difficult, if not impossible, to know which actor is carrying out each respective processing activity. In order to ascertain which authority is responsible for supervision, close cooperation between the DPAs will become increasingly relevant.[225]

In order to ensure efficient supervision, DPAs should be able to follow data flows across the different networks instead of looking at each specific controller separately. In order to achieve an effective supervision of the complex network of different processors, closer cooperation between national DPAs and the EDPS to better understand the steps behind certain decision-making processes and to better handle complaints is a move in the right direction.[226] Just like the merging of previously disconnected AFSJ databases under the Interoperability Regulations

[223] Article 62(4) of Regulation (EU) 2018/1725. Coordinated Supervision Committee, 'Rules of Procedure of the Coordinated Supervision Committee' (adopted on 19 December 2019), available at: https://edpb.europa.eu/system/files/2021-04/cscropfinal_en.pdf.

[224] Simona Demková and Teresa Quintel, 'Allocation of Responsibilities in Interoperable Information Exchanges: Effective Review Compromised?' (2020), https://ceec.ut-capitole.fr/cahiers-jean-monnet-n-6-actes-des-ateliers-doctoraux-2019-l-etat-de-droit-de-l-universite-degli-studi-di-milano-et-de-la-european-school-of-law-toulouse-centre-d-excellence-europe-capitole-862062.kjsp?RH=1572513344545.

[225] ibid.

[226] ibid.

and the increased exchanges of personal data between different authorities, supervisory authorities should gain a better overview of the connected systems in order to be able to provide more effective supervision.[227] Yet, national supervisory authorities often lack powers and resources to enforce, and have only weak powers in the law enforcement context. In addition, the EDPS has relatively weak enforcement powers or may be constrained at a political level, and cooperation between national DPAs and the EDPS is still far from being satisfactory, particularly in the law enforcement context.

VII. Conclusion

Interoperable systems are supposed to enable competent authorities to take better-informed decisions obtained from all the available data processed in the different AFSJ databases. Aiming to enhance the efficiency and effectiveness of information sharing within the EU, interoperability pursues a complete information awareness approach by granting access to numerous authorities at different levels. However, within an interoperable system, issues that already exist in the currently established AFSJ databases might be magnified, particularly where different authorities at both the national and EU levels are competent to insert and access data in the databases.[228]

The sharing of personal data in an interoperable system and between various authorities generates concerns regarding the quality of the data that are being inserted into the underlying AFSJ databases and then merged within the networked system. Although the interoperable system is supposed to improve decision-making processes and increase the accuracy of data, this assumption contradicts several reports, which show that most of the operational AFSJ databases contain erroneous data.[229] With interoperability, those existing errors would be multiplied and, instead of enhancing information sharing between different authorities, lead to an overload of wrong matches, which the competent authorities would have to rectify.

Consequently, connecting the AFSJ databases could multiply wrong matches and maximise (incorrect) hits that would be shown to the querying user(s). Instead of simply verifying the result of individual hits, the competent user would be confronted with large numbers of matches, each of which would have to be reviewed for its accuracy and correctness.

In order to avoid such a burdensome workload for the commonly understaffed authorities, all inaccurate data currently held in the operational systems would have to be either corrected or deleted. Moreover, data in national databases

[227] ibid.

[228] Quintel (n 197).

[229] EDPS, 'Opinion 4/2018 on the Proposals for Two Regulations Establishing a Framework for Interoperability between EU Large-Scale Information Systems' (2018) point 36.

should be assessed in accordance with their continuous relevance and the level of quality in order to achieve similar standards across Member States. Thus, national and operational AFSJ databases would require meticulous assessment before being interconnected within the interoperability framework.

Interoperability will drastically change the way in which competent authorities may access, retrieve and process personal data stored in AFSJ databases. The interoperable system abandons the traditional silo-based approach, pursuant to which these databases were set up according to specific purposes, with precise time limits and strict access conditions. Hence, the interoperable system will introduce a game-changing playing field. Whether this game changer will be beneficial remains to be seen once interoperability becomes operational.

In the light of the above-mentioned developments, it is crucial to ensure that initiatives that are mainly driven by security-related concerns do not fall short of adequate legal protection. Hence, interoperable information sharing is, first and foremost, a matter of legal rather than technological constraints. However, the Interoperability Regulations seemingly disregard some of the most important data protection principles, as will be demonstrated below with regard to the purpose limitation principle.

With interoperability, access to the underlying databases as well as the interoperable components is given for new purposes that are disconnected from those that initially served the AFSJ databases. Thus, interoperability establishes new processing operations, which are neither covered by existing legal bases nor provide valid justifications for all access possibilities. This causes serious concerns in the light of the purpose limitation principle.[230]

In addition, interoperability may lead to an institutionalised function creep, where it might not always be sufficiently proven whether the data accessed and subsequently processed by LEAs are strictly necessary for their work. Admittedly, such concerns already existed with regard to the underlying AFSJ databases and in pre-interoperability times. However, as mentioned above, interoperability will establish new access possibilities to datasets that were created based on processing operations without sufficient justifications. These datasets will be generated by automated means from all underlying AFSJ databases. Therefore, the appropriate implementation of the purpose limitation principle in practice seems unrealistic where databases with originally different purposes are being merged into new, centralised components that create additional processing operations.

The purpose limitation principle is one of the cornerstones of data protection law and is enshrined in all important data protection legislation,[231] stipulating that personal data must be collected for 'specified, explicit and legitimate purposes and not further processed in a way incompatible with those purposes'.[232]

[230] ibid 11.

[231] Convention 108+ (the Convention omits the word 'further'), the EU Charter, the GDPR and the LED.

[232] *cf* Article 29 Data Protection Working Party, 'Opinion 03/2013 on Purpose Limitation' (2013) 3.

The purpose limitation principle was integrated into each of the underlying databases that were set up for specific purposes, along with the types of data that were stored, the periods for the retention and a limited number of recipients of those data. The link between processing operations and specific purposes was supposed to ensure foreseeability for data subjects and to help define safeguards to be adopted by the controller.[233] Over time, the founding acts of those databases, initially established for specific purposes and with strict access requirements, were revised in order to serve more purposes, retain additional categories of personal data and provide broader access possibilities to more authorities, in particular to LEAs.

Looking at the establishment of interoperability, it becomes apparent that even more purposes have been added to the initial ones and that increased law enforcement access was given as an ancillary objective. To that end, the legal bases of the existing AFSJ databases were changed so as to include police and judicial cooperation provisions.

In order to be able to precisely define the purposes of processing activities, both the legal bases and the objectives of a legal act should be unambiguous and confined in order to give an indication as to the context of processing, the types of personal data that may be processed and the categories of data subjects. Where the legal bases and the objectives of a legal act are multiplied and widened, the purposes of processing will likewise be propagated and widened instead of being strictly restricted and precisely defined as required by the CJEU.[234]

Another concern is that interoperability will diminish some key safeguards for access authorisation and review. First, the Interoperability Regulations abolish the cascading system of checking national systems prior to requesting access to AFSJ databases, and the relevant authorities will obtain a strengthened mandate to access and process personal data in the underlying AFSJ databases as well as in the interoperable system.[235] The prerequisite that authorisation for access must be validated by a court or an independent administrative authority, as required by the CJEU, may be circumvented in many instances. In addition, in many situations it will be difficult to review whether personal data were accessed in a justified and lawful manner, as the interoperable system will simply be too complex to allow for thorough scrutiny by supervisory authorities or courts.

This is also because data processing activities within the AFSJ by the relevant actors may be opaque to data subjects, for whom it may be difficult to ascertain who is processing their personal data and against whom to exercise their rights. Therefore, compliance with data protection principles and strict supervision are of utmost importance to ensure fundamental rights standards.

[233] ibid 4.

[234] *Digital Rights Ireland* (n 139) paras 61 and 65.

[235] European Commission, 'Factsheet: EU Information Systems – Security and Borders', https://ec.europa.eu/home-affairs/sites/default/files/what-we-do/policies/european-agenda-security/20190416_agenda_security-factsheet-eu-information-systems-security-borders_en.pdf.

The changes introduced by the reform of AFSJ databases and interoperability also led to intensified powers and expanded competences of EU Agencies engaged at the EU's external borders. The mandates of EU Agencies such as Europol and the EBCGA were broadened to strengthen the role of these agencies in the management of migration, border control and asylum.[236] Under the Interoperability Regulations, numerous provisions aim at fostering exchanges between competent (law enforcement) authorities even more in the future. Although each EU Agency and national authority must put procedures into place to monitor and log processing activities, this might not be sufficient.

The new layers that interoperability adds to the already complex system of AFSJ databases make it extremely difficult to scrutinise the way in which data are collected, accessed and shared. In order to achieve full supervision, cooperation must be stepped up between the supervisory bodies at the national and EU levels. For that purpose, a so-called coordinated supervision model has been codified in the legal instruments of many of the underlying AFSJ databases. Moreover, Article 62(1) of Regulation (EU) 2018/1725 puts forward a harmonised model of coordinated supervision between the EDPS (which is responsible for the supervision, inter alia, of EU Agencies) and the national DPAs to ensure an effective supervision of large-scale AFSJ databases.[237] It remains to be seen whether such coordinated supervision will be carried out effectively and in favour of data subjects stored in those databases.

The above considerations are important when acknowledging that interoperability, as it stands now, is by no means a finalised product; rather, it is a dynamic toolbox that may be extended at will, similar to an extendable Lego set. The recent proposal to reform the Prüm database and to connect it to the interoperable system is only one example to demonstrate such dynamics. Prüm, a law enforcement database, would be coupled with the CIR and queried via the ESP.[238] This extension further reinforces the blending of migration and criminal law enforcement matters. In that context, it is of utmost importance that this merging will not lead to a lowering of data protection standards where competent authorities accessing the interoperable system apply the LED instead of the GDPR when processing the personal data of TCNs.

The processing of personal data by LEAs under the Interoperability Regulations will require close scrutiny by the (national) supervisory authorities.[239] Whereas the GDPR provides very strong data subject rights, in the law enforcement context, transparency obligations towards the data subject are naturally less stringent, as

[236] Nikolai Atanassov, 'EPRS Briefing – Revision of the Schengen Information System for Border Checks', PE 599.341, 18 October 2018, https://www.europarl.europa.eu/thinktank/en/document/EPRS_BRI(2017)599341, 2.

[237] See EDPS, 'Supervision Coordination', https://edps.europa.eu/supervision-coordination_en.

[238] Article 39(1) and (2) of COM (2021) 784 final.

[239] Juraj Sajfert and Paul de Hert, 'The Role of the Data Protection Authorities in Supervising Police and Criminal Justice Authorities Processing Personal Data' in *The Needed Balances in EU Criminal Law: Past, Present and Future* (Bloomsbury, 2017).

providing the data subject with information about the processing might jeopardise ongoing investigations.[240] This would imply that data subject rights could be limited more easily and obligations for controllers would be less strict where police officers process personal data retrieved from the underlying AFSJ databases or the interoperability components within the scope of the LED.

Besides the provisions on data subject rights and on the obligations for controllers, many of the provisions are more flexible under the LED and often depend on the transposition in the national laws of the individual Member States. Many national legislators decided to allow for a broadening of the LED's scope by making numerous authorities subject to its personal scope and by including a broad range of processing activities within its material scope. This means that competent authorities under the LED may not always be traditional criminal law authorities, but may instead also include customs authorities or coast guards[241] that may process personal data for the prevention, investigation, detection or prosecution of criminal offences or the execution of criminal penalties, including the safeguarding against and the prevention of threats to public security.

[240] In accordance with art 13(2)(d) of Directive (EU) 2016/680, data subjects must be notified once notification can no longer jeopardise ongoing investigations. See also Teresa Quintel, 'Follow the Money, if You Can – Possible Solutions for Enhanced FIU Cooperation under Improved Data Protection Rules', https://papers.ssrn.com/sol3/papers.cfm?abstract_id=3318299.

[241] As is, for instance, the case in Sweden. See Datainspektionen, 'Tillsyn enligt brottsdatalagen (2018:1177) – Polismyndighetens rutiner för hantering av personuppgiftsincidenter, approved on 17 December 2020' 14.

3

The Overly Broad Application of Directive (EU) 2016/680

As demonstrated in the previous chapters on AFSJ databases and interoperability, the 'unprecedented influx of TCNs'[1] led to an unprecedented wave of proposals on the reform of EU databases and the adoption of two Regulations on the establishment of the interoperability between large-scale AFSJ information systems. At the same time, the narrative of migration being a threat to the EU's internal security cultivated demands for more efficient border management, as well as increased powers for LEAs to consult and access personal data in AFSJ databases. Hence, law enforcement access to those databases as well as to the interoperability components was progressively widened, as were the purposes for which LEAs would be granted access.

Whilst LEAs must abide by the same regime as private actors – the GDPR – when the processing of personal data pursues a general or administrative purpose, different rules apply for processing carried out in the law enforcement context. However, what *law enforcement processing* encompasses is not always crystal clear. Hence, while the management of migration or the administration of visas and asylum applications could be categorised as administrative processing, when it comes to border control, the boundaries start to be more blurred. Where border guards are obliged to check law enforcement databases such as the SIS II for all entries to the EU, or where national police officers are supposed to check AFSJ databases for the fight against illegal immigration, the lines become greyer.

The relationship between data protection and law enforcement is not always straightforward and at times is characterised by conflicting interests. Reconciling demands for security on the one hand and fundamental rights on the other is not an easy task. Finding the least privacy-intrusive means while fighting crime, particularly with the increasing use of artificial intelligence (AI) and other novel technologies in policing is challenging. Public expectation to keep the application of advanced technologies within the boundaries of key data protection principles, such as fairness or lawfulness, to better protect the individual from becoming

[1] Bruno Nascimbene and Alessia Di Pascale, 'The "Arab Spring" and the Extraordinary Influx of People Who Arrived in Italy from North Africa' (2011) 13 *European Journal of Migration and Law* 341.

subject to unfair processing is high. Yet, public expectation to be ensured a high level of security within the EU is by no means lower.[2]

This leads to the important balancing exercise within the auspices of the purpose limitation and data minimisation principles. How can meaningful information be extracted from huge datasets while upholding the fundamental rights of individuals?

Within the law enforcement community, it is commonly argued that data protection rules impede effective operational work, as processing activities are constrained, and data may not be exploited without following a targeted aim. Yet, what is often forgotten is that solid and well-implemented data protection rules can serve as a means to help LEAs to better structure their files and hence carry out their tasks more efficiently. Therefore, it is essential that the law provides clear limits in order to protect individuals, particularly those that might not be aware of their rights.

Evidently, this should not mean that LEAs must refrain from using advanced technologies to support their work. However, certain conditions and rules should be followed prior to, during and after the personal data of potential perpetrators, victims of crime or witnesses are processed by LEAs. Therefore, a consistent application of data protection rules, while giving LEAs sufficient space for the performance of their tasks, is of paramount importance. This also means that the boundaries are not stretched in such a way as to allow LEAs to discretionally apply more flexible data protection rules for processing carried out in the law enforcement context. Instead, processing activities should follow specific purposes in order to achieve a clear goal, while only interfering with the privacy of individuals when this is necessary and proportionate. Whenever such purposes are not of a law enforcement nature, competent LEAs should apply the general data protection framework with its strong transparency requirements in order to enable individuals whose personal data are processed to be informed about all steps of the processing. Only then will the trust in good police work be sustained and individuals be willing to accept privacy intrusions.

In order to set certain legal limits for law enforcement processing, the GDPR is accompanied by the LED, which seeks to achieve more coherence when national LEAs in the EU Member States process personal data for the purpose of the prevention, investigation, detection and prosecution of crime. The LED has two aims: on the one hand, the Directive seeks to better protect individuals' personal data processed by competent authorities; on the other hand, it aims to achieve a more efficient and effective exchange of personal data between those authorities by harmonising the rules in the Member States.

[2] See, for instance, Survey requested by the European Commission, Directorate-General for Migration and Home Affairs, and coordinated by the Directorate-General for Communication, 'Special Eurobarometer 464b: Europeans' Attitudes towards Security, Wave EB87.4' (2017).

The LED replaced the DPFD from 2008, thereby expanding the scope of EU data protection law applicable in the area of police and criminal justice. Being applicable to both cross-border and domestic processing, the LED should be seen as an improvement in comparison to the data protection rules that existed under the DPFD. However, while some see the LED as having made great achievements in an area that had previously not been regulated by EU law,[3] others view the prospect of the LED attaining a higher level of data protection as less promising.[4]

Moreover, other than the GDPR, the LED is not directly applicable and sets out minimum standards, allowing the Member States to provide higher data protection safeguards than those under the Directive.[5] Hence, since the Directive is not a full harmonisation instrument, its scope and application depend on the transposition in the individual Member States.[6] Consequently, there are crucial differences concerning the national transposition acts of the LED, which may lead to an application of the Directive in some Member States where in fact the processing should fall within the scope of the GDPR. Such an overly broad interpretation of the Directive's scope may, in certain situations, lead to unfair processing practices. One of those situations – migration-related processing being turned into law enforcement processing – will be the subject of this chapter.

When determining whether the LED applies to certain processing operations by the competent authorities, the application of the Directive depends on whether both personal and material scopes are satisfied. This means that the personal data in question must be processed by a competent authority (personal scope) for the purposes of the prevention, investigation, detection or prosecution of criminal offences or the execution of criminal penalties (material scope). Hence, if either the personal or the material scope is not satisfied, the GDPR should apply, including where personal data are processed by competent authorities,[7] although in practice, such a conceptual separation is not always that evident.

In addition, national legislators had a wide margin of appreciation when deciding on what to encompass within the LED's scope. With regard to the material scope, neither the LED nor national legislation provides an explicit answer as to what should be included within the definition of a criminal offence and could apply coherently throughout the EU. While the LED suggests that a criminal

[3] Juraj Sajfert and Teresa Quintel, 'Data Protection Directive (EU) 2016/680 for Police and Criminal Justice Authorities' (1 December 2017), https://ssrn.com/abstract=3285873.

[4] See intervention by Vagelis Papakonstantinou during the 2019 Computers, Privacy & Data Protection (CPDP) conference: CPDPConferences, 'CPDP 2019: Law Enforcement and Data Subjects' Rights: Is the EU Legal Framework a …' (2019), https://www.youtube.com/watch?v=b8ab7oU4ZC0.

[5] Article 1(3) of Directive (EU) 2016/680.

[6] Teresa Quintel, 'Follow the Money, if You Can – Possible Solutions for Enhanced FIU Cooperation under Improved Data Protection Rules', https://papers.ssrn.com/sol3/papers.cfm?abstract_id=3318299.

[7] For instance, when LEAs process HR data; see Juraj Sajfert and Teresa Quintel, 'Data Protection Directive (EU) 2016/680 for Police and Criminal Justice Authorities' (1 December 2017), https://papers.ssrn.com/sol3/papers.cfm?abstract_id=3285873.

offence should be an 'autonomous concept of Union law as interpreted by the Court of Justice of the EU',[8] the criminal codes of the Member States are not harmonised. Thus, what types of offences fall within the remit of the LED depends on each national system. Consequently, whereas the LED applies to minor offences in some Member States, other national systems provide a clear division between administrative and criminal law, whereby administrative law would fall under the GDPR, while criminal law would be covered by the Directive.[9]

Similar concerns arise regarding the personal scope of the Directive. The competent authorities that may apply the LED to their processing activities may differ from Member State to Member State, which results in variations regarding the application of the LED. While in some Member States, the LED strictly applies only to traditional 'Third Pillar LEAs',[10] other Member States include a variety of bodies with prosecutorial powers on a variety of offences within the scope of the Directive.[11]

Overall, the divergent application of the LED, where some Member States include different criminal offences or additional competent authorities within the Directive's scope, impedes the harmonisation of data protection rules in the area of police and criminal justice.[12] Ultimately, where national law either expands the list of what constitutes a criminal offence or includes an extensive number of competent authorities under the definition in the LED, or both, this leads to the Directive's application to processing activities for which it was not foreseen.

Moreover, national divergences render a clear delineation between the scope of the LED and the GDPR more difficult and may ultimately affect data subject rights. Where the competent authorities apply the LED instead of the GDPR, many of the rights and obligations may be restricted or applied in a more flexible manner than under the Regulation. Hence, the extension of the Directive's scope may ultimately lead to a more limited scope of the GDPR, and the data subject rights enshrined therein.

The challenges that emerge when determining the legal instrument applicable to the processing of personal data in the area of migration, border control and asylum, as well as the differences between the relevant provisions under the GDPR and the LED and the consequences thereof for individuals whose personal data are processed, will be the focus in this chapter.

[8] Recital 13 of Directive (EU) 2016/680.

[9] Commission expert group on Regulation (EU) 2016/679 and Directive (EU) 2016/680 (E03461), 'Minutes of the Third Meeting of the Commission Expert Group on Regulation (EU) 2016/679 and Directive (EU) 2016/680' (7 November 2016).

[10] Commission expert group on Regulation (EU) 2016/679 and Directive (EU) 2016/680 (E03461), 'Minutes of the Seventh Meeting of the Commission Expert Group on Regulation (EU) 2016/679 and Directive (EU) 2016/680' (7 March 2017).

[11] Commission expert group on Regulation (EU) 2016/679 and Directive (EU) 2016/680 (E03461), 'Minutes of the Fifth Meeting of the Commission Expert Group on Regulation (EU) 2016/679 and Directive (EU) 2016/680' (18 January 2017).

[12] Sajfert and Quintel (n 3).

I. Directive (EU) 2016/680: Structure and Overview

As previously mentioned, the numerous changes introduced by the Lisbon Treaty in 2009 also had an impact on the means by which the EU was henceforth able to legislate in the area of data protection. On the one hand, data protection, as a fundamental right, was constitutionalised under the EU Treaties when the EU Charter became a binding source of EU primary law.[13] Besides Article 7 of the EU Charter, which enshrined the right to privacy, Article 8 introduced the right to the protection of personal data and thereby devoted an individual provision to that right, which had previously been included under Article 8 ECHR.

On the other hand, Article 16 TFEU provided an unusually strong legal basis to legislate broadly in areas relating to data protection.[14] The very limited exceptions that were left outside the scope of Article 16 TFEU were national security and the EU's common security and defence policy, the latter to be regulated in accordance with Article 39 TEU. Article 16 TFEU thus required the EU legislators to enact more comprehensive rules that would, at the same time, respect the fundamental rights aspect of data protection.

In addition, the Lisbon Treaty transferred more competences to the EU to regulate within the field of judicial cooperation in criminal matters and police cooperation. However, with regard to data protection, Declaration 21, which is attached to the Lisbon Treaty, acknowledged that in the fields of judicial cooperation in criminal matters and police cooperation, specific rules may prove necessary because of the particular nature of these fields.[15] Hence, this political intention of the drafters of the Treaties provided the direction in which regulation in the area of data protection should go in the future to both the Commission and the co-legislator.

At the same time, the Lisbon Treaty made the repeal of all Framework Decisions necessary, as the abolition of the pillar structure transferred the right of initiative to the Commission. The Framework Decision, which had been the most important instrument to regulate data protection in Third Pillar matters until then, was the legal instrument that provided certain rules in the field of judicial cooperation in criminal matters and police cooperation. Yet, the constitutional amendments of the EU legal order under the Lisbon Treaty meant that the DPFD had to be reviewed only four years after it had entered into force after a very lengthy and difficult process of negotiations.

[13] European Parliament, 'The Protection of Fundamental Rights in the EU', https://www.europarl.europa.eu/factsheets/en/sheet/146/euroopan-unionin-perusoikeuskirja.

[14] Hielke Hijmans, *The European Union as Guardian of Internet Privacy: The Story of Art 16 TFEU* (Springer, 2016).

[15] Treaty of Lisbon amending the Treaty on European Union and the Treaty establishing the European Community, 13 December 2007 – A. Declarations concerning provisions of the Treaties – 21. Declaration on the protection of personal data in the fields of judicial cooperation in criminal matters and police cooperation [2007] OJ C306, 17 December 2007.

Yet, the mandate received under the new treaty was clear and thus made the review of the DPFD as well as that of the 95 Data Protection Directive inevitable. In addition, technology had developed at an unprecedented pace during the preceding decade, so that an updated and more comprehensive data protection framework was necessary in response to the numerous challenges such development had brought about. On the one hand, the 95 Data Protection Directive was transposed differently in the Member States. On the other hand, the weakness of the DPFD had become more and more visible, and contributed even more to a fragmented data protection landscape within the EU.

In November 2010, the Commission presented a Communication on 'A comprehensive approach on personal data protection in the European Union',[16] concerning which the EDPS issued his opinion on 14 January 2011.[17]

In the Communication, the Commission addressed the impact of new technologies[18] as well as the globalised nature of international data transfers, which necessitated a stronger institutional arrangement for the effective enforcement of data protection rules. In light of these new challenges, a more coherent data protection framework would, according to the Commission, be imperative.[19] In the same vein, the Commission stressed the need for harmonisation between Member States' legislation on data protection, strengthened data subject rights,[20] and clarification of the status and powers of national DPAs, including the concept of 'complete independence'.[21]

In addition, the Commission envisaged the revision of the data protection rules applicable in the area of police and judicial cooperation in criminal matters,[22] acknowledging that the Lisbon Treaty abolished the previous pillar structure of the EU and, with Article 16 TFEU, introduced a new and comprehensive legal basis for the protection of personal data across EU policies. Against that background, the Commission affirmed that a more comprehensive legally binding instrument in that area was a prerequisite.[23]

[16] European Commission, 'Communication from the Commission to the European Parliament, the Council, the Economic and Social Committee and the Committee of the Regions: A Comprehensive Approach on Personal Data Protection in the European Union' COM (2010) 609 final, Brussels, 4 November 2010.

[17] Also taking into account the Article 29 Data Protection Working Party, 'The Future of Privacy – Joint Contribution to the Consultation of the European Commission on the Legal Framework for the Fundamental Right to Protection of Personal Data, Adopted on 01 December 2009'. See also EDPS, 'Opinion of the European Data Protection Supervisor on the Communication from the Commission to the European Parliament, the Council, the Economic and Social Committee and the Committee of the Regions – "A Comprehensive Approach on Personal Data Protection in the European Union"' (2011) 3.

[18] European Commission, 'Communication from the Commission to the European Parliament, the Council the Economic and Social Committee and the Committee of the Regions: A Comprehensive Approach on Personal Data Protection in the European Union' COM (2010) 609 final, Brussels, 4 November 2010, 3.

[19] ibid 4.

[20] European Commission (n 16).

[21] ibid 18.

[22] ibid 13.

[23] ibid.

At first, the Commission considered an extension of the rules under a general data protection instrument also to the area of police and judicial cooperation in criminal matters, including for processing at the domestic level.[24] At the same time, harmonised limitations to certain data protection rights of individuals would be possible. Hence, the Commission sought to examine the need to introduce specific and harmonised provisions in a new general, all-encompassing data protection framework. This should be achieved by introducing new rules on the processing of genetic data for criminal law purposes or distinguishing between categories of data subjects in the area of police cooperation and judicial cooperation in criminal matters.[25]

In addition, the need to align existing sector-specific rules adopted at the EU level for police and judicial cooperation in criminal matters in specific instruments with the new general legal data protection framework was to be assessed.[26] With regard to international transfers of personal data, the Commission acknowledged that the 2008 DPFD did not require an adequacy decision by the Commission.[27] Therefore, any new rules applicable in the area of law enforcement should be legally binding and, other than the DPFD, include domestic processing.[28]

Finally, the Commission acknowledged that instruments governing the functioning of Europol, Eurojust and the SIS II were governed by non-binding legal instruments,[29] which affected the possibilities for individuals to exercise their data protection rights effectively.[30] In the long term, the Commission therefore sought to assess the need to adapt the remaining legal instruments to the new general legal framework. For that purpose, Regulation 45/2001/EC was to be examined in order to be adapted in a second round of amendments.[31]

The EDPS, in his Opinion from February 2011,[32] generally welcomed the Commission's Communication and agreed on the need for a review of the EU legal data protection framework.[33] He recalled that in his 2007 Opinion for a

[24] The DPFD was applicable only where personal data were processed outside of the national sphere – for instance, when transmitted to other EU Member States or transferred to third countries.

[25] COM (2010) 609 final, 14.

[26] ibid 15.

[27] Like the one required by the 95 Data Protection Directive; see ibid 15. Article 13(4) DPFD merely stated that 'the adequacy of the level of protection referred … should be assessed in the light of all the circumstances surrounding a data transfer operation or a set of data transfer operations'.

[28] ibid.

[29] Namely, Recommendation No R (87) 15.

[30] European Commission, 'Communication from the Commission to the European Parliament, the Council the Economic and Social Committee and the Committee of the Regions: A Comprehensive Approach on Personal Data Protection in the European Union' COM (2010) 609 final, Brussels, 4 November 2010, 8.

[31] ibid 19.

[32] EDPS (n 17).

[33] ibid 4.

better implementation of the 95 Data Protection Directive,[34] he had identified key elements for future amendments to the EU data protection framework.

With regard to data protection in the area of police and justice, the EDPS recommended including such rules in a general instrument, while taking into account specificities of this sector, in line with Declaration 21 attached to the Lisbon Treaty.[35] The EDPS stressed the importance of a clear, simple and consistent legal framework, in particular with regard to the proliferation of the regimes applicable to Europol, Eurojust and the SIS II.[36] Hence, the EDPS strongly recommended a comprehensive data protection instrument that would cover all sectors.[37] In order to achieve a high level of data protection while improving consistency, the EDPS considered a two-step approach, which would first introduce a general instrument applicable to all processing activities, including those in the area of police and judicial cooperation. In a second step, the sector-specific data protection regimes should be aligned with the general instrument.[38]

On 25 January 2012, the Commission adopted a package to reform the European data protection framework, comprising a Communication,[39] a Proposal for a Regulation[40] and a Proposal for a Directive.[41] With the proposal for a Directive applicable to data protection in the police and criminal justice sector, alongside a general Regulation, the Commission sought to propose more harmonised and binding data protection rules in the area of criminal justice and police cooperation. However, the reform package included two separate legal instruments instead of one all-encompassing one. In the Impact Assessment, the Commission argued that in light of the principle of proportionality, a Directive would be the most appropriate instrument to ensure harmonisation at the EU level, while at the same time leaving the necessary flexibility to the Member States.[42]

On the one hand, the separation between two legal instruments should be interpreted as a simple continuation of the traditionally separated areas, while taking into account the disposition under Declaration 21. On the other hand, the pressure from within the Commission to impose strong rules in the form

[34] EDPS, 'Opinion of the European Data Protection Supervisor on the Communication from the Commission to the European Parliament and the Council on the Follow-up of the Work Programme for Better Implementation of the Data Protection Directive (2007/C 255/01)' (2007).

[35] EDPS (n 17).

[36] ibid 27.

[37] ibid 28.

[38] ibid.

[39] European Commission, 'Communication from the Commission to the European Parliament, the Council, the European Economic and Social Committee and the Committee of the Regions – Safeguarding Privacy in a Connected World: A European Data Protection Framework for the 21st Century' COM (2012) 9 final, Brussels, 25 January 2012.

[40] 'Proposal for a Regulation on the protection of individuals with regard to the processing of personal data and on the free movement of such data' COM (2012) 11 final, 25 January 2012.

[41] 'Proposal for a Directive on the protection of individuals with regard to the processing of personal data by competent authorities for the purposes of prevention, investigation, detection or prosecution of criminal offences or the execution of criminal penalties, and the free movement of such data' COM (2012) 10 final, 25 January 2012.

[42] COM (2012) 10 final, 6.

of a general Regulation, while neglecting the remaining areas, might have contributed to this separation. Yet, most decisive for the two-law solution was arguably the unwillingness of the Member States to give up their national procedural autonomy[43] and their sovereignty in the area of criminal justice and police cooperation.[44]

The result of such attitudes was consultations that largely focused on the Regulation[45] and a minimum harmonisation Directive that should apply in the area of police and criminal justice and that had not only been watered down already before it was proposed, but had also received further attenuation during the negotiations.

In accordance with Article 16(2) TFEU, the European Parliament exercised its legislative powers and consensus was reached during the trialogue negotiations that took place in the course of the Luxembourgish Presidency from July to December 2015. While the GDPR had been discussed and amended for four years – from 2012 when it was proposed until 2016 – negotiations on the LED only genuinely started during the second half of 2015.[46]

A. The Structure of Directive (EU) 2016/680: An Overview of its Provisions

At this point, it seems important to clarify in which areas and to what types of processing the LED does not apply. First, and as will further be demonstrated below, the Directive does not cover the processing of personal data that fall within the scope of the GDPR.[47] Moreover, and as stipulated under Article 2(3) LED, the Directive may not regulate processing of personal data that is carried out in the course of an activity that falls outside the scope of EU law. In accordance with Recital 14 LED, Article 2(3) LED is to be understood as relating to activities concerning national security, activities of agencies dealing with national security or military and defence issues, and the processing of personal data by the Member States when carrying out activities that fall within the scope of Chapter 2 of Title V of the TEU.[48]

In addition, the Directive does not cover the processing of personal data by EU institutions, bodies, offices and agencies within its scope. To be more

[43] See, for instance, Paul Craig and Gráinne de Búrca, *EU Law: Text, Cases, and Materials* (Oxford University Press, 2011). See also Hijmans (n 14).

[44] Elaine Fahey, 'External Norm Primacy and EU Law: AFSJ Directives in the Post-Lisbon Legislative Cycle' in *The Global Reach of EU Law* (Taylor & Francis, 2016).

[45] COM (2012)10 final, 3.

[46] Academy of European Law, 'Data Protection and the Law Enforcement Directive Challenges in Transposition and Compliance, 18–19 June 2020' (June 2020), https://www.era.int/upload/dokumente/22411.pdf.

[47] Article 9(1) and (2) of Directive (EU) 2016/680. See also Recitals 9, 11, 12 and 34 of Directive (EU) 2016/680.

[48] Recital 16 of Regulation (EU) 2016/679.

precise, such processing continued to be governed by the scope of application of Regulation 45/2001/EC, which was repealed in 2018 by Regulation (EU) 2018/1725.[49]

Lastly, the LED does not regulate the processing of personal data that falls within Chapter 2 TEU on the Common Foreign and Security Policy. In accordance with Article 39 TEU, such processing is to be governed by rules adopted by the Council.[50] However, currently, no Council Decision exists to lay down rules that would regulate the processing of personal data in that area, which creates concerns in situations when cooperation between CFSP teams and national authorities or EU Agencies takes place.[51]

The LED comprises 10 chapters in total, hence one chapter less than the GDPR. The first five chapters define the subject matter and the scope of the Directive, the general principles relating to processing, the rights of the data subject, the obligations of controllers and processors, technical and organisational measures to be implemented, and finally the rules on transfers of personal data to third countries or international organisations and on international cooperation.[52]

The second part of the LED – Chapters VI–VIII – regulates the establishment, tasks, competences and powers of the national supervisory authorities, and establishes the right to lodge a complaint with such authorities and the right to an effective judicial remedy against a decision of a DPA. Moreover, the rules on the right to an effective judicial remedy against a controller or processor, the possibility for organisations to lodge a complaint on behalf of a data subject, the right to compensation for material or non-material damage as a result of an unlawful processing of personal data and the penalties applicable to infringements of the LED are included in that part of the Directive. Chapters IX and X concern implementing acts and final provisions.

B. An Overview of Directive (EU) 2016/680: Chapter by Chapter

While Chapter I on general provisions, Chapter IV on controllers and processors, and Chapter VI on independent supervisory authorities are largely similar to

[49] Costanza Di Francesco Maesa, 'Balance between Security and Fundamental Rights Protection: An Analysis of the Directive 2016/680 for data protection in the police and justice sectors and the Directive 2016/681 on the use of passenger name record (PNR)', http://rivista.eurojus.it/balance-between-security-and-fundamental-rights-protection-an-analysis-of-the-directive-2016680-for-data-protection-in-the-police-and-justice-sectors-and-the-directive-2016681-on-the-use-of-passen.

[50] On art 39 TEU, see European Parliamentary Research Service, 'Unlocking the Potential of the EU Treaties: An Article by Article Analysis of the Scope for Action' (2020) PE 651.934.

[51] For instance, within the framework of the CSDP mission: EEAS, 'Factsheet: EULEX KOSOVO EU Rule of Law Mission in Kosovo'. See also Teresa Quintel, 'The Impact of Interoperability on the Processing of (Biometric) Data of Third Country Nationals by Europol' (2018) 101 *Kritische Vierteljahresschrift für Gesetzgebung und Rechtswissenschaft* 332.

[52] Di Francesco Maesa (n 49).

the corresponding chapters under the GDPR, the individual provisions include particularities that distinguish the rules of the Directive from those under the Regulation. Some of those will be further discussed in the more detailed analysis in the subsequent sections, together with an assessment of Chapters II, III and V of the Directive.

i. Chapters I and II

In the first chapter, Article 1 (subject matter and objectives), Article 2 (scope) and Article 3 (definitions) are particularly crucial when it comes to ascertaining the applicability of the LED. While the principles under Article 4 LED generally pursue the same objectives as the principles under Article 5 GDPR, the requirements on transparency and regarding the data minimisation principle have been adapted to the needs of competent authorities under the Directive. Because those two principles are of particular importance in the field of migration and asylum, they will be dealt with in the analysis below.

Beyond Article 4 on principles, Chapter II of the Directive encompasses several provisions that are non-existent under the GDPR. For instance, Article 5 LED foresees time limits for the storage and review of personal data, while Articles 6 and 7 LED require a distinction between different categories of data subjects and personal data based on facts to be distinguished from personal data based on personal assessment.

Moreover, while the GDPR foresees six legal bases, processing under the LED is lawful in accordance with Article 8 LED when laid down in EU or national law and if it is carried out by a competent authority for the purposes of the prevention, investigation, detection or prosecution of criminal offences. Article 9 LED seeks, inter alia, to clarify the relationship between the scope of application of the LED and the GDPR. In addition, Article 9 allows the competent authorities to impose specific conditions when transmitting personal data, unless the recipients are competent authorities in other EU Member States. Article 10 LED, which foresees specific rules when processing of special categories of data is carried out, and Article 11, on automated individual decision-making and profiling, play a pivotal role in the context of migration and asylum, and will be addressed below in more detail.

ii. Chapter III

Chapter III on the rights of data subjects is not only crucial with regard to the differences compared to the GDPR but also when considering the importance that those rights play in the context of migration management, border control and asylum. Especially when taking into account data subject rights with respect to access and rectification to and of personal data retrieved from AFSJ databases by competent national authorities, the applicable data protection instrument plays a significant role, not only in terms of transparency towards the data subject but also regarding data protection principles and requirements for subsequent processing.

iii. Chapter IV

Out of 16 articles under Chapter IV, the general obligations for controllers and processors (Articles 19–23), record keeping and logging of processing operations (Articles 24 and 25), cooperation with the national DPA, Data Protection Impact Assessments (DPIAs) and prior consultation with the DPA (Articles 26–28), security of processing and data breach notification (Articles 29–31) as well as the designation, position and tasks of the DPO (Articles 32–34) will be discussed in more detail below.

In particular, the two provisions on record keeping and logging of specific processing operations in automated processing systems are of specific importance when it comes to access to and the subsequent processing of personal data by competent authorities. The risk-based approach, the obligations for controllers and processors (on DPIAs, data breach notification and security requirements), and the data protection by design and by default requirement resemble those under the GDPR.

iv. Chapter V

In contrast, Chapter V on transfers of personal data to third countries or international organisations enshrines a very different approach compared to that under the GDPR. While the cascading system under the Regulation, which allows for international transfers first on the basis of an adequacy decision, second on the basis of appropriate safeguards and lastly by way of derogations, is replicated under the LED, Articles 35–39 provide more flexibility to competent authorities while weakening important safeguards for data subjects. In particular, Article 37 LED, on transfers subject to appropriate safeguards, will be discussed in more detail, as this provision may also have an impact on the transfer of personal data of TCNs, for instance, to their countries of origin.

v. Chapter VI

The final important element of the EU data protection model includes the establishment of an independent supervisory authority entrusted with the task of monitoring the application of data protection law within the respective Member State. Chapter VI on independent supervisory authorities lays down similar requirements to those stipulated under the GDPR, for instance, concerning DPA independence or the appointment of the members of a DPA.

However, under the Directive, Member States may choose to either establish one supervisory authority for the supervision of processing activities under both the GDPR *and* the LED or to establish two separate DPAs, each of which shall supervise either GDPR or LED processing operations. Moreover, the powers of the DPAs under the LED are much weaker than those under the GDPR. While some of the tasks of the supervisory authority concerning the certification, accreditation or approval of codes of conduct, contractual clauses and binding corporate rules under the GDPR evidently do not form part of the DPA tasks under the LED, many of the core DPA activities are alike under both instruments. This makes particular sense in Member States where one authority supervises compliance with both the LED and the GDPR.

Nevertheless, while the tasks may be regarded as being similar, the enforcing powers of DPAs are much weaker under the LED than under the GDPR. On the one hand, this is due to the fact that Member States were given the choice, under Article 83(7) GDPR, to exempt public authorities from administrative fines. Such exemption evidently applies to competent authorities under the LED and was made use of by several Member States. On the other hand, and besides the possibility of imposing administrative fines, the list of powers granted to the supervisory authorities under the Directive only provides for a minimum harmonisation of those powers.[53]

vi. Chapters VII–X

Chapters VII–X deal with cooperation, remedies, liability and penalties, and refer to the necessary implementing acts as well as the standard final provisions. In addition, Articles 60 and 62(2) under Chapter X are important with regard to the assessment of EU legal acts dealing with the processing of personal data in the law enforcement context, which were to be reviewed by May 2019.

II. Specific Rules under Directive (EU) 2016/680 for Data Protection in the Law Enforcement Context

One of the goals of the EU Data Protection Reform was to achieve more harmonisation among the national data protection laws and to establish more legal certainty with regard to a consistent application of data protection rules.[54]

[53] See Juraj Sajfert and Paul de Hert, 'The Role of the Data Protection Authorities in Supervising Police and Criminal Justice Authorities Processing Personal Data' in *The Needed Balances in EU Criminal Law: Past, Present and Future* (Bloomsbury, 2017).

[54] Bart van der Sloot, 'Legal Consistency after the General Data Protection Regulation and the Police Directive' (2018) 9 *European Journal of Law and Technology* 1.

In addition, both the GDPR and the LED seek to ensure the free movement of personal data within the EU[55] and, in the case of the LED, to facilitate the unrestricted exchange of personal data by the competent authorities.[56] However, while many of the definitions, principles, obligations and safeguards are very similar under both instruments, the different contexts in which GDPR and LED apply require, at times, different rules.

This means that, on the one hand, certain provisions under the LED are established to set boundaries or to provide additional safeguards when LEAs process personal data within the scope of the Directive. On the other hand, the LED leaves more leeway and flexibility to both national legislators and LEAs to transpose and apply its rules. This is not only due to the choice of legal instrument (in fact, the GDPR, with its numerous opening clauses, could be regarded as a kind of Directive). The flexibility regarding transposition and/or application of the LED is particularly apparent with regard to the determination of the Directive's scope,[57] certain provisions on data subject rights, the rules on international transfers[58] and the provisions on supervision.[59]

In order to achieve both the protection and the free flow of personal data, the GDPR introduced a risk-based approach,[60] incorporated stringent rules on supervision and DPA cooperation,[61] and established a system of heavy sanctions for non-compliance.[62] The GDPR includes innovative mechanisms like the one-stop shop,[63] confers strong corrective powers on national supervisory authorities and imposes high administrative fines for data breaches.[64] Moreover, the Regulation strengthened the rights of data subjects,[65] established strict

[55] Article 1(3) GDPR and, for instance, Recital (15) of Directive (EU) 2016/680.

[56] Article 1(2)(b) of Directive (EU) 2016/680.

[57] Jan Dirk Roggenkamp, '§ 21 Datenschutz und präventive Tätigkeit der Polizei' in Louisa Specht and Reto Mantz (eds), *Handbuch Europäisches und deutsches Datenschutzrecht* (CH Beck, 2019).

[58] Sajfert and Quintel (n 3).

[59] Sajfert and de Hert (n 53).

[60] Including the accountability principle and mandatory DPIAs for certain processing operations, *cf* Raphaël Gellert, 'Understanding the Notion of Risk in the General Data Protection Regulation' (2018) 34 *Computer Law & Security Review* 279; I Böröcz, 'Risk to the Right to the Protection of Personal Data' (2016) 2 *European Data Protection Law Review* 467; Claudia Quelle, 'Enhancing Compliance under the General Data Protection Regulation: The Risky Upshot of the Accountability and Risk-Based Approach' (2018) 9 *European Journal of Risk Regulation* 502.

[61] *cf* Hijmans (n 14).

[62] See, generally, Christopher Kuner, Lee A Bygrave and Christopher Docksey (eds), *The EU General Data Protection Regulation (GDPR): A Commentary Digital Pack: A Commentary* (Oxford University Press, 2020); Paul Voigt and Axel von dem Bussche, *The EU General Data Protection Regulation (GDPR): A Practical Guide* (Springer, 2017); Specht and Mantz (n 57).

[63] Paolo Balboni, Enrico Pelino and Lucio Scudiero, 'Rethinking the One-Stop-Shop Mechanism: Legal Certainty and Legitimate Expectation' (2014) 30 *Computer Law & Security Review* 392. However, the one-stop shop mechanism has also been harshly criticised for its inefficiency; see 'What Happened to the One-Stop Shop?', https://iapp.org/news/a/what-happened-to-the-one-stop-shop.

[64] Robert Baker, 'Is GDPR Compliance Essential? Ignoring the EU's New Online Privacy Rules Could Be a Big Gamble' (2018) 40 *New Hampshire Business Review* 23.

[65] For instance, with regard to transparency requirements, rules regarding individuals' consent, the right to object or the right to data portability.

obligations for controllers[66] *and* processors,[67] and introduced a system for demonstrating compliance with the GDPR rules by way of certification.[68]

The rules on international transfers under the GDPR[69] follow the guidance of the CJEU in its jurisprudence,[70] which was also encoded in other innovative provisions.[71] Moreover, the GDPR de facto extends its territorial scope to non-EU-based companies whenever these process personal data of individuals within the EU – for instance, by offering goods and services or when profiling EU citizens.[72]

In contrast, the provisions under the LED seem much weaker when looking at the data protection principles, the rights of data subjects, the obligations for controllers or the powers that national supervisory authorities have at their disposal. For instance, the transparency requirements under the Directive are far less pronounced than those under the GDPR, and data subject rights may be restricted more flexibly under the Directive. When it comes to the notification of data breaches or the assessment whether international transfers may be carried out, competent authorities have more leeway under the Directive. Moreover, cooperation between national DPAs is much more limited and administrative fines cannot be imposed on competent authorities in most Member States.

Nevertheless, when considering the particular area of law where the LED applies, it is logical that data subjects cannot expect the same rights as under the GDPR and that Member States are much more reluctant to allow other DPAs to get involved in the data processing practices of their national competent authorities. On the whole, the LED could very well serve as a strong data protection instrument, and it could even be argued that its scope applies extraterritorially

[66] For instance, the right to data portability; *cf* Stephanie Elfering, *Unlocking the Right to Data Portability* (Nomos, 2019); Lachlan Urquhart, Neelima Sailaja and Derek McAuley, 'Realising the Right to Data Portability for the Domestic Internet of Things' (2018) 22 *Personal and Ubiquitous Computing* 317.

[67] CJEU, Case C-210/16, *Unabhängiges Landeszentrum für Datenschutz Schleswig-Holstein v Wirtschaftsakademie Schleswig-Holstein GmbH*, ECLI:EU:C:2018:388, 5 June 2018; CJEU, Case C-673/17, *Bundesverband der Verbraucherzentralen und Verbraucherverbände – Verbraucherzentrale Bundesverband eV v Planet49 GmbH*, ECLI:EU:C:2019:801, 1 October 2019.

[68] Article 42 GDPR. *cf* Mraznica Erne, 'GDPR: A New Challenge for Personal Data Protection' (2017) 46 *Bankarstvo* 166.

[69] Paul van den Bulck, 'Transfers of Personal Data to Third Countries' (2017) 18 *ERA Forum* 229.

[70] Xavier Tracol, 'EU–US Privacy Shield: The Saga Continues' (2016) 32 *Computer Law & Security Review* 775.

[71] For instance, the 'right to be forgotten' that was inspired by the *Google Spain* case; *cf* Paul Lambert, *The Right to Be Forgotten: Interpretation and Practice* (Bloomsbury, 2019); Johannes Caspar, 'The CJEU *Google Spain* Decision' (2015) 39 *Datenschutz und Datensicherheit* 589.

[72] Gert Vermeulen and Eva Lievens, *Data Protection and Privacy under Pressure: Transatlantic Tensions, EU Surveillance, and Big Data* (Maklu, 2017); Adèle Azzi, 'The Challenges Faced by the Extraterritorial Scope of the General Data Protection Regulation' (2018) 9 *Journal of Intellectual Property, Information Technology and E-Commerce Law* 126; Imran Ahmad, 'Extraterritorial Scope of GDPR: Do Businesses outside the EU Need to Comply?' [2018] *Business Law Today* 1; Dan JB Svantesson, 'Extraterritoriality and Targeting in EU Data Privacy Law: The Weak Spot Undermining the Regulation' (2015) 5 *International Data Privacy Law* 226.

where the competent authorities may attach conditions to how onward transfers should be handled by non-EU recipients.[73]

Yet, even if the LED could be seen as the first comprehensive data protection instrument offering high data protection standards applicable to the processing of personal data performed in the area of law enforcement, it should not be regarded as an adequate instrument for processing carried out in the migration context. First, in accordance with the objective set out in Declaration 21 TFEU, the Directive's rules are meant to apply to the fields of judicial cooperation in criminal matters and police cooperation. Second, TCNs should not be regarded as perpetrators per se, solely because a small percentage arrive in the EU with forged documents or crossed the external borders irregularly.

In order to illustrate both the specificities of the LED and some of the differences compared to the GDPR, the following section will first address those provisions that are decisive with regard to the scope of application of the LED. Thereafter, relevant provisions of the Directive will be compared to the equivalent articles under the GDPR.

III. Scoping Exercise: The Scope of Application of Directive (EU) 2016/680

In order to understand the logic leading to the separation between the Regulation (the GDPR) and the Directive (the LED), and ultimately the importance of a clear delineation between the GDPR and the LED, it is crucial to take into account the policy fields that were included in the Third Pillar under the Maastricht Treaty. Some of those policy fields became First Pillar matters under the Treaty of Amsterdam and were eventually integrated within Title V TFEU. However, the separation between First and Third Pillar matters has remained visible to the present day.

At times, it is argued that the abolition of the pillar structure should allow more convergent data-sharing possibilities, including the interlinking of all policy areas included under Title V TFEU.[74] This would mean that policies on border checks, migration and asylum would be treated in the same way as judicial cooperation in criminal matter or police cooperation when it comes to the protection of personal data. On the other hand, when the tables are turned and Member States are required to surrender part of the national sovereignty, the argument is

[73] Article 39(1)(e) LED. Article 9(3) LED states that Member States shall, where EU or Member State law applicable to the transmitting competent authority provides specific conditions for processing, provide for the transmitting competent authority to inform the recipient of such personal data of those conditions and the requirement to comply with them.

[74] Intervention by Christiane Höhn (Principal Advisor to the EU Counter-Terrorism Coordinator) at *CPDP 2020: Interoperability in the AFSJ and Data Protection: What Is Missing?* https://www.youtube.com/watch?v=77AXC6T7KBo&t=588s.

quite different and Member States struggle to give up on their competences.[75] Yet again, one of the areas that Member States seem less reluctant to delegate powers to the EU level is the securitisation of borders and migration.[76] Paradoxically, the repurposing of the AFSJ databases and thereby accelerating the dilution between migration and law enforcement appears to fall back on the pre-Amsterdam pillar structure on the one hand, while being increasingly dealt with on the EU level on the other.[77]

As previously mentioned, the historical structure of the Treaties is one essential aspect in explaining why different data protection instruments apply to either former First Pillar (GDPR) matters or to former Third Pillar (LED) matters. However, it is important to take into consideration that already under the Amsterdam Treaty, policies on immigration, asylum and border control had been moved to the First Pillar, as it became clear that the creation of an AFSJ could not be achieved using the intergovernmental method.[78] Hence, the Amsterdam Treaty rendered matters on immigration, asylum and border control subject to the Community method, while police and judicial cooperation remained integrated within the Third Pillar. Only under the Lisbon Treaty did both former Justice and Home Affairs (JHA) policies and immigration, asylum and border control become part of the AFSJ under Title V TFEU and from then on subject to the same decision-making process.

The separation into pillars under the previous Treaty remained visible too with regard to the separation between the GDPR and the LED. This separation clearly indicates that both policies are to be treated distinctly. Maintaining the separation between First and Third Pillar matters for the GDPR and the LED could thus lead to two different arguments regarding the applicability of the two instruments to migration-related processing.

On the one hand, it could be argued that the scope of the LED should indeed include certain processing operations relating to migration matters as, historically, these were included under the Third Pillar. In addition, the 95 Data Protection Directive was adopted *before* the policies on immigration, asylum and border control were integrated into the First Pillar. Therefore, the GDPR's predecessor theoretically did not apply to those Third Pillar policies until they were included within the community method under the First Pillar. On the other hand, the national laws of the Member States generally recognised the applicability of the 95 Directive to migration-related processing, as did the purely migration-related parts of the AFSJ databases. Moreover, shortly after the entry into force

[75] 'Europe and Sovereignty: Reality, Limits and Outlook', https://www.robert-schuman.eu/en/european-issues/0410-europe-and-sovereignty-reality-limits-and-outlook.

[76] Dean Wilson, 'Marginalizing Migrants: Illegality, Racialization, and Vulnerability' in Erich Goode (ed), *The Handbook of Deviance* (Wiley-Blackwell 2015).

[77] Maegan Hendow, Alina Cibea and Albert Kraler, 'Using Technology to Draw Borders: Fundamental Rights for the Smart Borders Initiative' (2015) 13 *Journal of Information, Communication and Ethics in Society* 39.

[78] Craig and de Búrca (n 43) 925.

of the 95 Data Protection Directive, the Amsterdam Treaty made immigration, asylum and border control policies subject to the Community method, hence 10 years before the policy areas of judicial and police cooperation were *de-pillarised*. Therefore, the initial inclusion of migration, asylum and border control within the Third Pillar should not lead to the application of the LED to processing relating to those matters. In addition, Declaration 21 only refers to specific rules on the protection of personal data applicable 'in the fields of judicial cooperation in criminal matters and police cooperation'.

Yet, while that Declaration only refers to judicial and police cooperation, it does not exclude border control, migration and asylum from the applicability of those rules. Hence, where certain acts[79] relating to border control, migration and asylum are criminalised (at a national level), any related processing of personal data will be carried out for law enforcement purposes. Logically, the LED would then apply to such processing operations.

While the WP29 marginally mentioned and warned about such a possibility,[80] the application of the LED to processing in the context of asylum or border control was only voiced once during discussions in the Commission Expert Group on the GDPR and the LED.[81] Both the WP29 and the Commission Expert Group made the EU and national legislators aware that the line between the two data protection instruments should be clear in order to avoid a possible application of the LED to non-law enforcement matters. However, such a possibility was either simply not anticipated at that time or Member States deliberately sought to keep that possibility open. The applicability of the LED to migration-related processing fits the evolution that has been illustrated in the previous chapters. The developments with regard to AFSJ databases and interoperability seem to accept the dilution between migration and criminal law, and somehow naturally presume a flexibly adjustable delineation between data protection laws that apply in each area.

The delineation between the GDPR and the LED is a controversial topic as, on paper, the scope of application of each instrument is supposed to apply seamlessly. Consequently, the GDPR should apply for any 'general processing', whereas any 'law enforcement processing' would fall within the scope of the LED. Yet, in practice, such a distinction is difficult to identify, which often leads to an overly broad interpretation of the LED, thereby infringing upon the application of the GDPR. This is the case in the border control, migration and asylum context in

[79] For instance, document forgery and fraud are criminal offences, but so are irregular entry, illegal entry or stay.

[80] In its Opinion 1/2012 on the data protection reform proposals, the WP29 stated that 'account should be taken of the different traditions in the Member States to define the activities of their authorities as related to law enforcement purposes or merely administrative (for example, in the areas of customs, immigration, environmental affairs)'; see Article 29 Data Protection Working Party, 'Opinion 01/2012 on the Data Protection Reform Proposals, Adopted on 23 March 2012' (2012) 26.

[81] Commission expert group on Regulation (EU) 2016/679 and Directive (EU) 2016/680 (E03461) (n 9).

many Member States. While for processing carried out in the context of migration, border control and asylum, the GDPR should be applicable in a general manner subject to exceptions, the LED should only apply when both its personal and material scopes are satisfied. Article 1(1) LED stipulates that the Directive:

> [L]ays down the rules relating to the protection of natural persons with regard to the processing of personal data by competent authorities for the purposes of the prevention, investigation, detection or prosecution of criminal offences or the execution of criminal penalties, including the safeguarding against and the prevention of threats to public security.

Article 1(1) LED uses very broad language, which makes it challenging to define the Directive's material scope. The Article contains much information while not providing a clear explanation of what the scope actually includes. While the personal scope is defined under Article 3(7) LED,[82] the material scope is determined by the purpose for which the personal data are processed. Where processing is carried out for one of the purposes under Article 1(1) LED, competent authorities as determined under national law can apply the LED.

The question that a competent authority should therefore always be asking before applying the LED is *why* personal data are being processed. In order for the material scope to be fulfilled, processing must be carried out for the prevention, investigation, detection or prosecution of criminal offences. If processing is not carried out for those 'law enforcement purposes', the material scope is not satisfied and instead of the LED, the GDPR should apply in most cases. Any scenario where the LED would be out of scope, besides the area of application of the GDPR, should be understood in a restrictive manner. As mentioned above, the only situations where neither the GDPR nor the LED applies arise when processing falls outside the scope of EU law[83] or is covered by Regulation (EU) 2018/1725.[84] Whilst the former refers to processing carried out by national intelligence agencies or military agencies for national security purposes,[85] or where specific provisions on the common foreign and security policy apply,[86] the latter governs the processing carried out by EU institutions, bodies, offices and agencies.

An authority might be competent under the national law transposing the LED, but might not process personal data for the prevention, investigation, detection or prosecution of criminal offences or the execution of criminal penalties.

[82] This article defines a competent authority as 'any public authority competent for the prevention, investigation, detection or prosecution of criminal offences or the execution of criminal penalties, including the safeguarding against and the prevention of threats to public security; or any other body or entity entrusted by Member State law to exercise public authority and public powers for the purposes of the prevention, investigation, detection or prosecution of criminal offences or the execution of criminal penalties, including the safeguarding against and the prevention of threats to public security'.

[83] Article 2(3)(a) of Directive (EU) 2016/680.

[84] ibid art 2(3)(b).

[85] ibid Recital 14.

[86] ibid referring to ch 2 of Title V TEU.

As a result, depending on the purpose(s) of the processing, an authority that qualifies as competent under the LED might have to apply the GDPR for one processing operation while the Directive is applied to another. This could be the case where the police are managing different databases, some for law enforcement and others for non-law enforcement purposes – for instance, in Member States where the police authority is competent to both add, correct or erase data in a migration database *and* to access that database for law enforcement purposes.[87]

In that case, the GDPR would apply where processing would be carried out for the former purpose, whereas the LED would apply to the processing of personal data retrieved from those databases for law enforcement purposes. At the same time, a competent authority could process personal data within the scope of the GDPR, but later discover a link to a criminal offence, which would then allow that authority to subsequently apply the LED. Consequently, each processing entity competent under the LED needs to determine which of the two laws applies in a particular situation, taking into account the purpose(s) of the processing. This is not always a simple task, given the fact that in many areas, the boundaries between 'general' and 'law enforcement' processing are not always clear-cut.

Against that background, the wording of key provisions and essential definitions accords wide room for interpretation to national legislators. As previously demonstrated, this is particularly true for the material scope, which leaves a wide margin for interpreting the purposes to be included within the LED, a situation that may ultimately be used to determine the personal scope of the LED. Certain Member States[88] used the interpretative liberty provided under the LED in order to include minor offences or activities that *may* lead to a criminal offence within the scope of the Directive. In the same vein, Recital 12 of the Directive to some extent supports such a flexible interpretation, stating that activities falling within the scope of the LED may include coercive measures such as police activities at demonstrations, major sporting events and riots.

[87] This is, for instance, the case in Luxembourg, where the Police Grand-Ducale is both the designated authority for the access, correction and erasure of data recorded in Eurodac, and also the designated authority to access Eurodac for law enforcement purposes. The verifying authority in those cases is the police DPO. See 'List of Competent Authorities Notified to the Commission in Accordance with Article 43 of Regulation (EU) No 603/2013 of the European Parliament and of the Council on the Establishment of "Eurodac" for the Comparison of Fingerprints for the Effective Application of Regulation (EU) No 604/2013 Establishing the Criteria and Mechanisms for Determining the Member State Responsible for Examining an Application for International Protection Lodged in One of the Member States by a Third-Country National or a Stateless Person and on Requests for the Comparison with Eurodac Data by Member States' Law Notices from the Member States: Enforcement Authorities and Europol for Law Enforcement Purposes, and Amending Regulation (EU) No 1077/2011 Establishing a European Agency for the Operational Management of Large-Scale IT Systems in the Area of Freedom, Security and Justice (2019/C 56/01)' (2019) OJ C 56/1; and 'List of Designated Authorities Which Have Access to Data Recorded in the Central System of Eurodac Pursuant to Article 27(2) of Regulation (EU) No 603/2013, for the Purpose Laid down in Article 1(1) of the Same Regulation, (2015/C237/01)' (2015) OJ C237/1.

[88] For instance, Austria, Denmark, Estonia and Germany.

Taking the above example, a police authority in a Member State processing personal data for administrative offences may be permitted to do so within the scope of the Directive due to the wide material scope in the national transposition act. The latter example could easily lead to a further expansion of the material scope under national law where a competent authority has a wide margin of appreciation to include additional processing operations within its tasks. In countries where minor offences are criminalised, any processing relating to such offences could then be carried out within the scope of the LED. For instance, where a TCN during a random police check refuses to give his or her name to a competent authority, or gives a false statement, this could then be dealt with as a criminal offence.

Albeit referring to 'other law enforcement authorities', Recital 12 LED is primarily aimed at police authorities in order to permit the application of one legal instrument to most of their processing activities. However, this may lead to problems with regard to the differentiation between preventive and repressive police functions. In numerous Member States, administrative law applies whenever the police exercise preventive functions, whereas only repressive police functions are governed by criminal procedural law. This separation is supposed to safeguard the rights of the accused while ensuring both effective protection against threats and criminal prosecution in the area of serious crime.[89]

In the same vein, it seems illogical to treat data protection law as an exception and to apply the LED to all types of preventive processing activities. The inclusion of preventive processing within the scope of the LED, and thus a potential widening of the Directive's scope into the sphere of administrative law, would then also have an impact on those data subjects whose personal data are processed in the course of preventive police measures. Besides demonstrations and sporting events as mentioned in Recital 12 LED, those preventive measures could very well be applied to the processing of personal data carried out in the migration context. For instance, in a situation where a person was unable to identify himself or herself during a stop and search operation and the competent authority processing his or her data suspected that the individual had committed a migration-related offence,[90] that authority could process the personal data within the scope of the LED.

At the same time, problems may arise where the material scope of the LED eventually defines the personal scope. This would be the case where the material scope would suffice to automatically include an authority within the personal scope. This would mean that an authority that would generally not be considered a competent authority under Article 3(7) LED would nevertheless be able to carry out processing within the scope of the LED based on the tasks that it may perform.

[89] Dorothee Karbe, Charlotte Jawurek and Philipp Sarder, 'Legendierte Polizeikontrollen: Judgment from the German Federal Court of Justice (Bundesgerichtshof) of April 26, 2017, 2 StR 247/16' (2020) 21 *German Law Journal* 756.

[90] For instance, the use of fraudulent travel documents.

Where an authority would occasionally process personal data for the prevention, investigation, detection or prosecution of criminal offences, it could become competent under the LED for those isolated processing operations.

Especially in Member States where the criminalisation of minor offences leads to a situation where non-law enforcement authorities become competent under the LED, solely because they process personal data relating to those minor offences, this is problematic. For instance, a border guard might traditionally not be considered a competent authority under the personal scope of the LED, but may be authorised to process personal data for certain law enforcement purposes within the material scope of the Directive. In some Member States, this would suffice in order to render that border guard competent under the LED.

Although the LED, under Recital 15, suggests that harmonised data protection rules should ensure the same level of protection for all natural persons throughout the EU and prevent divergences that could hamper the exchange of personal data between competent authorities, such divergences remain. While Recital 13 LED clarifies that a criminal offence within the meaning of the LED should be an autonomous concept of EU law as interpreted by the CJEU, no such autonomous concept has so far been developed and the national criminal codes, as well as the catalogue of criminal offences in the Member States, remain diverse.

The number of authorities that are competent under the LED varies in the different Member States, as the Directive does not stipulate which national authorities shall be included within the definition of Article 3(7) LED. Therefore, the national legal framework not only plays an important role in terms of specifying which types of processing activities fall within the scope of the Directive, but is also decisive in terms of determining which authority qualifies as competent under the LED. Ultimately, in order to determine the scope of application of the Directive, the national transposition acts must be assessed in terms of both their material and personal scope.

In addition, it is important to take into consideration the sectoral laws applicable to competent authorities when processing personal data. On the one hand, this includes those laws that apply in areas where the national legislative body has detected a particular need to further regulate certain aspects with regard to the processing of personal data. Here, it may very well be that competent authorities are bound by stricter rules under national law than those provided by the LED. For instance, a police law could stipulate stricter notification requirements and maximum deadlines for the obligation to notify a data subject of processing that has been carried out with his or her personal data. On the other hand, many sectoral laws are much vaguer and widely interpretable, thereby leaving more flexibility than the LED.

Nevertheless, processing carried out in the context of migration management, asylum and border control should generally be governed by the rules in the GDPR, as the processing operations undertaken by national authorities in those areas are innately of administrative in nature. Following that logic, even if a competent national authority fulfilling the personal scope of the LED processed personal data for the purposes of immigration, asylum or border control, that authority would nevertheless have to apply the GDPR. For instance, a national police authority checking the identity of TCNs entering the Schengen Area would have to carry out those checks within the scope of the GDPR. Likewise, in Member States where border guards are considered competent authorities under Article 3(7) LED but do not process personal data for the prevention, investigation, detection or prosecution of crime, these border guards would not be permitted to apply the Directive to their processing activities. If applied in such a restrictive manner, the scope of the Directive is supposedly more constrained, which should in turn signify that most migration-related processing activities are subject to the GDPR rules, unless exceptions apply.

Evidently, where processing is carried out for law enforcement purposes and by a competent authority, the LED should apply in order to provide sufficient leeway and flexibility to those authorities, including in a migration-related context. Yet, often the connection between criminal and migration law matter is deceptive and interpreted in a misleading manner. Consequently, the line between law enforcement and non-law enforcement processing is thin and may be transgressed easily.

As has been shown, any discursive application of criminal law in migration management and border control matters inevitably affects the data protection instrument that applies to the processing of personal data. In instances where the LED applies to processing, more leeway and flexibility will be given to competent authorities, for instance, with regard to the restriction of data subject rights. This is logical in a criminal law context, as, for instance, processing cannot be based on the consent of a suspect, data subjects might not be informed of ongoing investigations and controllers should be able to restrict rights if investigations would otherwise be jeopardised.

The following sections will present an overview of those provisions under the LED that provide particular rules that apply to law enforcement processing. While many principles and key provisions under the Directive were indeed inspired by the GDPR, other rules are non-existent under the Regulation and therefore merit a more detailed discussion. While some of the principles under the LED will be discussed in terms of differing from those under the GDPR, those provisions that provide specific rules in the law enforcement context will be explained in more detail thereafter. The discussion will thereby bear in mind the consequences for data subjects whenever their personal data are processed under the Directive instead of the GDPR.

As previously mentioned, with regard to the effectiveness of the LED, it is essential not only to scrutinise the national transposition acts but also to take into account sectoral laws at the national level that intersect with the Directive. For instance, with regard to data subject rights, a national criminal code may allow police officers to restrict data subject rights for a broad range of offences. On the other hand, sectoral laws may provide specific safeguards that the LED did not foresee. Consequently, sectoral laws are important for assessing either the effectiveness of, or the gaps in, the LED transposition acts completely. However, because this discussion focuses on the Directive and how it could be applied by the competent authorities, an assessment of the sectoral laws of the Member States was not carried out.

IV. Provisions Specifically Designed for the Processing of Personal Data in the Law Enforcement Context

In the law enforcement context, certain rules need to be adjusted to the needs of the competent authorities, while at the same time protecting the rights and freedoms of those whose personal data might be processed within the scope of the LED. On the one hand, this means that more flexibility is granted with regard to certain principles, the restriction of data subject rights, obligations for controllers and processors, or the rules on international transfers. On the other hand, the level of transparency is reduced, and processing operations may be more intrusive when processing of personal data takes place in the law enforcement context. This can certainly entail negative consequences for data subjects, who might not be aware that their personal data are being processed and therefore cannot exercise their data subject rights effectively. The LED foresees certain safeguards, for instance, regarding the categorisation of data subjects, automated decision making, the right to request the DPA to exercise the right of access on the behalf of a data subject, or the keeping of logs for certain processing operations. Those safeguards are not included under the GDPR and will be assessed in more detail below.

A. Principles: More Flexibility for Competent Authorities

The principles under Article 4 LED[91] are similar to those under the GDPR in the sense that all of them exist under the Directive, albeit being adapted to the specific context in which the LED applies. The most striking differences between the GDPR and the LED in terms of principles are to be found in the transparency requirements, the purpose limitation and the data minimisation principles.

Nevertheless, differences also exist with regard to the remaining principles, particularly as to their wording and level of detail. Whilst the wording of the principle of accuracy and that of integrity and confidentiality are identical under both the LED and the GDPR, the storage limitation principle is much

[91] The principle of data protection by design and by default under art 20 of Directive (EU) 2016/680 (art 25 of Regulation (EU) 2016/679) will be discussed in more detail below.

less comprehensive under the Directive.[92] This is for obvious reasons. Where personal data initially processed within the scope of the LED were processed for archiving purposes, in the public interest, for historical research or for statistical purposes, the GDPR applies.[93]

i. Transparency, Accountability and Fairness

The principle of transparency is not included under Article 4(1)(a) LED, and hence that provision only refers to fairness and lawfulness. This is logical since criminal investigations can seldom be carried out effectively while full transparency is provided to the data subject. While under the GDPR, the data subject should be aware of every step of the processing carried out with his or her personal data, under the LED, the controller is only required to make some general information[94] available – for instance, on the website of the competent authority.[95] Only in specific cases must the data subject be provided with additional information.[96] Under the GDPR, the principle of transparency is both a key element and an overarching obligation to ensure fair processing towards the data subject.[97] Transparency, when adhered to by data controllers, empowers data subjects to hold data controllers and processors accountable and to exercise control over their personal data.[98]

The principle of transparency is closely connected to the principle of accountability, which under the GDPR is an additional tool for safeguarding fairness towards the data subject. While the principle of accountability,[99] which

[92] Article 4(1)(e) of Directive (EU) 2016/680 simply states that personal data shall be kept in a form which permits identification of data subjects for no longer than is necessary for the purposes for which they are processed.

[93] See also Article 9(2) of Directive (EU) 2016/680.

[94] 'a) the identity and the contact details of the controller;
(b) the contact details of the data protection officer, where applicable;
(c) the purposes of the processing for which the personal data are intended;
(d) the right to lodge a complaint with a supervisory authority and the contact details of the supervisory authority;
(e) the existence of the right to request from the controller access to and rectification or erasure of personal data and restriction of processing of the personal data concerning the data subject.'

[95] Article 13(1) and Recital 42 of Directive (EU) 2016/680.

[96] Article 13(2) of Directive (EU) 2016/680.

[97] With regard to the Internet of Things, *cf* Sandra Wachter, 'The GDPR and the Internet of Things: A Three-Step Transparency Model' (2018) 10 *Law, Innovation and Technology* 266.

[98] WP29, 'Article 29 Working Party Guidelines on Transparency under Regulation 2016/679 Adopted on 29 November 2017 as Last Revised and Adopted on 11 April 2018 (WP260 Rev.01)' (2018) 5. For example, where the data subject may provide or withdraw his or her informed consent and action his or her data subject rights. See also Opinion of AG Cruz Villalon, Case C-201/14, *Smaranda Bara and Others v Preşedintele Casei Naţionale de Asigurări de Sănătate, Casa Naţională de Asigurări de Sănătate, Agenţia Naţională de Administrare Fiscală (ANAF)*, 9 July 2015, ECLI:EU:C:2015:461, para 74.

[99] *cf* Hielke Hijmans and Charles Raab, 'Ethical Dimensions of the GDPR', https://papers.ssrn.com/sol3/papers.cfm?abstract_id=3222677.

requires controllers to put in place appropriate technical and organisational measures and to be able to demonstrate compliance with data protection rules,[100] is also codified under the LED, holding the controller accountable may prove more challenging in the law enforcement context.

Ultimately, transparency and accountability will ensure fair processing and should be read together. However, since the principle of transparency is non-existent in the form of a provision under the LED, the principle of fairness under Article 4(1)(a) LED must be secured in other ways. In order to remedy the absence of transparency, the accountability principle is therefore vital in order to fill this gap. In a similar vein, the role of data protection supervisory authorities to ensure compliance with data protection rules as well as with the principle of accountability is essential. Yet, the powers of DPAs under the LED are much weaker than under the GDPR, for instance, with regard to the possibility of issuing administrative fines. Therefore, it could be argued that under the LED, the level of responsibility to establish trust from the side of the data subject that lies with the controller to ensure fairness without being transparent is greater under the LED than under the GDPR.

ii. Purpose Limitation and Subsequent Processing

In accordance with the purpose limitation principle under Article 4(1)(b) LED, data must be collected for specified, explicit and legitimate purposes, and not be processed in a manner that is incompatible with those purposes. In the law enforcement context, this means that processing is lawful if it is carried out for the purposes stipulated under Article 1(1) LED, namely for the prevention, investigation, detection or prosecution of criminal offences or the execution of criminal penalties, including the safeguarding against, and the prevention of, threats to public security. Other than the GDPR,[101] Article 8 of the Directive only provides for one legal basis, namely if processing is necessary for the performance of a task carried out by a competent authority for the purposes under Article 1(1) LED and based on EU or Member State law.[102]

[100] EDPS, 'Accountability', https://edps.europa.eu/data-protection/our-work/subjects/accountability_en.
[101] Article 6(1) of Regulation (EU) 2016/679 provides for six different legal bases for processing: (1) the data subject has given consent; (2) processing is necessary for the performance of a contract to which the data subject; (3) processing is necessary for compliance with a legal obligation to which the controller is subject; (4) processing is necessary in order to protect the vital interests of the data subject or of another natural person; (5) processing is necessary for the performance of a task carried out in the public interest; and (6) processing is necessary for the purposes of the legitimate interests pursued by the controller or by a third party.
[102] Quintel, 'Follow the Money, If You Can – Possible Solutions for Enhanced FIU Cooperation under Improved Data Protection Rules' (n 6).

Hence, under the LED legal bases such as consent, the vital interest of the data subject,[103] or the legitimate interest of the controller are not deemed adequate legal bases for the processing of personal data by the competent authorities. Instead, the performance of the tasks of preventing, investigating, detecting or prosecuting criminal offences institutionally conferred by law to the competent authorities allows them to order natural persons to comply with requests made. Consequently, where the data subject is required to fulfil a legal obligation, he or she has no genuine and free choice. Against that background, consent should not provide a legal ground for the processing of personal data by the competent authorities subject to the LED.[104] Nevertheless, several Member States use consent as a legal basis for processing under the Directive, as is the case under the German LED transposition act.[105]

The fact that the LED only provides for one legal basis facilitates any assessment on whether or not personal data may be processed by the competent authorities. Where no legal ground is provided by law that enables the processing of personal data, processing may simply not take place. In addition, no choice between different legal bases has to be made by the competent authorities covered within the scope of the LED.

Ultimately, Articles 4 and 8 LED read together provide for more discretion regarding the purpose limitation principle than the provisions under the GDPR.[106] Nevertheless, the competent authorities must be given a specific mandate under EU or national law to process personal data in a particular situation and within the purposes set out in Article 1(1) of the LED. Hence, Article 8(1) requires a legal basis under EU or Member State law, which defines the conditions for processing. Evidently, such a legal basis must satisfy the quality of law criteria, namely, to be clear, accessible and foreseeable for the data subject. As a minimum and in accordance with Article 8(2) LED, Member State law providing for processing to be lawful based on Article 8(1) LED must specify the objectives, the personal data to be processed and the purposes of the processing.

Article 4(2) LED lays down the conditions that apply when so-called subsequent processing is carried out by the same or another controller for any of the purposes set out in Article 1(1) LED. Hence, subsequent processing is carried out for purposes other than those for which the data were initially collected, but

[103] As understood under Regulation (EU) 2016/679. Recital 35 Directive (EU) 2016/680 states that the prevention, investigation, detection or prosecution of criminal offences or the execution of criminal penalties activities should cover the protection of vital interests of the data subject.

[104] Recital 35 Directive (EU) 2016/680. Nevertheless, this should not preclude Member States from providing, by law that the data subject may agree to the processing of his or her personal data for the purposes of this Directive, such as DNA tests in criminal investigations or the monitoring of his or her location with electronic tags for the execution of criminal penalties.

[105] Article 51 of the Bundesdatenschutzgesetz vom 30. Juni 2017 (BGBl. I S. 2097), das durch Artikel 12 des Gesetzes vom 20. November 2019 (BGBl. I S. 1626) geändert worden ist.

[106] Sajfert and Quintel (n 3).

uses the same legal basis under the LED. For instance, evidence gathered by the police that is subsequently transmitted to the prosecutor and then to the criminal court, which prepares the trial, would fall within the scope of Article 4(2) LED. Consequently, the purpose changes from one to the other controller, but remains within the scope of the Directive, which presupposes the compatibility of purposes by different controllers for as long as they remain within the realm of Article 1(1) LED.[107]

This means that when a competent authority within the meaning of the LED discovers correlations to a different investigation, personal data used in an initial file for one type of crime may be used for that additional investigation. It could also mean that a person who was initially categorised as a witness could turn out to be a suspect. A third scenario could be that a different competent authority, which received personal data under the LED, uses those data for another investigation than the competent authority that first collected the data. In those cases, the same or another controller, competent to process personal data within the scope of the LED in accordance with Article 4(2)(a), may base the subsequent processing on Article 4(2) of the Directive. Under Article 4(2)(b) LED, any subsequent processing must be necessary and proportionate to the new purpose in accordance with national or EU law. Hence, either EU or Member State law must provide for a legal basis as set out in Article 8 LED. The presumption of compatibility of purpose in the law enforcement context for subsequent processing facilitates the work of competent authorities, as it provides for more flexibility when personal data are processed for investigative purposes.

Subsequent processing by the same or another controller under Article 4(2) LED must derive from any initial processing that took place within the scope of the LED. Accordingly, only where a competent authority initially collected the data may Article 4(2) LED be used. This means that personal data initially processed within the scope of the GDPR – for instance, by private entities – will not fall within the scope of Article 4(2) LED.[108] Because private companies cannot satisfy the personal scope of the Directive, any data received and processed by competent authorities that were initially collected by private entities under the GDPR should be seen as initial processing under the LED.[109]

[107] See Advocate-General Opinion in Case C-180/21, *VS v Inspektor v Inspektorata kam Visshia sadeben savet*, ECLI:EU:C:2022:406, 19 May 2022.

[108] *cf* Nadezhda Purtova, 'Between the GDPR and the Police Directive: Navigating through the Maze of Information Sharing in Public–Private Partnerships' (2018) 8 *International Data Privacy Law* 52.

[109] On different views regarding processing of personal data by the competent authorities initially collected by private entities, see Catherine Jasserand, 'Law Enforcement Access to Personal Data Originally Collected by Private Parties: Missing Data Subjects' Safeguards in Directive 2016/680?' (2018) 34(1) *Computer Law & Security Review* 154; Catherine Jasserand-Breeman, 'Reprocessing of Biometric Data for Law Enforcement Purposes: Individuals' Safeguards Caught at the Interface between the GDPR and the "Police" Directive?' (thesis, University of Groningen, 2019).

iii. Data Minimisation

Another principle under the LED that diverges from the wording of the GDPR is that of data minimisation. The data minimisation principle under Article 4(1)(c) LED stipulates that processing must be adequate, relevant and *not excessive* in relation to the purposes for which the data are processed. Compared to Article 5(1)(c) GDPR, which stipulates that personal data shall be adequate, relevant and *limited to what is necessary*, the LED grants more leeway to competent authorities to establish the types and amount of data that are needed for the performance of their tasks. This allows competent LEAs to determine the relevance of collected information for an investigation and, where certain data later prove to be unnecessary, simply discard them without having to justify why those data were initially collected.

Nevertheless, processing must remain within the boundaries of Article 8 LED, and therefore processing operations for which at least objectives, data to be processed and purposes cannot be established prior to the commencement of the processing should be seen as problematic. With regard to predictive policing or the use of AI technologies for criminal investigations, Article 8 LED therefore sets clear limits for those processing activities. Defining a clear objective, specific purposes for processing and the types of data to be processed may prove difficult, if not impossible for such processing.

Both the purpose limitation principle and the data minimisation principle under the LED grant more flexibility to competent authorities in the performance of their tasks compared to the requirements of the corresponding provisions under the GDPR.[110] Where the LED would be applied in a migration-related context, this could lead to broader interpretation of both principles and, ultimately, unfair processing towards the data subjects concerned.

B. Time Limits for the Storage and Categorisation of Personal Data

While the GDPR links potential time limits for the storage of personal data to the storage limitation principle under Article 5(1)(e),[111] the LED encompasses a specific provision that sets out the rules regarding time limits for the storage and

[110] Sajfert and Quintel (n 3).

[111] Personal data shall be kept in a form which permits identification of data subjects for no longer than is necessary for the purposes for which the personal data are processed; personal data may be stored for longer periods insofar as the personal data will be processed solely for archiving purposes in the public interest, scientific or historical research purposes or statistical purposes in accordance with Article 89(1) subject to implementation of the appropriate technical and organisational measures required by this Regulation in order to safeguard the rights and freedoms of the data subject ('storage limitation').

review of personal data. This is particularly important in the area of law enforcement, where data retention periods must often be specified in a stricter manner than under the GDPR. Pursuant to Article 5 LED, Member States are to establish time limits for the erasure, storage and periodic review of the need to store personal data.[112] The Directive therefore provides for a built-in safeguard for data subjects that might not be aware of the fact that their personal data are being processed by a competent authority.

While the transparency obligations under the GDPR to continuously keep the data subject informed about all processing operations are very strong, such transparency can evidently not be afforded in the context of the LED. Hence, the controller must carry out periodic reviews and justify why certain data need to be kept. Time limits for storage diverge between the Member States and in accordance with different situations, types of data or data subjects.[113] Already before the entry into application of the Directive, many national laws provided for review mechanisms, which have proved to be a useful organisational tool for keeping criminal databases well ordered. Where police and other law enforcement databases are structured in accordance with data protection rules, this may thus facilitate the work of competent authorities.

In addition to the periodic review obligation under Article 5 LED, Article 6 introduces a specific obligation for controllers to establish a clear distinction between the personal data of different categories of data subjects.[114] Hence, competent authorities must clearly distinguish between suspects, convicts, victims, witnesses and other persons that could provide relevant information for investigations.[115] Well-structured files are particularly important regarding dynamic cases, where a victim may turn out to be a suspect and will then have to be shifted into a different category. Keeping good track of any change of category is essential, as different rights are attached to different statuses and retention periods may change. Just like retention periods, many Member States had already implemented rules on such categorisation prior to the entry into force of the LED, and often such categorisation is done by LEAs based on internal guidelines that require rules similar to those stipulated under Article 6 LED *by default*.

Alongside Article 5 LED, the provision on the categorisation into different types of data subjects represents an additional safeguard and, at the same time,

[112] Quintel (n 6).

[113] In Germany, data storage duration is limited depending on the types of persons: 10 years for adults, five years for adolescents and two years for children (under art 35 of the old Data Protection Act). Data on whistleblowers and informants can only be stored for one year, but can be extended to three years. In the Netherlands, the storage of personal data by the police is limited to one year, which can be extended to five years if the data are necessary for the police tasks (art 8 of Wet Politiegegevens). In the UK, s 39(2) of the Data Protection Act 2018 requires that appropriate time limits must be established for the periodic review of the need for the continued storage of personal data for any of the law enforcement purposes; see Mark Leiser and Bart Custers, 'The Law Enforcement Directive' (2019) 5 *European Data Protection Law Review* 367.

[114] Quintel (n 6).

[115] Recital 31 of Directive (EU) 2016/680.

codifies the right of the presumption of innocence guaranteed by the Charter[116] as well as by ECtHR case law.[117] Any clear distinction between the personal data of different categories of data subjects will likewise ensure well-structured criminal files, provide additional safeguards for data subjects and facilitate the sharing of information with other competent authorities, in line with the Directive's objectives. Being intrinsically linked to the mandatory review under Article 5 LED, the rules under Article 6 may therefore facilitate investigations in accordance with the principles of necessity and proportionality.

Both the rules on periodic review and those on the categorisation into different types of data subjects should be seen as safeguards for the protection of the fundamental rights of data subjects and a facilitation tool for the work of competent authorities. In addition, Articles 5 and 6 LED ensure compliance with both the EU Charter and the ECHR, as well as with ECtHR case law.[118] With regard to processing that takes place in a border control and migration-related context, it is of utmost importance that the need to retain data is thoroughly reviewed and that data subjects are correctly categorised. For instance, where competent authorities investigate cases of migrant smuggling or document fraud, databases should clearly separate victims (those who were smuggled) from perpetrators (those who were smuggling humans or who forged documents).

Evidently, when analysing large and complex datasets in order to find correlations between different investigations or perpetrators, any categorisation pursuant to Articles 6 LED seems unrealistic, as such processing presupposes a certain margin of flexibility to process personal data outside the categories defined under that provision.

Nevertheless, when reading the principles under Article 4 LED together with Articles 5, 6 and 8, the competent authorities should only process personal data that are relevant for their investigations and discard any irrelevant information as soon as they become aware of it. For that purpose, national law, in accordance with Article 5 LED, should lay down appropriate time limits for review so as to oblige competent authorities to erase any personal data for which the need for continued storage cannot be justified.

C. The Distinction between Personal Data and Verification of Quality of Personal Data

Aligned with the objectives of Articles 5 and 6 LED, Article 7 stipulates that personal data based on facts should be separated from personal data that relate to personal assessments. For example, where police officers or investigators process

[116] ibid.
[117] See *S and Marper v United Kingdom*, App Nos 30562/04 and 30566/04 (ECtHR, 4 December 2008).
[118] On divergent standpoints, see Leiser and Custers (n 113).

fingerprints that were collected at a crime scene or video material that recorded a crime, those data must be distinguished from witness testimonies or statements made by potential suspects or perpetrators. Hence, a competent authority, before filing certain evidence in a criminal database, must establish to which of the (two) categories the data belong.

Evidently, there might be certain subcategories that may require additional distinctions. One such subcategory could, for instance, be inferences generated by automated processing or by way of data mining. An inference is not a fact yet; however, additional information, added to the inference, might transform an inference into a fact. This will logically not only have an impact on the distinction between personal assessment and fact, but may also affect the categorisation of data subjects and consequently the periods for review. The change of differentiation/categorisation would have to be justified by the competent authority or police officer and would, in a best-case scenario, be subject to scrutiny by the DPA, or at least the authority's Data Protection Officer (DPO).

This proves that the obligations enshrined in Articles 5–7 LED are not to be seen as burdensome, but in fact as support tools for the competent authorities in performing their tasks effectively. With the increasing use of digital means, well-functioning categorisation will become even more relevant and probably automated. Just like the periodic review and the categorisation into different data subjects, Article 7 LED contributes to better-structured police working files and provides for safeguards for data subjects.

Ultimately, the competent authorities must organise their law enforcement databases in accordance with specific review and deletion periods and must categorise collected information into different data subjects and distinguish between levels of reliability of information. These provisions are better fitted to processing operations carried out in the law enforcement context than to those under the GDPR, which are not as explicit in that regard. Nevertheless, the effectiveness of these provisions also depends on how these conditions are scrutinised by the national supervisory authorities and how the latter enforce their investigative, monitoring and corrective powers.[119]

D. Specific Processing Conditions

Article 9 LED consists of four paragraphs that seek to further clarify the scope and application of the LED, while at the same time referring to quite disconnected subjects. While paragraphs (1) and (2) explain the Directive's applicability towards the GDPR, paragraphs (3) and (4) refer to conditions that may or may not apply where personal data are transmitted. Both sets of paragraphs – (1) and (2) as well as (3) and (4) – should be read together.

[119] On this, see Sajfert and de Hert (n 53).

In order to avoid an overly broad application of the Directive at the expense of the GDPR, Article 9(1) and (2) LED further specifies the Directive's scope. The first paragraph emphasises that the competent authorities shall not process personal data for purposes other than the prevention, detection, investigation or prosecution of crime, unless EU or national law provides for an adequate legal basis. In addition, the paragraph states that whenever the processing of personal data by the competent authorities is carried out for purposes other than the prevention, investigation, detection or prosecution of crime, the GDPR applies. Only where the processing of personal data falls outside the scope of EU law does neither the GDPR nor the LED apply. This is, for instance, the case where processing operations are carried out by national intelligence agencies, which are generally regulated by national law only.[120]

The second paragraph of Article 9 LED further specifies that in situations where competent authorities are entrusted by law to process personal data for tasks other than the prevention, investigation, detection or prosecution of crime, such processing should fall within the scope of the GDPR. As examples, Article 9(2) LED lists archiving purposes, processing in the public interest, scientific or historical research purposes or statistical purposes, and once again refers to the exception that applies to processing that is performed outside the scope of EU law. Read together, paragraphs (1) and (2) of Article 9 LED may seem to be superfluous and merely serving to provide an additional clarification as to the delineation between the LED and the GDPR.

Paragraph (3) of Article 9 LED requires competent authorities that transmit personal data to inform the recipient of any specific conditions that may apply to the processing under EU or national law. The recipient must then comply with those conditions. Paragraph (4) stipulates that no further specific conditions shall be applied to recipients in other Member States or EU Agencies, offices or bodies than those that apply to the transmitting authority. While the logic under paragraph (3) is the same as the one that applies to international transfers under Chapter V LED, paragraph (4) clarifies that any transmission of personal data within the EU should be deemed safe and not requiring specific conditions imposed by individual Member States.

E. Processing of Special Categories of Personal Data

Article 10 LED addresses the protection of personal data of a particularly sensitive nature, ie, the processing of special categories of personal data.[121] Since the

[120] However, in some Member States, certain provisions of Regulation (EU) 2016/679 or Directive (EU) 2016/680 apply to the processing of personal data by national intelligence agencies.

[121] Article 10 defines special categories of personal data as personal data revealing racial or ethnic origin, political opinions, religious or philosophical beliefs, or trade union membership, and the processing of genetic data, biometric data for the purpose of uniquely identifying a natural person, data concerning health or data concerning a natural person's sex life or sexual orientation.

misuse of these types of data may entail defamatory or discriminatory consequences for data subjects, the processing of special categories of personal data requires additional safeguards. Recital 51 of the Directive acknowledges both the sensitivity and the risks linked to the processing of special categories of personal data. In the same vein, Recital 37 of the LED suggests the provision of appropriate safeguards, such as the possibility of collecting special categories of personal data only in connection with other data on the natural person concerned, the possibility of securing the data collected adequately, stricter rules on access of staff and the prohibition of transmission of those data. While the recital generally considers the processing of special categories of personal data to be lawful if the data subject has explicitly agreed to processing that is particularly intrusive to him or her, it acknowledges that the consent of the data subject should not provide in itself a legal ground for the processing of such sensitive personal data by the competent authorities.

Other than Article 9 GDPR (the equivalent provision to Article 10 LED), which stipulates a general prohibition of the processing of special categories of personal data, subject to certain exceptions, the Directive allows such processing under certain conditions. Pursuant to Article 10 LED, the processing of special categories of personal data must first and foremost be strictly necessary and subject to appropriate safeguards for the rights and freedoms of the data subject.

Further, Article 10 LED foresees three scenarios for the processing of special categories of personal data: (a) where authorised by EU or Member State law; (b) to protect the vital interests of the data subject or of another natural person; or (c) where such processing relates to data that are manifestly made public by the data subject.

It is important to note that these three options should be regarded as additional safeguards and not as an alternative legal basis. Instead, Article 8 LED continues to apply and to require a separate legal basis under EU or Member State law *before* special categories of personal data may be processed. Consequently, special categories of personal data may only be processed where national or EU law provides for a legal basis under Article 8 LED and at least one of the options under Article 10 LED is fulfilled. With regard to Article 10(a) LED, the processing of special categories of personal data may be allowed, for instance, where fingerprints are stored in a criminal database that was established by national law, which lays down both the objectives and purposes of the processing and which defines the personal data to be processed.

The second option under paragraph (b) – to process special categories of personal data to protect the vital interest of the data subject – should be interpreted in line with the definition of 'vital interest' under Article 6(1)(d) GDPR, meaning that it refers to circumstances regarding life or death. In other words, where the contemplated processing of personal data is vital to an individual's (the data subject) survival, special categories of personal data may be processed under Article 10(b) LED.[122] This could be the case where a perpetrator has been lethally injured in a shooting and his or her DNA traces are on another perpetrator's weapon. With regard to the interpretation of the notion under paragraph (b), several Member States rely on their own national understanding of vital interest, which very often is more extensive than the notion of a life and death situation.[123] This may be the case where fingerprints of a murderer are collected at a crime scene and checked against other fingerprints in order to protect potential victims.

The third option, under Article 10(c) LED, which allows for the processing of personal data where those are manifestly made public by the data subject, seems to be the most obvious. For instance, where a suspect has posted his or her religious beliefs on a public online forum, these data could be collected by competent authorities in order to create a profile of that person. However, the third option under Article 10(c) LED raises questions regarding the foreseeability of a processing measure, as well as the rights that are attributed to a person once he or she is under suspicion.

At first sight, the provision on the processing of special categories of personal data under the GDPR seems more restrictive than the one under the LED, as Article 9 GDPR sets out a prohibition, whereas Article 10 LED allows processing only where certain conditions are fulfilled. However, given the numerous exceptions that the GDPR provides in order to derogate from the general prohibition, it almost seems as if the Directive provides for stricter limits to the processing of special categories of personal data. In addition, it is noteworthy that where the GDPR acknowledges that the processing of photographs should not systematically be considered to be processing of special categories of personal data,[124] the LED does not make such a concession. Hence, the processing of photographs is to be regarded as processing of special categories of personal data under the Directive and must fulfil the requirements under Article 10 LED.

Nevertheless, the provision of adequate safeguards for processing performed with special categories of data within the scope of the LED is of utmost importance, as any breach or misuse of data in the law enforcement context could lead to significant consequences for the data subject. However, some Member States suggest that there are other legal bases for the processing of special categories of personal data, such as the consent of the data subject.[125] Yet, just like under

[122] 'Vital Interests', https://iapp.org/resources/article/vital-interests.

[123] Anna Moscibroda, Policy Officer, Data Protection Unit, DG Justice and Consumers, European Commission, 'Data Protection and the Law Enforcement Directive', online seminar at 'ERA – Academy of European Law' conference, https://www.era.int/cgi-bin/cms?_SID=NEW&_sprache=en&_bereich=artikel&_aktion=detail&idartikel=129633.

[124] '[A]s they are covered by the definition of biometric data only when processed through a specific technical means allowing the unique identification or authentication of a natural person.' See Recital 51 of Regulation (EU) 2016/679.

[125] Moscibroda (n 123).

Article 8 LED, consent cannot serve as a legal basis for processing in the law enforcement context. Hence, the consent of the data subject should only serve as an additional safeguard besides the conditions under paragraphs (a), (b) and (c) of Article 10 LED. For example, in the context of sexual violence, it would be possible that the victim agrees to releasing certain sensitive data, such as a DNA test, as suggested in Recital 35 LED. In the area of migration, a TCN could consent to his or her fingerprints being taken during an identity check. However, this would not be the legal basis on which processing could be based, and any such taking of fingerprints would have to be regulated by a legislative measure.

F. Automated Individual Decision-Making

Combining different processing techniques, such as data mining,[126] data matching[127] and predictive analytics,[128] often conflict with key data protection principles and rights.[129] These techniques are commonly used by the police and other law enforcement authorities for predictive policing purposes.[130] Needless to say, profiling and data matching techniques are also used for border control and migration management purposes.

Due to the potentially intrusive nature of decision-making that is based on solely automated means, Article 11 LED sets out a general prohibition of those types of processing when they produce an adverse legal effect concerning the data subject or otherwise significantly affect him or her.[131] In that regard, the LED differs from the wording under Article 22 GDPR, which states that data subjects shall have the *right* not to be subject to automated decision-making.[132] Hence, the

[126] Toon Calders and Bart Custers, 'What is Data Mining and How Does it Work?' in Bart Custers et al (eds), *Discrimination and Privacy in the Information Society: Data Mining and Profiling in Large Databases* (Springer, 2013).

[127] Tal Z Zarsky, 'The Data Mining Balancing Act' in Serge Gutwirth et al (eds), *European Data Protection: In Good Health?* (Springer Netherlands, 2012); Walter L Perry et al, *Predictive Policing: The Role of Crime Forecasting in Law Enforcement Operations* (RAND Corporation, 2013); Bilel Benbouzid, 'From Situational Crime Prevention to Predictive Policing: Sociology of an Ignored Controversy' (2015) XII *Champ pénal*, https://doi.org/10.4000/champpenal.9066.

[128] Generally, *cf* Eric Siegel, *Predictive Analytics: The Power to Predict Who Will Click, Buy, Lie, or Die* (Wiley, 2016).

[129] Sajfert and Quintel (n 3).

[130] Vlad Niculescu-Dinca, 'Managing Suspicion and Privacy in Police Information Systems' in Serge Gutwirth et al (eds), *European Data Protection: In Good Health?* (Springer Netherlands, 2012).

[131] Article 11 of Directive (EU) 2016/680 states that 'Member States shall provide for a decision based solely on automated processing, including profiling, which produces an adverse legal effect concerning the data subject or significantly affects him or her, to be prohibited'. Sajfert and Quintel (n 3).

[132] The wording of art 11 suggests that the Directive could, hypothetically, provide stronger data protection standards regarding automated processing than the GDPR. While the latter stipulates, in art 22, that data subjects 'shall have the right not to be subject to a decision based solely on automated processing, including profiling, which produces legal effects concerning him or her or similarly significantly affects him or her', art 11 LED prohibits such processing if it 'produces an adverse legal effect concerning the data subject or significantly affects him or her'. See Sajfert and Quintel (n 3).

legislator recognised that automated decision-making may lead to more severe repercussions in the area where the Directive applies. Whether the individual must seek the right under Article 22 GDPR, whereas under the Directive automated decision-making leading to adverse legal effects for data subjects is prohibited by default, remains unclear.[133] Admittedly, the WP29 argued that Article 22 GDPR does indeed set out a prohibition,[134] yet the different wording of the LED and the GDPR is striking and could suggest a different interpretation.

Automated individual decision-making is permitted only where several conditions are satisfied. Such processing must be authorised by EU or Member State law, must provide for appropriate safeguards and must allow the data subject to obtain human intervention on the part of the controller.[135] In addition, and as mentioned above, any purely automated decision may not have an adverse legal effect on the data subject concerned[136] (or significantly affect him or her). In that regard, the LED differs from the wording of the GDPR, which is not limited to adverse legal effects, but includes all results that legally affect data subjects as the outcome of the automated decision-making processing.[137]

In order to carry out automated decision-making, national or EU law must provide for such an option. Where a legal basis is non-existent, the controller may not use processing techniques which are based solely on automated means to generate decisions. Since the conditions that must be fulfilled to process personal data by way of automated decision-making are cumulative, the law allowing for such processing must provide for all appropriate safeguards for the rights and freedoms of the data subject.

Human intervention under Article 11(1) LED should be seen as a minimum safeguard, which should be complemented by additional measures.[138] According to Recital 38 LED, the provision of specific information to the data subject, an explanation of a decision that has been taken concerning him or her and the right to challenge such a decision should be available.[139] Yet, already under the GDPR,

[133] Mario Martini, 'Art 22 DSGVO – Automatisierte Entscheidungen Im Einzelfall Einschließlich Profiling' in Boris P Paal and Daniel Pauly (eds), *Datenschutz-Grundverordnung* (CH Beck, 2017).

[134] WP29, 'Guidelines on Automated Individual Decision-Making and Profiling for the Purposes of Regulation 2016/679 (Wp251rev.01) – Adopted on 3 October 2017, as Last Revised and Adopted on 6 February 2018' (2018).

[135] With regard to art of 22 Regulation (EU) 2016/679, *cf* Sandra Wachter, Brent Mittelstadt and Luciano Floridi, 'Why a Right to Explanation of Automated Decision-Making Does Not Exist in the General Data Protection Regulation' (2017) 7 *International Data Privacy Law* 76. See also Bryce Goodman and Seth Flaxman, 'European Union Regulations on Algorithmic Decision-Making and a "Right to Explanation"' (2016), https://arxiv.org/abs/1606.08813.

[136] Jacques Bus et al, 'The Dawn of a Critical Transparency Right for the Profiling Era' in *Digital Enlightenment Yearbook 2012* (IOS Press, 2012).

[137] Sajfert and Quintel (n 3); Martini (n 133) fn 28. Martini questions whether the GDPR refers to adverse legal effects and mentions the German Bundesdatenschutzgesetz, which only includes negative legal effects and finds that the GDPR's wording is less clear in that regard.

[138] See also CJEU, Opinion 1/15 on the Draft PNR Agreement between the EU and the US, ECLI:EU:C:2017:592, 26 July 2017, para 141. The CJEU sees human intervention as a mandatory safeguard when processing of personal data is carried out solely by automated means.

[139] Sajfert and Quintel (n 3) 11.

the effectiveness of the right to obtain information concerning the existence of automated decision-making and the logic involved in such processing may be doubted.[140] In the law enforcement context, where naturally more discretion is granted to the controller, the right to information is less likely to have the same (or even a lower) standing as that under Article 15(h) GDPR.[141]

In addition, the right to an explanation of decisions taken as referred to under Article 11 LED is merely suggestive, as only set out in the recitals.[142] Most importantly with regard to the processing of personal data under the LED, providing an explanation of the logic involved in the respective algorithms used for processing might give insights into the strategies of LEAs and could potentially jeopardise ongoing investigations.[143] In the migration context, this could become a problem where the competent authorities use the LED to process personal data of TCNs due to their irregular stay as criminalised under national law. In those cases, the concerned TCNs would be less able to be provided with an explanation concerning a decision that was taken about them than under the GDPR. Thus, the above constraints limit the possibility of challenging a decision that is based on automated decision-making under Article 11 LED.[144]

As previously mentioned, other than the LED, the GDPR does not refer to *adverse* legal effects, but includes effects that may be beneficial for data subjects.[145] This would substantiate the above argument that Article 11 LED refers to a prohibition of automated decision-making, while the GDPR rather provides for a right.[146] Neither Article 11 LED nor its recitals define what constitutes an adverse legal effect. It may, however, be assumed that the Directive refers to results of automated processing that 'alter or determine a person's legal rights or duties either partly or entirely'[147] in a negative sense. Conversely, this could mean that a positive decision that was taken by automated means would not be covered by Article 11 LED, and hence the mandatory safeguards that are attached to that provision would not have to be applied.

Admittedly, the provision mentions effects significantly affecting the data subject. Yet, deciding on where to set a threshold in order to determine whether a decision indeed *adverse* or *significantly affected the data subject* may prove difficult. In addition, the subjective needs of data subjects may clash with the interests of LEAs, which might instead choose to argue that a decision had a positive (or at least not adverse) effect on the individual.

[140] Wachter, Mittelstadt and Floridi (n 135).

[141] Sajfert and Quintel (n 3).

[142] ibid 10.

[143] Sajfert and Quintel (n 3). See also Wachter, Mittelstadt and Floridi (n 135).

[144] Sajfert and Quintel (n 3).

[145] This could be welfare decisions; see WP29 (n 134).

[146] *cf* Bart Custers, 'Profiling as Inferred Data: Amplifier Effects and Positive Feedback Loops' in Emre Bayamlioglu et al (eds), *Cogitas Ergo Sum: 10 Years of Profiling the European Citizen* (Amsterdam University Press, 2018).

[147] Lee A Bygrave, 'Minding the Machine: Art 15 of the EC Data Protection Directive and Automated Profiling' (2000) 7(4) *Privacy Law and Policy Reporter* 67.

Evidently, any police officer should be held accountable for his or her decision concerning the impact of Article 11 decisions on individuals. In addition, both police DPOs and DPAs are supposed to thoroughly monitor compliance with all data protection rules. Yet, while the DPO forms part of the same organisation as the controller to be held accountable under the LED (and therefore might not be entirely impartial), there may be doubts concerning the capacity of DPAs to effectively overview all Article 11 processing activities in accordance with Article 46 LED.

It is important to acknowledge the difference between forms of profiling as such and decision-making solely based on automated means. Processing operations and different forms of profiling that take place *before* the automated decision-making comes into play are covered by other provisions of the Directive.[148] Article 11 LED only applies where decision-making is solely based on automated means. Any type of processing that is not based on automated means should not fall within the scope of that provision. Thus, where processing involves decision-making that is not solely based on automated means, any *preliminary profiling* will not be covered under Article 11 of the Directive.[149]

However, this also means that Article 11 LED also covers other processing operations such as data mining, data matching and similar operations, as long as they are purely automated. For instance, where a profile is created and subsequently processed by solely automated means, this will trigger the applicability of Article 11 LED.[150] In turn, other principles and data subject rights apply to 'preliminary profiling' (not solely based on automated means), while such preliminary profiling might not be covered within the scope of Article 11 LED. Referring to the right to be informed, the WP29 similarly suggested distinguishing clearly between these types of processing.[151] Ultimately, processing to create a profile in order to take a decision (either with or without human intervention) will trigger other provisions, but only from the moment where data (whether an already created profile or 'raw data') are used for automated decision-making, which does not involve human intervention will Article 11 LED apply.

Article 11(2) LED states that automated decisions shall not be based on special categories of personal data, as referred to in Article 10 LED, unless suitable measures to safeguard data subject rights, freedoms and legitimate interests are in place. Hence, automated individual decision-making based on special categories of personal data is allowed under the LED, subject to certain conditions. Recital 37 LED suggests collecting special categories of data only in connection with other data on the natural person concerned, securing the data collected adequately, implementing stricter rules regarding the access to sensitive data

[148] Articles 4, 8, 10 and 13–17.

[149] Sajfert and Quintel (n 3). See also WP29 (n 134) 23.

[150] Sajfert and Quintel (n 3).

[151] WP29 (n 134).

by law enforcement staff and prohibiting the transfer of such data.[152] A general prohibition of automated decision-making to be contained in Article 11 LED was proposed by the European Parliament after the first reading[153] and was recommended by the EDPS,[154] but was not maintained in the final text of the Directive.[155]

In return, Article 11(3) LED stipulates an absolute prohibition of discriminatory profiling based on special categories of personal data, a provision that is non-existent under Article 22 GDPR.[156] This provision is to be welcomed, as the risk of discriminatory and racial profiling seems to be particularly high not only in the context of processing activities within the scope of the LED, but also in the context of migration and asylum. On the other hand, that paragraph may be seen as redundant, as discrimination is generally prohibited under EU law.[157] In addition, even if special categories of data are deleted during the data collection phase, the aggregation of 'non-sensitive' data may easily allow conclusions to be drawn about data subjects that reveal similar information.[158]

Hence, several issues remain. On the one hand, it may prove difficult to ascertain precisely when a certain processing operation was carried out by purely automated means. Consequently, the moment at which additional safeguards as required by Article 11 LED must be provided could be contested.

In addition, any human intervention in an automated decision-making process makes the latter no longer *solely* automated.[159] Hence, without an indication of what constitutes 'true' human intervention, that requirement is ambiguous, if not futile. Ultimately, where processing based on automated decision-making takes place without a decision being taken, the result of that processing operation could in theory be used for subsequent processing operations.[160] Finally, group profiling[161] is often part of related processing operations, but is covered neither by the GDPR nor by the Directive, and thus illustrates a loophole in EU data

[152] Sajfert and Quintel (n 3).

[153] European Parliament, 'Texts Adopted – Wednesday, 12 March 2014 – Processing of Personal Data for the Purposes of Crime Prevention *** I – P7_TA(2014)0219', https://www.europarl.europa.eu/sides/getDoc.do?pubRef=-//EP//TEXT+TA+P7-TA-2014-0219+0+DOC+XML+V0//EN.

[154] EDPS, 'Opinion 6/2015: A Further Step towards Comprehensive EU Data Protection – EDPS Recommendations on the Directive for Data Protection in the Police and Justice Sectors' (2015) 7.

[155] Sajfert and Quintel (n 3).

[156] ibid 14.

[157] Raphaël Gellert et al, 'A Comparative Analysis of Anti-discrimination and Data Protection Legislations' in Custers et al (n 125).

[158] Sajfert and Quintel (n 3).

[159] ibid 11.

[160] ibid 13.

[161] Bart Custers, 'The Power of Knowledge Ethical, Legal and Technological Aspects of Data Mining and Group Profiling in Epidemiology', https://papers.ssrn.com/sol3/papers.cfm?abstract_id=3186639; Linda E Fisher, 'Guilt by Expressive Association: Political Profiling, Surveillance and the Privacy of Groups' (2004) 46 *Arizona Law Review* 621.

protection law.[162] Particularly in the area of migration and border control, individuals are commonly profiled in groups, which may eventually have an impact on their rights under data protection legislation.

V. Data Subject Rights

One of the main differences between the GDPR and the LED concerns the right to information, as closely tied to transparency, and the right of access to personal data, as well as the restriction of these rights. If these rights were exercised to a similar extent to that under the GDPR within the ambit of criminal law, this would make criminal investigations effectively impossible.[163] Against that background, the restriction of data subject rights under the LED may evidently be exercised more flexibly by controllers and leaves room for discretion to be exercised by the national competent authorities.

Nevertheless, under the Directive, the rights of data subjects were strengthened compared to the rights that existed under the 2008 DPFD. For instance, other than under the DPFD, the LED obliges controllers to provide direct access to data subjects where its predecessor gave a choice to the national legislator to allow individuals to access their data either directly or indirectly.

The set of rights under the LED is almost the same as that under the GDPR, with the difference that the rights under the GDPR are much stronger and more detailed. In addition, GDPR rights such as the right to data portability[164] or the right to object to processing[165] do not exist under the Directive. Furthermore, the rights under the LED were adjusted to the specific context in which the Directive applies. Hence, the transparency obligation, which on the one hand raises awareness of individuals and on the other hand increases accountability on the side of the controllers, is much weaker under the LED. This means that data subjects might not always be aware of the fact that their personal data are processed, which may affect other data subject rights, such as the right of access or the right to rectification and erasure.[166]

The differences between the LED and the GDPR take into account the needs of the competent authorities that process personal data within the scope of the LED

[162] Wim Schreurs et al, 'Cogitas, Ergo Sum. The Role of Data Protection Law and Non-discrimination Law in Group Profiling in the Private Sector' in Mireille Hildebrandt and Serge Gutwirth (eds), *Profiling the European Citizen: Cross-Disciplinary Perspectives* (Springer Netherlands, 2008).

[163] Di Francesco Maesa (n 49).

[164] Article 20 of Regulation (EU) 2016/679.

[165] ibid art 21.

[166] For instance, in Case C-553/07, *College van burgemeester en wethouders van Rotterdam v MEE Rijkeboer*, ECLI:EU:C:2009:293, 7 May 2009, Advocate General Ruiz-Jarabo Colomer held that the purpose of the right of access is to provide data subjects with transparency about processing by ensuring that they are aware of the information stored about them.

in order to enable them to carry out their tasks efficiently. This means that the competent authorities must be able to hold back certain information that could reveal to someone that he or she is under investigation, or details about investigative measures used. Hence, as will be explained in section V.A, the rules under the LED differ, for instance, with regard to the transparency requirements in the law enforcement area. Consequently, associated rights, such as the right to information, which is laid down under Article 13 LED, follow this approach.

A. The Right to be Informed

Article 13(1) LED lists the information that is to be made available by the controller to any potential data subject in a general manner.[167] Such general information could be published in an easy-to-understand, clear and plain language on the website of a police authority or other authority competent under the Directive.[168] Evidently, such information will not reveal any processing techniques, but is supposed to enable the data subject to exercise his or her rights.

For that purpose, the generally accessible information should include the contact details of the controller as well as those of the DPO. In addition, the purposes of the processing should be communicated in accordance with Article 13(1)(c) LED. Further, individuals should be made aware of their additional rights as well as the possibility of lodging a complaint with the competent supervisory authority. Hence, the right to information is the first step in enabling the exercise of other data subject rights.

Besides the basic information to be provided to the data subject in accordance with Article 13(1) LED, under Article 13(2) LED, the controller is required to proactively provide the data subject with additional information in specific cases.[169] Such additional information should, for instance, be provided to victims, witnesses, experts, convicts and suspects. However, the time at which the information is to be provided to the data subject may differ, as informing a suspect could jeopardise ongoing investigations. In addition, data that may lead to the

[167] Under Article 13(1) LED, the controller must inform the data subject about: (a) the identity and the contact details of the controller; (b) the contact details of the data protection officer, where applicable; (c) the purposes of the processing for which the personal data are intended; (d) the right to lodge a complaint with a supervisory authority and the contact details of the supervisory authority; and (e) the existence of the right to request from the controller access to and rectification or erasure of personal data and restriction of processing of the personal data concerning the data subject.

[168] As suggested in Recitals 39 and 42 of Directive (EU) 2016/680.

[169] Under Article 13(2) LED, the controller must inform the data subject about: (a) the legal basis for the processing; (b) the period for which the personal data will be stored, or, where that is not possible, the criteria used to determine that period; (c) where applicable, the categories of recipients of the personal data, including in third countries or international organisations; and (d) where necessary, further information, in particular where the personal data are collected without the knowledge of the data subject.

identification of other natural persons should not be disclosed, particularly if the sources are to remain confidential or concern vulnerable persons such as victims.[170]

The information to be provided in specific cases to the data subject under Article 13(2) LED may be delayed, restricted or omitted, subject to strict conditions. However, as soon as providing the data subject with the information under Article 13(2) LED no longer jeopardises the investigation, he or she should be given the information to enable the exercise of his or her rights.[171] Thus, the right to information is the basis for exercising other data subject rights. If the data subject is not aware that his or her personal data are potentially being processed, he or she cannot request access to, or rectification or erasure of, his or her data.

B. The Right of Access

The importance of the right of access is evidenced by its inclusion in Article 8(2) of the EU Charter.[172] In general terms, the right of access is essential to allow data subjects to exercise control over their personal data and for the way in which these are processed.[173] Hence, the right of access is an enabling right to achieve transparency, supervision and monitoring of the lawfulness of processing, or to raise awareness and address unlawful processing.[174] Hence, data subjects generally have a legitimate interest in finding out what information about them is processed by the controller, including, but not exclusively, the aim of exercising sequential rights.[175]

However, there are some important differences between the right of access in general terms and in the context of law enforcement processing. Hence, where data are being processed within the scope of the LED, data subjects might not always be in full control over their personal data, as this might hamper the work of the competent authorities. At the same time, it is particularly important that individuals have the possibility to access and potentially correct their data when the latter are processed for law enforcement purposes, as any incorrect data may lead to adverse effects for the data subject.[176]

[170] Diana Dimitrova and Paul de Hert, 'The Right of Access under the Police Directive: Small Steps Forward' in Manel Medina et al (eds), *Privacy Technologies and Policy* (Springer International Publishing, 2018) 119.

[171] Sajfert and Quintel (n 3) 13.

[172] For an excellent analysis of the right of access under Directive (EU) 2016/680, see Dimitrova and de Hert (n 170).

[173] ibid 111.

[174] ibid 114.

[175] Opinion of Advocate General in Case C-434/16, *Peter Nowak v Data Protection Commissioner*, ECLI:EU:C:2017:582, 20 July 2017, paras 36–38.

[176] See also in that respect *Khelili v Switzerland*, App No 16188/07 (ECtHR, 18 October 2011).

Article 14(1) LED enshrines the right of access, according to which the data subject has the right to obtain from the controller confirmation as to whether or not his or her data are being processed. Without prejudice to the limitations set out in Article 15 LED, the controller should always confirm whether or not data about the requesting person are processed and, if that is the case, inform him or her of six different elements concerning the processing.[177]

It seems particularly important that data subjects are provided with information on the origin as well as potential recipients of the data in order to be able to exercise their right of access against other controllers.[178] Yet, the Directive allows controllers to merely disclose categories of recipients to whom the personal data have been disclosed.[179] Hence, the data subject might have to file multiple requests (including blind requests) with several controllers in order to build up a more complete picture about the processing operations that are carried out with his or her personal data.[180]

In addition, it is essential that the data subject is informed about his or her right to request the controller to rectify or erase his or her personal data and to have the possibility to restrict processing if there is any doubt over whether the processed data are correct.[181] Finally, the controller should always inform the data subject about the option to lodge a complaint with the supervisory authority and provide him or her with the latter's contact details.[182]

The Directive excludes public authorities from the definition of 'recipient'. Hence, public authorities may receive personal data within the framework of a particular inquiry in accordance with Member State law, but shall not be regarded as recipients.[183] This exclusion is based on a similar practice in the French legal system and therefore is not made use of in other national frameworks. However, in the migration context, this exclusion could hypothetically be used in order to conceal information about recipients where data are sent from a competent authority to a migration authority, which may affect the way in which individuals may exercise their rights.

[177] '(a) [T]he purposes of and legal basis for the processing; (b) the categories of personal data concerned; (c) the recipients or categories of recipients to whom the personal data have been disclosed, in particular recipients in third countries or international organisations; (d) where possible, the envisaged period for which the personal data will be stored, or, if not possible, the criteria used to determine that period; (e) the existence of the right to request from the controller rectification or erasure of personal data or restriction of processing of personal data concerning the data subject; (f) the right to lodge a complaint with the supervisory authority and the contact details of the supervisory authority; (g) communication of the personal data undergoing processing and of any available information as to their origin.'

[178] As mentioned above, data that could lead to the identification of other natural persons should not be disclosed, particularly if the sources are to remain confidential or concern vulnerable persons such as victims or witnesses.

[179] Article 14(c) of Directive (EU) 2016/680.

[180] Dimitrova and de Hert (n 170) 118.

[181] Article 14(e) of Directive (EU) 2016/680.

[182] ibid art 14(g).

[183] ibid art 3(10).

Several elements of information that are to be provided under the GDPR[184] when access to personal data is requested (and granted) are not listed under Article 14 LED: for instance, the communication of a possible change of the purpose of processing,[185] the existence of profiling[186] and the obligation for the controller to provide the data subject with a copy of the personal data undergoing processing.[187]

However, with regard to the communication of a change of purpose, any comparison with the GDPR cannot be carried out, as the latter is based on the concept of further processing, while the LED follows the concept of subsequent processing, as illustrated above.[188] Hence, the same data may be subsequently processed based on the same legal basis by different controllers under the LED, following the chain of custody under criminal procedural law.[189]

With respect to the communication of the existence of profiling, this might seem logical in the law enforcement context in order not to reveal investigative methods of the police or other competent authorities. Yet, the existence of profiling is to be communicated to the competent supervisory authority in accordance with the obligation to record processing activities pursuant to Article 24(1)(e) LED. This offers the opportunity for the supervisory authority to scrutinise the processing operations of the controller, while not revealing any investigative techniques to the data subject. A similar logic applies to the right to obtain a copy of the data processed, which, under the Directive, is reduced to a summary of the data undergoing processing.[190]

The right of access is a precondition for the exercising of other data subject rights, such as the right to rectification or erasure, or the right to the restriction of processing. Hence, the right of access is always directly linked to the quality of data in a law enforcement system. Particularly in the law enforcement context, high standards in terms of the quality of personal data are essential not only for the operational work of competent authorities, but also with regard to the rights of the individual concerned.

[184] In accordance with art 13 of Regulation (EU) 2016/679 on the information to be provided where personal data are collected from the data subject and art 15 of Regulation (EU) 2016/679 on the right of access.

[185] Article 13(3) of Regulation (EU) 2016/679 states that: 'Where the controller intends to further process the personal data for a purpose other than that for which the personal data were collected, the controller shall provide the data subject prior to that further processing with information on that other purpose and with any relevant further information as referred to in paragraph 2.'

[186] Article 15(1)(h) of Regulation (EU) 2016/679. As explained above, automated decision-making is generally prohibited under the LED; therefore, it is assumed that the Directive only refers to profiling under art 24, whereas Regulation (EU) 2016/679 also refers to automated decision-making.

[187] Article 15(1)(3) of Regulation (EU) 2016/679.

[188] For instance, where the police process personal data for the purpose of collecting evidence and thereafter the prosecutor processes the same data for the purpose of building the indictment, processing will be based on the same legal basis.

[189] In that regard, Regulation (EU) 2016/679 could be compared to Regulation 45/2001/EC, which also incorporated the change of purpose concept.

[190] Recital 43 of Directive (EU) 2016/680.

Therefore, a data subject access request is also always a test of the quality of the data that are processed by the competent authorities. The right of access may be exercised by the data subject regardless of whether or not he or she has received any notification that his or her data are being processed. Hence, any person could contact a police or other competent authority in order to determine whether his or her personal data are being processed and that authority would be obliged to respond to that request.[191]

Access to data should generally be granted to the fullest extent, unless exceptions apply. Hence, by default, a data subject should be provided with all data concerning him or her and any restriction should be duly justified. Data subject access requests will not have to be replied to in the event the controller applies limitations to the right of access, or if a request is manifestly unfounded or excessive.[192]

The reply to a data subject access request logically only includes the information that exists at the moment of the request. Thus, data that were processed in the past but were deleted due to a legal obligation will not be included in the reply. Moreover, although the data subject should be informed about the envisaged period of the processing, this might not always be possible in all instances. If there are doubts about the identity of a person, the competent authorities are usually permitted to request a copy of the data subject's ID card or passport in order to verify whether the person is who he or she claims to be. Any background searches, either from public sources or in other databases, to establish the identity of the data subject should be prohibited, as such processing would not be based on a valid legal basis.

There are different scenarios that may follow a data subject access request. The first scenario would be that no data about that person are processed, in which case the data subject should receive a reply indicating that no personal data are being processed about him or her. There may be exceptional circumstances, for instance, when two family members send an access request and one of them is stored in the database of the requested competent authority. In that case, both individuals may receive different replies. For instance, one person could receive a reply in which the competent authority confirms that no data are being processed, whereas the other person would be informed that he or she cannot be provided with any information about him or her. In those cases, the data subjects might know that the likelihood that personal data about the second person are processed is quite high. However, such scenarios are rare.

In a second scenario, personal data concerning the person who sent the access request are stored in the system and the information is available. In such

[191] ibid Recital 42.

[192] For instance, where the data subject unreasonably and repetitiously requests information or where the data subject abuses his or her right to receive information, for example, by providing false or misleading information when making the request, the controller should be able to charge a reasonable fee or refuse to act on the request. See ibid Recital 49.

cases, there would be a need to establish whether or not such information may be provided to the data subject, if this has not already been done. There would be a possibility to provide a partial reply, such as 'we would like to inform you that we have x information about you, but apart from that information, there is no further information that we can provide you with'.[193]

In a third scenario, data about the requesting person are stored in the system of the competent authority, but there are justified reasons why those data cannot be provided to the data subject. In such a case, the data subject will receive a 'neither confirm nor deny' reply, hence 'we can neither confirm nor deny that we are processing your personal data'. In those cases, the data subject will not be able to know whether his or her data are being processed and whether they are correct. For such situations, Article 17 LED provides for the right to indirect access, which will be explained below.

If the data subject receives a reply indicating that his or her personal data are being processed, this enables him or her to make use of the right to rectification or erasure of personal data and restriction of processing.

C. The Right to Rectification or Erasure of Personal Data and to the Restriction of Processing

The right to rectification or erasure of personal data and the right to restriction of processing are set out in Article 16 LED. These rights allow the data subject to obtain from the controller the rectification of inaccurate data, the completion of incomplete data or the restriction of processing. For instance, where the processing infringes any of the principles under Article 4 LED, is not based on a proper legal basis as required under Article 8 LED or violates the rules regarding the processing of special categories of personal data, the controller must erase those data without undue delay.

Where the accuracy of the data is contested by the data subject but cannot be ascertained,[194] or in the event that the personal data must be maintained for the purposes of evidence, the LED provides for the option to restrict the processing of personal data instead of deleting them. Consequently, when the accuracy of personal data is contested, restriction of processing could mean that the data in question be moved to a different working file, be made unavailable or be restricted by other technical means. In addition, any rectification, erasure and restriction should be communicated to all recipients and/or to those who initially collected the data in question.[195]

[193] Daniel Drewer, 'Data Protection and the Law Enforcement Directive', https://www.era.int/cgi-bin/cms?_SID=NEW&_sprache=en&_bereich=artikel&_aktion=detail&idartikel=129633.

[194] Article 16(3)(a) of Directive (EU) 2016/680.

[195] ibid Recital 47.

The restriction or 'soft deletion' of personal data could also mean that some of the operational staff may no longer use those data for analysis purposes, while the data will not be irreversibly deleted from the system. This could be necessary in cases where the data subject would need the information, for instance, as evidence against the controller before a court.[196]

Notwithstanding the particular field in which the Directive applies, it seeks to establish a robust system of data subject rights, at least on paper. All rights generally apply and may only be restricted if such restriction is justified by the competent authority. Hence, as a general rule, individuals must be informed (at least indirectly) about possible situations in which competent authorities could process their personal data. In addition, persons whose data are processed as part of a criminal investigation need to be provided with additional information concerning the processing.

Moreover, individuals have the right to inquire as to whether their data are being processed and to ask a controller to get access to their data, as long as such requests are not manifestly unfounded or excessive. All those rights are generally free of charge and should be responded to without undue delay.[197]

However, in the law enforcement context, the competent authorities are granted the privilege not to disclose information if this could impede criminal investigations. This privilege is bound by conditions and any restriction of data subject rights under the Directive needs to be justified. Furthermore, restrictions of data subject rights should be limited as far as possible.

D. Restriction of Data Subject Rights

The approach towards data subject rights and their possible limitations under the LED seeks to find a balance between the rights of the individual under Articles 13, 14 and 16 on the one hand, and the needs of competent authorities on the other.[198] In other words, although the Directive's main objective is the protection of the fundamental right to the protection of personal data, this must be done in a way that does not impede the work of the competent authorities and the exchange of personal data between those authorities. The LED allows for a restriction of the rights only for as long as is necessary and proportionate. At the same time, the Directive leaves sufficient leeway for competent authorities to prevent information from being given to the data subject that could otherwise compromise their work,

[196] Drewer (n 193). However, whether the controller will indeed retain data that might be used against him or her in the future might not always be that self-evident, although deletion of personal data must be logged.

[197] Recital 49 of Directive (EU) 2016/680. However, where the data subject abuses his or her right to receive information – for example, by providing false or misleading information when making the request – the controller should be able to charge a reasonable fee or refuse to act on the request.

[198] Sajfert and Quintel (n 3).

as in certain cases, the mere response that no information may be provided could hamper ongoing investigations.[199]

The controller may limit the right to specific information being given to the data subject,[200] the right of access[201] and the right to obtain information about the possible refusal of rectification, erasure or restriction of processing[202] in a similar way to that under Article 23 GDPR.[203] Hence, where informing the data subject could jeopardise ongoing investigations or obstruct official inquiries, or might threaten public security or the rights and freedoms of others, the right to information, the right of access and the right to rectification, erasure and restriction of processing may be restricted for as long as necessary.

Like under the GDPR, all restrictions of data subject rights under the LED must be based on a separate legislative measure. The horizontal wording under Articles 13(3), 15 and 16(4) LED is not sufficient to provide for a restriction of the rights under the LED. This means that where Member States did not implement national laws allowing for the limitation of data subject rights, any restriction to data subject rights that is based solely on the provisions under the LED should be seen as unlawful. The LED understands the possibility of restricting data subject rights as an option that the national legislators can choose to adopt in their transposition acts. Hence, Member States *may* adopt legislative measures that allow controllers to either wholly or partly restrict the rights of individuals.

Articles 13(3), 15 and 16(4) LED lay down the conditions under which the right to be informed, the right of access and the right to rectification, erasure and restriction of processing may be restricted. The provisions stipulate that a restriction must be laid down in law, must respect the essence of the fundamental rights and freedoms of the data subject, and must constitute a necessary and proportionate measure in a democratic society.[204] Consequently, the controller must carry out a balancing test between the interests at stake *before* restricting data subject rights. Moreover, Articles 13(3), 15 and 16(4) LED indicate that once investigations are over and/or providing the data subject with information and access would no longer compromise investigative measures, the limitations must be lifted, and the data subject must be notified about the processing. Although this is not explicitly spelled out in the provisions, the wording *for as long as necessary* denotes that once the restriction is no longer necessary, all data subject rights fully apply, and the data subject must be informed and may then exercise his or her right of access.

[199] ibid 13.

[200] Article 13(1) of Directive (EU) 2016/680.

[201] ibid art 14.

[202] ibid art 16.

[203] Sajfert and Quintel (n 3) 7. See also Quintel (n 6).

[204] Quintel (n 6). See also EDPS, 'Opinion 1/2017 Opinion on a Commission Proposal Amending Directive (EU) 2015/849 and Directive 2009/101/EC. Access to Beneficial Ownership Information and Data Protection Implications' (2 February 2017), 2, 5.

While it is true that under the GDPR, the transparency obligations for controllers and processors are far stronger than under the LED, it could be argued that the restrictions of data subject rights under Article 23 GDPR are not accompanied by the same notification safeguards as under the LED. Logically, the threshold for restricting data subject rights under the GDPR is much higher than that under the LED, due to each instrument's respective area of application. In addition, because of the strong transparency obligations, data subjects whose personal data are being processed within the scope of the GDPR should be informed about any processing activity by default, which reduces the possibility for controllers to impose restrictions.

However, while under the GDPR controllers are, like under the LED, required to carry out a balancing test before restricting data subjects' rights, Article 23(2)(h) lays down that data subjects shall not be informed about the restriction if this would impair the purpose of the restriction. This paragraph does not stipulate that data subjects must be notified of the restriction once the purpose of the restriction can no longer be impaired. It might be the case that, due to criminal investigations, private companies processing personal data pursuant to Article 23 GDPR will not be permitted to inform the data subject of any restrictions until ordered to do so by the competent authority.[205]

On the one hand, the standards under the Directive regarding data subject rights are generally lower than those under the GDPR, as the rights may be restricted more flexibly under the former and because the latter's focus on transparency is evidently much more pronounced. Due to the particular area in which the LED applies, transparency obligations towards data subjects are naturally less strict than under the framework of the GDPR.[206] In line with the same logic, the threshold for controllers to restrict data subject rights is lower under the LED since, in the field of law enforcement, more flexibility when processing personal data may be the key to a successful investigation. On the other hand, the LED provides for specific obligations that are non-existent under the GDPR, as in the case of the notification obligation under Articles 13(3), 15 and 16(4) LED.

Because the rights under the Directive are closely related, any restriction of one right will affect the exercising of the other rights. Hence, where the controller decides that no specific information shall be provided to the data subject in accordance with Article 13(2) LED, that person can only exercise his or her right of access by means of a blind access request. In such a situation, the person would send the request to the controller based on a suspicion that his or her personal

[205] See, for instance, the provisions for notification of data subjects under the e-evidence proposal: art 11(2) of 'Proposal for a Regulation of the European Parliament and of the Council on European Production and Preservation Orders for electronic evidence in criminal matters' COM (2018) 225 final, Strasbourg 17 April 2018. For a preliminary analysis of the e-evidence proposals, see Mark D Cole and Teresa Quintel, 'Transborder Access to e-Evidence by Law Enforcement Agencies' (2018), https://papers.ssrn.com/sol3/papers.cfm?abstract_id=3278780.

[206] Quintel (n 6).

data are being processed. A meaningful reply would, however, be unlikely, as otherwise the restriction to the right to information would have been unnecessary. Consequently, the data subject would not be provided with the full set of his or her personal data and would not be able to ascertain whether the personal data processed are (in)accurate.

If the controller refuses the right to rectification or erasure of personal data or restriction of processing under Article 16(4) LED, he or she shall inform the data subject in writing of any such refusal. However, Member States were able to adopt legislative measures to allow controllers to refrain from informing the data subject in cases where doing so would impair ongoing investigations, could threaten public or national security, or might harm the rights and freedoms of others.[207]

The Directive seeks to find a balance between the rights of individuals whose data are processed within the scope of the LED and the interests of competent authorities that may not want to disclose information relating to their investigative measures. Any restriction of data subject rights must be preceded by a careful balancing between the different fundamental rights and the interests at stake. Hence, the competent authority restricting data subject rights must justify the reasons for the restriction and may be held accountable for unjustified restrictions. In addition, any restriction must be based on national or EU law, which means that ad hoc restrictions are not permissible. Finally, data subjects must be informed about the processing of their personal data once such notification may no longer impact ongoing investigations or reveal investigative techniques in order to be able to exercise their remaining rights. Consequently, the notification requirement codified landmark judgments from both the CJEU[208] and the ECtHR.[209]

E. The Right to Indirect Access: Exercise of Data Subject Rights by the Data Protection Authority

Pursuant to the LED, the exercise of data subject rights, as well as their restriction, is more specific than the approach chosen under the GDPR, which

[207] If such a restriction constitutes a necessary and proportionate measure in a democratic society with due regard for the fundamental rights and legitimate interests of the natural person concerned.

[208] CJEU, Joined Cases C-293/12 and C-594/12, *Digital Rights Ireland Ltd* (C-293/12) *and Seitlinger* (C-594/12), ECLI:EU:C:2014:238, 8 April; CJEU, Case C-362/14, *Maximillian Schrems v Data Protection Commissioner*, ECLI:EU:C:2015:650, 6 October 2015.

[209] *Roman Zakharov v Russia*, App No 47143/06 (ECtHR, 4 December 2015) or *Máté Szabó and Beatrix Vissy v Hungary*, App No 37138/14 (ECtHR, 12 January 2016); for a detailed case analysis, see Mark D Cole and Annelies Vandendriessche, 'Case Note: From *Digital Rights Ireland* and *Schrems* in Luxembourg to *Zakharov* and *Szabó/Vissy* in Strasbourg: What the ECtHR Made of the Deep Pass by the CJEU in the Recent Cases on Mass Surveillance *Roman Zakharov v Russia* (App No 47143/06) and *Szabó and Vissy v Hungary* (App No 37138/14)' (2016) 2(1) *European Data Protection Law Review*, https://edpl.lexxion.eu/article/EDPL/2016/1/18.

foresees a horizontal provision for the restriction of rights. Particularly in the law enforcement context, a robust system for the exercise of data subject rights is important, as any incorrect data, misuse or data breach may have a severe impact for the individual whose data are being processed. Therefore, the Directive foresees, as a specific safeguard, the exercise of data subject rights by the supervisory authority on behalf of the data subject.[210] Hence, the national supervisory authority, when requested by the data subject, will act as intermediary and verify whether all processing operations regarding that person are carried out in compliance with the LED.

Generally, the exercise of data subject rights, including their restriction, may be described in a three-step approach.[211] In the first step, the data subject would be fully granted all data subject rights, meaning that he or she would proactively be provided by the controller with all information concerning the processing in accordance with Article 13(2) LED and could subsequently exercise his or her right of access, and, possibly, the right of rectification, erasure or restriction of processing.

In the second step, some information could be withheld from the data subject. In such cases, the controller would, for instance, refuse to provide information concerning the origin of the personal data or the categories of recipients of the data in question. This might be necessary in order to protect informants or not to reveal any cross-border elements of an investigation.

In the third step, the controller would entirely restrict the right of access and respond to an access request with a 'neither confirm nor deny' reply. After receiving such a reply, the data subject would neither know whether data about him or her are being processed nor if those data are correct or should be corrected/erased.

For those cases in particular, but also for situations in which the data subject has only received a partial reply, the Directive foresees a fourth step that enables the *indirect* exercise of data subject rights. Under Article 17(1) LED, Member States that have availed themselves of the option to provide for the restriction of data subject rights must adopt legislative measures that offer the opportunity to exercise those rights through the competent supervisory authority. This means that where a data subject has received an unsatisfactory or neutral reply to an access request from a competent authority, the supervisory authority may exercise the right of access on behalf of the data subject.

Hence, where data subject rights have been restricted and the competent authority can only give a neutral reply, the supervisory authority may act as a proxy for the data subject in order to verify whether the processing is carried out

[210] The ECtHR held on several occasions that the decision not to grant direct access should be reviewed by an independent authority; see, for instance, *Gaskin v United Kingdom*, App No 10454/83 (ECtHR, 7 July 1989) or ECtHR, *Ammann v Switzerland*, App No 27798/95 (ECtHR, 16 February 2000). *cf* Dimitrova and de Hert (n 170) 123.

[211] Sajfert and Quintel (n 3) 13.

in compliance with the LED. The supervisory authority should then carry out all necessary checks as to whether the competent authority is processing the personal data in question in compliance with the rules of the LED.

The DPA could, for instance, verify the legal basis of the processing, whether personal data should be rectified or whether the storage period has been transgressed. However, in certain instances, it might prove challenging to check the accuracy of all data – for example, where the supervisory authority cannot reconfirm with the data subject whether or not data are correct, or where the competent authority stores personal data that are based on inferences. In those cases, the DPA should ensure that all data are categorised in a correct manner and that deadlines for deletion are complied with. Yet, any reply to the data subject by the supervisory authority should not reveal the reasons as to why the competent authority restricted the data subject rights. Therefore, a reply by the supervisory authority could simply state that all necessary checks have been carried out. In any event, the data subject should be informed of his or her right to seek an effective judicial remedy against the decision of the supervisory authority in accordance with Article 53 LED.[212]

The provision on indirect exercise of data subject rights under the LED has no equivalent provision under the GDPR. However, the right under Article 17 LED is not completely new, but already existed under the 2008 DPFD. However, the DPFD offered Member States the option to grant data subjects the right of either direct or indirect access, or both. Most Member States chose the second option and only in some Member States was it possible for individuals to seek their rights by directly contacting the controller.

The provisions on data subject rights under Chapter III of the Directive now grant individuals the opportunity to address controllers directly with access requests or requests for the rectification or erasure of personal data or the restriction of processing. Moreover, there is no more choice left to the national legislators, but direct access became the general rule under the LED. As an additional safeguard and in a second step, data subjects may seek redress via the supervisory authority.

The strengthened data subject rights under the Directive are very progressive when compared to the situation that existed in many Member States before. Often, competent authorities could carry out ad hoc or blanket restrictions of their entire work files and even the supervisory authorities had no power to sanction. However, in reality, the situation often only looks good on paper, while the provisions on the restrictions are often transposed incorrectly and the supervisory authorities lack effective investigatory and sanctioning powers. This is unfortunate, particularly with regard to migration-related processing, where individuals often do not know how to exercise their data subject rights and are therefore more dependent on the DPAs to scrutinise whether processing operations were carried out in accordance with the law.

[212] ibid 14.

VI. Obligations for Controllers and Security of Personal Data

A. Records of Processing Activities and Logging Requirements

Two key obligations for controllers that were reinforced under the LED compared to the 2008 DPFD are the record keeping and the logging requirements, stipulated in Articles 24 and 25 LED, respectively. Due to its limited scope of application, the Directive's predecessor did not oblige controllers to keep records of their domestic processing activities and merely required logging *or* documentation for cross-border transmissions of personal data.[213]

The LED introduced two separate provisions in order to enable the national supervisory authorities to verify the lawfulness of the processing carried out by the competent authorities.[214] Thus, the choice given to the controllers under the DPFD to *either* document *or* log their processing operations was strengthened under the Directive and both were turned into an obligation. While controllers are now obliged to maintain a record of all categories of processing activities under their responsibility, the types of processing operations to be logged were expanded from one under the DPFD to six under the Directive.[215]

In accordance with Article 24(1)(a) to (i) LED, each record to be kept by a controller subject to the LED must contain at least nine elements relating to the processing operation. These include, inter alia, the contact details of the controllers and their DPO, the categories of data subjects, personal data, transfers and recipients, the purposes of the processing, the legal basis for processing and, where possible, the time limits for erasure and a general description of the technical and organisational security measures. In addition, controllers shall record whether profiling is used as a processing method.[216]

Article 24 makes a distinction between controllers under paragraph (1) and processors under paragraph (2). The latter merely requires processors to maintain records of the contact details of processors and their DPO, the categories of processing, any transfers to third countries and, where possible, a general description of the technical and organisational security measures. Hence, the list of information to be recorded by controllers and processors under Article 24 LED is similar to the information to be provided to the data subject under Article 13(1) and (2) LED, with the exception that Article 24 LED adds profiling to the list of records.

[213] Article 10 of Framework Decision 2008/977/JHA.

[214] Articles 24(3) and 25(3) of Directive (EU) 2016/680.

[215] Under Framework Decision 2008/977/JHA, only transmissions of personal data were to be logged or documented.

[216] Article 24(e) of Directive (EU) 2016/680.

It could be argued that the obligation to keep records of processing activities is relatively general and already in existence under Article 13 LED, in the sense that those records will have to be kept in order for controllers to be able to provide individuals with adequate information and to respond to data subject access requests. Only when reading the requirement to keep records in conjunction with the logging obligation jointly do these become effective and an adequate safeguard against misuse or unauthorised access.

While the obligation to maintain records of processing activities exists under Article 30 GDPR, an equivalent provision to the logging requirement under Article 25 LED is absent in the Regulation.[217] Hence, the obligation to keep logs of six processing operations in automated processing systems is a very distinct feature of the Directive.[218] The LED consolidated the obligation to keep records that previously existed under the founding acts of the SIS II and the VIS.[219] Recently, the EES,[220] the SIS III Regulations,[221] the recast VIS Regulation,[222] the ETIAS,[223] the ECRIS-TCN[224] and the Interoperability Regulations[225] have all included provisions on the keeping of logs. The wording regarding the provisions on logging diverges under the founding acts of the different databases. While the EES and the ETIAS require the logging of all processing operations, but refer to certain processing operations being logged,[226] the SIS III and the VIS keep the wording more general.

In accordance with Article 25(1) LED, every processing operation involving the collection, alteration, consultation, disclosure, transfer, combination or erasure of personal data shall be logged. Normally logs should be kept for

[217] Sajfert and Quintel (n 3).

[218] ibid 15.

[219] Article 34 of the VIS Regulation and art 12 of the SIS II Decision.

[220] Article 46 of Regulation (EU) 2017/2226 for the keeping of logs by eu-LISA and Member States.

[221] See, for instance, art 12 of Regulation (EU) 2018/1862 for the keeping of logs at the national level and art 18 for the keeping of logs at the central level.

[222] Article 34 of Regulation (EU) 2021/1134 of the European Parliament and of the Council of 7 July 2021 amending Regulations (EC) No 767/2008, (EC) No 810/2009, (EU) 2016/399, (EU) 2017/2226, (EU) 2018/1240, (EU) 2018/1860, (EU) 2018/1861, (EU) 2019/817 and (EU) 2019/1896 of the European Parliament and of the Council and repealing Council Decisions 2004/512/EC and 2008/633/JHA, for the purpose of reforming the Visa Information System [2021] OJ L248/11.

[223] Article 69 of Regulation (EU) 2018/1240.

[224] Article 31 of Regulation (EU) 2019/816.

[225] See, for instance, art 10 of Regulation (EU) 2019/817 and Regulation (EU) 2019/818 on the keeping of logs of all processing operations in the ESP, art 16 on the keeping of logs of all processing operations in the BMS, art 24 on the keeping of logs of all processing operations in the CIR, and art 36 on the keeping of logs of all processing operations in the MID.

[226] For the EES: (a) the purpose of access; (b) the date and time; (c) the data transmitted; (d) the data used for interrogation; (e) the name of the authority entering or retrieving the data of art 46 Regulation (EU) 2017/2226. For the ETIAS: a) the purpose of the access; (b) the date and time of each operation; (c) the data used for the automated processing of the applications; (d) the hits triggered while carrying out the automated processing; (e) the data used for the verification of identity stored in the ETIAS Central System or other information systems and databases; (f) the results of the verification process; (g) the staff member having performed it.

between one[227] and three years[228] in order to enable the competent authorities, on the one hand, and the independent supervisory authorities, on the other, to verify whether processing was carried out in a lawful manner. The logging obligation is aimed at helping to detect data protection or security breaches, such as unauthorised and unusual access, or more generally any misuse of the systems.[229]

Consequently, whenever competent authorities collect, alter, consult, disclose, combine or erase personal data in their systems, those processing operations must be logged. For logs on consultation and disclosure, the Directive requires controllers to indicate in the logs the date and time of the processing operations, the person who consulted or disclosed the data and the identity of any recipients of those data. Hence, for those two particularly high-risk processing operations, controllers are required to log additional details.

Article 25 LED applies to all automated processing systems, which means that all law enforcement databases must be in compliance with the obligation to keep logs.[230] The logging requirement thus plays a crucial role in ensuring that law enforcement databases are not accessed without prior authorisation or for unjustified purposes.[231] At the same time, it is important that the logs are stored in compliance with the highest security standards, as each log contains a large amount of highly confidential information. This concerns not only personal data about the accessing of police officers, but also information about their working methods as well as the persons stored in the databases of competent authorities. Therefore, logs should only be kept for the purposes of verifying the lawfulness of processing, self-monitoring, integrity and security of the personal data and for criminal proceedings.[232]

Self-monitoring may include disciplinary proceedings against law enforcement officers who break or bend the rules, for instance, when consulting databases for personal reasons.[233] In addition, logs may be used for criminal proceedings, serving as evidence in such proceedings or against a perpetrator of another type of crime.[234] By matching consultation logs of a border control database, conclusions can be reached about the movements of a suspect. However, logs are above

[227] Under the Interoperability Regulations, the logs of the CIR shall be kept for one year: art 24(7) of Regulation (EU) 2019/817.

[228] There is no such time limit stipulated under Directive (EU) 2016/680, due to the nature of the legal instrument and the political decision not to go into that much detail. Hence, the individual time periods for the retention of logs need to be found either in the national transposition acts of the LED or the internal rules of procedure of the respective competent authority.

[229] Sajfert and Quintel (n 3).

[230] Quintel (n 6).

[231] ibid 16.

[232] Article 25(2) of Directive (EU) 2016/680.

[233] See intervention by Marit Hansen: 'CPDP 2020: DPAs, Policing and Law Enforcement', https://www.youtube.com/watch?v=0tJ0WV3sdU0&t=17s.

[234] Sajfert and Quintel (n 3).

all safeguards and should not lead to further interferences with the right to privacy and data protection.[235] When reading Article 25(2) LED closely, the use of logs in criminal proceedings would only be adequate when the lawfulness of a data processing operation is being challenged, when there is a security breach or when the integrity of personal data is at stake.[236]

The requirements that are linked to the logging obligation are presumed to be costly for the Member States and may prove difficult to implement, particularly in older automated processing systems. Therefore, Article 63(2) and (3) LED grants Member States a longer transposition period to implement Article 25(1) LED for databases set up before the entry into force of the Directive.[237] Exceptionally, Member States may take an additional five or even eight years to transpose this provision by 2023 or 2026, respectively, if the transposition causes massive costs or jeopardises the functioning of the database as such.[238] However, any new law enforcement system must include the logging possibility by default.

B. Data Protection Impact Assessment, Prior Consultation and Security of Processing

Chapter IV LED sets out the obligations for controllers and processors that fall within the scope of the Directive. Besides Article 20 LED, which requires Member States to implement the data protection by design and by default principles for all types of processing, the chapter also stipulates mandatory DPIAs and the prior consultation of the national DPA for certain types of processing operations, as well as the implementation of appropriate security measures.

Pursuant to Article 27 LED, the national legislator is supposed to make DPIAs[239] mandatory for high-risk processing operations or operations expected to lead to a high risk to the rights and freedoms of data subjects. In any event, a DPIA is to be carried out when a controller or processor intends to use new technologies, in order to be able to obtain a general overview of the impact that such processing may have on the rights and freedoms of the data subjects concerned. When carrying out their assessment, controllers are supposed to take into account the nature, scope, context and purpose of processing.[240] For instance, it should be considered whether the processing involves different types of data subjects (such as

[235] ibid.

[236] ibid. See also WP29, 'Opinion on Some Key Issues of the Law Enforcement Directive (EU 2016/680), Adopted on 29 November 2017'; and Teresa Quintel, 'Article 29 Data Protection Working Party Opinion on the Law Enforcement Directive' (2018) 4 *European Data Protection Law Review* 104.

[237] Sajfert and Quintel (n 3).

[238] ibid 17.

[239] In accordance with art 27(1) LED, a DPIA is an assessment of the impact of the envisaged processing operations on the protection of personal data.

[240] Article 27(1) of Directive (EU) 2016/680.

victims, perpetrators or witnesses) or special categories of personal data, whether the processing includes a large number of data subjects, whether there needs to be context-specific safeguards and whether the purpose could be achieved by other, less intrusive means.

In addition, DPIAs are also important where existing systems are updated or expanded, for instance, with new technological means for processing. At the same time, controllers may rely on an existing DPIA if it covers a similar processing operation with similar risks to the one envisaged.[241]

DPIAs should be beneficial for both controllers and processers, for multiple reasons. On the one hand, DPIAs may contribute to increasing awareness of any potential data protection issues that should be solved prior to engaging in new and risky processing operations. On the other hand, they may be very useful for establishing supplementary measures and adequate safeguards if these are necessary to achieve compliance with the LED.

In the same vein, the DPIA contributes to the accountability principle and supports compliance with another general obligation, the data protection by design and default principles.[242] Yet, it is crucial that the outcomes of a DPIA are integrated into the processing plan, which is to be reviewed and reassessed, if necessary, together with the DPA. For that purpose, the LED mandates the DPIA to include *at least* a general description of the envisaged processing operations, an assessment of the risks to the rights and freedoms of data subjects, the measures envisaged to address those risks, and safeguards, security measures and mechanisms to ensure the protection of personal data and to demonstrate compliance with this Directive.[243]

Compared to Article 35 GDPR,[244] the provision on DPIAs under the LED is far less detailed and neither requires the DPO to be involved when carrying out the DPIA[245] nor the DPA to establish a public list of the types of processing operations for which a DPIA shall be carried out.[246] Logically, the EDPB is not involved in the adoption of the list of processing operations that require a DPIA under the LED.[247] In addition, the LED does not refer to codes of conduct[248] and does not

[241] 'What is a DPIA?' (20 July 2020), https://ico.org.uk/for-organisations/guide-to-data-protection/guide-to-the-general-data-protection-regulation-gdpr/data-protection-impact-assessments-dpias/what-is-a-dpia.

[242] ibid.

[243] Article 27(2) of Directive 2016/680.

[244] See, for instance, O'Reilly Media, EU *General Data Protection Regulation (GDPR): An Implementation and Compliance Guide*, (IT Governance Publishing, 2016); Legitech and Lexing Belgique, *Protection des données personnelles: recueil de textes: textes de référence – guidelines – jurisprudences européennes et nationales* (Legitech, 2019); Shakila Bu-Pasha, 'The Controller's Role in Determining "High Risk" and Data Protection Impact Assessment (DPIA) in Developing Digital Smart City' (2020) 29 *Information & Communications Technology Law* 391.

[245] Article 35(2) of Regulation (EU) 2016/679.

[246] ibid art 35(4).

[247] As stipulated under ibid art 35(5), (6) and (7).

[248] ibid art 35(8).

require the views of data subjects or their representatives on the intended processing to be taken into account.[249]

While the obligation to carry out DPIAs did not exist under the 2008 Framework Decision, the latter had already included the prior consultation of national DPAs, albeit in a condensed form. This obligation was reinforced under Article 28 LED, which requires the controller to consult the national DPA prior to processing, which will form part of a new filing system to be created in two situations. First, the DPA must be consulted where the results of a DPIA suggest that processing would result in a high risk.[250] The second situation in which the supervisory authority must be consulted is when the type of processing, in particular where new technologies, mechanisms or procedures are being used, involves a high risk to the rights and freedoms of data subjects.[251] In addition and in accordance with Article 28(2) LED, the DPA is to be consulted during the preparation of a proposal for a legislative measure, or of a regulatory measure based on such a legislative measure that relates to the processing of personal data.

Article 28(3), (4) and (5) LED emphasises the possibility of supervisory authorities establishing a list of processing operations that require prior consultation, clarifies that controllers shall provide the DPA with information about high-risk processing operations and the results of DPIAs, and recalls that the supervisory authorities should use their powers[252] in the event that processing infringes the LED or identified risks have not been mitigated. Article 38 LED is worded in a similar way to Article 36 GDPR on prior consultation and, with the possibility of the DPA establishing a list of processing operations that require prior consultation, even confers an additional capability to the supervisory authority that the GDPR does not foresee. Yet, as will be shown below, the powers of the supervisory authorities under the Directive are weaker than those under the GDPR, and hence it might be more difficult to enforce Article 28 LED in a vigorous manner.

What might have a negative impact on data protection standards is the indication that for processing that complies with EU law applicable prior to the date of entry into force of the LED, the requirements of the Directive concerning the prior consultation of the supervisory authority do not apply.[253]

Similarly to the GDPR, the recitals of the LED suggest that the implementation of appropriate technical and organisational measures should not depend solely on economic considerations.[254] Such measures should take into account the results of any DPIA carried out in accordance with the LED. In addition, controllers subject to the Directive should adopt internal policies and implement measures

[249] ibid art 35(9).
[250] Article 28(1)(a) of Directive (EU) 2016/680.
[251] ibid art 28(1)(b).
[252] The powers of supervisory authorities under ibid art 47 will be discussed below.
[253] ibid Recital 96.
[254] Recital 83 of Regulation (EU) 2016/679 and Recital 53 of Directive (EU) 2016/680.

that adhere in particular to the principles of data protection by design and data protection by default, which are stipulated under Article 20 LED.[255]

Article 29 LED sets out the requirement for both controllers and processors to implement appropriate technical and organisational measures that correspond to the risk of a particular processing operation. Hence, the technical and organisational measures are to be adjusted to the risks that different processing operations may pose for data subjects' rights and freedoms, and according to the probability and severity of those risks. Due to their sensitive nature and the increased risk that arises when special categories of personal data are processed, Article 29(1) LED explicitly refers to Article 10 LED.

Where personal data are processed in an automated manner, Article 29(2) LED requires the controller and processor to evaluate the risk of the processing and, furthermore, to implement a set of measures to avert 10 incidents that would lead to data breaches. Paragraphs 2(a)–(j) of Article 29 LED list these incidents in detail: (a) denying unauthorised access; (b) preventing the unauthorised reading, copying, modification or removal of data; (c) preventing the unauthorised input of personal data and the unauthorised inspection, modification or deletion of stored personal data,; (d) preventing the use of automated processing systems by unauthorised persons; (e) ensuring that persons authorised to use an automated processing system have access only to the personal data covered by their access authorisation; (f) ensuring that it is possible to verify and establish the bodies to which personal data have been or may be transmitted; (g) ensuring that it is subsequently possible to verify and establish which personal data have been input into automated processing systems and when and by whom the personal data were input; (h) preventing the unauthorised reading, copying, modification or deletion of personal data during transfers of personal data or during transportation of data media; (i) ensuring that installed systems may, in the case of interruption, be restored; and (j) ensuring that the functions of the system perform, that the appearance of faults in the functions is reported and that stored personal data cannot be corrupted by means of a malfunctioning of the system.

Article 29 LED provides for higher security standards than its equivalent provision under the GDPR. On the one hand, Article 32 GDPR does not refer to special categories of personal data. On the other hand, this provision is worded in more general terms and where the Directive sets out a detailed list of incidents that shall be prevented, the GDPR suggests a rather broad checklist that needs to be complied with. The more detailed list under the Directive is to be welcomed and, at the same time, seems logical, given the fact that processing in the law enforcement context may lead to more severe incidents – for instance, if personal data are accessed by an unauthorised person. Therefore, Article 29 LED should be seen as an important provision that may contribute to a more secure processing

[255] Recital 53 of Directive (EU) 2016/680.

environment and that takes into account different types of data and different risks for individuals.

For both the provision on DPIAs and that on prior consultation, the LED mandates the national legislator to adopt a separate legal basis that provides for the DPIA and for the prior consultation requirements. The same holds true for the implementation of appropriate security measures under Article 29 LED and the notification of a personal data breach to the supervisory authority and the data subject,[256] which will be discussed below. Unfortunately, this makes it more likely that the provisions are not transposed in a correct manner and that the data subjects will find it more challenging to assert their rights under the Directive.

C. Notification of Data Breaches

The provisions under Article 30 LED on the notification of a personal data breach to the competent supervisory authority are more or less identical to those under Article 33 GDPR, with the exception that the Directive adds an additional safeguard under paragraph 6 that obliges controllers to inform other controllers of those data breaches where personal data have been transmitted.

Like the GDPR, the LED foresees a minimum set of information to be included in the data breach notification, which shall likewise be communicated to controllers to whom the personal data were transmitted.[257] In addition, and in accordance with paragraph 5 of Article 30 LED, the controller must document any personal data breach in order to provide such documentation to the supervisory authority on request to enable the latter to assess whether the controller acted in accordance with Article 30 LED.

Article 31 LED, the provision on the notification of data breaches to the data subject, likewise is equivalent to the provision under the GDPR. However, under paragraph 5 of that Article, the Directive allows controllers to delay, restrict or omit the notification of data subjects, given that the conditions and the grounds referred to in Article 13(3) LED are fulfilled. Thus, notification of data breached to data subjects may be delayed, restricted or omitted for as long as such a restriction/omission constitutes a necessary and proportionate measure in a democratic society with due regard for the fundamental rights and the legitimate interests of the natural person concerned, and only in order to avoid obstructing official or

[256] ibid arts 30 and 31.

[257] Under ibid art 30(3), controllers shall include the following information in the notification to the supervisory authority: (a) the nature of the personal data breach, including, where possible, the categories and approximate number of data subjects concerned and the categories and approximate number of personal data records concerned; (b) the name and contact details of the data protection officer or other contact point where more information can be obtained; (c) the likely consequences of the personal data breach; and (d) the measures taken or proposed to be taken by the controller to address the personal data breach, including, where appropriate, measures to mitigate its possible adverse effects.

legal inquiries, investigations or procedures, to avoid prejudicing the prevention, detection, investigation or prosecution of criminal offences or the execution of criminal penalties, or to protect public security national security or the rights and freedoms of others.

This paragraph is non-existent under the GDPR, but may prove useful in the law enforcement context – for instance, where personal data about suspects or perpetrators who are not aware that their data are being processed have been accessed in an unlawful manner. In such cases, the data subjects may not be informed of a potential data breach, so that Article 30 LED represents a safeguard in the sense that the national DPA should thoroughly examine all data breaches, in particular of those data subjects who were not informed of the breach.

VII. International Transfers of Personal Data

Because of the different level of data protection standards in the EU compared to other parts of the world, any data transfer outside the EU can only take place if certain conditions are fulfilled.[258] This is all the more important in the law enforcement context.[259]

Because the processing of personal data in the police and criminal justice area was, to a large extent, left outside the scope of EU law, a majority of the EU Member States adopted bilateral agreements with third countries to exchange information for law enforcement-related purposes.[260] The Directive does little to affect those bilateral agreements already in place, basically turning all existing agreements into definite ones.

Pursuant to Article 61 LED, agreements involving the transfer of personal data to third countries or international organisations that were concluded prior to 6 May 2016 remain in force until amended, provided that they complied with EU law before the adoption of the LED. In a nutshell, these agreements only need to comply with the Directive's standards if Member States decided to amend them after May 2018. National legislators are only encouraged, but not obliged, to amend these bilateral agreements in the near future. Consequently, if Member States do not take action, the prolonged existence of those bilateral agreements will lead to the application of lower standards than are required by the LED. This could undermine the framework set up for international data transfers under the Directive.[261] In the context of migration and border control where cooperation

[258] On this, see the following recent judgment: CJEU, Case C0311/18, *Data Protection Commissioner v Facebook Ireland Ltd and Maximilian Schrems*, ECLI:EU:C:2020:559, 16 July 2020 (hereinafter '*Schrems II*').

[259] This part of the analysis is mainly based on the following article: Sajfert and Quintel (n 3).

[260] ibid.

[261] Di Francesco Maesa (n 49).

takes place, for instance, with INTERPOL or third states, which are the countries of origin of TCNs, this represents a loophole. Where bilateral agreements between the Member States and those third countries were not reformed in order to satisfy the requirements under the LED, this leads to concerns regarding the rights of individuals whose personal data are transferred under those agreements.

A. General Principles Applicable to International Transfers

Under the LED, international transfers shall, as a general rule, be allowed only from one LEA to another,[262] subject to authorisation by the originating Member State. This rule also applies to any onward transfer from the receiving third country to another third country, which must seek prior authorisation from an authority in the Member State from which the original transfer was carried out.[263] As a side note, those specific conditions are applied to transfers of personal data to third countries only. The Member State from which the data originated may not impose conditions on recipients in EU Member States other than those applicable within its own jurisdiction.[264]

A transfer should be carried out only by competent authorities acting as controllers, except where processors are explicitly instructed to transfer personal data on behalf of controllers. In addition, the controller in the third country or international organisation must be an authority competent within the meaning of the Directive,[265] hence a public authority competent in the prevention, investigation, detection or prosecution of criminal offences or the execution of criminal penalties, including the safeguarding against (and the prevention of) threats to public security, or any other body or entity entrusted by Member State law to exercise public authority and public powers for the purposes of the prevention, investigation, detection or prosecution of criminal offences or the execution of criminal penalties, including the safeguarding against, and the prevention of, threats to public security. While this definition already causes difficulties within the EU Member States, it might include an even broader number of competent authorities in third countries.

The LED incorporates the three-step cascading system that was adopted under Articles 45–49 GDPR for international transfers.[266] Thus, under Article 36 LED,

[262] This provision in the Directive is similar to art 13 of its predecessor, the 2008 Framework Decision, but, other than under the Framework Decision, and as an important novelty, is subject to certain derogations. See Juraj Sajfert and Teresa Quintel, 'Data Protection Directive (EU) 2016/680 for Police and Criminal Justice Authorities', 1 December 2017, https://ssrn.com/abstract=3285873.

[263] Article 35(1)(e) of Directive (EU) 2016/680.

[264] ibid Recital 36.

[265] ibid Recital 64.

[266] Quintel (n 6).

transfers are carried out on the basis of an adequacy decision,[267] Article 37 LED permits transfers based on appropriate safeguards,[268] Article 38 LED allows for derogations from the general rules provided appropriate safeguards are in place and Article 39 LED introduces a provision under which transfers are allowed from EU LEAs to private entities in third countries.

B. The Self-Assessment Derogation

The approach of transferring personal data by way of appropriate safeguards gives more flexibility to controllers, as they may carry out a self-assessment of the safeguards available and the circumstances surrounding the international transfer.[269] This means that, on the one hand, Article 37(1) LED offers fewer options to controllers to transfer personal data by way of appropriate safeguards than the GDPR, while, on the other hand, the self-assessment provides a lot of leeway to the controller.

The procedure under Article 37(1) LED lays down two options to provide appropriate safeguards. Under paragraph (a), appropriate safeguards may be provided for in a legally binding instrument, such as an international agreement. Pursuant to paragraph (b), such a transfer may take place after the controller has assessed all the circumstances surrounding the transfer and has concluded that appropriate safeguards exist in the third country or international organisation.[270]

Under Article 37(2) and (3) LED, additional requirements with regard to the self-assessment of reporting obligations apply. Those obligations do not have to be fulfilled regarding transfers that are based on an international agreement. Under Article 37(2) LED, the controller shall report to the supervisory authority the categories of transfers that are carried out by way of self-assessment. Under Article 37(3) LED, transfers based on self-assessment must be documented and such documentation is to be made available to the supervisory authority on

[267] An adequacy decision is to be taken by the EU Commission, which must assess whether the third country in question ensures an adequate level of protection. In order to make such a decision, the Commission takes into account, inter alia, the rule of law, the respect for human rights or relevant data protection legislation and its implementation. On 2 February 2021, the EDPB adopted Recommendations on the adequacy referential under the LED. The aim of the Recommendation is to provide a list of elements to be examined when assessing the adequacy of a third country under the LED. The document recalls the concept and procedural aspects of adequacy according to the LED and the case law of the CJEU, and lays down the EU standards for data protection for police and judicial cooperation in criminal matters. See EDPB, 'Recommendations 01/2021 on the Adequacy Referential under the Law Enforcement Directive, Adopted on 2 February 2021'.

[268] For instance, legally binding bilateral agreements which have been concluded by the Member States and implemented in their legal order and which could be enforced by their data subjects, ensuring compliance with data protection requirements and the rights of the data subjects, including the right to obtain effective administrative or judicial redress; see Recital 71 of Directive 2016/680.

[269] Article 37(1)(b) of Directive (EU) 2016/680.

[270] Quintel (n 6).

request. Any such documentation must include the date and time of the transfer, information about the receiving competent authority, the justification for the transfer and the personal data transferred.

This means that supervisory authorities should strictly observe and scrutinise transfers that are carried out by way of self-assessment under Article 37(1)(b) LED. The CJEU in the *Schrems II* judgment also referred to the task of the supervisory authority to actively supervise the legality of transfers to third countries. Hence, there could be an interesting parallel drawn between the self-assessment provision under the LED and the Standard Contractual Clauses (SCCs) under the GDPR.[271] In addition, competent LEAs should take into account supplementary measures, as recommended by the EDPB, when carrying out transfers under Article 37(1)(b) LED.[272]

For the time being, there is only one international agreement in place that establishes a framework for the protection of personal data when transferred outside of the EU. The EU-US Umbrella Agreement[273] is supposed to provide for appropriate safeguards when international transfers between the EU and the US are being carried out.[274] However, other legally binding instruments concluded with third countries or international organisations may include provisions on appropriate safeguards too.[275]

Since there is no international agreement with INTERPOL currently in place, controllers use Article 37(1)(b) LED to transfer personal data to INTERPOL. Unfortunately, the first CJEU judgment on the LED in which the Court was asked to look at the question on whether transfers to INTERPOL are in conformity with

[271] In the aftermath of the *Schrems II* judgment, the EDPB issued recommendations on measures to supplement transfers of personal data that are subject to appropriate safeguards. Some of the points in the recommendations could be applied to transfers carried out by way of self-assessment under art 37 LED. See EDPB, 'Recommendations 01/2020 on Measures That Supplement Transfer Tools to Ensure Compliance with the EU Level of Protection of Personal Data' (2020), https://edpb.europa.eu/our-work-tools/public-consultations-art-704/2020/recommendations-012020-measures-supplement-transfer_en. See Theodore Christakis, '"Schrems III"? First Thoughts on the EDPB Post-*Schrems II* Recommendations on International Data Transfers (Part 1)' (*European Law Blog*, 13 November 2020), https://europeanlawblog.eu/2020/11/13/schrems-iii-first-thoughts-on-the-edpb-post-schrems-ii-recommendations-on-international-data-transfers-part-1.

[272] EDPB, Recommendations 01/2020 on measures that supplement transfer tools to ensure compliance with the EU level of protection of personal data (version 2.0, adopted on 18 June 2021).

[273] Agreement between the United States of America and the European Union on the protection of personal information relating to the prevention, investigation, detection, and prosecution of criminal offences [2016] OJ L336/3, 10 December 2016.

[274] On divergent opinions, see Meijers Committee, 'CM1613, Note on the EU-US Umbrella Agreement' (2016), https://www.statewatch.org/media/documents/news/2016/nov/meijers-committee-umbrella-agreement-note.pdf; Electronic Privacy Information Center, 'EPIC – EU-US Umbrella Agreement & Judicial Redress Act', https://epic.org/privacy/intl/data-agreement.

[275] Recital 71 refers to other legally binding instruments: 'Such legally binding instruments could, for example, be legally binding bilateral agreements which have been concluded by the Member States and implemented in their legal order and which could be enforced by their data subjects, ensuring compliance with data protection requirements and the rights of the data subjects, including the right to obtain effective administrative or judicial redress.'

the LED did not shed new light on the admissibility of the LED self-assessment regime regarding international transfers.[276] However, in the recent *Schrems II* judgment,[277] the CJEU provided several conditions applicable to international transfers under the GDPR that could also apply to such transfers carried out under the Directive. In light of this judgment, the Court suggested new guidance for controllers on how to carry out the self-assessment to identify appropriate safeguards in a third country.

C. General Derogations

The final step of the cascade on international transfers is Article 38 LED, under which the Directive allows Member States, in certain situations, to derogate from the conditions under Articles 36 and 37 LED. Article 38 LED provides a solution to carry out transfers on a case-by-case basis – for instance, in the case of immediate threats. In such a scenario, a transfer or a category of transfers to a third country or an international organisation may take place if it is necessary and certain conditions are fulfilled.

First, the derogation under Article 38 LED may only be used where neither an adequacy decision under Article 36 LED nor adequate safeguards in accordance with Article 37 LED are in place. Second, derogations are only permitted in individual cases and solely if they serve to protect the vital interests of the data subject or another person,[278] if they are instrumental in the prevention of an immediate threat in a Member State or a third country,[279] for the purposes under Article 1(1) LED,[280] or for the establishment, exercise or defence of legal claims.[281]

Under Article 38(2) LED, the transferring authority shall carry out a balancing test if it intends to transfer personal data based on paragraphs (d)[282] or (e).[283] Where the fundamental rights and freedoms of the data subject prevail over the public interest, international transfers on the basis of Article 38 LED may not take place.[284] Whether the fundamental rights and freedoms of the data subject prevail over the public interest is to be determined by the transferring authority. For obvious reasons, it is in that authority's interests to carry out the transfer. Therefore,

[276] CJEU, Case C-505/19, *WS v Bundesrepublik Deutschland*, ECLI:EU:C:2021:376, 12 May 2021.
[277] *Schrems II* (n 258).
[278] Article 38(1)(a) Directive (EU) 2016/680.
[279] ibid art 38(1)(c).
[280] ibid art 38(1)(d) – hence, for the purposes of the prevention, investigation, detection or prosecution of criminal offences or the execution of criminal penalties, including the safeguarding against and the prevention of threats to public security.
[281] ibid art 38(1)(e)
[282] In individual cases for the purposes set out in art 1(1).
[283] In an individual case for the establishment, exercise or defence of legal claims relating to the purposes set out in art 1(1).
[284] Sajfert and Quintel (n 3).

the transferring competent authority might be inclined to transfer the data, even if fundamental rights concerns may prevail.

In addition, the balancing test only needs to be carried out for two types of transfers, as all other grounds for transfers are deemed sufficiently urgent to justify the transfer based on Article 38 LED. As a counterbalance and safeguard, any transfers based on Article 38(1) LED shall be documented and made available to the supervisory authority on request.[285] The documentation shall include a justification for the transfer, the time and date of the transfer, and information about the receiving authority in the third country.

With regard to the derogation under Article 38 LED, the EDPB guidelines on derogations under Article 49 GDPR[286] could be used mutatis mutandis with regard to determining in which situations those provisions on derogations under both the LED and the GDPR may apply. In addition, the guidelines may prove useful with regard to the balancing test, which also has to be carried out for certain types of transfers under the GDPR.[287] For instance, in order to consider the rights and freedoms of the data subject, the possible negative effects[288] have to be carefully predicted and assessed by taking into account their likelihood and severity.[289] In addition, the role of 'suitable safeguards' in the context of balancing the interests of controllers and data subjects should be considered.[290] For the assessment of 'suitable safeguards' for the rights and freedoms of the data subject, the EDPB suggests in particular taking into account the nature of the data, the purpose and duration of the processing as well as the situation in the third country, and, if any, the country of final destination of the transfer.[291] It could also be argued that derogations under Article 38 LED should not, like those under the GDPR, be used in a repetitive manner, although the Directive, unlike the GDPR, does not explicitly exclude such an option.

The obligation to document the transfers that are carried out based on Article 38 LED should not, similarly to the obligation under the GDPR to inform the supervisory authority of transfers carried out by way of derogation, be seen as requiring the transfer to be authorised by the supervisory authority. Rather, the documentation should serve as a means to enable the supervisory authority to assess the data transfer as to its possible impact on the rights and freedoms of the data subjects affected and act *ex post*.[292]

[285] Article 38(3) of Directive (EU) 2016/680.

[286] EDPB, 'EDPB Guidelines 2/2018 on Derogations of Article 49 under Regulation 2016/679, Adopted on 25 May 2018' (2018).

[287] For the balancing test, see ibid 15–16.

[288] That is, the risks of the data transfer on any type of (legitimate) interest of the data subject.

[289] EDPB (n 286). See also Recital 75 of Regulation (EU) 2016/679.

[290] On this, see EDPB, 'Opinion 06/2014 on the Notion of Legitimate Interests of the Data Controller under Article 7 of Directive 95/46/EC, Adopted on 9 April 2014' (2014).

[291] EDPB (n 284) 16. See also Recital 113 of Regulation (EU) 2016/679.

[292] ibid 17.

D. Asymmetrical Transfers of Personal Data

Under certain conditions, Article 39 LED provides for so-called *asymmetrical transfers* from an LEA in an EU Member State directly to private parties situated in third countries.[293] This provision may be very useful for competent authorities in situations where the competent authority in the third country is not able to reply to a request, or where transfers cannot be carried out via official channels. Article 39 LED could therefore be viewed as the most innovative provision under Chapter V,[294] as it serves as a means to send personal data directly to third country service providers in order to request information in return, without using the official channels.

Due to the often burdensome and lengthy procedures required to request information via official channels, asymmetrical transfers provide a solution that facilitates enhanced cooperation with service providers in third countries. Hence, Article 39 LED establishes a derogation, for individual and specific cases, from the obligation under Article 35 to use the official channels for transfers only.[295] In order for Article 39 to apply, all other conditions of the Directive need to be satisfied. First, the legal basis for Article 39 transfers must be laid down in EU or Member State law in accordance with Article 8 LED.[296] In addition, 'asymmetrical transfers' must be strictly necessary and must relate to the investigation of a particular crime. Consequently, bulk transfers are not permitted under this provision. As a result, a clear link between the key tasks of the transferring authority and the need to transfer personal data must exist. Paragraph 1(c) of Article 39 LED stipulates that the transferring competent EU authority must consider a transfer to the competent authority in the third country in accordance with the procedure laid down in the previous articles ineffective or inappropriate. This may be the case where the transfer cannot be achieved in a timely manner. However, the competent authority in the third country should be informed of the transfer, unless this is impracticable. The latter would be the case, for instance, in a failed or corrupted state.[297] In addition, the fundamental rights and freedoms of the data subject may not override the public interest in the purpose(s) for which the asymmetrical transfer is carried out.[298] Finally, the service providers must be informed about the specific purpose or purposes for which the data that were transferred may be processed. Whenever processing takes place, it must be necessary.[299]

In addition to the above conditions, Article 39 LED imposes further requirements on competent LEAs where requests to receive personal data are addressed

[293] Sajfert and Quintel (n 3) 7.
[294] ibid 19.
[295] ibid.
[296] ibid.
[297] See art 39(1)(d) of Directive (EU) 2016/680.
[298] ibid art 39(1)(b).
[299] ibid art 39(1)(e).

to service providers in third countries. First, transfers under Article 39 LED may only be carried out if they are strictly necessary for the investigation of a particular criminal offence and if all other options under Articles 36–38 LED to transfer the data are exhausted.[300] Second, the supervisory authority in the EU Member State of the transferring authority must be informed of the transfer and the latter must be documented for *ex post* review.[301]

Any 'asymmetrical transfers' that are carried out by way of derogation should be monitored by the national supervisory authorities. The latter, after having been notified whenever transfers under Article 39 LED take place,[302] may impose a temporary or definite limitation or ban on processing.[303] In order to guarantee an effective review, it would be advisable to invest sufficient resources into the national supervisory authorities in order to enable them to approach the respective national LEAs and other criminal justice authorities with greater authority and to carry out their work in a meaningful manner.[304]

The LED aims to balance the flexibility needed for carrying out transfers to third countries for the purposes set out in Article 1(1) LED with the data protection rights of the individuals concerned.[305] While such flexibility is required for the investigation of criminal offences and the safeguarding of public security, when personal data cross borders, this may put at increased risk the ability of natural persons to exercise their data protection rights and to protect themselves from the unlawful use or disclosure of their personal data.[306]

Oversight powers of supervisory authorities within the Member States are reduced once the data have left the EU. This is particularly true for onward transfers by third countries and international transfers that are carried out without establishing their basis on an adequacy decision. The execution of international transfers requires close overview by the Member States' supervisory authorities, strict interpretation of derogations and *ex post* review of documented transfers in order to protect data subjects' fundamental rights.

While the LED certainly contributes to a less fragmented general framework for international transfers, it cannot cover all the fields in which transfers of data might take place. Pursuant to Article 2(3)(a) of the Directive, transfers of personal data between authorities responsible for safeguarding national security will not be covered by the provisions, as these generally fall outside the scope of the Directive. This may become particularly problematic in Member States where intelligence

[300] Sajfert and Quintel (n 3) 19.
[301] Article 39(4) of Directive (EU) 2016/680.
[302] ibid art 39(3).
[303] ibid art 47(1)(c).
[304] Sajfert and Quintel (n 3) 20.
[305] ibid.
[306] Recital 74 of Directive 2016/680.

agencies and LEAs form part of the same organisational structure and data are commonly exchanged between these authorities.[307]

The provisions on international transfers facilitate exchanges between the EU competent authorities and their counterparts in third countries, while providing higher data protection standards than the LED's predecessor. However, when comparing the rules under the LED with those under the GDPR, much leeway is given to the competent authorities to transfer personal data even without the existence of an adequacy decision or an international agreement. For instance, the self-assessment option under Article 37 LED provides broad powers to the competent authorities to apply that provision discretionally. Hence, Article 37 LED could be used in order to circumvent stricter provisions.

In the migration context, the competent authorities might find ways to transfer personal data under Article 37 LED where such transfers should normally be carried out within the scope of the GDPR. For instance, for returns of rejected asylum seekers, a competent authority could argue that the personal data of a person who has also committed a crime could be transferred for both purposes conjointly under the LED, despite the fact that returns are generally a purely administrative task.

Moreover, with regard to Article 39 LED on 'asymmetrical transfers', there is a risk that third-country authorities would demand reciprocal commitments and require private companies in the EU to likewise disclose personal data directly to their LEAs, although those obliged entities would nevertheless have to comply with the rules under the GDPR, and there are currently provisions on the table for similar transfers in other areas between public and private bodies.[308] Therefore, it is important that the supervisory authorities exercise their monitoring powers vigorously in order to prevent any misuses of the possibility to carry out 'asymmetrical transfers'.

VIII. The Role of Data Protection Supervisory Authorities

Not much has been written about data protection supervisory authorities,[309] and even less about DPAs supervising police and criminal justice authorities within

[307] For instance, in Lithuania, Poland and Sweden. See Sajfert and Quintel (n 3).

[308] For instance, the US CLOUD Act, the EU Commission's e-Evidence proposal and the amendments to the CoE Cybercrime Convention; see Cole and Quintel (n 205).

[309] See, for instance, Hijmans (n 14); Şandru Şandru and Simona Şandru, 'Le Contrôle des Règles sur la Protection des Données à Caractère Personnel par l'intermédiaire des Autorités Administratives Indépendantes' [2015] *Revista Română de Drept Comparat* 165; Ulrik Fredrik Thyve, 'One-Stop-Shop – or Not? The Regulation of Competent Supervisory Authority in the New EU General Data Protection Regulation: Does the One-Stop-Shop Mechanism Live up to its Promise?', https://www.duo.uio.no/handle/10852/54556; David Barnard-Wills, Cristina Pauner Chulvi and Paul de Hert, 'Data Protection Authority Perspectives on the Impact of Data Protection Reform on Cooperation in the EU' (2016) 32 *Computer Law & Security Review* 587; Francis Aldhouse, 'A Reflection on the Priorities of a Data

the scope of the LED.[310] The same holds true for existing jurisprudence at the EU level, which comprises three cases on supervisory authorities – all under Directive 95.[311] On the one hand, this is rather disappointing and may reflect the perception of a general public that sees the role of DPAs as negligible. On the other hand, it is logical that not many publications exist on DPAs in the law enforcement context, as the 95 Directive did not apply in that area and only a few Member States had established DPAs that were also competent to supervise police and criminal justice authorities.

DPAs serve a role of independent administrative authorities and are unique organisations that perform a pivotal function in defending fundamental rights.[312] The entry into force of the EU Charter, and particularly Article 8(3) thereof, emphasises the importance of independent supervision in order to guarantee an effective right to the protection of personal data. Logically, this applies to all processing of personal data that would fall within the scope of EU law and hence also the processing of personal data by competent LEAs.

Yet, the separation between the GDPR and the LED – general and law enforcement processing – also continued the separation between supervisory authorities that are provided with different competences and powers that already existed under the 95 Directive and the 2008 DPFD. Evidently, particularities with regard to the supervision of the police and other law enforcement or criminal justice authorities exist.

On the one hand, the police are one of the most regulated public authorities and are subject to strict rules on how they may process personal data. On the other hand, there are a large number of areas where much discretion is given to the police. This also applies with regard to the processing of personal data – for instance, when police apply predictive policing techniques or profiling tools. Because these types of processing operations may be particularly harmful for individuals, effective supervision in the area where the LED applies seems *at least*

Protection Authority' (2018) 34 *Computer Law & Security Review* 816; European Union Agency for Fundamental Rights, *Strengthening the Fundamental Rights Architecture in the EU.II, Data Protection in the European Union: The Role of National Data Protection Authorities* (Publications Office, 2010); and European Union Agency for Fundamental Rights, *Access to Data Protection Remedies in EU Member States* (Publications Office, 2013). In addition, the activity reports of the supervisory authorities in the Member States may be a useful source of information, albeit often neglecting Directive (EU) 2016/680 in comparison to Regulation (EU) 2016/679.

[310] Sajfert and de Hert (n 53).

[311] For instance, CJEU, Case C-518/07, *European Commission v Federal Republic of Germany*, ECLI:EU:C:2010:125, 9 March 2010; or CJEU, Case C-614/10, *Action under Article 258 TFEU for failure to fulfil obligations, brought on 22 December 2010*, ECLI:EU:C:2012:631, 16 October 2012. For case comments, see, for instance, Alexander Balthasar, '"Complete Independence" of National Data Protection Supervisory Authorities; Second Try: Comments on the Judgment of the CJEU of 16 October 2012, C-614/10, with Due Regard to its Previous Judgment of 9 March 2010, C-518/07' (2013) 9 *Utrecht Law Review* 26. It needs to be noted that the CJEU in the *Schrems* cases as well as in the case *Facebook Ireland Ltd. v Gegevensbeschermingsautoriteit* acknowledges the crucial role of supervisory authorities, see: CJEU, Case C-654/19, *Facebook Ireland Ltd. v Gegevensbeschermingsautoriteit*, ECLI:EU:C:2021:483, 15 June 2021.

[312] Sajfert and de Hert (n 53) 247.

as important as GDPR supervision. Therefore, it is to be welcomed that the Directive seeks to strengthen DPA competences and powers.

In terms of supervision, the LED departs significantly from the provisions of the GDPR.[313] Whilst under the GDPR, the list of powers granted to the supervisory authorities is quite extensive, the Directive only provides for the minimum harmonisation of those powers.[314] Hence, while Article 58 GDPR grants substantive investigative, corrective, authorisation and advisory powers, the LED leaves more leeway to the Member States to regulate the powers of their supervisory authorities. Consequently, the effectiveness of the powers of the national supervisory authorities very much depends on whether and how those authorities make use of them. Nevertheless, Article 47 of the Directive stipulates that the supervisory authority shall have *effective* investigative, corrective and advisory powers. Moreover, the LED obliges controllers to consult the supervisory authority where new filing systems may lead to high-risk processing operations.[315]

The LED puts more emphasis on the role of competent supervisory authorities than its predecessor. It acknowledges that more than one authority might be needed to meet the particular circumstances of different legal systems and that specific supervisory authorities whose activity is limited to a specific area may be put in place.[316] At the same time, Member States are free to establish one supervisory authority that is competent for the supervision of both the LED and the GDPR.[317] The vast majority of EU Member States have chosen the latter option, with only Belgium having established two different DPAs – one competent to supervise the application of the GDPR and the other responsible within the scope of application of the LED. It is debatable whether the choice to set up two different DPAs is to be recommended.

Just like under the GDPR, DPAs supervising the police and criminal justice authorities must act in complete independence in the performance of their tasks and powers.[318] Complete independence when supervising public authorities may be more challenging for DPAs than when supervising private companies under the GDPR. Being public authorities themselves, supervisory authorities might be more lenient towards other public authorities than towards companies that generate profit by processing personal data.

In order to secure their independence, each supervisory authority is to be equipped with sufficient technical, financial and human resources, as well as with the necessary premises and infrastructure in order to enable it to perform its tasks and powers in accordance with the provisions under the LED. Hence,

[313] ibid.
[314] ibid 251.
[315] Article 27(a) of Directive (EU) 2016/680.
[316] ibid art 41(1).
[317] ibid art 41(3).
[318] ibid art 42(1) and (2).

Article 42 LED on DPA independence is similar to the equivalent provision under the GDPR.[319]

Besides the rules on the appointment of the members of the supervisory authority, which are set out under Articles 43 and 44 LED and are similar to the conditions set out under the GDPR, one important factor of DPA independence is that supervisory authorities are equipped with sufficient funding as well as with an independent budget that is free from governmental influence. In addition, a lack of funding represents a significant challenge to the effective exercise of DPAs' tasks.[320]

For a while, the lack of adequate funding of supervisory authorities has been an issue and highlighted as a problem in many Member States.[321] While this may have been explainable with a less stringent legal framework under the 95 Directive and the 2008 DPFD, respectively,[322] both the GDPR and the LED[323] certainly reinforced and strengthened the role of national supervisory authorities, including requiring that the DPA be provided with sufficient funding. However, already in 2020, a report from found that half of the EU supervisory authorities, besides other structural issues, are provided with an insufficient budget that amounts to less than €5 million.[324] Although the report refers only to supervisory authorities dealing with GDPR compliance, it is to be assumed that the picture does not look better for the LED.

First, most Member States established one DPA for the supervision of both the GDPR and the LED, and thus the funding would have to be distributed within that authority. Second, looking at the importance attributed to the GDPR in relation to the LED, it would be surprising if LED supervision were to be given more funding. In addition, although there are no statistics available concerning data breaches under the LED, these are less likely to be reported and probably less severely prosecuted than those under the GDPR, as most Member States chose to exclude public authorities, including LEAs, from receiving administrative fines.

In the same vein, it seems essential that supervisory authorities are sufficiently funded in order to be able to perform their tasks independently and effectively.

[319] Article 52 of Regulation (EU) 2016/679.

[320] European Union Agency for Fundamental Rights, *Strengthening the Fundamental Rights Architecture* (n 307) 20.

[321] See ibid.

[322] Neither Directive 46/95/EC nor Framework Decision 2008/977/JHA mentions the funding of supervisory authorities.

[323] Article 52(4) of Regulation (EU) 2016/679 and Article 42(4) of Directive (EU) 2016/680 state that: 'Each Member State shall ensure that each supervisory authority is provided with the human, technical and financial resources, premises and infrastructure necessary for the effective performance of its tasks and exercise of its powers.'

[324] A total of 14 DPAs receive budgets of under €5 million according to a study. For instance, Estonia's government allocated the third-smallest annual budget (€750,331) in 2019 and made no increase to this in 2020. Although Estonia is a small Member State, this amount seems to be very low. See Johnny Ryan, 'New Data on GDPR Enforcement Agencies Reveal Why the GDPR is Failing' (*Brave Browser*, 27 April 2020), https://brave.com/dpa-report-2020 (hereinafter Brave Report').

This should include not only financial resources but also the equipment, well-trained staff and technical expertise. As the 2020 Brave Report revealed, only six of the 28 national supervisory authorities have more than 10 tech specialists within their staff, which means that there is no genuine capacity to investigate new processing techniques.[325] With regard to law enforcement processing, and especially when it comes to advanced predictive policing and AI technologies that may increasingly be used by LEAs in the future, it is important that DPAs will be able to scrutinise such systems. In addition, thorough knowledge of the legal framework is of utmost importance. Hence, DPAs should assume the role of assisting the police to transpose and implement the LED, for instance, by organising training sessions together with police DPOs.

Article 45 LED sets out the competence of supervisory authorities within the scope of the LED and recognises the integrity and independence of the judiciary by clarifying that DPAs are not competent to supervise courts and other independent judicial authorities when these are acting in their judicial capacity.[326] In turn, this means that if the latter is not the case, DPAs are competent to supervise the processing activities of courts and other judicial authorities.[327]

It would be advisable to interpret this provision restrictively, as in some Member States, certain competent authorities obtain the same independent status as judges.[328] In addition, problems may arise with regard to the extension of the meaning of 'supervision of courts acting in their judicial capacity'. In certain Member States, where courts may give orders to the police, prosecutors or other LEAs, the latter may be regarded as acting in their judicial capacity as conferred by the those courts.[329] This is highly problematic, as those authorities would then be able to claim that they do not fall within the scope of the LED as long as they carry out court orders. Hence, there is a need for an alternative supervision mechanism, such as internal judicial supervisory panels, in situations where supervisory authorities are not competent to scrutinise processing activities by courts.[330]

While under the GDPR, supervisory authorities obtained six investigative,[331] 10 corrective[332] and 10 advisory powers,[333] the LED merely provides for a minimum harmonisation of investigative powers,[334] some advisory powers[335] and three corrective powers.[336] Consequently, and although DPA powers under the LED

[325] ibid.

[326] Article 57(a) of Regulation (EU) 2018/1725 foresees a similar exemption for the CJEU when the Court acts in its judicial capacity. Its predecessor, Regulation (EC) 45/2001, set out this exemption in its Article 46(c).

[327] Sajfert and de Hert (n 53) 248–49.

[328] For instance, public prosecutors in Italy. See ibid 249.

[329] This is the case, for instance, in Belgium.

[330] Sajfert and de Hert (n 53) 249.

[331] Article 58(1) of Regulation (EU) 2016/679.

[332] ibid art 58(2).

[333] In accordance with ibid art 58(3).

[334] Article 47(1) of Directive (EU) 2016/680.

[335] ibid art 47(2).

[336] ibid art 47(3).

are supposed to be *effective*, the list of powers of supervisory authorities competent under the LED is very much reduced compared to the list under the GDPR, which demonstrates the reluctance of the Member States to make their national LEAs subject to independent supervision.[337] In addition, there is no cooperation between DPAs envisaged under the LED such as the EDPB cooperation under the GDPR, except for the provision on mutual assistance in Article 50 LED.

Under the LED, DPAs have exclusive territorial jurisdiction, meaning that each of the supervisory authorities is only competent to supervise its 'own' national LEAs. Although data subjects may approach a supervisory authority from another Member State with their access request, that authority would then forward the request to the DPA that is in charge under the LED. Hence, the complaint handling framework under Articles 52–55 LED deviates from the one under the GDPR in the sense that it is based on the reality that LEAs and other criminal justice authorities operate, unlike multinational companies that process personal data within the scope of the GDPR, within their national jurisdiction only. Consequently, the GDPR sought to remedy the circumstance that companies had to be acquainted with 28 different laws and deal with 28 different DPAs, whereas the area in which the LED applies does not concern entities that operate across borders in most of the cases.[338]

Nevertheless, overall, the complaint-handling framework that the Directive established is quite comprehensive and has strengthened data subjects' ability to exercise their right with the national supervisory authorities. Besides the right to lodge a complaint with a supervisory authority[339] and the opportunity to seek an effective judicial remedy against the decision of a DPA[340] and against the controller or processor,[341] data subjects have the right to mandate non-profit organisations to represent their case,[342] and a right to compensation.[343] In addition, with Article 50 LED on mutual assistance, the legislator also recognised that a minimum amount of cooperation among DPAs under the Directive is needed, given the increasing cross-border operations in criminal cases at an EU level. Against that background, it is regrettable that the EDPB did not issue one single document on cooperation under the LED. Particularly in the context of migration and border management, TCNs such as asylum seekers might not be able to read or write, let alone know about their data subject rights under EU data protection law. Therefore, the DPAs play an important role in terms of assisting and even acting on behalf of such vulnerable group of data subjects.

[337] In addition, DPAs under Directive (EU) 2016/680 did not obtain the power to initiate court proceedings against controllers or processors who violated the provisions under the Directive; hence, the Directive did not establish an improvement when compared to Framework Decision 2008/977/JHA. See Sajfert and de Hert (n 53) 253.

[338] ibid 254.

[339] Article 52 of Directive (EU) 2016/680.

[340] ibid art 53.

[341] ibid art 54.

[342] ibid art 55.

[343] ibid art 56.

IX. Existing EU Legal Acts and Commission Reports

On 24 June 2020, the Commission issued a Communication on the way forward on aligning the former Third Pillar *acquis* with data protection rules.[344] In the Communication, the Commission set out its intention to conduct a review of EU legal acts in the field of judicial cooperation in criminal matters that regulate the processing of personal data between Member States, as well as instruments governing access by national authorities to EU databases and which do not comply with the provisions of the LED. The Communication builds on Article 62(6) LED,[345] which requires the Commission to conduct such a review in order to bring the applicable personal data protection rules laid down in other EU acts in line with the Directive to ensure a consistent approach to the protection of personal data within the scope of the LED.[346]

Article 62(2) LED requires the review to be conducted in a much broader and more general manner, while leaving it up to the Commission to assess whether the proposal of changes to the legal acts in question is necessary. Hence, Article 62(2) LED does indeed foresee, in a more general manner, a review of such acts and provides for legislative changes where these are deemed necessary by the Commission. Such a review had evidently been neglected, given that the Communication was issued with more than a one-year delay.[347] In addition, the Communication was published at the same time as the Commission report that is required under Article 97(1) GDPR,[348] which left the LED Communication virtually unnoticed.

Based on a study that was carried out as part of the European Parliament Pilot Project 'Fundamental Rights Review of EU Data Collection Instruments and Programmes',[349] the Commission identified 26 EU legal acts falling under the review exercise.[350] Out of these 26, the Commission concluded that 16 would not

[344] 'Communication from the Commission to the European Parliament and the Council: Way Forward on Aligning the Former Third Pillar Acquis with Data Protection Rules' COM (2020) 262 final (hereinafter 'the Communication').

[345] In contrast, art 60 LED provides for a 'grandfathering' clause by which the specific provisions for the protection of personal data in certain EU legal acts that were adopted prior to 6 May 2016 shall remain unaffected. Article 60 LED is worded in a quite specific manner, referring only to those provisions of legal acts that deal with the protection of personal data and access by designated authorities.

[346] COM (2020) 262 final (n 344) 1.

[347] Article 62(2) of Directive (EU) 2016/680 anticipated the review for 6 May 2019.

[348] That report had only been delayed by a few weeks, as it was supposed to be published by 25 May 2020.

[349] The Pilot Project was requested by the European Parliament, managed by the Commission and carried out by a contractor (group of independent experts). The Commission selected the contractor on the basis of criteria defined by the European Parliament. The deliverables of the project reflect the views and opinions only of the contractor, and the Commission cannot be held responsible for any use which may be made of the information contained therein. The results can be viewed at https://www.fondazionebrodolini.it/en/projects/pilot-project-fundamental-rights-review-eu-data-collection-instruments-and-programmes.

[350] The legal acts regulating the processing of personal data by the competent authorities adopted or already amended after entry into force of the LED do not fall under this review as these acts already

need to be revised,[351] while 10[352] of them were not fully in line with the LED and would therefore require amendments.[353] In order to align these 10 legal instruments with the rules under the LED, the Commission proposed targeted amendments between the end of 2020 and the last quarter of 2021.[354]

The rather disappointing delay in the following-up on amending legal acts that are not in conformity with the provisions of the LED fits too well within the Commission's poor track record in starting infringement proceedings against Member States for the non-transposition of the Directive, or the commonly incomplete national transposition acts. Evidently, it was to be expected that the LED would receive much less attention than the GDPR, due to the smaller number of individuals affected by processing carried out within the scope of the Directive. However, given the impact of such processing on the rights and freedoms of data

took into account the requirements of the LED; see 'Communication from the Commission to the European Parliament and the Council: Way Forward on Aligning the Former Third Pillar Acquis with Data Protection Rules' COM (2020) 262 final, 2.

[351] Out of these 16, seven do not contain specific data protection rules and Directive (EU) 2016/680 applies, three refer to the Framework Decision 2008/977/JHA (Directive (EU) 2016/680 states in its art 59 that references to Council Framework Decision 2008/977/JHA shall be construed as references to Directive (EU) 2016/680) and do not contain specific data protection rules beyond the reference to Framework Decision 2008/977/JHA, two are currently under negotiation (Eurodac and the VIS) and four are international agreements that contain rules on the processing of personal data by competent authorities for purposes of law enforcement and are subject to national laws transposing Directive (EU) 2016/680.

[352] Council Framework Decision 2002/465/JHA of 13 June 2002 on joint investigation teams [2002] OJ L162/1; Council Decision 2005/671/JHA of 20 September 2005 on the exchange of information and cooperation concerning terrorist offences [2005] OJ L253/22; Council Decision 2006/960/JHA of 18 December 2006 on simplifying the exchange of information and intelligence between law enforcement authorities of the Member States of the European Union [2005] OJ L386/89; Council Decision 2007/845/JHA of 6 December 2007 concerning cooperation between Asset Recovery Offices of the Member States in the field of tracing and identification of proceeds from, or other property related to, crime [2007] OJ L332/103; Council Decision 2008/615/JHA of 23 June 2008 on the stepping up of cross-border cooperation, particularly in combating terrorism and cross-border crime [2008] OJ L210/1 and Council Decision 2008/616/JHA of 23 June 2008 on the implementation of Decision 2008/615/JHA on the stepping up of cross-border cooperation, particularly in combating terrorism and cross-border crime [2008] OJ L210/12; Council Decision 2009/917/JHA of 30 November 2009 on the use of information technology for customs purposes [2009] OJ L323/20; Agreement between the European Union and Japan on mutual legal assistance in criminal matters [2010] OJ L39/20; Directive 2014/41/EU of the European Parliament and of the Council of 3 April 2014 regarding the European Investigation Order in criminal matters [2014] OJ L130/1; Directive (EU) 2015/413 of the European Parliament and of the Council of 11 March 2015 facilitating cross-border exchange of information on road-safety-related traffic offences [2015] OJ L68/9; and Directive (EU) 2016/681 of the European Parliament and of the Council of 27 April 2016 on the use of passenger name record (PNR) data for the prevention, detection, investigation and prosecution of terrorist offences and serious crime [2016] OJ L119/132. See Annexes to the Communication from the Commission to the European Parliament and the Council: Way Forward on Aligning the Former Third Pillar Acquis with Data Protection Rules' COM (2020) 262 final, Brussels, 24 June 2020.

[353] 'Communication from the Commission to the European Parliament and the Council: Way Forward on Aligning the Former Third Pillar Acquis with Data Protection Rules' COM (2020) 262 final, 2.

[354] However, at the time of writing, those proposals that were issued have not been adopted. An analysis of the implementation of Directive (EU) 2016/681 was already initiated in the last quarter of 2019. See ibid 12.

subjects, not only in the context of law enforcement but also where the criminalisation of migration takes place, it is dangerous to ignore the lack of transposition in the Member States or to neglect the revision of legal acts in the field of law enforcement.

X. Conclusion

This chapter has illustrated some of the main improvements that came about with the adoption of the LED in terms of fundamental rights of individuals when their personal data were processed by competent EU LEAs for law enforcement purposes. Despite being a minimum harmonisation instrument, the Directive represents a major amelioration when compared to the 2008 DPFD regarding many provisions. This holds true not only for data subject rights and obligations for controllers, but also concerning the rules on international transfers and regarding the role of data protection supervisory authorities. Even when compared to the GDPR, some of the Directive's provisions may offer a higher degree of protection – for instance, with regard to the categorisation of personal data, automated decision-making or security measures that are to be implemented by the controller.

At the same time, the preceding sections exemplified some of the main differences between the LED and the GDPR in order to demonstrate the potentially negative effects for individuals if their personal data are processed within the scope of the Directive instead of the GDPR. In short, while the Directive introduced considerable improvements regarding the rights and freedoms of data subjects for processing in the law enforcement context, this observation changes when personal data are processed within the grey areas between the LED and the GDPR. Hence, in situations where it is not entirely clear whether the Directive may be applied or whether processing should be carried out within the scope of the GDPR, it is questionable whether the competent authorities could revert to the 'weaker' instrument and thereby lower data subject rights and data protection standards.

In addition, it is essential to take into account the laws transposing the LED in order to ascertain its scope of application at a national level and to locate potential gaps where the provisions were not transposed correctly. On the one hand, it is crucial to identify the authorities that may fall within the scope of Article 3(7) LED, and thus the definition of competent authorities that may process personal data within the scope of the Directive in a Member State. On the other hand, it is important to look at the national laws to determine what is included in the processing of personal data for the 'prevention, investigation, detection and prosecution of criminal offences' and in order to ascertain for what kind of processing activities the LED may be applied in each Member State. Moreover, sectoral laws may intersect with both the GDPR and the LED, and thus allow LEAs to process personal data within the scope of the Directive on separate grounds.

As has been illustrated, one of the grey areas between the GDPR and the LED is the area of border control, migration and asylum. Particularly in the migration context, the blurred scope between the GDPR and the LED may lead to the processing of personal data of migrants and other TCNs within the scope of the Directive. This may be the case where competent LEAs access and subsequently process personal data from AFSJ databases or, in the future, the interoperability components. LEAs could also attempt to process personal data of TCNs within the scope of the LED when carrying out random identity checks. Depending on the grounds for return, and whether the authority carrying out such a return is a competent authority within the scope of the LED in a Member State, personal data could even be transferred to third countries within the scope of the Directive instead of the GDPR. Finally, when exchanging personal data with EU Agencies – for instance, within the framework of EUROSUR – border guards who are defined as competent authorities under the LED could apply the latter and use the more flexible rules to exchange personal data.

In instances where it is not clear for what purpose personal data are processed, or where LEAs may argue that the processing of TCNs' personal data is carried out for law enforcement purposes, many national transposition acts leave a wide margin of appreciation for LEAs to apply the Directive and thus risk a lowering of data protection rights for TCNs.

4

The Blurred Line between EU Law Enforcement Agencies and EU Migration Agencies

With the establishment of the AFSJ and the entry into force of the Lisbon Treaty, many EU Agencies were attributed new competences in order to pool both technical and specialised expertise at the EU level with a view to enhancing cooperation among Member States, and between the EU level and the national level.[1]

With the 2015 migration crisis, certain EU Agencies started to play a more pivotal role in migration and border management. Instead of only national authorities handling the implementation of the EU asylum policy, the institutionalisation of practical cooperation through EU Agencies brought players such as the EBCGA, the then European Asylum Support Office (since 2021, the European Union Agency for Asylum (EUAA)) and Europol to the forefront of such matters.[2] These Agencies became increasingly involved in information exchange and the training of national staff such as border guards and asylum officers, but also in the identification, security screenings and risk analysis of TCNs, as well as in assistance for return operations.[3] While operationally assisting the national competent authorities in the Member States, these EU Agencies often further developed their expertise and naturally expanded their own mandate, which was later codified either in the form of specialised centres at the respective agency or through legislation and by amending the agency's constituting act.

The increasing opportunities for those Agencies to process the personal data of TCNs went hand in hand with the initiatives on the expansion of AFSJ databases and facilitated data exchanges through interoperability. Two EU Agencies in particular, the EBCGA and Europol, were not only engaged physically in

[1] Anne Weyembergh, Ines Armada and Chloe Briere, 'Competition or Cooperation: State of Play and Future Perspectives on the Relations between Europol, Eurojust and the European Judicial Network' (2015) 6 *New Journal of European Criminal Law* 258, 259.

[2] Evangelia Tsourdi, 'Holding the European Asylum Support Office Accountable for its Role in Asylum Decision-Making: Mission Impossible? Border Justice: Migration and Accountability for Human Rights Violations' (2020) 21 *German Law Journal* 506, 507.

[3] Kimara Davis, 'The European Union's Dublin Regulation and the Migrant Crisis Notes' (2020) 19 *Washington University Global Studies Law Review* 261, 281.

the hotspots[4] or participated in different missions. Both Agencies also progressively engaged in the processing of personal data of TCNs, being responsible for the identification, registration and carrying out of secondary security checks on TCNs.[5] Furthermore, both Agencies are supposed to contribute to tackling cross-border crime such as migrant smuggling and trafficking in human beings, thereby collecting, analysing and exchanging personal data with Member State authorities and additional EU bodies.[6]

This chapter analyses some of the discrepancies that may arise in a context where systematic data exchanges take place between actors that apply different data protection regimes when processing personal data for migration management, border control and security purposes. For that purpose, this section will address those EU Agencies that are active in the AFSJ, namely Europol, the EBCGA and Eurojust. The following sections will give an overview of these AFSJ agencies, their role in the context of AFSJ databases, illustrate the major changes introduced to their mandates to process personal data and highlight certain inconsistencies between the data protection regimes applicable to the EBCGA, Europol and Eurojust.

I. Overview of the Respective Agencies

A. The European Border and Coast Guard Agency

The European Border and Coast Guard, composed of the European Border and Coast Guard Agency (Frontex)[7] and the national competent authorities responsible for border management, is the central pillar of the EU's integrated border management.[8] Frontex, as the European Agency for the Management

[4] See, for instance, the definition under art 2(10) of Regulation (EU) 2016/1624: 'hotspot area' means an area in which the host Member State, the Commission, relevant EU agencies and participating Member States cooperate, with the aim of managing an existing or potential disproportionate migratory challenge characterised by a significant increase in the number of migrants arriving at the external borders. On the hotspot approach, see A Vradis et al, 'Governing Mobility in Times of Crisis: Practicing the Border and Embodying Resistance in and beyond the Hotspot Infrastructure' (2020) 38 *Environment and Planning D: Society and Space* 981; and Katharyne Mitchell and Matthew Sparke, 'Hotspot Geopolitics versus Geosocial Solidarity: Contending Constructions of Safe Space for Migrants in Europe' (2020) 38 *Environment and Planning D: Society and Space* 1046.

[5] Europol, 'Europol Setting up Team of 200 Investigators to Deploy to Migration Hotspots', https://www.europol.europa.eu/newsroom/news/europol-setting-team-of-200-investigators-to-deploy-to-migration-hotspots.

[6] See, for instance, Council of the European Union, Final Report Future Group on Travel Intelligence and Border Management, Annex: Europol and Frontex Final Report (The Hague/Warsaw, 16 September 2021), EDOC 1182065/Frontex No 9870, Brussels, 3 March 2022, 53.

[7] This section is based on the following article: Teresa Quintel, 'Interoperable Data Exchanges within Different Data Protection Regimes: The Case of Europol and the European Border and Coast Guard Agency' (2020) 26 *European Public Law* 205.

[8] Anja Radjenovic, 'Protection of EU External Borders, PE 630.316' [2019] *EPRS Briefing* 2.

of Operational Cooperation at the External Borders of the EU, was established on 26 October 2004.[9] In 2011, the Frontex Founding Act was revised and was finally replaced in 2016 by Regulation (EU) 2016/1624,[10] renaming the Agency the European Border and Coast Guard Agency.[11] Only two years after the entry into force of the 2016 Regulation, the Commission issued a proposal, on 9 September 2018, for the revision of the EBCGA, which was agreed upon in April 2019 and adopted by the Council in November 2019.[12]

In light of this chapter, the EBCGA is a particularly interesting case, because it was established as a border control agency with an arguably limited mandate, which turned into a powerful information hub alongside Europol. Relatively quickly, the EBCGA developed into one of the fastest-growing EU Agencies in terms of budget and staff.[13] Effectively, its initial mandate was expanded to not focus exclusively on migration management and the monitoring of irregular border crossings, but also to safeguarding the security of the external EU borders.[14]

Frontex's most significant boost in competences came in the aftermath of the 2015 *migration crisis*, when, after only about one year of negotiations, the Agency was turned into the EBCGA.[15] The Agency was attributed a greater role for return operations of irregular migrants and more responsibilities to counter organised crime and the smuggling of human beings. Fairly quickly, the EBCGA experienced an expansion of competences with the creation of Rapid Border Intervention Teams (RABITs) to provide operational assistance to the Member States and other EU Agencies.[16] In the same vein, cooperation with Europol was strengthened in

[9] Council Regulation (EC) No 2007/2004 of 26 October 2004 establishing a European Agency for the Management of Operational Cooperation at the External Borders of the Member States of the European Union [2004] OJ L349/1.

[10] Regulation (EU) No 2016/1624 of the European Parliament and of the Council of 14 September 2016 on the European Border and Coast Guard and amending Regulation (EU) 2016/399 of the European Parliament and of the Council and repealing Regulation (EC) No 863/2007 of the European Parliament and of the Council, Council Regulation (EC) No 2007/2004 and Council Decision 2005/267/EC [2007] OJ L251/1.

[11] European Union Agency for Fundamental Rights, 'Under Watchful Eyes – Biometrics, EU IT-Systems and Fundamental Rights' (2018), https://fra.europa.eu/sites/default/files/fra_uploads/fra-2018-biometrics-fundamental-rights-eu_en.pdf.

[12] European Parliament, 'Legislative Train Schedule: Regulation on the European Border and Coast Guard', https://www.europarl.europa.eu/legislative-train.

[13] *cf* Arne Niemann and Johanna Speyer, 'A Neofunctionalist Perspective on the "European Refugee Crisis": The Case of the European Border and Coast Guard' (2018) 56 *Journal of Common Market Studies* 23; Francesca Ferraro and Emilio de Capitani, 'The New European Border and Coast Guard: Yet Another "Half Way" EU Reform?' (2016) 17 *ERA Forum* 385; Jorrit Rijpma, 'The Proposal for a European Border and Coast Guard: Evolution or Revolution in External Border Management? Study for the LIBE Committee' (2016), https://www.europarl.europa.eu/RegData/etudes/STUD/2016/556934/IPOL_STU(2016)556934_EN.pdf; Philippe de Bruycker, 'The European Border and Coast Guard: A New Model Built on an Old Logic' (2016) 1 *European Papers: A Journal on Law and Integration* 559.

[14] Udo Bux, 'Protection of EU External Borders: Achievements during the Legislative Term 2014–2019: The Role of the European Parliament, Briefing Requested by the LIBE Committee, Directorate-General for Internal Policies' PE 608.876 (April 2019) 12.

[15] Niemann and Speyer (n 13) 33.

[16] Florian Trauner and Irina Angelescu, '10,000 Border Guards for Frontex: Why the EU Risks Conflated Expectations' (September 2018), https://www.epc.eu/en/publications/10000-border-guards-for-Frontex-Why-the-EU-risks-conflated-expectati~2070b0.

the hotspot areas and with Europol's specialised European Migrant Smuggling Centre (EMSC).

i. Data Protection Rules Applicable to the EBCGA

Just like its predecessor, the 2019 EBCGA Regulation was proposed, negotiated and adopted within an extremely short timeframe and without an Impact Assessment. The Regulation suggests strengthening the Agency with a new mandate and increased powers to protect the EU's external borders, to carry out returns more effectively and to cooperate with third countries in the area of border protection.[17] In addition, the Regulation builds upon the increasing number of tasks and responsibilities of the EBCGA regarding irregular secondary movements and the Agency's role in (forced) returns of TCNs. Overall, the EBCGA's activities in relation to the management of the external borders was, once again, broadened.[18] Moreover, the deployment of migration management support teams will not be restricted to 'situations of disproportionate migratory challenges', which needed to be demonstrated under Regulation (EU) 2016/1624.[19]

Increased attention is given to inter-agency cooperation, including information exchanges to tackle cross-border crime. Under its current regulation, the EBCGA obtained more opportunities to process personal data and to engage more actively in cooperation with other EU Agencies to facilitate the exchange of information.[20] To that end, Article 88(1)(d) of the EBCGA Regulation stipulates that the Agency shall process personal data for the purpose of facilitating the exchange of information with national LEAs, Eurojust and Europol. These processing activities shall fall within the scope of Article 90a of the EBCGA Regulation, which refers to the processing of so-called operational data by the Agency.

As mentioned above, processing activities by the EBCGA fall within the scope of Regulation (EU) 2018/1725, which entered into force in November 2018 and repealed a Regulation from 2001. Regulation (EU) 2018/1725 aligns the rules at the EU level with those that apply in the Member States in a forward-thinking way, combining provisions of both the GDPR and of the LED into one instrument. Under Chapter IX of Regulation (EU) 2018/1725, EU Agencies, such as the EBCGA, may apply specific rules on operational data whenever processing personal data for law enforcement purposes.

As a *quasi*-EU LEA, the EBCGA will play a decisive role in the practical application of Regulation (EU) 2018/1725 in terms of the delineation between the general rules (ie, processing for migration management) and the provisions

[17] Radjenovic (n 8) 8.

[18] ibid.

[19] European Union Agency for Fundamental Rights (FRA), 'FRA Opinion 5/2018 [EBCG]: The Revised European Border and Coast Guard Regulation and its Fundamental Rights Implications, Vienna, 27 November 2018' (2018).

[20] Article 10(19) and (20) and art 88(1)(c) of COM (2018) 631 final.

on operational data (ie, cooperation with Europol and other LEAs). Since both Europol and Eurojust apply, besides Chapter IX, a *lex specialis* regime to their processing activities of operational personal data, the EBCGA was, until the entry into force of the EUAA's foundation regulation in 2021, the only Agency could apply both sets of rules under Regulation (EU) 2018/1725 without an additional tailor-made data protection regime to its processing activities. Thereby, the EBCGA should set high standards for the delineation between the rules applicable to law enforcement and non-law enforcement processing under Regulation (EU) 2018/1725 and could serve as a model for processing by national LEAs (ie, the delineation between the GDPR and the LED), as the rules at the EU and national levels are now more aligned than was the case under the previous data protection regimes.

In addition, the EBCGA should set the standards for other EU Agencies, which process personal data within the scope of Regulation (EU) 2018/1725, such as the new EUAA. Despite being focused on asylum-related matters, the EUAA may process personal data for the purpose of facilitating the exchange of information with the competent national authorities: the EBCGA, Europol or Eurojust.[21] This does not necessarily mean that the EUAA would be permitted to process the personal data in question within the remit of Chapter IX of Regulation (EU) 2018/1725 on operational personal data. Nevertheless, certain analogies may be drawn between the analysis concerning the EBCGA's processing operations and those carried out by the EUAA.

ii. EUROSUR: The European Border Surveillance System

EUROSUR provides a common framework for the exchange of information and cooperation between Member States' border surveillance authorities and the EBCGA. For that purpose, so-called National Coordination Centres (NCCs) and the EBCGA exchange information, data and intelligence in situational awareness pictures to detect and monitor unauthorised crossings of the external Schengen borders.[22] The majority of the EUROSUR NCCs are hosted either by the national police, the border guard or the border police of the Member States,[23] and exercise command and control functions in that capacity. In order to ensure timely awareness and reaction capabilities, the NCCs cooperate with various authorities such as the police, customs, coastguards, the navy, tax authorities, fishery control and transport authorities, maritime authorities, migration and asylum authorities, the Ministry of Defence, the army and the intelligence services.[24]

[21] Article 31(1)(c) of Regulation (EU) 2021/2303.

[22] Commission Staff Working Document: Evaluation of the Regulation (EU) No 1052/2013 of the European Parliament and of the Council of 22 October 2013 establishing the European Border Surveillance System (Eurosur) SWD (2018) 410 final, 7.

[23] ibid 13.

[24] ibid 15.

While EUROSUR and the EBCGA were established by two different legal instruments,[25] under the 2019 EBCGA Regulation, EUROSUR was integrated within the EBCGA's central structure, although the exact architecture and content are not explicitly regulated. Above that, EUROSUR is tasked with fostering information exchanges between the national, regional and EU levels,[26] as well as with (neighbouring) third countries via bilateral cooperation.[27]

While the majority of processing operations within EUROSUR are currently based on non-personal data, the EBCGA Regulation opens up possibilities for EUROSUR to increasingly process personal data – for instance, within the framework of EUROSUR Fusion Services[28] and national situational pictures.[29] Hence, Articles 29(g) and 90(1) of the EBCGA Regulation refer to both the GDPR and the LED for the processing of personal data by NCCs.[30] Although the processing of personal data other than ship and aircraft identification numbers will be strictly limited to what is necessary for the purposes of EUROSUR,[31] numerous provisions clearly indicate that the processing of personal data will become a greater part of EUROSUR's tasks. Finally, the EUROSUR Fusion Services will use analyses derived from large-scale information systems for the purpose of detecting changing routes and methods used for illegal immigration and cross-border crime.[32]

While from a strategical point of view, enabling the NCCs to better connect and exchange information gathered seems logical, from a data protection perspective, the sharing of personal data between authorities that adhere to different data protection rules may entail risks regarding different standards. First, national LEAs and immigration authorities apply either the GDPR or the LED to their processing activities, which requires a clear delineation between the scopes of the two instruments, as under the LED, data subject rights may be restricted more flexibly than under the GDPR, and certain obligations for controllers are less stringent

[25] Regulation (EU) No 1052/2013 of the European Parliament and of the Council of 22 October 2013 establishing the European Border Surveillance System (Eurosur) [2013] OJ L295/11; and Regulation (EU) 2016/1624.

[26] SWD (2018) 410 final, 11.

[27] See, eg, art 76 of Regulation (EU) 2019/1896.

[28] Article 29 of Regulation (EU) 2019/1896. The EUROSUR Fusion Services include automated vessel tracking and detection capabilities, software functionalities allowing complex calculations for detecting anomalies and predicting vessel positions, as well as precise weather and oceanographic forecasts. Fusion Services use optical and radar satellite technology to locate vessels suspected to be engaged in people smuggling that often puts the lives of migrants in danger. Many of the services are delivered in cooperation with the European Maritime Safety Agency (EMSA) and the EU Satellite Centre (SatCen). See 'Information Management', https://frontex.europa.eu/we-know/situational-awareness-and-monitoring/information-management.

[29] Article 90 of Regulation (EU) 2019/1896.

[30] Although the previous EUROSUR Regulation also referred to Directive 95/46/EC and Framework Decision 2008/977/JHA, the list of processing tasks for EUROSUR was considerably extended.

[31] Article 90(2a) of Regulation (EU) 2019/1896.

[32] ibid art 29(2)(h).

under the former than under the latter.[33] Second, closer cooperation where information from national and European situational pictures is merged[34] and further shared with other organisations, agencies[35] and authorities in third countries leads to additional complexity with regard to processing activities and the applicable data protection frameworks. In addition, with interoperability, it will be extremely challenging to reconstruct which actor accessed a system and further exchanged the retrieved data.[36]

The extended competences for the EBCGA, the integration of EUROSUR into the EBCGA and the broadened access rights to EU databases for both clearly indicate increasingly intertwined channels for the exchange of personal data between national and EU LEAs to ensure the gapless surveillance of those crossing the EU's external borders. While improved data exchanges between EU Agencies and national authorities should definitely be seen as a step forward regarding cooperation in the AFSJ, concerns remain with respect to the different data protection regimes applicable to the different actors. For instance, while with the adoption of Regulation (EU) 2018/1725, the rules applicable to the EBCGA and the national competent authorities have been aligned and contribute to more coherent standards, Europol continues to process personal data within its stand-alone data protection regime. Although under its recast Regulation, Europol was subjected to the rules under Regulation (EU) 2018/1725, the data protection rules under its revised founding act further strengthened its processing capabilities and doubts remain regarding the data protection safeguards accompanying these new processing capabilities.

B. Europol

After the entry into force of the Lisbon Treaty, Europol was transformed into a full EU Agency[37] and, from January 2010,[38] its mandate included organised transnational crimes relating to immigration, such as migrant smuggling and illegal immigration. Only two years later, negotiations to reform the Europol Regulation were initiated to extend its competences.[39] The objective of the reform was to

[33] The processing of personal data by national intelligence or military services is not regulated by EU law and is subject to national legislation.

[34] Into specific situational pictures; see art 28(2) of Regulation (EU) 2019/1896.

[35] Inter alia, Europol, Eurojust, eu-LISA, INTERPOL or the OSCE. See art 69 of Regulation (EU) 2019/1896.

[36] Quintel (n 7).

[37] Europol, 'Europol's New Regulation', https://www.europol.europa.eu/newsroom/news/europols-new-regulation.

[38] Council Decision 2009/371/JHA of 6 April 2009 establishing the European Police Office (Europol) [2009] OJ L212/37.

[39] Sabine Gless and Thomas Wahl, 'A Comparison of the Evolution and Pace of Police and Judicial Cooperation in Criminal Matters: A Race between Europol and Eurojust?' in Chloé Brière and Anne Weyembergh (eds), *The Needed Balances in EU Criminal Law* (Hart Publishing, 2017).

increase the EU's internal security by making Europol a stronger hub for information exchanges.[40]

On 1 May 2017, the revised Europol Regulation entered into force and introduced a number of structural changes, inter alia, regarding the Agency's data protection rules. First, and in contrast to other EU institutions and bodies that apply Regulation (EU) 2018/1725[41] to their processing activities, Europol continued to processes operational personal data within the framework of its stand-alone data protection regime.[42] This solution was supposed to take into account Europol's specific requirements as an EU LEA. Hence, Europol maintained a *sui generis* data protection framework, tailored to the specific processing law enforcement tasks of the Agency,[43] to enable it to operate as a forum that connects and analyses information and personal data that it receives, by applying data analytics within broadly defined purposes.[44]

Second, under the 2016 Regulation, Europol progressively developed into a data-driven 'intelligence analyst', competent to exchange information with national LEAs and other EU Agencies, as well as with third countries and international organisations such as INTERPOL.[45] For that purpose, the 2016 Europol Regulation shifted the purpose limitation away from Europol's databases and instead attached the purposes to the processing activities by the Agency.[46]

Europol's databases were henceforth no longer separated between different purposes and crimes, but instead the purposes became connected to the actual processing by the Agency. This allowed Europol to retain all datasets in one single repository and carry out data mining for different types of law enforcement purposes.[47] These capabilities provided Europol with a remarkably broad scope and flexibility to process personal data,[48] and enabled the Agency to process

[40] Julia Ballaschk, 'In the Unseen Realm: Transnational Intelligence Sharing in the European Union – Challenges to Fundamental Rights and Democratic Legitimacy' (2015) 51 *Stanford Journal of International Law* 19; Robin Hofmann, 'Europäische Kriminalpolitik und die neue europäische Sicherheitsarchitektur' in Robin Hofmann (ed), *Flucht, Migration und die neue europäische Sicherheitsarchitektur: Herausforderungen für die EU-Kriminalpolitik* (Springer, 2017).

[41] Europol applies Regulation (EU) 2018/1725 to administrative data, but not to operational data.

[42] In accordance with art 46 of Regulation (EU) 2016/794, administrative data held by Europol are to be processed within the scope of Regulation (EU) 2018/1725.

[43] Juraj Sajfert, 'New Data Protection Regulation for EU Bodies: Another Piece of the Puzzle Completed' (2018) 4 *European Data Protection Law Review* 213.

[44] Robert Wainwright, 'The "Uberisation" of International Work', (23 January 2016), https://www.linkedin.com/pulse/uberisation-international-police-work-rob-wainwright.

[45] Sabine Gless, 'Europol' in Valsamis Mitsilegas (ed), *Research Handbook on EU Criminal Law* (Edward Elgar, 2016).

[46] Daniel Drewer and Vesela Miladinova, 'The BIG DATA Challenge: Impact and Opportunity of Large Quantities of Information under the Europol Regulation' (2017) 33 *Computer Law & Security Review* 298.

[47] SWD (2013) 99 final, 5.

[48] Teresa Quintel, 'The Impact of Interoperability on the Processing of (Biometric) Data of Third Country Nationals by Europol' (2018) 101 *Kritische Vierteljahresschrift für Gesetzgebung und Rechtswissenschaft* 332.

information more flexibly, allowing it to cross-check, link and classify personal data in a more unconstrained manner.[49]

Beyond the updated legal framework to allow Europol to implement more sophisticated processing capabilities, the Agency set up several centres focusing on different areas of crime. Those centres are supposed to provide operational support to national investigations in prioritised cases.[50] Besides centres on serious and organised crime,[51] cybercrime,[52] counter-terrorism,[53] or financial and economic crime,[54] one area of crime for which the Agency set up a dedicated centre aimed at preventing the smuggling of migrants. In February 2016, the EMSC, a platform to foster the exchange of information concerning migrant smuggling between Europol and the Member States, as well as with the EBCGA and Eurojust, was launched at Europol to further codify the Agency's engagement in the area of border control and immigration-related cross-border crimes. The activities carried out by the EMSC built upon Europol's tasks within the hotspots and similar joint operations, further expanding the Agency's operational tasks to crime areas concerning people-smuggling networks and intelligence in related fields of crime.[55]

The EMSC's principal area of interest is the disruption of migrant smuggling networks, but EMSC staff also work on document and identity fraud, analysing online content relating to migrant smuggling and financial investigations.[56] The EMSC closely cooperates with national LEAs and other EU Agencies dealing with border management to receive and exchange information. As part of Europol, EMSC staff have access to EU databases as well as the relevant interoperability components, as all types of crime dealt with by the Centre are defined as serious crime under Annex I of the Europol Regulation. Whereas the legal basis to establish the EMSC under the 2016 Europol Regulation was absent, or at least unclear, the recast Europol Regulation from 2022 captures and codifies all those processing operations for which the previous legal framework did not explicitly allow.

[49] Tomasz Safjański and Adrian James, 'Europol's Crime Analysis System: Practical Determinants of its Success' (2020) 14 *Policing: A Journal of Policy and Practice* 469.

[50] Europol, 'European Serious and Organised Crime Centre – ESOCC', https://www.europol.europa.eu/about-europol/european-serious-and-organised-crime-centre-esocc.

[51] ibid.

[52] Europol, 'European Cybercrime Centre – EC3', https://www.europol.europa.eu/about-europol/european-cybercrime-centre-ec3.

[53] Europol, 'European Counter Terrorism Centre – ECTC', https://www.europol.europa.eu/about-europol/european-counter-terrorism-centre-ectc.

[54] Europol, 'European Financial and Economic Crime Centre – EFECC', https://www.europol.europa.eu/about-europol/european-financial-and-economic-crime-centre-efecc.

[55] Europol, 'European Migrant Smuggling Centre – EMSC', https://www.europol.europa.eu/about-europol/european-migrant-smuggling-centre-emsc.

[56] Europol, 'Tackling the Organised Criminal Groups Profiting from Migrant Smuggling', https://www.europol.europa.eu/about-europol/european-serious-and-organised-crime-centre-esocc/european-migrant-smuggling-centre-emsc.

With its reformed legal framework, broadened access rights to the AFSJ databases and the interoperability components, Europol will have even greater opportunities to utilise its processing capabilities in the area of border control, migration management and asylum.

As mentioned above, in December 2020, the Commission proposed a new Europol Regulation, which was adopted in February 2022. The recast Europol Regulation substantially transformed Europol's mandate and the nature of the Agency – in particular, the way in which Europol may process large datasets including the personal data of individuals regarding whom there is no established link to a criminal activity.[57] In addition, the recast Regulation created a new alert category to be entered into the SIS III, which permits Europol to propose to the Member States to enter so-called information alerts[58] in the database.[59] Moreover, the proposal is supposed to strengthen the Agency's role in research and innovation and to further codify Europol's cooperation with third countries and private parties. Finally, the recast Europol Regulation retroactively legalises the processing of datasets, which the EDPS had ordered[60] the Agency to delete as they contained personal data concerning innocent individuals including, inter alia, asylum seekers and other TCNs.

C. Eurojust

Compared to Europol, Eurojust developed in a very different manner, in particular with regard to the processing of personal data both in terms of processing capabilities and the legal mandate attributed under the Agencies' founding acts. Initially both being tasked with facilitating the exchange of information and providing support to Member State authorities in cross-border criminal cases, Europol evolved into a more autonomous agency, while Eurojust remained limited to carrying out data-driven analyses. These developments also raise important

[57] To address the so-called 'Big Data challenge' following Europol's admonishment by the EDPS in September 2020 (see Letter from the EDPS, Wojciech Wiewiórowski, to Catherine de Bolle, 'EDPS Decision on the Own Initiative Inquiry on Europol's Big Data Challenge' Brussels, 18 September 2020'). See Niovi Vavoula and Valsamis Mitsilegas, 'Strengthening Europol's Mandate A Legal Assessment of the Commission's Proposal to Amend the Europol Regulation' PE 694.200 (May 2021) 84, 8.

[58] The term 'information alert' is not defined under the Regulation; however, these alerts concerns persons involved in terrorism or serious and organised crime.

[59] Article 4(r) of the recast Europol Regulation. *cf* Niovi Vavoula and Valsamis Mitsilegas, 'Strengthening Europol's Mandate: A Legal Assessment of the Commission's Proposal to Amend the Europol Regulation' PE 694.200 (May 2021) 84, 10.

[60] EDPS, 'EDPS Orders Europol to Erase Data Concerning Individuals with No Established Link to a Criminal Activity', https://edps.europa.eu/press-publications/press-news/press-releases/2022/edps-orders-europol-erase-data-concerning_en. The full text of the EDPS order is available at: https://edps.europa.eu/system/files/2022-01/22-01-10-edps-decision-europol_en.pdf. The Frequently Asked Questions information sheet is available at: https://edps.europa.eu/system/files/2022-01/22-01-10-europol-order_faqs_en.pdf.

questions regarding differences in autonomy and accountability.[61] Both Europol and Eurojust adopted (and were granted via their legal framework) dissimilar operational capabilities with regard to the analysis of personal data and the tasks falling within each Agency's competence. For instance, Eurojust's involvement in cross-border cases still strongly depends on the initiative of the Member States to request support from the Agency,[62] although Eurojust may request investigations at the national level and Member States are under the obligation to justify any non-compliance with such requests.[63] Hence, while Europol and the EBCGA developed into more self-standing data processing Agencies, Eurojust remained more 'traditional' in its coordinating role.

As mentioned above, Eurojust's part in migration-related cases is (so far) rather marginal compared to the role that the EBCGA or Europol plays. However, already some time ago, the Agency was being called an important actor with regard to the judicial dimension of migrant smuggling.[64] Calls for Eurojust to develop and promote a tailor-made model for joint investigation teams (JITs) in migrant smuggling cases and to facilitate the networking of practitioners to exchange best practices in investigating and prosecuting migrant smuggling cases were put forward.[65]

In 2019 alone, Eurojust supported 187 investigations dealing with migrant smuggling. In addition, the Agency supported 12 JITs focusing on migrant smuggling cases, often with the involvement of third countries. Furthermore, Eurojust assists national authorities to develop links with relevant European and international organisations such as Europol's EMSC, the EBCGA, the CSDP mission EUNAVFOR MED[66] and INTERPOL, and is supposed to involve new partners.[67] Eurojust supports a focus group of specialised prosecutors from all Member States that deals with migrant smuggling in order to share best practices, analyse new trends and gather input from different judicial practitioners.[68]

[61] *cf* Madalina Busuioc and Martijn Groenleer, 'Beyond Design: The Evolution of Europol and Eurojust' (2013) 14 *Perspectives on European Politics & Society* 285.

[62] Ángeles Gutiérrez Zarza, 'Eurojust' in Ángeles Gutiérrez Zarza (ed), *Exchange of Information and Data Protection in Cross-border Criminal Proceedings in Europe* (Springer, 2015), 57– 90.

[63] On the initiative function of Eurojust under the 2009 Decision, see Jörg Monar, 'Eurojust's Present and Future Role at the Frontline of European Union Criminal Justice Cooperation' (September 2013) 14(2) *ERA Forum* 187–200.

[64] For some case examples, see ibid.

[65] General Secretariat of the Council, 'Council Document 14576/1/18/ REV 1, Enhancing the Response to Migrant Smuggling Networks: A Comprehensive and Operational Set of Measures, Brussels, 6 December 2018', 5, https://data.consilium.europa.eu/doc/document/ST-15250-2018-INIT/en/pdf.

[66] Eurojust, 'Migrant Smuggling', https://www.eurojust.europa.eu/crime-types-and-cases/crime-types/migrant-smuggling.

[67] General Secretariat of the Council, 'Council Document 14576/1/18/ REV 1, Enhancing the Response to Migrant Smuggling Networks: A Comprehensive and Operational Set of Measures, Brussels, 6 December 2018', 8, https://data.consilium.europa.eu/doc/document/ST-15250-2018-INIT/en/pdf.

[68] Eurojust (n 66).

Admittedly, the information used by Eurojust primarily focuses on personal data relating to perpetrators of crime such as persons smuggling migrants and not the migrants, asylum seekers or refugees themselves. However, cases concerning migrants will inevitably also include personal data about migrants or other types of smuggled persons, even if they are the *victims* of a particular crime. Categories of data subjects and of personal data that Eurojust may process are restricted,[69] and data of persons who are not under investigation are rather limited. In practice, the Agency has little information on those who are not being investigated or prosecuted. Nevertheless, different sources of information about TCNs, including personal data, are at the disposal of Eurojust. On the one hand, these data will be obtained through cooperation with national authorities and the respective networks in which Eurojust operates. On the other hand, strengthened cooperation with the EBCGA and Europol (in particular within the framework of the EMSC) will generate more data about TCNs that may be processed by Eurojust.

With regard to AFSJ databases and the interoperability framework, Eurojust plays a negligible role. Nevertheless, information from different systems, either held by the Agencies themselves at a central EU level or by national authorities, may also include personal data from AFSJ databases to which Eurojust might not have direct access. In particular, where data-matching techniques are applied to find correlations between different types of suspects or different crimes, it may very well be the case that the result of such processing operations will be subsequently used by additional actors. Where cooperation between the EBCGA, Europol and Eurojust will be reinforced and data exchanges facilitated, personal data processed by one Agency, albeit in a modified form, will most likely also be available to another. Therefore, the applicable data protection framework, including the supervision of different processing operations, will be increasingly important.

II. Access to EU Databases and the Interoperability Components by EU Agencies

A. The European Border and Coast Guard Agency

During the past few years, the EBCGA in particular was given an entirely new role with regard to access and searches in AFSJ databases, which was mainly established under the ETIAS Regulation and with interoperability. The so-called ETIAS Consequential Amendments, which expand the scope of the underlying AFSJ databases, underpinned that role of the EBCGA.

[69] Article 27 and Annex II of Regulation (EU) 2018/1727.

Both the ETIAS and the Interoperability Regulations signified an essential step up for the EBCGA with regard to accessing, searching, comparing and verifying personal data stored in both the AFSJ databases and the interoperability components. The EBCGA was granted new operational tasks when the ETIAS Regulation established the ETIAS Central Unit, which will be operated within the EBCGA and will be actively involved in the processing of personal data of TCNs. If automated processing reveals a hit, then Articles 21 and 22 of the ETIAS Regulation provide that the ETIAS Central Unit shall be consulted to verify the hit.[70] In addition, and in accordance with the ETIAS Consequential Amendments, the ETIAS Central Unit shall be granted access to other AFSJ databases in order to verify any hits that occurred when a query was launched in the ETIAS.[71] These amendments, under Article 50a and b of the ETIAS Regulation, also foresee that the ETIAS Central Unit will, for the purpose of performing the tasks conferred upon it, be granted access to the relevant SIS III data.[72]

In accordance with the ETIAS consequential amendments, the EBCGA was added as a competent authority within the definitions under Article 3 of the ETIAS Regulation. Thereby, the Regulation encloses the Agency in the same definitions with the remaining competent authorities – Eurojust, Europol and the EPPO.[73] Evidently, this does not automatically mean that the EBCGA obtained the same tasks as the other three Agencies, or that it may carry out law enforcement processing. However, it seems natural to assume that with the inclusion of the EBCGA in that definition, the Agency could indeed carry out similar processing operations to Eurojust, Europol or the EPPO.

In addition, under the Interoperability Regulations, the ETIAS Central Unit is supposed to carry out multiple identity detection[74] and thus will have access to the Multiple Identity Detector for the purpose of the manual verification of different identities of TCNs.[75] In those cases, the ETIAS Central Unit will act as the data controller.[76] The multiple identity detection will also allow for access to the underlying AFSJ databases that contain data leading to a match, as well as to the relevant Interoperability components.[77]

The above-mentioned examples are only a few of the new tasks that the EBCGA was granted under the adopted instruments that established the added AFSJ databases and interoperability. In reality, the setting-up of those new systems

[70] Niovi Vavoula, *The European Commission Package of ETIAS Consequential Amendments: Substitute Impact Assessment, PE 642.808 – December 2019* (Publications Office, 2019) 3.

[71] Amendment 3 of Annex I, Amendment 2 of Annex IV, Amendment 5 of Annex V and Amendment 3 of Annex VI.

[72] See Amendment 3 of Annex I of the ETIAS consequential amendments.

[73] See Amendment 3 of the ETIAS Consequential Amendments.

[74] See, for instance, Recital 70 of Regulation (EU) 2019/817.

[75] ibid art 57.

[76] ibid art 40(3)(a).

[77] On that topic, see Teresa Quintel and Diana Dimitrova, 'Technological Experimentation without Adequate Safeguards? Interoperable EU Databases and Access to the Multiple Identity Detector by SIRENE Bureaux' in Paul de Hert et al (eds), *Data Protection and Privacy Data Protection and Artificial Intelligence* (Bloomsbury, 2020).

will also add changes regarding the way in which the Agency may access the already-existing AFSJ databases. In particular, the Interoperability Regulations and the consequential ETIAS amendments amplify the new role of the EBCGA. In addition, under Article 50 of the SIS III Regulation on police and judicial cooperation in criminal matters, EBCGA teams obtained access to SIS III data insofar as necessary for the performance of their tasks, such as return operations. Ultimately, these new access possibilities will lead, in many cases, to an increased dilution of the boundaries between immigration and criminal law.[78]

B. Europol

A similar situation arises with regard to Europol. Like the EBCGA, Europol was attributed a greater role to add, search, access and retrieve data from the AFSJ databases as well as the interoperability components. Already before the Interoperability Regulations were proposed, Europol's access to AFSJ databases became somehow self-evident and both the Interoperability Regulations and the recast Europol Regulation codify the Agency's role in the context of migration management and border control. The outcome is the same as that regarding the EBCGA, just in reverse: while the EBCGA as an EU border and coast guard obtained more law enforcement tasks, Europol as an EU LEA obtained more and more tasks in migration management and border control, which eventually resulted in a blurring of boundaries between migration and criminal law.

Besides adding its own datasets, Europol may, for the purpose of fighting serious crime, be granted access to EU databases as well as to the interoperability components.[79] Europol access will be subject to prior verification by a specialised unit of Europol officials to access the ETIAS.[80] Similarly, to be granted access to the EES,[81] the VIS[82] and Eurodac,[83] a Europol central access point will verify whether all access requirements are met. The SIS III[84] and the ECRIS-TCN[85] grant Europol direct access. However, verification by units that are established within the Agency itself casts doubts on whether such prior verification can be truly independent. If verification is carried out within the same organisation as the authority that requested access to AFSJ databases, independence may be jeopardised by prejudiced interests.

Systematic data exchanges between Europol, the EBCGA and the national competent authorities have been intensified for several years, and structural data

[78] See also Vavoula (n 70) 22.
[79] See, for instance, arts 6, 7, 9, 17 and 22 of Regulation (EU) 2019/817 and 818.
[80] Article 53(3) of Regulation (EU) 2018/1240 (ETIAS).
[81] Article 30(2) of Regulation (EU) 2017/2226.
[82] Article 22l(2) of COM (2018) 302 final.
[83] Article 8(2) of COM (2016) 272 final.
[84] For instance, art 48(1) of Regulation (EU) 2018/1862.
[85] Article 14(2) of Regulation (EU) 2019/816.

exchanges are being implemented not only between Europol, the EBCGA and national LEAs, but also within wider structures that include additional actors. For instance, the EMSC is supposed to be developed into a multi-stakeholder platform to provide a 'full intelligence picture by data fusion' with the involvement of other 'key partners'.[86]

The 2022 recast Europol Regulation, which will be the subject of discussion below, paves the way for the Agency to process personal data not only of criminals or other persons who may be involved in or linked to a criminal activity; by allowing Europol to engage in the processing of large datasets without having to carry out a data subject categorisation prior to inserting those data into the Agency's data environment, Europol may theoretically process the personal data of innocent people, including asylum seekers, refugees and other TCNs.

C. Eurojust

As has been mentioned above, the role of Eurojust regarding access to AFSJ databases is marginal. Under the Interoperability Regulations, the Agency may appoint a representative to attend meetings of the Interoperability Advisory Group and the meetings of the Management Boards of the different AFSJ databases.[87] However, neither the Eurodac Proposal and the new VIS Regulation nor the ETIAS or the EES Regulations mention Eurojust in terms of access. Nevertheless, it should be noted that the ETIAS consequential amendments *do* define Eurojust as a competent authority, which would theoretically grant more opportunities to the Agency in terms of access to the databases. Whether such access will be used to a similar extent to what will probably be the case regarding Europol and the EBCGA remains to be seen, but it is rather unlikely, as Eurojust pursues a very different data strategy and disposes of processing capabilities that are less advanced. However, it is important that while this is currently the case, Eurojust's processing capabilities may be further elaborated in the future, in the context of the Digital Justice Project.[88]

[86] See, for instance, Council Document 10944/18, 3, https://www.statewatch.org/news/2018/jul/eu-council-europol-note-migrant-smuggling-action-10944-18.pdf. These include, for instance, the EBCGA, Interpol or the military operation EUNAVFOR, an European External Action Service (EEAS) mission launched within the framework of the European Common Security and Defence Policy (CSDP). Similar cooperation schemes exist within the so-called Crime Information Cell, which is hosted by the EUNAVFOR MED operation Sophia and was codified in May 2018. The Cell is to establish a coordination mechanism between relevant Member State authorities and EU Agencies such as Europol, the EBCGA, Eurojust, the European Asylum Support Office (EASO) and CSDP missions to facilitate the receipt, collection and transmission of information, including personal data. Under which legal framework those actors would be able to cooperate and exchange data remained open, as currently no data protection regime for CSDP missions in such a constellation exists.

[87] See, for instance, art 62 of Regulation (EU) 2019/817.

[88] Eurojust, 'Digital Justice Project Phases', https://www.eurojust.europa.eu/digital-justice-project-phases.

Only the SIS III Regulations[89] and the ECRIS-TCN Regulation[90] include stand-alone provisions that specifically regulate access to personal data by Eurojust. With regard to the SIS III, Eurojust access to data is limited, as searches are reserved for Eurojust national members and issuing Member States will be informed of the existence of alerts. In addition, Eurojust may only transfer personal data with the consent of the issuing Member State. In the case of ECRIS-TCN, Eurojust will have access to the database in order to identify the Member States holding criminal records information on a TCN[91] for the purpose of support and for strengthening coordination and cooperation between national investigating and prosecuting authorities in accordance with Article 2 of the Eurojust Regulation.

In addition, Eurojust will serve as a contact point for third countries and international organisations, which may address the Agency, for the purpose of criminal proceedings, in order to ascertain whether Member States hold criminal records of TCNs.[92] However, the Member State holding a criminal record must give its consent before Eurojust may share any information with a third country or international organisation.[93] In addition, how this mechanism will work in practice is still currently under discussion.

Ultimately, the opportunities of Eurojust to access, search and process personal data in AFSJ databases are much more confined than those attributed to Europol and the EBCGA. On the one hand, Eurojust's rights to access those systems are much more limited than those of the other two agencies. On the other hand, the Agency is much more dependent on the instructions that it receives from the Member States. Whilst Europol and the EBCGA may access and use personal data in AFSJ databases in a more autonomous manner, Eurojust relies on the consent given by the respective Member State that issued an alert or input data within a database. In addition, the Agency is (for the time being) far less involved in matters concerning migration and border control and hence does not use personal data from the AFSJ for its daily operations. This seems logical given the role of Eurojust, which only starts when a judicial investigation or prosecution is envisaged, which is much later in the process.

The sharing of personal data in an interoperable system and between various bodies that apply different data protection frameworks not only raises doubts regarding data protection standards per se; such data exchanges also constitute concerns regarding function creep. Europol and the EBCGA in particular may illustrate such creep, as the former engages increasingly in migration and border

[89] See, for instance, art 49 of Regulation (EU) 2018/1862 on police cooperation and judicial cooperation in criminal matters.

[90] Article 14(1) of Regulation (EU) 2019/816.

[91] ibid art 7(3).

[92] ibid art 17(1).

[93] ibid art 17(3).

management functions, despite being an LEA, whereas the latter was attributed a role of a competent authority, despite having been established as a border guard agency that was supposed to merely play an assisting role.

The reformed roles for EU Agencies and, in particular, Europol and the EBCGA, as well as the complexity of the system of AFSJ databases, render the supervision of the processing operations increasingly challenging, not only in terms of different data protection rules that apply to different actors, but also because the supervisory authorities at the national and EU levels must coordinate their activities in order to be able to supervise all processing activities on these levels.

III. The Fragmentation of Applicable Data Protection Rules

Because Regulation (EU) 2018/1725 merely covers the processing of personal data by EU institutions, offices, bodies and Agencies, its scope is rather limited. In addition, and as will be demonstrated in the subsections below, further data protection rules apply to Eurojust and Europol.[94] Both Agencies apply Regulation (EU) 2018/1725 as *lex generalis* and the specific data protection rules enshrined in their founding acts as *lex specialis*. At the time when Regulation (EU) 2018/1725 was negotiated, the 2016 Europol Regulation had just entered into force one year earlier. This allowed the Agency to continue applying its stand-alone data protection regime to the processing of operational (law enforcement) personal data, while applying Regulation (EU) 2018/1725 only when processing so-called administrative data, such as HR or other non-operational data.

With regard to Eurojust, the Agency was made subject to Regulation (EU) 2018/1725 when the latter entered into force in December 2018, but retained and further refined more specific rules for the processing of operational data under its own Regulation. This was, inter alia, due to the fact that Chapter IX on operational personal data under Regulation (EU) 2018/1725 remained underdeveloped, for instance, with regard to international transfers or supervision.

Out of the three Agencies discussed in this chapter, the EBCGA is the only one that applies Regulation (EU) 2018/1725 as the sole data protection instrument to its processing activities without being subject to tailor-made rules under its founding act. While the Agency traditionally should not be understood as an LEA, the EBCGA, under its new Regulation from 2019, may indeed be able to process operational or law enforcement data in certain situations. This means that the EBCGA could, in certain situations, be able to argue in favour of an application of Chapter IX to its processing activities. Such application would have significant

[94] As well as to the EPPO under Council Regulation (EU) 2017/1939 of 12 October 2017 implementing enhanced cooperation on the establishment of the European Public Prosecutor's Office ('the EPPO') [2017] OJ L283/1.

implications. First, this would mean that the EBCGA would be able to process personal data within the scope of Chapter IX despite the underdeveloped rules on international transfers and supervision, which in turn could involve repercussion for data subjects. Second, any practical delineation between the general rules in Regulation (EU) 2018/1725 and the rules under Chapter IX would have to be compared and evaluated against the delineation between the GDPR and the LED at the national level in order to ensure a coherent application of national and EU data protection rules. Third, the EU legislator should closely monitor whether the potential application of Chapter IX by the EBCGA would require a refining of the underdeveloped provisions, also with a view to other Agencies that might be able to apply that chapter in the future, such as the EUAA.

A. A Regulation for EU Bodies, Offices and Agencies

With its entry into force in December 2018, Regulation (EU) 2018/1725 repealed Regulation 45/2001/EC. The latter Regulation for its part was adopted a few years after the start of the application of Directive 95, at a time before the Lisbon Treaty had entered into force. Hence, Regulation 45/2001/EC governed *community* institutions, bodies and agencies, as opposed to Directive 95, which was directed to the Member States for transposition to regulate internal market matters. The adoption of Regulation 45/2001/EC allowed for the establishment of the EDPS, with the Regulation itself being the founding act of that new institution. The EDPS in turn would be responsible for the supervision of those entities that fell within the scope of Regulation 45/2001/EC – EU institutions, bodies, offices and agencies.

The reform of Regulation 45/2001/EC became necessary for similar reasons to those that required the EU Data Protection Reform package that became applicable at the Member State level. Yet, while there could have been one set of data protection rules applicable at both the EU and national levels, the EU legislator opted for maintaining the two-level regime. The reasons for adopting a separate new regulation instead of also applying the national rules at the EU level were partly of a political and partly of a legal nature. Indeed, during the GDPR negotiations between 2012 and 2016, there were discussions on whether the GDPR could also apply to the EU institutions, bodies and agencies. However, instead of being applicable on all levels, a new fully fledged Regulation that, like Regulation 45/2001/EC, would only cover the EU institutions, bodies and Agencies should be adopted in order to put an emphasis on the transparency of, and rules within, those institutions.

As it turned out later, Regulation (EU) 2018/1725 as a separate instrument allowed for stricter data protection rules, at least with regard to the provisions under the 'general' parts of the Regulation (meaning all provisions except those under Chapter IX on operational data), as the Council was probably less eager to negotiate, and the lobbying on the co-legislator was negligible. In addition, Recital 17 of the GDPR states that Regulation 45/2001/EC should be adapted to the rules under the GDPR, thereby making a clear distinction between the two instruments while requiring an alignment.

However, against this background, a separate regulation was adopted with Regulation (EU) 2018/1725 that should be closely aligned with the GDPR. Ultimately, this led to large parts of the GDPR being copied and pasted into the new Regulation, in order to keep the coherence between the two instruments high. Although the negotiations did not end at the same time as those of the GDPR, there was a gap of only six months between the application of the GDPR and of Regulation (EU) 2018/1725.[95]

While the definitions, as well as Chapter II on rights and Chapter V on transfers under Regulation (EU) 2018/1725, are fully aligned with the provisions under the GDPR, a second category of rules emerged as a concept that previously existed neither under Directive 95 nor for the EU institutions, bodies and agencies, but only emerged under the GDPR and was then incorporated under Regulation (EU) 2018/1725. These rules were the risk-based approach, the principle of accountability and the provisions concerning data protection by design and default.

In addition, the provisions on the obligations for controllers were reinforced:[96] for instance, the provision on record keeping, the task for Data Protection Officers (DPOs) to monitor compliance with the Regulation, the requirement to carry out a DPIA for certain processing operations[97] and the provisions on data breach notification to the competent DPA[98] – in the case of Regulation (EU) 2018/1725, the EDPS.[99] Contrary to Directive 95/46/EC, Regulation 45/2001/EC already included the compulsory DPO, which meant that in that sense the institutions, agencies and bodies were 'pioneers'.

A third category of rules under Regulation (EU) 2018/1725 differs entirely from those under the GDPR because those rules under Regulation (EU) 2018/1725 provide, in a very specific manner, a higher level of protection than those under the GDPR. This was a consequence of the Commission's unwillingness to lower the level of protection under Regulation (EU) 2018/1725 only for the sake of alignment. At the same time, the higher level that had already been introduced by Regulation 45/2001/EC was to be kept. As mentioned above, the DPO culture within the institutions, bodies and agencies was highly developed and the rules under Regulation 45/2001/EC, which were more detailed than those under the GDPR, were kept under the new Regulation. Another article under

[95] Regulation (EU) 2018/1725 entered into application in December 2018.

[96] See also Veronique Cimina, 'The Data Protection Concepts of "Controller", "Processor" and "Joint Controllership" under Regulation (EU) 2018/1725' (2021) 21 *ERA Forum* 639.

[97] Article 39 of Regulation (EU) 2018/1725.

[98] ibid art 40.

[99] See also Tihomir Katulic and Nikola Protrka, 'Information Security in Principles and Provisions of the EU Data Protection Law' [2019] *42nd International Convention on Information and Communication Technology, Electronics and Microelectronics (MIPRO)* 1420, 1425.

Regulation (EU) 2018/1725 provides specific protection to whistleblowers within the institutions and is non-existent under the GDPR.[100]

Evidently, those provisions under the GDPR that give a certain leeway to the national legislators, the so-called opening clauses, were not adopted under the data protection regime for EU institutions, bodies and Agencies. This was, for instance, the case with regard to the rules on the age of children,[101] for which the GDPR left a certain margin to the national legislator to determine that age.

In addition, the revision of Regulation 45/2001/EC brought some major changes and new provisions, some of which will be discussed below. However, the most important change for the discussion here is the introduction of Chapter IX, which regulates the processing of operational data by EU bodies, offices and agencies when carrying out activities that fall within the scope of Chapter 4 or Chapter 5 of Title V of Part Three TFEU, ie, judicial cooperation in criminal matters and police cooperation.

Chapter IX is important insofar as it may be seen as somewhat equivalent to the rules governing law enforcement processing under the LED at the national level. Therefore, a parallel between the issues and concerns regarding the delineation between the GDPR and the LED at the national level may be drawn with regard to the delineation between the general chapters under Regulation (EU) 2018/1725 and Chapter IX for processing at the EU level.

B. Some Main Changes under Regulation (EU) 2018/1725

One of the key changes that took place with the entry into force of Regulation (EU) 2018/1725 was the role of the EDPS. The latter was granted strengthened tasks and powers, which may be seen as almost equivalent to those of national DPAs under the GDPR.[102]

Interestingly, under Article 66 of Regulation (EU) 2018/1725, just like national DPAs under the GDPR, the EDPS may now issue administrative fines to EU institutions, bodies and agencies, albeit with a lower threshold than the fines that may be imposed against controllers under Article 83 GDPR.[103] This means that an EU body may issue a fine against another EU body, which is a novelty. However, that provision will not be further discussed in the subsequent sections.

Instead, the following subsections will focus on Article 25 of Regulation (EU) 2018/1725, on the restriction of data subject rights. This provision sends a strong

[100] Article 68 of Regulation (EU) 2018/1725 on complaints by EU staff.

[101] ibid art 8.

[102] Magdalena Kędzior, 'GDPR and beyond: A Year of Changes in the Data Protection Landscape of the European Union' (2019) 19 *ERA Forum* 505.

[103] The threshold for fines for infringements under art 66(2) of Regulation (EU) 2018/1725 was set at €25,000 per infringement and €250,000 per year. For infringements under art 66(3) of Regulation (EU) 2018/1725, the threshold was set at €50,000 per infringement and €500,000 per year.

message on how the restriction of the rights of data subjects should be carried out under Article 23 GDPR. Evidently, because the logic of the restriction of data subject rights under the LED is the same as that under the GDPR, the restriction of rights under Regulation (EU) 2018/1725 may, or should, also serve as a model for Articles 13(3), 15 and 16(4) of the Directive. Nevertheless, the Regulation for EU institutions, bodies and agencies places a particular focus on the principle of transparency, which does not exist under the LED. The restriction of data subject rights and the specific provisions concerning the transparency principle will be discussed below, before turning the discussion towards Chapter IX of Regulation (EU) 2018/1725 on the processing of operational (law enforcement) personal data by EU LEAs.

i. Restriction of Data Subject Rights

Under Regulation 45/2001/EC, Article 20 allowed for the restriction of data subject rights in a direct manner. For example, the European Anti-Fraud Office (OLAF), when receiving an access request from a data subject, was able to rely on Article 20 of Regulation 45/2001/EC to restrict, in a very broad manner, the right of access in an ad hoc manner. Under Regulation (EU) 2018/1725, the EU legislator took Article 23 GDPR as a blueprint. As explained in Chapter 3 on the LED, Article 23 GDPR (as well as Articles 13(3), 15 and 16(4) LED) does not allow for direct or ad hoc restrictions, but requires Member States to adopt legislative measures that must be based on one of the grounds under Article 23 GDPR (and Articles 13(3), 15 and 16(4) LED).[104] Only where these legislative measures were adopted may data subject rights be restricted in limited cases. Hence, during the legislative discussions, there was a strong will to ensure alignment with both the GDPR and with the EU Charter (as well as with the LED), which both require the prior adoption of a legislative measure in order to allow for the restriction of fundamental rights.[105]

However, one evident difficulty linked to the restriction of fundamental rights in the context of Regulation (EU) 2018/1725 was that the EU would legislate on EU institutions, bodies and agencies restricting individual rights, which is generally problematic and not permissible in the light of the Charter. In addition, at the EU level, the procedure to adopt a legislative measure is generally more challenging and lengthier than at the national level. Therefore, Regulation (EU) 2018/1725 allows for the restriction of data subject rights either by legal acts adopted on the basis of the Treaties or by internal rules laid down by the respective EU institution, body or agency.[106] The possibility of adopting internal rules instead of a

[104] As demonstrated in the previous chapter, art 23 of Regulation (EU) 2016/679 (just like the restrictions under Directive (EU) 2016/680) is in many Member States not properly implemented, but was simply copied and pasted from Regulation (EU) 2016/679.

[105] Intervention by Juraj Sajfert during a seminar on Data Protection in the European Institutions (4–5 February 2020), https://era-comm.eu/data-protection/data-protection-in-the-european-institutions.

[106] Article 25(1) of Regulation (EU) 2018/1725.

legislative measure is inspired by Recital 41 GDPR.[107] Nevertheless, the conditions that need to be fulfilled in order to restrict data subject rights under Regulation (EU) 2018/1725 could be regarded as being less restrictive than those under the GDPR or the LED.

Consequently, under Regulation (EU) 2018/1725, data subject rights may be restricted either if they are based on a legislative measure or on internal rules if approved by the highest level of management of the respective institution, body or agency and after consultation with the EDPS.[108] In addition, the internal rules providing for the restrictions of data subject rights need to be published in the Official Journal of the EU.[109] Finally, the legislative measure must be a separate one from the legal bases under Article 5 of Regulation (EU) 2018/1725[110] and the internal rules may not serve as a legal basis for processing.[111]

A legal act adopted pursuant to Article 25(1) of Regulation (EU) 2018/1725, or internal rules allowing for the restriction of data subject rights, could serve as a blueprint for Member States to adopt legislative measure to restrict data subject rights under both the GDPR and the LED. Hence, ECtHR case law on the quality of law requirement (discussed in relation to law enforcement access to the interoperability components) and Strasbourg jurisprudence more generally should serve as conditions for the adoption of legislative measures to restrict data subject rights under Regulation (EU) 2018/1725. Any such measure that would allow for the restriction of data subject rights must be published in the Official Journal of the EU in order to be foreseeable and accessible and must be sufficiently detailed.

ii. The Principle of Transparency under Regulation (EU) 2018/1725

The transparency principle was incorporated under Regulation (EU) 2018/1725 as an entirely new principle that did not exist under Regulation 45/2001/EC. As mentioned above, the right to information is the only right that data subjects do not have to exercise proactively. Hence, certain information, such as the contact

[107] Recital 41 of Regulation (EU) 2016/679 reads as follows: 'Where this Regulation refers to a legal basis or a legislative measure, this does not necessarily require a legislative act adopted by a parliament, without prejudice to requirements pursuant to the constitutional order of the Member State concerned. However, such a legal basis or legislative measure should be clear and precise and its application should be foreseeable to persons subject to it, in accordance with the case-law of the Court of Justice of the European Union (the "Court of Justice") and the European Court of Human Rights.' See also Sajfert (n 43) 215.

[108] See also EDPS, 'Guidance on Article 25 of the Regulation 2018/1725 and Internal Rules Restricting Data Subjects Rights (Updated 24 June 2020)' (2020), https://edps.europa.eu/sites/default/files/publication/20-06-24_edps_guidance_on_article_25_of_the_new_regulation_and_internal_rules_en.pdf.

[109] Article 25(5) of Regulation (EU) 2018/1725.

[110] Under Regulation (EU) 2016/679, the lawfulness of processing (legal bases) is set out under art 6, while under Directive (EU) 2016/680, art 8 provides for the legal basis for processing.

[111] Article 41(2) of Regulation (EU) 2018/1725. See also Juraj Sajfert, 'New Data Protection Regulation for EU Bodies: Another Piece of the Puzzle Completed' (2018) 4 *European Data Protection Law Review* 213, 215.

details of the controller,[112] the legal basis and the purposes of processing,[113] or the existence of data subject rights and how to exercise them,[114] need to be provided by the controller to the data subject once their personal data have been processed.

This means that under both the GDPR and Regulation (EU) 2018/1725, the controller should inform data subjects of any new purposes for which their personal data will be processed. As mentioned earlier, the LED diverges substantially from both the GDPR and Regulation (EU) 2018/1725 with regard to the transparency principle due to the particular area in which the Directive applies. Therefore, while the general details concerning the processing of personal data must be communicated, for instance, on the controller's website, whether a particular data subject is to be informed about specific processing activities depends on whether or not the conditions under Article 13(3) LED are fulfilled. If notification could jeopardise ongoing investigations, the person will not be informed of any processing measures until the investigation is terminated.

In addition, under Article 35 of Regulation (EU) 2018/1725, controllers are – besides their obligation to notify the EDPS (under Article 34 of Regulation (EU) 2018/1725) – required to communicate personal data breaches to the data subject if such breaches are likely to result in a high risk to the rights and freedoms of the data subjects concerned.

These new provisions are an essential element to put the data subject in control of their data and in order to allow him or her to understand what is happening to his or her data, and to enable him or her to exercise his or her rights.[115] At the same time, Regulation (EU) 2018/1725 contains a new chapter, which refers to the processing of so-called operational personal data. In a nutshell, Chapter IX foresees specific provisions that apply in the law enforcement context, where competent EU LEAs process personal data for law enforcement purposes. Chapter IX is therefore a separate regulation within Regulation (EU) 2018/1725, and replicates many rules from the LED. The specificities of that chapter and how it might be applied (and by whom) in the future will be discussed in the subsequent sections.

IV. Chapter IX of Regulation (EU) 2018/1725 on Operational Personal Data

The so-called 'law enforcement chapter' applies to EU bodies, offices and agencies processing operational personal data (law enforcement data) when carrying out activities that fall within the scope of Chapter 4 or Chapter 5 of Title V of

112 Article 16(1)(a) of Regulation (EU) 2018/1725.
113 ibid art 16(1)(c).
114 ibid art 16(2)(b).
115 On the principles of transparency under Regulation (EU) 2018/1725, see also Sajfert (n 43) 216.

Part Three TFEU. Those two chapters of Title V encompass provisions on judicial cooperation in criminal matter (Chapter 4, Articles 82–86) and police cooperation (Chapter 5, Articles 87–89). Hence, Chapter IX governs the processing of personal operational data in the area of the former Third Pillar regarding EU police cooperation and judicial cooperation in criminal matters.

For the time being, the only EU bodies acting in this area and that could be called EU law enforcement agencies are Europol, Eurojust and the EPPO.[116] In addition, Frontex, with its renewed mandate under the 2019 EBCGA Regulation, gained new tasks and an extended mandate, some of which include cooperation with Europol and Eurojust[117] or to contribute to the detection, prevention and combating of cross-border crime at the EU's external borders.[118] Hence, when the EBCGA carries out those newly gained tasks, the Agency might, in certain circumstances, be able to base its processing activities on the rules of Chapter IX.

With Chapter IX, the EU legislator sought to incorporate another regulation in the actual Regulation (EU) 2018/1725, thereby mirroring the GDPR and the LED, which apply at the national level in *one* legal instrument. As explained above, the different data protection rules in the area where the LED applies were fragmented and consisted of a patchwork of rules that were adopted in different times and for different purposes. Similarly, the landscape of data protection rules that existed before the entry into force of Regulation (EU) 2018/1725 at the EU level was, due to its fragmented nature, practically unreadable. Therefore, the approach of incorporating another chapter that would mirror the rules of the LED within the Regulation that was almost identical to the GDPR was logical in the sense that all data protection rules would gradually be aligned at both the EU and the national levels.

With regard to Eurojust, Regulation (EU) 2018/1725 introduced a *lex generalis, lex specialis* regime, in the sense that the rules under the Regulation became the general data protection regime applicable to the Agency, whereas under the 2018 Eurojust Regulation,[119] more specific rules than those under Regulation (EU) 2018/1725 and, in particular, Chapter IX were established. With the adoption of the recast Europol Regulation in February 2022, a similar solution was found for Europol, albeit with more opportunities for Europol to process large datasets more flexibly than Eurojust. Nevertheless, following the entry into force of Regulation

[116] There may be divergent views regarding the definition on what is meant with 'law enforcement'. Some more restrictive notions would not encompass Eurojust, Europol and the EPPO into that definition – the first two because they do not exercise coercive powers as such, but rather support/coordinate national authorities' activities (it should be noted that the boundaries between coercive and non-coercive have become rather blurred, especially for Europol). In any case, Eurojust, and in the future Europol (and the EBCGA), will apply the rules under Chapter IX and therefore be treated as law enforcers within this dissertation.

[117] Article 68(b) and (e) of Regulation (EU) 2019/1896.

[118] Article 1 of Regulation (EU) 2019/1896.

[119] Regulation (EU) 2018/1727.

(EU) 2018/1725, both Europol and the EPPO were only made subject to the Regulation when processing administrative data, while continuing to apply their own data protection rules to operational processing activities.

One of the reasons why Europol and the EPPO maintained – or were granted – their own *sui generis* data protection rules at the time of the adoption of Regulation (EU) 2018/1725 was that Chapter IX remained underdeveloped.[120] While the EPPO's data protection rules are similar to those under the LED, the rules that were applicable under the 2016 Europol Regulation were rather different in their stand-alone data protection provisions. This allowed the Agency to carry out more sophisticated analyses of large datasets without having to take into account some of the limitations imposed by additional data protection rules applicable to other agencies. The recast Europol Regulation did not introduce much of a change in that regard, as will be further illustrated in section VI below.

A. The Underdeveloped Nature of Chapter IX: The Most Problematic Provisions

Many of the data protection concerns that were described with regard to the LED apply regarding the processing of operational personal data by EU Agencies within the scope of Chapter IX of Regulation (EU) 2018/1725. Because most parts of Chapter IX were replicated from the LED,[121] this subsection will not discuss the individual provisions in detail, but rather will refer the reader to the previous chapter dealing with potential shortcomings under the LED. Nevertheless, it needs to be taken into account that Regulation (EU) 2018/1725 did not have to be transposed into different legal systems, and thus the concerns that may apply with regard to the wrongful transposition of the Directive do not occur at the EU level.

However, some of the provisions under Chapter IX are underdeveloped and not sufficiently elaborated, so the chapter should not be regarded as an adequate data protection regime to be applied by EU Agencies for the processing of operational personal data if no additional *lex specialis* regime to fill the gaps under Chapter IX applies. On the one hand, this is particularly true because those EU Agencies that currently process operational personal data did have more developed data protection rules within their constituting legal acts. This explains the *lex specialis* solution for Eurojust under its 2018 Regulation and the upholding of Europol's stand-alone data protection regime (as well as the *sui generis* data protection regime under the EPPO Regulation). However, also with regard to newly mandated agencies such as the EBCGA, the adoption of Chapter IX would have been a perfect opportunity

[120] In addition, Europol had just implemented new rules and the EPPO rules had just been adopted.

[121] Some rules were, just like the LED, inspired by the rules under the Europol Regulation. See Sajfert (n 43).

to harmonise all data protection rules applicable to EU bodies and agencies, and, furthermore, to render EU and national rules more compliant. This would, for instance, have been more beneficial with regard to the coordinated supervision system under Article 62 of Regulation (EU) 2018/1725, in particular where more data exchanges take place between the national and EU levels.

Instead, this opportunity to avoid double standards between national and EU rules was missed, Europol and the EPPO maintained their own data protection regimes, and the data protection rules for CSDP missions were completely neglected.[122] This led to a situation in which the recast Europol Regulation granted the Agency even more leeway to process operational personal data than its predecessor did without a subsequent completion of the rules under Chapter IX. An additional reason to leave Chapter IX underdeveloped was the argument that the only EU LEAs (Europol, Eurojust and the EPPO) that would apply Chapter IX already had their own (stricter) data protection rules. However, this argument ignored the possibility that other EU Agencies, such as the EBCGA, eu-LISA or the EUAA, could eventually argue that they may be eligible to carry out processing under Chapter IX.

While this discussion will not further refer to such possibilities with regard to eu-LISA and the EUAA, section V below will discuss situations in which the EBCGA could process personal data (of TCNs) within the scope of Chapter IX. Although it will be assumed that similar shortcomings to those at the national level with regard to the provisions under the LED apply, two even more problematic sets of rules in Chapter IX, Article 94 on international transfers and the question of supervision will be addressed below.

i. International Transfers

International transfers of operational personal data by EU institutions, bodies, offices and agencies are hardly regulated under Chapter IX of Regulation (EU) 2018/1725. Rather, the provisions allowing for such transfers rely on more specific provisions regarding the conditions for international transfers of operational personal data laid down in the founding acts of those EU institutions, bodies, offices and agencies that may carry out such transfers.[123]

With regard to Europol, Eurojust and the EPPO, all three bodies must adhere to stricter rules under their respective regulations. Transfers of operational personal data under the 2019 EBCGA Regulation are not explicitly envisaged. For most transfers, the EBCGA is supposed to apply the rules on international transfers under Chapter V of Regulation (EU) 2018/1725, which correspond with the rules

[122] On the other hand, rules that apply to activities carried out by EU institutions, bodies, offices and agencies always have to be based on art 16 TFEU, even if their processing is carried out within the framework of CSDP missions. See ibid 216.

[123] Article 94(2) of Regulation (EU) 2018/1725.

under the GDPR. Consequently, the 2019 EBCGA Regulation does not foresee any more specific rules on international transfers of operational personal data. Yet, there may be limited opportunities for the EBCGA to nevertheless carry out transfers of operational personal data within the scope of Chapter IX. On those limited occasions, it could theoretically use the underdeveloped rules under Article 94 of Regulation (EU) 2018/1725.

In accordance with Article 94(1) of Regulation (EU) 2018/1725, transfers of operational personal data to third countries and international organisations may take place in three constellations. First, an international transfer may be based on a Commission adequacy decision adopted in accordance with Article 36(3) of the LED, finding that a third country or a territory ensures an adequate level of data protection.[124] Second, where no adequacy decision exists (which for the moment is the case for most third countries[125] and may become a big issue in practice), international transfers may be carried out if an international agreement pursuant to Article 218 TFEU has been concluded between the EU and the third country or international organisation to which the data will be transferred. Such international agreements based on Article 218 TFEU must include adequate safeguards with respect to the protection of privacy and the fundamental rights and freedoms of individuals.[126] Third, and only where no adequacy decision or international agreement exists, an international transfer may be based on a cooperation agreement that allows for the exchange of operational personal data.[127] Such a cooperation agreement must be concluded before the date of application of the legal act establishing the EU body, office or agency concerned between that EU body, office or agency and the third country in question.

Pursuant to paragraph 3 of Article 94 of Regulation (EU) 2018/1725, the controller shall publish on its website and keep up to date a list of adequacy decisions and of agreements, administrative arrangements and other instruments relating to the transfer of operational personal data. In addition, paragraph 4 of the same provision establishes an obligation to keep detailed records of all transfers that were carried out pursuant to Article 94 of Regulation (EU) 2018/1725.

When comparing the provisions on international transfers under Chapter IX of Regulation (EU) 2018/1725 to those rules that exist under Chapter V of the Regulation, or the provisions under the GDPR and the LED, evident gaps are recognisable. Whereas Chapters V of Regulation (EU) 2018/1725, the GDPR and the LED contain detailed provisions on the cascading system regarding international transfers and provide specific conditions for when such transfers are carried out, Chapter IX merely includes one single article on transfers of operational personal

[124] ibid art 94(1)(a).

[125] For the moment, the only third country that obtained adequacy under the LED is the UK. See Commission, 'Implementing Decision of 28.6.2021 pursuant to Directive (EU) 2016/680 of the European Parliament and of the Council on the adequate protection of personal data by the United Kingdom' COM (2021) 4801 final, Brussels, 28 June 2021.

[126] ibid art 94(1)(b).

[127] ibid art 94(1)(c).

data to third countries and international organisations. Moreover, any obligation to carry out a proportionality assessment, to perform a balancing exercise of the rights of the data subjects or to provide necessary justifications for carrying out a particular transfer are missing under Article 94 of Chapter IX of Regulation (EU) 2018/1725. In addition, requirements on the assessment of appropriate safeguards and the documentation to be produced by controllers or information to be provided to the EDPS are non-existent under that article. Although controllers carrying out international transfers under Chapter IX might still have to take into account certain requirements on international transfers established by the CJEU, Article 94 is lacking important details, which could allow for a more profound system for transfers.

ii. Supervision by the European Data Protection Supervisor

The provisions on supervision like those that exist under Chapters VI,[128] VII[129] and VIII[130] of Regulation (EU) 2018/1725 are lacking with regard to the processing of operational personal data under Chapter IX. While some tasks and powers of the EDPS also exist for Chapter IX, most supervision powers are only laid down in the previous chapter and in the founding acts of the EU Agencies that were originally determined to apply Chapter IX.

Chapter IX indirectly provides for the right to lodge a complaint[131] and the possibility of data subjects to have their rights exercised by the EDPS, and stipulates that the EDPS may verify whether personal data were processed in accordance with Regulation (EU) 2018/1725.[132] In addition, some of the obligations of controllers, such as the logging requirement under Article 88, the obligations to carry out a DPIA for certain processing operations under Article 89, the prior consultation obligation under Article 90 and the notification of data breaches under Article 92 of Regulation (EU) 2018/1725, require a certain amount of contribution by the EDPS. A particular section that exclusively deals

[128] Chapter VI of Regulation (EU) 2018/1725 deals with the establishment (art 52) and appointment (art 53), as well as with the independence (art 55), professional secrecy (art 56), tasks (art 57) and powers (art 58) of the EDPS. These provisions are very similar to the provisions on national DPAs under Regulation (EU) 2016/679. In addition, Chapter VII includes more specific provisions on regulations and general conditions governing the performance of the European Data Protection Supervisor's duties, staff and financial resources (art 54) and on the obligation of controllers and processors to react on warnings, reprimands and referrals of cases to the European Parliament, the Council and the Commission (art 59), which do not exist under Regulation (EU) 2016/679/Directive (EU) 2016/680, as these would rather be set out under national law.

[129] Chapter VII of Regulation (EU) 2018/1725 includes two provisions concerning cooperation between the EDPS and national DPAs (art 61) as well as the coordinated supervision mechanism by the EDPS and national DPAs of large-scale IT systems and of EU Bodies, offices and agencies (art 62(2)).

[130] Chapter VIII, art 63–69 of Regulation (EU) 2018/1725 deals with remedies, liability and penalties.

[131] Under arts 79 (right to information), 80 (right of access) and 81 (limitations to the right of access), the controller shall notify the data subject of the possibility of lodging a complaint with the EDPS.

[132] Article 84(3) of Regulation (EU) 2018/1725.

with supervision is missing for the processing of operational personal data and the EDPS would not even be involved with regard to international transfers.

While both the Eurojust Regulation[133] and the recast Europol Regulation[134] contain specific provisions on supervision by the EDPS, the EBCGA Regulation does not include any provisions on EDPS supervision. On the one hand, this could be interpreted in a way that would make Chapter IV of Regulation (EU) 2018/1725 on supervision applicable to all processing operations by the EBCGA, including the processing of operational personal data.

Consequently, it could be argued that, unlike Eurojust and Europol, which only apply Article 3 and Chapter IX of Regulation (EU) 2018/1725 to the processing of operational personal data,[135] the EBCGA should apply Regulation (EU) 2018/1725 *whenever* processing personal data[136] and may *only* process operational personal data within the scope of Chapter IX when cooperating with Europol and Eurojust or when supporting Member States in the fight against cross-border crime and terrorism.[137] Hence, with regard to the EBCGA, the rules on supervision laid down in Chapter VI of Regulation (EU) 2018/1725 would then apply in all situations and provide for a robust system of oversight by the EDPS.

On the other hand, it could be argued that for all processing operations that involve operational personal data, only Chapter IX would be applicable and that, consequently, Chapter VI on EDPS supervision would not apply in those situations. Because the rules on supervision under Chapter IX are missing, this represents a substantial gap for those agencies whose founding acts lack rules on supervision. This is not only the case for the EBCGA, but would be the case regarding all EU Agencies that may process operational personal data within the scope of Chapter IX.

Against this background, it could be argued that because the rules on supervision are lacking in Chapter IX, the EBCGA Regulation should instead have included such rules in a similar way as the Europol, Eurojust or EPPO Regulations. However, if that were to be the case, this would mean that any newly established EU Agency that could theoretically process personal data within the scope of Chapter IX would have to include specific data protection rules (particularly on supervision and international transfers) in its founding act. Since this would make Chapter IX redundant, a more logical solution would be to update the rules (on international transfers and supervision) under Chapter IX in order to allow for safeguards with regard to the application of that Chapter to any EU Agency processing operational personal data.

[133] Chapter IV (processing of information) of Regulation (EU) 2018/1727 includes provisions on supervision by the EDPS (art 40), professional secrecy of the EDPS (art 41), cooperation between the EDPS and national DPAs (art 42), the right to lodge a complaint with the EDPS if operational personal data are processed (art 43) and the right to judicial review against the EDPS (art 44).

[134] Chapter VI (data protection) of the recast Europol Regulation.

[135] Article 26(1) of Regulation (EU) 2018/1727.

[136] Article 86(1) of Regulation (EU) 2019/1896.

[137] Article 90(1) of Regulation (EU) 2019/1896.

In addition, where data exchanges take place on different levels and between different agencies that apply different data protection regimes and are subject to different rules on supervision, the powers of the EDPS may be undermined once another authority subsequently processes certain operational personal data. Both the EBCGA and EUROSUR obtained a strengthened mandate to process personal data and to engage in cooperation with other EU Agencies and national authorities. Not only will it be more challenging for national DPAs and the EDPS to supervise the increased data exchanges on different levels, but the high standards that exist under one data protection instrument may also be undermined where another data protection regime includes different, less strict rules and the data may simply be exchanged between authorities in order to apply the least strict data protection framework.

V. The European Border and Coast Guard Agency Processing Personal Data: The Extended Mandate under the 2019 Regulation[138]

Distinguishing between the 'general Regulation' and Chapter IX of Regulation (EU) 2018/1725 is more straightforward than the delineation between the LED and the GDPR at the national level, as the latter depends very much on the national transposition of both the GDPR opening clauses and the LED. However, there are grey areas with regard to the definition of what constitutes EU bodies, offices and agencies that may process operational personal data under Chapter IX. As mentioned above, the material scope of Chapter IX defines its personal scope. This means that any EU body, office or agency processing operational personal data within the scope of Chapter 4 or 5 of Title V Part Three TFEU could apply Chapter IX.

On the one hand, this solution ensures that all EU bodies, offices and agencies that would be able to process operational personal data would have to adhere to the rules under Chapter IX without introducing specific data protection rules in their own founding acts. On the other hand, this opens up possibilities to interpret Chapter IX's scope in a broad manner that could allow for the inclusion of all those bodies, offices and agencies that may carry out processing activities within the scope of Chapters 4 or 5 of Title V of Part Three TFEU. However, which precise processing operations could be included within processing activities carried out for judicial cooperation in criminal matters or police cooperation might not always be clearly definable. This may, in particular, be the case in the context of

[138] In the future, cooperation will be drastically strengthened between the EBCGA and all kinds of national, EU and third-country authorities, but this section will only attempt to illustrate the issues related to data protection, which may also easily be applied to exchange of information with other authorities.

migration management and border control. Under the new EBCGA Regulation, some of the Agency's activities may be considered law enforcement activities, and for those purposes, the EBCGA could become – at least on a sporadic basis – an EU LEA and process operational personal data within the scope of Chapter IX.

During the last few years, numerous legislative texts have been introduced that provide a broader mandate to the EBCGA to process personal data. This mandate was codified, on the one hand, with the revision of existing databases, the adoption of new systems and the interoperability framework. On the other hand, the EBCGA Regulation changed the Agency from one that was to assist the Member States and would merely sporadically process personal data into one that would be able grow more and more into an information hub with executive powers.

A further initiative followed within the framework of the New Pact on Migration and Asylum, which was presented in September 2020[139] and included, inter alia, suggestions to further develop the procedures on pre-entry screening of TCNs.[140] Such procedures were further elaborated in the proposal for a so-called Screening Regulation,[141] which was issued on the same date as the New Pact on Migration and Asylum.

The following section illustrates how the 2019 EBCGA Regulation set up the provisions to allow for the restriction of data subject rights, including the transparency requirements, and further assesses the extent to which the Agency could apply Chapter IX of Regulation (EU) 2018/1725 to its processing activities. Both the restriction of data subject rights and the limitation of the transparency provisions may be provided for in internal rules adopted by the Agency.[142]

A. The 2019 European Border and Coast Guard Agency Regulation: More Possibilities for Processing Personal Data for More (Law Enforcement) Purposes

As illustrated above, the 2016 EBCGA Regulation established a new legal basis for the EBCGA to process personal data of individuals and transformed the Agency from a support agency into one that, since then, has gained additional competences to assist, together with Europol, in the identification and registration of TCNs, including the assessment of potential security threats and processing personal data when consulting EU databases.[143] While the 2004 and

[139] European Commission, 'Communication from the Commission to the European Parliament, the Council, the European Economic and Social Committee and the Committee of the Regions on a New Pact on Migration and Asylum, COM (2020) 609 final, Brussels, 23 September 2020' (2020).

[140] ibid 4.

[141] Proposal for a Regulation of the European Parliament and of the Council introducing a screening of third country nationals at the external borders and amending Regulations (EC) No 767/2008, (EU) 2017/2226 and (EU) 219/817, COM (2020) 612 final, Brussels, 23 September 2020.

[142] Article 86(2) of Regulation (EU) 2019/1896.

[143] Radjenovic (n 8) 8. See also Quintel (n 7).

the 2011 Frontex Regulations foresaw an assisting role for the Agency, the 2016 Regulation upgraded the EBCGA's mandate and competences, making return operations one of its primary tasks.[144] However, already in September 2018, while the EBCGA was still implementing the changes introduced with the 2016 Regulation, the Commission proposed yet another upgrade to its constituting legal framework.

The new Regulation was agreed by the co-legislator in April 2019, after only six months of negotiations, presumably so that it could be adopted before the European elections that took place in May 2019.[145] Under the 2019 Regulation, the EBCGA's budget was drastically increased and its mandate was reinforced compared to the 2016 Regulation. For instance, its tasks were augmented and broadened, ranging from the monitoring of migratory flows and the external borders[146] to providing operational assistance to Member States and third countries,[147] assisting in all stages of the return process,[148] cooperating with Europol and Eurojust,[149] third countries[150] and other EU Agencies,[151] managing and operating the False and Authentic Documents Online (FADO) database,[152] and fulfilling the EBCGA's tasks and obligations with regard to the ETIAS.[153] In total, Article 10 of the 2019 Regulation comprises 33 partially broadly formulated tasks, stretching from paragraph (a) to paragraph (ag).

In terms of personnel, the EBCGA will have its own European Border and Coast Coastguard Standing Corps,[154] which is supposed to increase to 10,000 members of staff by 2027.[155] The standing corps will be established by

[144] For an in-depth analysis of the 2016 EBCGA Regulation, including the Agency's role regarding (forced) returns, see, for instance, Sergio Carrera et al, *The European Border and Coast Guard: Addressing Migration and Asylum Challenges in the Mediterranean?* (*CEPS*, 1 February 2017); Sergio Carrera and Leonard den Hertog, 'A European Border and Coast Guard: What's in a Name?' (*CEPS*, 8 March 2016); Jorrit Rijpma, 'External Migration and Asylum Management: Accountability for Executive Action outside EU Territory' (24 November 2017), https://www.europeanpapers.eu/en/e-journal/external_migration_and_asylum_management_accountability_for_executive_action.

[145] Mariana Gkliati, 'EU Law Analysis: The New European Border and Coast Guard: Do Increased Powers Come with Enhanced Accountability?' (*EU Law Analysis*, 17 April 2019), https://eulawanalysis.blogspot.com/2019/04/the-new-european-border-and-coast-guard.html.

[146] Paragraphs (1)(a) and (d) of art 10 of Regulation (EU) 2019/1896.

[147] ibid art 10(1)(i).

[148] ibid art 10(1)(n).

[149] ibid art 10(1)(q).

[150] ibid art 10(1)(u).

[151] For instance, with the EASO or the FRA; see paras (1)(r) and (s) of art 10 of Regulation (EU) 2019/1896.

[152] FADO refers to the Falso and Authentic Documents Online system that is supposed to support the Member States to detect document fraud. See art 10(ae) of Regulation (EU) 2019/1896.

[153] Article 10(1)(af) of Regulation (EU) 2019/1896.

[154] Frontex, 'Legal Basis', https://frontex.europa.eu/about-frontex/legal-basis.

[155] Jane Kilpatrick, 'Analysis: Frontex Launches "Game-Changing" Recruitment Drive for Standing Corps of Border Guards' (*Statewatch*, March 2020), 3, https://www.statewatch.org/media/documents/analyses/no-355-frontex-recruitment-standing-corps.pdf; Chris Jones, 'Monitoring "Secondary Movements" and "Hotspots": Frontex is Now an Internal Surveillance Agency' (*Statewatch*, December 2019), https://www.statewatch.org/media/documents/analyses/no-348-frontex-internal-surveillance.pdf.

different categories of EBCGA operational staff[156] that are to carry out tasks relating to the identification, screening, registration and return of TCNs.[157] For these purposes, profiles such as *border guard officers*, *information officers*, *forced return escorts* and *support officers* as well as *return specialists* are supposed to be made available to the EBCGA's standing corps.[158] The activities of these staff members include risk analyses, vulnerability assessments and integrated planning projects together with other authorities.[159] Hence, the tasks of the different staff members are manifold and range from forgery detection and motor vehicle crime detection[160] to logistical and health support,[161] field press support[162] and operating aerial or maritime assets.[163]

Admittedly, not all of these tasks entail the processing of personal data, let alone operational personal data. Yet, many staff members will deal with information that may also include personal data. For instance, the so-called information officers are supposed to collect, monitor, process, update and validate operational information in near or real time, including through the execution of EUROSUR Fusion Services, or to contribute to the proper implementation of operational information gathering in the field, based on information issued by the EBCGA.[164]

Other staff members may even process special categories of personal data such as fingerprints. For instance, one of the tasks carried out by the EBCGA border guard officers is to perform screening interviews with TCNs who do not possess valid identification documents,[165] taking and recording fingerprints of TCNs crossing external borders illegally, and interviewing TCNs applying for asylum.[166] In addition, these border guard officers are tasked with contributing to the detection of cross-border crime and the identification of persons suspected of being involved in cross-border crime activities. The latter task comprises supporting the prevention and detection of cross-border crime, including migrant smuggling,

[156] (1) Statutory staff deployed in operational areas and staff responsible for the functioning of the European Travel Information and Authorisation System (ETIAS) Central Unit; (2) long-term staff seconded from the Member States; (3) staff from Member States who can be immediately deployed on short-term secondment to the EBCGA; and (4) reserve staff from the Member States for rapid border interventions. See Kilpatrick (n 155).

[157] ibid.

[158] Frontex, 'Annex to the Frontex Management Board Decision 1/2020 of 4 January 2020 on Adopting the Profiles to Be Made Available to the European Border and Coast Guard Standing Corps, Reg No 14060', https://frontex.europa.eu/assets/Key_Documents/MB_Decision/2020/MB_Decision_1_2020_adopting_the_profiles_to_be_made_available_to_the_EBC....pdf.

[159] Recital 26 of Regulation (EU) 2019/1896.

[160] Point 7.1 of Annex to the Frontex Management Board Decision 1/2020 of 4 January 2020 on adopting the profiles to be made available to the European Border and Coast Guard Standing Corps, Reg No 14060.

[161] ibid Point 9.2.2.

[162] ibid Point 9.2.4.

[163] ibid Point 13.1.

[164] ibid Point 3.2.

[165] ibid Point 2.2.3.

[166] ibid Point 2.2.4.

trafficking in human beings and terrorism, supporting the collection of information concerning the apprehension of TCNs, and supporting the preservation of evidence when detecting illicit or smuggled goods or during the apprehension of individuals.[167]

Likewise, so-called cross-border crime detection officers are required to contribute to crime detection and to the identification of suspected persons. Yet, unlike the border guard officers, cross-border crime detection officers not only have to support the collection of information and the preservation of evidence, and facilitate inter-service collaboration, but also have to prevent and detect cross-border crime, including migrant smuggling and the trafficking in human beings and terrorism.[168]

Whilst with regard to the tasks of border guard officers, it could be argued that their (processing) activities solely serve the auxiliary purpose of supporting the work of the *actual* LEAs, the functions of cross-border crime detection officers could be seen as *real* law enforcement activities.

The rules on the processing of personal data by the EBCGA are laid down in section 2 of the 2019 EBCGA Regulation. Articles 86–91 of the Regulation provide the legal basis for processing personal data for regular EBCGA staff. The provisions set out the general rules on processing,[169] the purposes for which the Agency may process personal data[170] and the conditions that apply when EBCGA staff process personal data that were collected during JITs, return operations, pilot projects, rapid border interventions and migration management support team deployments.[171] In addition, Articles 89 and 90 set out the rules on the processing of personal data in the EUROSUR framework and on the processing of operational personal data, respectively. Finally, Article 91 of the EBCGA Regulation deals with the retention of personal data by the EBCGA or in the systems operated by the Agency.

The general rules on processing under Article 86 of the EBCGA Regulation refer to Regulation (EU) 2018/1725 as the applicable data protection instrument and set out the conditions that apply with regard to the restriction of data subject rights as well as to international transfers.

The purposes of processing that may be carried out by the EBCGA are wide-ranging, presumably to match the Agency's tasks that are set out in Article 10 of the EBCGA Regulation. Besides processing personal data while organising and coordinating different missions,[172] the Agency may process personal data for the purposes of supporting the Member States and third countries in return

[167] ibid Point 2.2.5.
[168] ibid Point 6.2.
[169] Article 86 of Regulation (EU) 2019/1896.
[170] ibid art 87.
[171] ibid art 88.
[172] ibid art 87(1)(a).

operations and to operate return management systems,[173] in order to carry out risk analyses,[174] to operate the FADO system[175] and for administrative tasks.[176]

B. The Question of Applicable Data Protection Rules: The Same Dilemma as at the National Level?

The system of data protection rules at the EU level under Regulation (EU) 2018/1725 follows a similar logic to the one that applies at the national level within the framework of the GDPR and the LED. Hence, for the general processing of personal data, the GDPR applies at the national level and Regulation (EU) 2018/1725 at the EU level, with the exception of Chapter IX. For the processing of law enforcement/operational personal data carried out by competent authorities or by EU bodies, offices and agencies when carrying out activities that fall within the scope of Chapter 4 or Chapter 5 of Title V of Part Three TFEU, the LED or Chapter IX apply, respectively.

At the national level, the delineation between the GDPR and the LED is not always clear-cut due to both the definition of what constitutes a competent authority under Article 3(7) LED and the broad range of processing activities that may fall within the meaning of law enforcement processing. At the EU level, the situation is different, as the authorities that may process operational personal data within the scope of Chapter IX are not specifically defined.

Instead, the scope of Chapter IX of Regulation (EU) 2018/1725 is defined solely by making reference to the processing of operational personal data. This means, in essence, that when either the founding act of a newly established agency or amendments to the founding act of an existing agency allow for the processing of such operational personal data, that agency (body or office) may theoretically process those data within the scope of Chapter IX. Ultimately, this means that the scope of Chapter IX, despite the criticisms that were voiced in the previous chapter regarding the unclear scope of the LED, is even less clear than the scope under the Directive. Hence, similar problems to those at the national level arise with regard to the scoping exercise and the applicability between the 'general' Regulation and Chapter IX.

Because of the above-mentioned amendments to the founding act of the EBCGA that changed the character of its processing activities profoundly, the EBCGA could serve as an example for the problematic application of Chapter IX. With the entry into force of the new EBCGA Regulation, which confers upon the Agency many new tasks that may also be interpreted as *quasi*-law enforcement

[173] ibid art 87(1)(b).
[174] ibid art 87(1)(e).
[175] ibid art 87(1)(g).
[176] ibid art 87(1)(h).

tasks, any processing of personal data related to such tasks could fall within the scope of Chapter IX. In combination with the political incentive to shape the EBCGA more into a law enforcement agency, it is likely that any lack of clarity with regard to the scope of Chapter IX will lead to an application of the latter to various processing operations of the EBCGA in the future.

VI. Europol and Eurojust: Solutions after the Adoption of Regulation (EU) 2018/1725

At the time that Regulation (EU) 2018/1725 was adopted, different solutions for Eurojust and Europol as regards their adherence to the data protection rules under that regulation were found. While the Eurojust Council Decision was repealed by a Regulation that incorporated *lex specialis* rules in addition to Regulation (EU) 2018/1725,[177] Europol maintained its own data protection regime. The explanation to justify such different treatment was simple: the Eurojust Decision had needed to be reformed for a while, and not only regarding its data protection rules, while the Europol Regulation had just been adopted two years earlier.

Because of the underdeveloped nature of Chapter IX, the 2018 Eurojust Regulation required more specified rules with regard to the processing of operational personal data. Therefore, Chapter IX applies as *lex generalis* to Eurojust, while the Eurojust Regulation specifies individual provisions in its *lex specialis* regime, such as the rules on the DPO,[178] on the notification of data breaches to the authorities concerned,[179] on supervision,[180] on the rights of data subjects with regard to the EDPS[181] and on international transfers. In addition, it was considered particularly important to keep the rules on the Eurojust Case Management System,[182] the time limits[183] and the issue of consultation of national authorities regarding access to personal data requests.[184]

On 9 December 2020, the Commission issued a Proposal for a Regulation to amend the 2016 Europol Regulation.[185] The Proposal was adopted in February

[177] As well as the Rules of Procedure on the Processing and Protection of Personal Data at Eurojust [2020] OJ L50/10.

[178] Articles 36, 37 and 38 of Regulation (EU) 2018/1727.

[179] ibid art 39

[180] ibid arts 40, 41 and 42.

[181] The right to lodge a complaint with the EDPS with respect to operational personal data or the right to judicial review against the EDPS under arts 43 and 44 of Regulation (EU) 2018/1727, respectively.

[182] Articles 23, 24 and 25 of Regulation (EU) 2018/1727.

[183] ibid art 29.

[184] ibid art 31(3).

[185] Proposal for a Regulation of the European Parliament and of the Council amending Regulation (EU) 2016/794, as regards Europol's cooperation with private parties, the processing of personal data by Europol in support of criminal investigations, and Europol's role on research and innovation, COM (2020) 796 final, Brussels, 9 December 2020.

2022 and follows a similar solution to the one under the Eurojust Regulation with regard to the processing of personal data. Hence, while Regulation (EU) 2018/1725 had already been applicable to the processing of administrative personal data[186] by Europol, Chapter IX of that Regulation only became applicable to Europol with the reform of its 2016 founding act.[187] However, the solution found with regard to the Europol Proposal differs from the one under the Eurojust Regulation. While the rules under the Eurojust Regulation are more or less aligned with the rules under the LED, the recast Regulation Europol provides more leeway for the Agency to engage in undefined data analytics. Because the nature of the processing carried out by Europol and Eurojust varies in many ways, the recast Europol Regulation creates more opportunities to carry out processing in a very flexible manner.

As mentioned earlier, Europol underwent an impressive development regarding its operational capabilities to carry out data analytics, while Eurojust remained a more static Agency that works with files that are handled according to individual cases and only cross-matched on a case-by-case basis. Hence, Europol's capabilities with regard to data analytics are much further developed than those of Eurojust. Not only are the rules on receiving personal data from the national authorities different from those that apply to Eurojust, but Europol's own databases also allow it to engage in more sophisticated analytics of personal data, cross-checking and matching different pieces of information from different sources in order to identify connections or other relevant links between information.[188] While Eurojust's case management system only allows for the sharing of work files on a case-by-case basis, Europol's systems are by default more interconnected in order to let it find correlations between different cases. Hence, the processing of personal data by Europol takes place in a more fluent and less clearly defined manner in order to enable the 'finding of the needle in the haystack'.

A. The Recast Europol Regulation

The amendments to the 2016 Europol Regulations came early, as the latter foresaw an evaluation assessing the impact, effectiveness and efficiency of Europol only by May 2022.[189] The time until 2022 could have allowed for a reform of the provisions under Chapter IX of Regulation (EU) 2018/1725 in order to provide a harmonised framework that would be applicable to all EU law enforcement Agencies. Instead, the Europol Proposal lacked an Impact Assessment[190] and preceded the revision

[186] All those personal data, which are not operational personal data and are unrelated to criminal investigations.

[187] Recital 36 of the recast Europol Regulation. Regulation (EU) 2022/991 of the European Parliament and of the Council of 8 June 2022 amending Regulation (EU) 2016/794, as regards Europol's cooperation with private parties, the processing of personal data by Europol in support of criminal investigations, and Europol's role in research and innovation [2022] OJ L 169/1.

[188] Article 18(2) of Regulation (EU) 2016/794.

[189] COM (2020) 796, 2.

[190] The proposal was only accompanied by an Inception Impact Assessment. See ibid 8.

of Regulation (EU) 2018/1725. The Commission missed an important opportunity to strengthen the data protection rules applicable to processing by Europol in line with the processing capabilities that the Agency was granted under its recast Regulation.

Most importantly, however, the final text that was agreed by the co-legislators on 1 February 2022 includes changes to the Commission proposal, which retroactively make legal the processing operations that were sanctioned by an EDPS order from January 2022.[191] The text of the recast Europol Regulation substantiates the already questionable processing operations by the Agency by setting the focus on the analysis of large and complex datasets to address Europol's 'big data challenge'. In addition, the recast Regulation seeks to remedy an alleged lack of cooperation between private parties and Europol, and to strengthen Europol's role in research and innovation.[192] Finally, the recast Regulation foresees enhancing Europol's cooperation with third countries and the EPPO.[193]

While the recast text will not be discussed in detail, several provisions that are crucial regarding the new data protection rules applicable to Europol and the provisions on EDPS supervision merit a further assessment in the following subsections.

i. New Processing Capabilities

Article 18(6a) of the recast Europol Regulation[194] allows the Agency, prior to processing carried out for the purposes of cross-checking aimed at identifying connections,[195] to process personal data received for the sole purpose of performing a data subject categorisation. In order to achieve this, Europol may match those data against all information already in its possession for an extendable period of 18 months. Where that period is prolonged to a maximum of three years, Europol shall *inform* the EDPS and functionally separate the data in question from other data. Where it is established that the data to be categorised do not fall within the data subjects under Annex II, Europol must delete the data and inform the provider of the data, *where relevant*.

The new paragraph not only extends the period for the categorisation of data subjects by 12 months, but also provides a legal basis for Europol to cross-check the information of individuals against all datasets that it holds, before having

[191] EDPS (n 60).

[192] COM (2020) 796, 3. Although the provisions on research and innovation signify additional possibilities for Europol to engage in very undefined processing, these will not be further discussed here.

[193] ibid.

[194] This section is based on Teresa Quintel, 'The EDPS on Europol's Big Data Challenge in Light of the Recast Europol Regulation' (2022) 8 *European Data Protection Law Review* 90.

[195] Connections or other relevant links between information related to perpetrators or suspects and by way of analyses of a strategic or thematic nature and operational analyses; see art 18(2) of Regulation (EU) 2016/794.

established whether that data contain information on innocent individuals. Moreover, Europol is merely required to *inform* the EDPS of a decision to extend the processing period. Europol's Management Board shall further define access authorisation and storage periods after *consulting* the EDPS.[196] Hence, the supervisor essentially has no say regarding the proportionality of those decisions.

The new paragraph 5 in Article 18 of the recast Europol Regulation essentially abandons the data subject categorisation for processing carried out pursuant to the new Article 18a. The latter provision inserts additional opportunities for Europol to engage in the processing and analysis of large and complex datasets, and to carry out pre-analyses of personal data received in order to determine whether the data contain information about data subjects related to crimes that fall within the competence of Europol.[197]

Moreover, Article 18a explicitly authorises Europol to process personal data *outside* the categories of data subjects listed in Annex II.B if such processing is in support of a specific criminal investigation and received by a national competent authority, Eurojust or the EPPO. In such cases, Europol may process the data without having to take into account the limitations under Annex II.B by way of operational analysis or to cross-check the data in question[198] for as long as the processing supports an ongoing investigation.[199] Where Europol determines that it would not be feasible to carry out its operational analyses or cross-checking in compliance with the provisions on data subject categorisation, it may engage in such processing and disregard the categorisation obligation. Once the processing is terminated, Europol shall send the assessment on the decision to disregard the data subject categorisation to the EDPS.[200]

The data must be functionally separated from other data and may only be accessed where necessary for the support of the specific criminal investigation for which they were provided. Europol itself would verify whether personal data received from a national competent authority, an EU Agency or, in specific cases a third country, could be necessary for supporting a specific criminal investigation, even if those personal data are not listed under the categories of data subjects that may be processed for the purpose of cross-checking under Article 18(2)(a) of the Europol Regulation.[201] In cases where data were provided by a third country authority, the Europol DPO may decide to notify the EDPS *where relevant*. In addition, Europol shall check whether the case file has been obtained in manifest violation of fundamental rights, in which case the Agency may not process the file.

[196] Article 18(6b) of Regulation (EU) 2022/991.
[197] COM (2020) 796 final, 14.
[198] Article 18a(1)(a)(i) and (ii) of Regulation (EU) 2022/991.
[199] ibid art 18a(2).
[200] ibid art 18a(1)(b).
[201] See point A of Annex II to Regulation (EU) 2016/794, listing the categories of personal data and categories of data subjects whose data may be collected and processed for the purpose of cross-checking as referred to in point (a) of art 18(2). See also art 18a(1) of COM (2020) 796 final.

However, exactly how Europol would be able to verify in what manner the third country authority obtained the case file remains unclear.

In other words, the recast Europol Regulation provides a legal basis to process personal data that would not have to be limited to persons who are suspected of having committed or having taken part in a criminal offence and persons regarding whom there are factual indications suggesting that they will commit criminal offences.[202] It thereby codifies those processing operations that were declared illegal in the EDPS order and even retroactively legalises the concerned processing activities.[203]

ii. New Data Protection Rules

According to the proposal for the Europol Regulation, the suggested amendments were supposed to further strengthen the data protection framework applicable to the Agency. The proposal emphasised five provisions that (allegedly) contribute to such strengthening of data protection standards.[204]

First, and with regard to the data protection rules applicable to the Agency, the recast Regulation makes Europol subject to Article 3 and Chapter IX of the Regulation (EU) 2018/1725. The latter shall govern the processing of personal data by Europol as *lex generalis*, while the tailor-made data protection rules under the Europol Regulation remain as *lex specialis*. The processing of administrative personal data by Europol continues to be covered by the remaining chapters of the Regulation (EU) 2018/1725.[205]

Second, the recast Regulation suggests adding biometric data within the meaning of special categories of personal data under Article 30(2) of the recast Europol Regulation. In essence, this would align the wording of that provision with other existing data protection laws, which customarily define biometric data as special categories of personal data. Hence, this inclusion was long overdue, as under the 2016 Europol Regulation, biometric data were not defined as special categories of personal data and could therefore be treated without the provision of additional safeguards. And yet again, while other special categories of personal data shall be subject to appropriate safeguards with regard to the rights and freedoms of the data subject and shall be processed only and if supplemented by other personal data processed by Europol, biometric data are excluded from such requirements.[206]

Third, with Article 33(a), the recast Europol Regulation asserts to put forward additional safeguards concerning the processing of personal data for research and

[202] See point A.1(a) and (b) of Annex II to Regulation (EU) 2016/794.

[203] See art 74a of Regulation (EU) 2022/991 regarding the transitional arrangements concerning the processing of personal data in support of a criminal investigation.

[204] COM (2020) 796 final, 14.

[205] Article 27a (1) of Regulation (EU) 2022/991.

[206] Article 30(2) final text of the recast Europol Regulation.

innovation. For instance, any anticipated project must be subject to prior authorisation by the Europol Executive Director and must be based on a description of the envisaged processing, the personal data to be processed, the retention period and the conditions to access the data undergoing processing. Yet, as the EDPS emphasised in his Opinion on the European Strategy of Data, the definitions and scope of key concepts related to research and innovation are not provided.[207]

Fourth, with Article 39a, the recast Europol Regulation seeks to introduce a new provision on keeping records of categories of data processing activities, which would signify an alignment with other data protection instruments, namely the GDPR, the LED and the EUDPR. Hence, this provision on record keeping would be a new safeguard under the Europol Regulation, albeit being routine under other existing EU data protection rules.

Finally, the recast Regulation adds more detail regarding the designation, position and tasks of the Data Protection Officer of Europol pursuant to Articles 41a–41c and supplements the powers of the EDPS. Under Article 43(1)(j), (k) and (l), the EDPS now has the power to order the controller or processor to bring processing operations into compliance with the provisions of the recast Europol Regulation, to order the suspension of data flows to a recipient in a Member State, a third country or to an international organisation, and to impose an administrative fine in the case of non-compliance by Europol. This is an important insertion, as the 2016 Europol Regulation lacked substantive corrective powers for the EDPS. However, where the EDPS is not informed about certain risky processing operations, it will be challenging for it to exercise its powers.

At first, the above provisions seem to be an essential improvement of the data protection rules applicable to Europol. However, after a second glance, it becomes apparent that all of the above novelties, with the exception of the provision on processing for research and innovation, already exist in the other data protection instruments that apply to national authorities as well as to EU law enforcement Agencies such as Eurojust and the EPPO.[208] Hence, the alleged amelioration under the Europol recast Regulation should be seen as gold-plating of the above provisions, as they merely align with already-existing rules.

iii. What Does Europol's New Data Protection Framework Mean in Practice?

The final text of the recast Europol Regulation includes a series of worrying provisions, which essentially and retroactively make legal the breaches that

[207] EDPS, 'Opinion 3/2020 on the European Strategy of Data' (16 June 2020) para 40. See also Niovi Vavoula and Valsamis Mitsilegas, 'Strengthening Europol's Mandate: A Legal Assessment of the Commission's Proposal to Amend the Europol Regulation' [2021] PE 694.200 (May 2021) 41.

[208] Although it should be mentioned that the EDPS has no power to impose administrative fines against Europol or the EPPO.

were sanctioned by the EDPS in his order of 3 January 2022.[209] New processing operations of large datasets will be widely authorised without any restriction and will be extended to cover any data collected in a broad context of any criminal investigation by a Member State.[210] The final section of this chapter will primarily comment on some of the worrying provisions linked to the EDPS order – most importantly, Article 18a of the recast Europol Regulation. Thereafter, it will address some of the additional concerns that arise in relation to Europol's way of handling personal data in more general terms.

Under the 2016 Europol Regulation, Europol was not permitted to temporarily process the personal data of individuals not falling within the categories of data subjects foreseen in Annex II.B for the purpose of verifying whether the personal data received fell into those categories.[211] Under the new Article 18a of the recast Europol Regulation, the Agency not only obtained a mandate to carry out processing of personal data outside the categories of data subjects listed in Annex II.B, but will also be permitted to match uncategorised data against all data already in its possession and to carry out processing of large and complex datasets by way of operational analysis. Article 18a(1)(b) of the recast Regulation even enables Europol to assess *itself* whether or not it is feasible to carry out an analysis for a specific investigation in compliance with the data subject categorisation requirement. The EDPS will merely have to be *informed* once the criminal investigation is terminated. However, where the EDPS is not aware of such processing operations, it will become more challenging to scrutinise the latter's legality. It will be up to the EDPS to conduct regular and thorough investigations. This de facto renders the role of the EDPS as advisory body and statutory authority dispensable. The requirement to only inform the EDPS of operational data processing after an investigation is over might take several years and would significantly decrease the capability of the EDPS' to scrutinise Europol's processing activities.

While the EDPS regarded the processing operations that are now being legalised as exceptional derogations from the rule,[212] such processing should be seen as unlawful and at odds with any general data protection principle. In addition, Europol will be able to process the personal data of individuals who do not have an established link to a criminal activity and thus originally never fell into its competence. Hence, such processing should not be an exceptional derogation or become the new standard under the recast Regulation.

The recast Europol Regulation will provide a new mandate and a legal basis for Europol to carry out processing activities in which it was already engaging,

[209] Wojciech Wiewiórowski, EDPS, 'Remarks at the LIBE Committee on Europol', https://edps.europa.eu/data-protection/our-work/publications/speeches-articles/remarks-libe-committee-europol_en, 3.

[210] Wojciech Wiewiórowski, EDPS, 'Presentation of the EDPS Annual Report 2021 before the European Parliament's Committee on Civil Liberties, Justice and Home Affairs (LIBE)', https://edps.europa.eu/press-publications/publications/speeches-articles_en, 2.

[211] EDPS Decision in Cases 2019-0370 and 2021-0699, point 4.15.

[212] Wiewiórowski (n 209) 3.

but which were admonished by the EDPS. Now, by codifying existing processing operations in the recast Regulation, the latter will legalise what Europol was already doing and for which it had no legal basis. Besides legalising the current processing practices, Article 18a further adds on the processing operations that the EDPS had ordered to be terminated.

Consequently, the final text legalises the processing operations that were declared in breach of the 2016 Europol Regulation, codifies and further strengthens the way in which the Agency may process large and complex datasets without having to carry out a data subject categorisation, and renders the supervisory powers of the EDPS close to meaningless with regard to those processing operations. In addition, pursuant to Article 39(1) of the recast Regulation, prior consultation shall not apply to specific individual operational activities that do not include any new type of processing. In other words, where the EDPS is of the opinion that the envisaged processing would infringe the Regulation (EU) 2018/1725, Europol may nevertheless initiate the processing if it is of substantial significance and necessary to prevent an immediate threat of a criminal offence prior to receiving written advice by the EDPS.[213]

However, while the recast Europol Regulation might give the Agency a mandate to continue its currently questionable processing activities, it could be argued that the Regulation (EU) 2018/1725, as *lex generalis* applicable to Europol, sets a higher threshold for the protection of personal data and thus, would not allow for the intended processing activities.[214]

While the EDPS solely looked at the data minimisation and storage limitation principles under Regulation (EU) 2018/1725, the other general principles under the Regulation should also be taken into account. One should ask oneself whether the processing carried out by Europol could be brought into compliance with the principles of fairness or purpose limitation where the data of innocent people are cross-checked against information of suspects and perpetrators – and, even if Europol now obtained a legal basis to carry out such processing, whether this would make it more fair or justifiable.

When taking into account further rules than only those related to the protection of data, one should also consider the right to the presumption of innocence under Article 48 of the Charter. Where personal data of individuals who are not linked to any criminal activity may be processed over a period of several years because Europol assesses that there is a need for such processing, this should not be seen as being in conformity with Article 48(1) of the Charter.

The new Europol Regulation offers a whole new range of processing capabilities that were already declared illegitimate prior to the 2022 EDPS order

[213] In accordance with art 90(4) of Regulation (EU) 2018/1725.

[214] See, by analogy, the analysis carried out with regard to such profiling under the LED: Juraj Sajfert and Paul de Hert, 'Variety, Velocity, and Volume of Personal Data in Criminal Investigations and Proceedings: The Limits Drawn by the Purpose Limitation and Data Minimization Principles in Directive (EU) 2016/680' in Valsamis Mitsilegas and Maria Bergström (eds), *Research Handbook on EU Criminal Law* (Edward Elgar, 2022).

(for instance, Europol had no legal basis to host FIU Net)[215] or processing operations for which it was questionable whether the 2016 Regulation provided a legal basis (for instance, Europol's EMSC)[216] to the Agency.

Another question is why law enforcement authorities in the Member State were sending uncategorised personal data to Europol despite Article 6 LED requiring national competent authorities to categorise these into different types of data subjects themselves. The goals of the Stockholm Programme to make Europol a hub for information exchange between the law enforcement authorities of the Member States[217] led to Europol receiving more and more data from those authorities. This generated a situation in which Europol, when receiving such large datasets, was often unable to ascertain whether all information contained in these large datasets was in compliance with the limitations under its own Regulation, since the content of the datasets is often unknown until the moment of extraction.

One of the underlying concerns that may be linked to the EDPS order against Europol is that investigative analyses of the Agency are increasingly carried out by way of AI-based algorithms, based on pre-determined criteria to identify suspicious individuals or criminal behaviour. Such processing requires large amounts of information that allows Europol to *connect the dots* by way of matching data from different sources. Europol seems to have developed from an information hub that was merely supposed to support national authorities into an Agency that carries out criminal analyses on its own.[218] Evidently, this may also affect TCNs in situations where Europol exchanges their personal data with the EBCGA, where their personal data in the interoperability components are matched against Europol data, or where national LEAs provide their personal data to Europol. Because of the way in which Europol may restrict data subject rights, this can entail serious repercussions for TCNs.

Presumably, Europol was able to develop more sophisticated processing capabilities than most of its national counterparts. However, Europol's strengthened mandate is not accompanied by adequate safeguards that would ensure sufficiently high data protection standards. This is unfortunate, as Europol as an EU Agency could have served as a primary example to demonstrate that strong data protection rules can go hand in hand with effective crime prevention. Instead, the EU legislator granted more and more powers to Europol to the extent that it has developed

[215] *cf* Eero Heinäluoma, Karel Lannoo and Richard Parlour, 'CEPS-ECRIT Task Force Report: Anti-money Laundering in the EU – Time to Get Serious (Centre for European Policy Studies (CEPS), January 2021) 13, https://www.ceps.eu/wp-content/uploads/2021/01/TFR_Anti-Money-Laundering-in-the-EU.pdf.

[216] Europol (n 55).

[217] Explanatory Memorandum to the Proposal for a Regulation of the European Parliament and of the Council on the European Union Agency for Law Enforcement Cooperation and Training (Europol) and repealing Decisions 2009/371/JHA and 2005/681/JHA, COM (2013) 173 final, 27 March 2013, Document No 52013PC0173.

[218] Wiewiórowski (n 210) 3.

an abundance of additional processing capabilities in order to analyse large and complex datasets. Whether this is in line with the mandate conferred upon it under Article 88 TFEU may be disputable.

VII. Conclusion

As has been shown throughout the previous sections, data exchanges among EU Agencies, between EU Agencies and national authorities, as well as with third countries or private parties have become increasingly intensified over the past few years.

Particularly within the AFSJ, data processing activities are often opaque, which makes it difficult for data subjects to ascertain who is processing their personal data. In addition, many TCNs whose personal data are being processed have difficulties comprehending the complex system of AFSJ databases, Agencies and authorities that may process their personal data. For those individuals, it is extremely challenging to exercise their data subject rights, not least because many TCNs who come to the EU do not know what rights they have under EU data protection legislation. The additional layers of complexity that have been added with the new AFSJ databases and interoperability, and the intensification of data exchanges between different authorities at different levels, make it even more difficult for those individuals to exercise their rights. Therefore, the first steps to ensure compliance with data protection principles and other fundamental rights are clearly defined processing activities and strict supervision.[219]

With regard to those EU Agencies that became increasingly involved in migration-related matters, the risks for a lowering of data protection standards as well as for data subject rights are manifold. On the one hand, the data flows between the different agencies became more and more incomprehensible, which makes it difficult to retrace the initial source of information and to identify the responsible controller. On the other hand, the Agencies became increasingly autonomous and were attributed new competences to process the personal data of TCNs. In addition, their mandates were broadened to accommodate new tasks and functions, reaching into additional fields. Particularly in the context of migration, such increased competences and mandates exacerbate the risk of function creep and foster the dilution between the migration and criminal law sphere.

In order to apply data protection rules in a consistent manner, clear boundaries between these two areas of law are essential, as different data protection rules will apply depending on the purpose for which the personal data are processed. Where authorities or agencies may process personal data for many different purposes and easily adapt the purpose of processing, it becomes more difficult to ascertain which

[219] Simona Demková and Teresa Quintel, 'Allocation of Responsibilities in Interoperable Information Exchanges: Effective Review Compromised?' (2020) 6 *Cahiers Jean Monnet* 589.

data protection rules should be applied. In addition, where data exchanges take place between agencies that apply different processing methods and may treat the information that they receive under different rules, this increases the likelihood of unlawful processing. If an agency receives data that are the result of processing that the agency itself would not have been permitted to carry out, this leaves doubts concerning both legality and accountability.

While Europol as an EU LEA became more involved in the field of migration, the EBCGA as a migration and border control agency obtained more tasks that are seemingly of a law enforcement nature. Under its new constituting act, the EBCGA shall increasingly engage in data exchanges with other EU Agencies as well as with national authorities. The recast Europol Regulation, on the other hand, broadens the Agency's possibilities of strengthening cooperation with other partners to engage in the analysis of large and complex datasets. This will foster any synergies between the two agencies and presumably contribute to further diluting the delineation between migration and law enforcement processing.

With regard to Eurojust, its role in migration-related processing is (at least for the moment) minor, as its mandate did not undergo a broadening of competences as did those of Europol and the EBCGA. Strictly speaking, Eurojust is arguably subject to the most stringent data protection standards, albeit having to deal with a rather complex set of rules. The EBCGA, on the other hand, could, in certain cases, process personal data within the scope of Chapter IX of Regulation (EU) 2018/1725, while not having to respect additional rules such as those under the *lex specialis* regime in the Eurojust Regulation. Europol maintained, even under the recast Europol Regulation, its stand-alone and more flexible data protection regime, and was given more opportunities to engage in the processing of extremely large datasets that may be analysed computationally to reveal patterns, trends and associations related to crime.

In addition, the interactions between Europol and the EBCGA with other competent authorities seem more fluid and less restrained than those in which Eurojust may engage. That is, after all, somehow inherent in the fact that Eurojust is deeply interconnected with judicial proceedings, where there are well-defined limits within which data may be processed. When it comes to police-like authorities such as Europol, the boundaries are by definition less strict, not least because – generally speaking and to the greatest extent possible – police also prevent crime, while prosecutors are mainly competent for pursuing crimes *after* they have been committed.

As mentioned above, intensified data exchanges take place not only among EU Agencies but also between authorities at the national and EU levels. At the national level, the competent authorities in the Member States apply either the GDPR or the LED, depending on the purpose of the processing. Hence, where data exchanges between the national and the EU levels take place, attention must be paid to the different applicable rules. The reform of Regulation 45/2001/EC was the ideal opportunity to harmonise the rules at the EU level with those that entered into force at the national level just a few months earlier. However, the solution reached during the negotiations on Regulation (EU) 2018/1725 first acquitted Europol of becoming subject to the rules under Chapter IX and instead led to the adoption of the recast Europol Regulation before Regulation (EU) 2018/1725 was revised.

Access to AFSJ databases and the interoperability components constitutes yet another building block in the construction of a complex framework that was built around the migration and border management structures within the EU. With the new databases and their connection via the interoperability project, more actors at both the national and EU levels will have access to the information stored in the interoperable system as well as the underlying AFSJ databases. The risk of such access possibilities leading to a dilution of processing activities is high and it will become increasingly challenging to identify the origin of the data or the different entities that processed them.

The reinforced processing possibilities for Europol under the recast Regulation and the increased mandate of the EBCGA to process personal data not only of an administrative nature add to this dilemma. The different regimes that apply to national and EU competent authorities, as well as the specific rules that apply to the different agencies at the EU level, make it difficult for data subjects to understand the way in which their personal data are processed and render the supervision of data flows extremely challenging.

A consistent and complete protection of data subject rights is key to a robust data protection regime. The blurred lines between migration and criminal law, and the fine nuances that exist between border management and security, lead to a dilution of responsibilities between different processing entities. This will make it increasingly challenging for supervisory authorities to draw a concrete picture of processing activities and the risks involved for individuals, in this case TCNs. In an environment in which data are continuously transmitted between different actors, it is important to ascertain who carried out which processing activity.

Therefore, supervisory authorities should be able to *follow* data flows between the different authorities instead of considering each specific controller separately. In order to achieve an effective supervision of the complex network of different processors, closer cooperation between national supervisory authorities and the EDPS to better comprehend the steps behind certain decision-making processes and to handle data subject requests effectively is of the utmost importance.[220]

[220] ibid.

Concluding Remarks

This volume aimed to address potential conflicts between different EU data protection laws within the wider spectrum of recent developments in the area of migration management, border control and asylum. The analysis specifically considered the way in which personal data of TCNs are processed by competent (law enforcement) authorities at both the national and EU levels.

Since the negotiations over the Schengen Agreement during the mid-1980s, which placed internal security at the heart of the abolition of internal borders, (irregular) immigration has been increasingly seen as presenting a new category of internal security challenge, as evidenced by the political agendas of the EU Member States. By including immigration, asylum and visa policies within the First Pillar, these policies became AFSJ matters. At the same time, the Hague Programme, which defined key priorities for the establishment of the AFSJ, placed, alongside the management of migration flows, a major emphasis on the strengthening of security measures within the EU.

Irregular migration and related crimes (such as migrant smuggling) steadily became a relevant topic at the EU level, resulting in the reinforcement of the EU's external borders (for example, through the fortification of fences at Ceuta, Melilla and elsewhere), the strengthening of relevant EU Agencies engaged in external border control and the installation of early-warning radar systems in pre-frontier areas. In recent years, and with the so-called *migration crisis*, migration management and border control has become an even more relevant element in the debate on internal security within the EU. In 2015, this security debate reached new heights in many Member States in the aftermath of the arrival of great numbers of individuals seeking asylum in the EU.

With the European Agendas on Security and on Migration, the Security Union Strategy and the New Pact on Asylum and Migration, the EU set out to address the parallel challenges of migration management, the fight against terrorism and organised crime. The call for an increased use of large-scale AFSJ databases set up at the EU level in order to improve the management of migration flows by facilitating information exchanges between relevant authorities was encouraged to a greater degree.

As one of the responses, the Commission proposed changes on the expansion of the main operational databases in order to enable the storage of additional information and to streamline access to personal data of TCNs by LEAs. As a final step, the Commission was tasked with examining the possibility of establishing a legal framework to enable the sharing of information among the different AFSJ databases. The long-term objective was to render all existing and anticipated AFSJ databases interoperable in order to use all data available to create exhaustive profiles of TCNs. The interoperability project was agreed upon by the co-legislator in May 2019 with the adoption of two Regulations that will interconnect all AFSJ databases and establish four new centralised components.

In the Member States, national legislation was amended in order to respond to the *migration crisis*, and, in many instances, asylum laws became stricter and often required the collection of additional personal data of TCNs. At the EU level, the role of EU Agencies was strengthened, for instance, with the entry into force of a new EBCGA Regulation and, in May 2022, the adoption of the recast Europol Regulation. With the changes to their founding acts, these EU Agencies were attributed a greater operational role in the processing of personal data, including (or particularly) those of TCNs.

The need for a revision of the data protection rules that existed under the old framework, namely the 95 Data Protection Directive and the 2008 DPFD, had already become visible prior to the changes to the AFSJ databases and the increase of powers of EU Agencies. With the abolition of the pillar structure, the EU not only obtained the right of initiative for former Third Pillar matters, but also the competence to legislate by way of Regulations and Directives of the European Parliament and the Council in that area. Conventions and Framework Decisions in the area of criminal justice were to be replaced, which made the revision of the 2008 DPFD necessary. In 2012, the European Commission presented a legislative package to reform the outdated data protection framework that was primarily based on the 95 Data Protection Directive. The EU Data Protection Reform comprised two legislative instruments, the GDPR and the LED, the latter being applicable in the police and criminal justice sector. Hence, while the 95 Data Protection Directive was repealed by the GDPR, the processing of personal data in the law enforcement context is regulated under the LED, replacing the DPFD.

In 2016, the EU Data Protection Reform had become both necessary and possible, seven years after the entry into force of the Lisbon Treaty and the EU Charter becoming legally binding. Since the entry into force of the Lisbon Treaty, the CJEU had progressively bolstered the rights of data subjects through its case law, relying on Articles 7 and 8 of the EU Charter. In addition to Articles 7 and 8 of the EU Charter, Article 16 TFEU became a strong legal basis for the EU to legislate on matters concerning data protection. Both the provisions that form part of the EU Data Protection Reform and the rights under Articles 7 and 8 of the EU Charter apply to everyone in the EU, irrespective of nationality. Yet, in the context of border control and migration management, where personal data are needed for the assessment of TCNs, the rights of those individuals are often seemingly of a secondary nature.

While a majority of TCNs might not consider the right to data protection as important or might not even be aware that that right exists and equally applies to them as to EU citizens, data protection is one of the last lines of defence for vulnerable individuals, such as migrants and asylum seekers approaching EU external borders.[1] Yet, while in theory the same data protection rights as those that apply to EU citizens should apply to TCNs, the practical application of the law often suggests differently.

In the context of migration management, border control and asylum, detecting the applicable data protection instrument is of particular importance. In EU data protection law, the purpose of the processing and the authority processing the data determine the applicability of different sets of rules. Hence, while EU data protection law grants strong rights to individuals in the field of border control, migration and asylum (the GDPR), in a security-related context, competent authorities need to be able to apply data protection rules in a more flexible manner and are granted more leeway to restrict data subject rights of individuals (the LED). However, the delineation between those different types of data protection rules may prove difficult, as the events that occurred in recent years and in the aftermath of the *migration crisis* have not only led to the above-mentioned revision of many legal instruments in that area, but have also blurred the line between migration and security, migration law and criminal law.

TCNs such as visa applicants, (irregular) migrants and asylum seekers are subject to certain types of profiling measures when they apply for a visa in the EU or are being registered in the receiving countries. In order to determine whether an individual may be granted a visa, the personal data of an applicant are examined by the respective authorities and matched against other datasets. In the case of asylum applications, information regarding the route via which the person applying for international protection arrived in the recipient state is thoroughly scrutinised. Such administrative processing for the determination of visa eligibility or refugee status should fall within the scope of the GDPR. On the other hand, for processing that is carried out for the prevention, investigation, detection or prosecution of criminal offences, the LED should apply. Therefore, where national competent authorities such as the police, prosecutors or criminal judges process personal data for preventative and investigatory purposes, or to prosecute perpetrators, such processing falls within the scope of the Directive.

Because the LED is a minimum harmonisation instrument, it is essential to take into account the laws transposing it in the Member States in order to ascertain its scope of application at the national level and to locate potential gaps where its provisions were not transposed correctly. In certain Member States, it seems difficult to clearly determine the authorities that may fall within the personal scope of the LED, and thus the definition of what constitutes a competent authority that may process personal data according to the rules under the Directive. In other Member States, the *prevention, investigation, detection and prosecution of criminal*

[1] EDPS, 'Opinion 9/2020 EDPS Opinion on the New Pact on Migration and Asylum (30 November 2020)' 6, point 7.

offences including the safeguarding against and the prevention of threats to public security may be interpreted widely so as to include migration-related processing in the broader sense. In addition, sectoral laws at the national level may intersect with both the GDPR and the LED, and thus allow LEAs to apply the Directive to their processing activities, thereby broadening its scope of application.

One of the grey areas between the GDPR and the LED is the area of border control, migration and asylum. Particularly in the migration context, the blurred scope between the GDPR and the LED may lead to the processing of personal data of migrants and other TCNs within the scope of the Directive. This may be the case where competent LEAs access and subsequently process personal data from AFSJ databases or, in the future, the interoperability components. LEAs could also attempt to process the personal data of TCNs within the scope of the LED when carrying out random identity checks. Depending on the grounds for return, and whether the authority carrying out such return is a competent authority within the scope of the LED in a Member State, personal data could be transferred to third countries within the scope of the Directive.

In addition, relevant actors at the EU level obtained strengthened mandates to access, process and exchange personal data from the relevant AFSJ databases as well as the interoperable system. Two EU Agencies that are increasingly involved in the processing of personal data of TCNs are Europol and the EBCGA. These two Agencies process personal data within the scope of different legal frameworks. The exchange of personal data between these agencies, as well as with national authorities, presents risks for data subjects, as the recast Europol Regulation in particular maintains *sui generis* rules. While Regulation (EU) 2018/1725 (applicable to the EBCGA) introduced a chapter that foresees more flexibility whenever EU Agencies process operational personal data for law enforcement purposes, the recast Europol Regulation takes into account the additional law enforcement needs of the Agency to process large and complex datasets, including the personal data of TCNs. In the same vein, the EBCGA's mandate to process personal data was widened, in particular under its new Regulation from 2019. This means that, in situations where the EBCGA processes operational personal data, it is important to establish a clear delineation between Regulation (EU) 2018/1725 and its Chapter IX.

The new opportunities to process and link personal data within the area of migration management, border control and asylum require close cooperation at both the national and EU levels to guarantee the gapless supervision and scrutiny of processing operations. This was recognised with the revision of Regulation (EU) 2018/1725, which provides some clarity regarding the coordinated supervision between the national DPAs and the EDPS. However, beyond the scrutiny by national and EU data protection supervisory authorities, the Commission should thoroughly review the national laws transposing the LED and launch infringements against Member States that have failed to correctly transpose its provisions.

I. Outlook

Improving the exchange of information between LEAs in the EU is of paramount importance for tackling cross-border crime. However, the question is whether this is done in the right way and in a necessary and proportionate manner. The assimilation of migration management, border control and asylum with security concerns first materialised through the revision of AFSJ databases. Rendering those databases interoperable is, for the time being, the last exemplification in a series of steps to manifest such assimilation. However, the interoperability project will certainly not be the final step. More and more information that may be repurposed is being collected and exchanged within different networks and among different actors across the EU.

Where personal data are being processed, adherence to the purpose limitation principle is of utmost importance, as the purpose may define the applicable data protection instrument. Particularly in the area of migration and border control, there is a risk that the personal data of TCNs can be repurposed and subsequently processed for law enforcement purposes. In addition, connecting more and more data from different sources makes it challenging to define clear purposes for which the data should be processed; rather, the connection of information from different sources leads to a broadening of purposes and dilution between different areas.

Interoperability will revolutionarily change the way in which AFSJ databases have been governed so far and raises concerns regarding data protection standards, in particular the purpose limitation principle, as well as the requirement that a legislative measure must be necessary and proportionate.

In the near future, one of the initiatives with the greatest impact on the right to the protection of personal data (apart from the interoperability of AFSJ databases) will be the pre-entry screening procedure that will take place at the external borders of the EU. Such screening is envisaged in the Proposal for a Screening Regulation. Should the Regulation be adopted in its current form, the screening procedure will apply to all TCNs who cross an external border without authorisation, who apply for asylum during checks at the border or who are disembarked after a search and rescue operation. The objectives of the screening procedure are diverse and include identification, health and security checks, and vulnerability assessments, as well as the registration of biometric data in accordance with the new proposal on the revision of the Eurodac database. This will signify a further defeat for the purpose limitation principle, as personal data from different areas are processed for general objectives instead of clearly defined purposes.

Where the personal data of TCNs are being made increasingly available to competent (law enforcement) authorities – for instance, through streamlined access to AFSJ databases – the risk of a function creep increases. In addition, where purposes are increasingly broadened or objectives are treated as purposes, the dilution between migration law enforcement and criminal law enforcement becomes inevitable. This dilution makes a clear delineation between the GDPR and the LED at a national level and between Regulation (EU) 2018/1725 and its Chapter IX at the EU level more challenging.

In order to prevent an implicit lowering of data protection standards for TCNs, it would be important to clearly define the purposes of each processing operation in accordance with the purpose limitation principle. This seems difficult, if not impossible, when looking at the recently amended and newly established AFSJ databases, the interoperability Regulations with its numerous add-ons or the envisaged Screening Regulation. These initiatives confuse purposes with objectives, widen the purposes for which personal data of TCNs may be used and thereby gradually bring an end to the purpose limitation principle. Because individual purposes are no longer recognisable, the personal data of TCNs originally processed in the migration context may undergo a change of purpose and eventually be processed for alleged law enforcement purposes.

The scope of application of those data protection laws that apply to the processing of personal data in the law enforcement context is generally more broadly defined and may often be applied discretionally. Where it is not clear whether a purpose is of a migration or of a law enforcement nature, a competent authority could apply the more flexible data protection rules.

Ultimately, it remains to be seen whether certain Member States will introduce amendments to their national LED transposition acts and if the co-legislator will materialise the mandate in Article 98 of Regulation (EU) 2018/1725 and will complete Chapter IX with the needed provisions. Moreover, time will tell whether the EBCGA or other EU Agencies will indeed progressively engage in the processing of operational personal data and apply Chapter IX to such processing operations. Taking into consideration the pace at which EU Agencies developed during the last few years, the upgrade to Europol's processing capabilities should have been accompanied by stronger data protection rules. As regards the EBCGA and EUROSUR, as well as the EUAA, the completion of Chapter IX seems both necessary and inevitable, since their processing activities, including those of operational personal data, can only increase in the future.

BIBLIOGRAPHY

Aden H, 'Interoperability between EU Policing and Migration Databases: Risks for Privacy' (2020) 26 *European Public Law* 93

Ahmad I, 'Extraterritorial Scope of GDPR: Do Businesses outside the EU Need to Comply?' [2018] *Business Law Today* 1

Albers M et al, *Digitalisierte Verwaltung – Vernetztes E-Government* (Erich Schmidt Verlag 2018)

Aldhouse F, 'A Reflection on the Priorities of a Data Protection Authority' (2018) 34 *Computer Law & Security Review* 816

Alonso Blas D, 'Ensuring Effective Data Protection in the Field of Police and Judicial Activities: Some Considerations to Achieve Security, Justice and Freedom' (2010) 11 *ERA Forum* 233

——, 'The New Council Decision Strengthening the Role of Eurojust: Does it Also Strengthen Data Protection at Eurojust?' in *Data Protection in a Profiled World* (Springer 2010)

——, *Data Protection at Eurojust: A Robust, Effective and Tailor-Made Regime* (Eurojust 2011)

Andersson R, 'Europe's Failed "Fight" against Irregular Migration: Ethnographic Notes on a Counterproductive Industry' (2016) 42 *Journal of Ethnic and Migration Studies* 1055

Apfl VM, '5. Kapitel: Verfassungsmäßigkeit der Verdachts- und Ereignisunabhängigen Personenkontrollen – Art. 3 GG' in *Racial Profiling in Deutschland? Eine Untersuchung zu §22Absatz1aBundespolizeigesetzausderPerspektivederGleichheitsdogmatikundKognitionswissenschaft* (Peter Lang 2018)

Argomaniz J, 'Post-9/11 Institutionalisation of European Union Counter-terrorism: Emergence, Acceleration and Inertia' (2009) 18 *European Security* 151

Atanassov N, 'EPRS Briefing: Revision of the Schengen Information System for Border Checks', PE 599.341, 18 October 2018

Azzi A, 'The Challenges Faced by the Extraterritorial Scope of the General Data Protection Regulation' (2018) 9 *Journal of Intellectual Property, Information Technology and E-Commerce Law* 1

Bäcker M and Hornung G, 'EU-Richtlinie für die Datenverarbeitung bei Polizei und Justiz in Europa. Einfluss des Kommissionsentwurfs auf das nationale Strafprozess-und Polizeirecht' (ZD 2012) 147–152

Baker R, 'Is GDPR Compliance Essential? Ignoring the EU's New Online Privacy Rules Could Be a Big Gamble' (2018) 40 *New Hampshire Business Review* 23

Balboni P, Pelino E and Scudiero L, 'Rethinking the One-Stop-Shop Mechanism: Legal Certainty and Legitimate Expectation' (2014) 30 *Computer Law & Security Review* 392

Baldaccini A, *Whose Freedom, Security and Justice?: EU Immigration and Asylum Law and Policy* (Hart Publishing 2007)

Baldwin-Edwards M, 'Immigration after 1992' (1991) 19 *Policy & Politics* 199

——, 'The Emerging European Immigration Regime: Some Reflections on Implications for Southern Europe' (1997) 35 *Journal of Common Market Studies* 497

Baldwin-Edwards M and Schain MA, *The Politics of Immigration in Western Europe* (Routledge 2013)

Ballaschk J, 'In the Unseen Realm: Transnational Intelligence Sharing in the European Union – Challenges to Fundamental Rights and Democratic Legitimacy' (2015) 51 *Stanford Journal of International Law* 19

Balthasar A, '"Complete Independence" of National Data Protection Supervisory Authorities; Second Try: Comments on the Judgment of the CJEU of 16 October 2012, C-614/10, with Due Regard to its Previous Judgment of 9 March 2010, C-518/07' (2013) 9 *Utrecht Law Review* 26

Balzacq T and Carrera S, *Migration, Borders and Asylum: Trends and Vulnerabilities in EU Policy* (Centre for European Policy Studies 2005)

Barak A, *Proportionality: Constitutional Rights and Their Limitations* (Cambridge University Press 2012)

Barker V, 'Global Mobility and Penal Order: Criminalizing Migration, a View from Europe' (2012) 6 *Sociology Compass* 113

Barnard-Wills D, Pauner Chulvi C and de Hert P, 'Data Protection Authority Perspectives on the Impact of Data Protection Reform on Cooperation in the EU' (2016) 32 *Computer Law & Security Review* 587

Basilien-Gainche M-L, 'The EU External Edges: Borders as Walls or Ways?' (2015) 2 The *Journal of Territorial and Maritime Studies* 97

Bazzocchi V, 'The European Charter of Fundamental Rights and the Area of Freedom, Security and Justice' in G di Federico (ed), *The EU Charter of Fundamental Rights* (Springer Netherlands 2011)

Beckerhoff P, 'Reform des europäischen Datenschutzrechts: Ein Überblick unter besonderer Berücksichtigung des Datenaustausches zwischen Polizei-, Strafjustiz- und Geheimdienstbehörden' [2017] *Eucrim* 88

Bellanova R and Duez D, 'Le Citoyen Face aux Nouvelles Pratiques Sécuritaires de l'Union Européenne : Enjeux Démocratiques d'une Sécurité par les Fichiers' (2013) 2012 *Espace populations sociétés* 49

——, 'The Making (Sense) of EUROSUR: How to Control the Sea Borders?' in R Bossong and H Carrapico (eds), *EU Borders and Shifting Internal Security: Technology, Externalization and Accountability* (Springer 2016)

Bellanova R and Fuster GG, 'Politics of Disappearance: Scanners and (Unobserved) Bodies as Mediators of Security Practices' (2013) 7(2) *International Political Sociology* 188

Bellanova R, de Hert P and Gutwirth S, 'Variations sur le thème de la banalisation de la surveillance' (2010) 62 *Mouvements* 46

Bellanova R, Webster W and Kirstie B, *Surveillance and Democracy: Sympathies and Antagonisms* (Routledge 2018)

Benbouzid B, 'From Situational Crime Prevention to Predictive Policing. Sociology of an Ignored Controversy' (*Champ pénal*, 9 June 2015), https://journals.openedition.org/champpenal/9066

Benraad M, 'Peut-on Vaincre Daesh ? – Politique Internationale, N° 148 – Été 2015', https://politiqueinternationale.com/revue/n148/article/peut-on-vaincre-daech

Bergström M and Cornell AJ, *European Police and Criminal Law Co-operation* (Bloomsbury 2014)

Bergström M, Gammeltoft-Hansen T and Albertsen KB, Achievements and Challenges towards a European Migration Policy : The Stockholm Programme and Beyond (Notre Europe 2010) in E Fabry (ed), *Think Global – Act European 2010*

Bigo D, 'Criminalisation of "Migrants": The Side Effect of the Weele to Control the Frontiers and Sovereign Illusion' [2004] *Irregular Migration and Human Rights: Theoretical, European and International Perspectives* 61

——, 'Liberty, Whose Liberty? The Hague Programme and the Concept of Freedom' in S Carrera and T Balzacq (eds), *Security versus Freedom? A Challenge for Europe's Future* (Ashgate 2006)

——, 'The Principle of Availability of Information, Briefing Paper PE: 378272 for Directorate-General Internal Policies Policy Unit C: Citizens' Rights and Constitutional Affairs, European Parliament' (20 January 2006). https://www.europarl.europa.eu/RegData/etudes/note/join/2006/378272/IPOL-LIBE_NT(2006)378272_EN.pdf

——, 'Towards a New EU Legal Framework for Data Protection and Privacy: Challenges, Principles and the Role of the European Parliament' (*CEPS*, 10 November 2011)

Bigo D, Carrera S and Guild E (eds), *Foreigners, Refugees or Minorities? Rethinking People in the Context of Border Controls and Visas* (Ashgate 2015)

Bigo D and Leveau R, 'L'Europe de la Sécurité Intérieure – Rapport de Fin d'étude Pour l'Institut des Hautes Etudes de la Sécurité Intérieure, Paris'. *L'Europe des polices et de la sécurité intérieure*, (Editions Complexe, April 1992)

Bilsdorfer MC, *Polizeiliche Öffentlichkeitsarbeit in sozialen Netzwerken* (Nomos 2019)

Blasi C, 'Fundamental Rights Implications of Interconnecting Migration and Policing Databases in the EU' (2021) 21 *Human Rights Law Review* 433

Boccardi I, *Europe & Refugees: Towards an EU Asylum Policy* (Kluwer 2002)

Boehm F, *Information Sharing and Data Protection in the Area of Freedom, Security and Justice: Towards Harmonised Data Protection Principles for EU Internal Information Exchange* (Springer 2012)

Bonditti P, 'From Territorial Space to Networks: A Foucaldian Approach to the Implementation of Biometry' (2004) 29 *Alternatives: Global, Local, Political* 465

Bonner D, 'Managing Terrorism While Respecting Human Rights? European Aspects of the Anti-terrorism Crime and Security Act 2001' (2002) 8 *European Public Law* 497

Borell A and Schindler S, 'Polizei und Datenschutz: Vorgaben der neuen JI-RL für technische und organisatorische Maßnahmen zur Gewährleistung datenschutzkonformer polizeilicher Datenverarbeitung' (2019) 43 *Datenschutz und Datensicherheit* 767

Böröcz I, 'Risk to the Right to the Protection of Personal Data' (2016) 2 *European Data Protection Law Review* 467

Bossong R, 'Intelligente Grenzen und interoperable Datenbanken für die innere Sicherheit der EU – Umsetzungsrisiken und rechtsstaatliche Anforderungen' [2018] *SWP-Studie* 36

Bosworth M, Parmar A and Vázquez Y (eds), *Race, Criminal Justice, and Migration Control: Enforcing the Boundaries of Belonging* (Oxford University Press 2018)

Bourbeau P, *Handbook on Migration and Security* (Edward Elgar 2017)

Brière C and Weyembergh A, *The Needed Balances in EU Criminal Law: Past, Present and Future* (Bloomsbury 2017)

Brkan M, 'The Concept of Essence of Fundamental Rights in the EU Legal Order: Peeling the Onion to its Core' (2018) 14 *European Constitutional Law Review* 332

——, 'Do Algorithms Rule the World? Algorithmic Decision-Making and Data Protection in the Framework of the GDPR and beyond' (2019) 27 *International Journal of Law and Information Technology* 91

——, 'The Essence of the Fundamental Rights to Privacy and Data Protection: Finding the Way through the Maze of the CJEU's Constitutional Reasoning' (2019) 20 *German Law Journal* 864

Broeders D, 'The New Digital Borders of Europe: EU Databases and the Surveillance of Irregular Migrants' (2007) 22 *International Sociology* 71

Broeders D and Brakel RV, 'Big Data and Security Policies: Towards a Framework for Regulating the Phases of Analytics and Use of Big Data' (2017) 33(3) *Computer Law & Security Review* 309

Brouwer E, 'The Other Side of Moon: The Schengen Information System and Human Rights: A Task for National Courts' [2008] *CEPS Working Document* 17

——, 'Fundamental Rights Analysis for the Ecorys Feasibility Study of the European Commission for Proposals on Lowering Fingerprinting Age Children and Storage of Travel Documents into the Visa Information System (VIS)' (March 2018)

——, *Digital Borders and Real Rights: Effective Remedies for Third-Country Nationals in the Schengen Information System* (Martinus Nijhoff 2008)

——, 'The Other Side of the Moons: The Schengen Information System and Human Rights: A Task for National Courts' (*CEPS*, 26 August 2009)

Brouwer J, van der Woude M and van der Leun J, '(Cr)Immigrant Framing in Border Areas: Decision-Making Processes of Dutch Border Police Officers' (2018) 28 *Policing and Society* 448

Bunyan T, 'The "Point of No Return": Interoperability Morphs into the Creation of a Big Brother Centralised EU State Database Including All Existing and Future Justice and Home Affairs Databases' (May 2018), https://www.statewatch.org/media/documents/analyses/eu-interop-morphs-into-central-database.pdf

——, 'Statewatch Analysis EU Data Protection in Police and Judicial Cooperation Matters: Rights of Suspects and Defendants under Attack by Law Enforcement Demands' (October 2006), https://www.statewatch.org/media/documents/analyses/no-57-eu-dp.pdf

Bu-Pasha S, 'The Controller's Role in Determining "High Risk" and Data Protection Impact Assessment (DPIA) in Developing Digital Smart City' (2020) 29 *Information & Communications Technology Law* 391

Bus J et al, 'The Dawn of a Critical Transparency Right for the Profiling Era' in *Digital Enlightenment Yearbook 2012* (IOS Press 2012)
Busuioc M and Groenleer M, 'Beyond Design: The Evolution of Europol and Eurojust' (2013) 14 *Perspectives on European Politics & Society* 285
Bux U, 'Protection of EU External Borders: Achievements during the Legislative Term 2014–2019: The Role of the European Parliament, Briefing Requested by the LIBE Committee, Directorate-General for Internal Policies' PE 608.876, April 2019
Bygrave LA, 'Minding the Machine: Art 15 of the EC Data Protection Directive and Automated Profiling' Privacy Law and Policy Reporter (2000) 7(4) *Private Law Reporter* 67
Caillault A, 'The Implementation of Coherent Migration Management through IOM Programs in Morocco' in M Geiger and A Pécoud (eds), *The New Politics of International Mobility* (Institut für Migrationsforschung und Interkulturelle Studien 2012)
Calders T and Custers B, 'What is Data Mining and How Does it Work?' in B Custers et al (eds), *Discrimination and Privacy in the Information Society: Data Mining and Profiling in Large Databases* (Springer 2013)
Cannataci J, 'Defying the Logic, Forgetting the Facts: The New European Proposal for Data Protection in the Police Sector' (2013) 4(2) *European Journal of Law & Technology* 1
Cannataci J and Caruana MM, 'Report : Recommendation R (87) 15: Twenty-Five Years down the Line' (Council of Europe 2013)
Cano MIG, 'Cesión y tratamiento de datos personales en el proceso penal. Avances y retos inmediatos de la directiva (UE) 2016/680' (2019) 5 *Revista Brasileira de Direito Processual Penal* 1331
Capitani E, 'Progress and Failure in the Area of Freedom, Security, and Justice' in F Bignami (ed), *EU Law in Populist Times: Crises and Prospects* (Cambridge University Press 2020)
——, 'The Schengen System after Lisbon: From Cooperation to Integration' (2014) 15 *ERA Forum* 101
Carlier J-Y, *Immigration and Asylum Law of the EU: Current Debates* (Bruylant 2005)
Carrapiço H and Trauner F, 'Europol and its Influence on EU Policy-Making on Organized Crime: Analyzing Governance Dynamics and Opportunities' (2013) 14 *Perspectives on European Politics & Society* 357
Carrera S, 'The Irregular Immigration Policy Conundrum: Problematizing "Effectiveness" as a Frame for EU Criminalization and Expulsion Policies' in A Ripoll Servent and F Trauner (eds), *The Routledge Handbook of Justice and Home Affairs Research* (Routledge 2017)
——, *The European Border and Coast Guard: Addressing Migration and Asylum Challenges in the Mediterranean?* (CEPS, 2017)
Carrera S and Apap J, 'Maintaining Security within Borders: Towards a Permanent State of Emergency in the EU?' (CEPS Policy Brief No 41, November 2003)
Carrera S and Bigo D, 'Mass Surveillance of Personal Data by EU Member States and its Compatibility with EU Law' (*CEPS*, 6 November 2013) <https://www.ceps.eu/ceps-publications/mass-surveillance-personal-data-eu-member-states-and-its-compatibility-eu-law/> accessed 23 May 2021
Carrera S and den Hertog L, 'Whose Mare? Rule of Law Challenges in the Field of European Border Surveillance in the Mediterranean' (*CEPS*, 27 January 2015)
——, 'A European Border and Coast Guard: What's in a Name?' (*CEPS*, 8 March 2016)
Carrera S, den Hertog L and Pamozzon M, *EU External Migration Policies in an Era of Global Mobilities: Intersecting Policy Universes* (Brill Nijhoff 2018)
Carrera S and Guild E, 'Rethinking Asylum Distribution in the EU: Shall We Start with the Facts?' (*CEPS*, 17 June 2016)
Carrera S et al, 'Security versus Freedom: A Challenge for Europe's Future' (*CEPS*, 26 August 2009)
——, *Europe's 21st Century Challenge: Delivering Liberty* (Ashgate 2013)
——, 'An Analysis of the Schengen Area in the Wake of Recent Developments' (*CEPS*, 30 June 2016)
——, 'The Future of the Schengen Area: Latest Developments and Challenges in the Schengen Governance Framework since 2016' (European Parliament Think Tank, 2018)
——, 'What is Happening to the Schengen Borders?' (*CEPS*, 2015)

Carrera S and Stefan M (eds), *Fundamental Rights Challenges in Border Controls and Expulsion of Irregular Immigrants in the European Union: Complaint Mechanisms and Access to Justice* (Routledge 2020)

Carian MM, 'The Reform of the EU Data Protection Framework in the Context of the Police and Criminal Justice Sector: Harmonisation, Scope, Oversight and Enforcement' (2019) 33 *International Review of Law, Computers & Technology* 249

Casagran CB, 'The Limits of European Data Protection Law in EU Border Control' [2015] *Revista CIDOB d'Afers Internacionals* 127

Caspar J, 'The CJEU Google Spain Decision' (2015) 39 *Datenschutz und Datensicherheit* 589

Cate FH, Cullen P and Mayer-Schönberger V, 'Data Protection Principles for the 21st Century – Revising the 1980 OECD Guidelines' (2013) Books & Book Chapters by Maurer Faculty, 23

Ceyhan A, 'Les technologies européennes de contrôle de l'immigration' (2010) 159 *Reseaux* 131

Cimina V, 'The Data Protection Concepts of "Controller", "Processor" and "Joint Controllership" under Regulation (EU) 2018/1725' (2021) 21 *ERA Forum* 639

Claes E, *Privacy and the Criminal Law* (Intersentia 2006)

Cole MD and Boehm F, 'Data Retention after the Judgement of the Court of Justice of the European Union' (30 June 2014), https://www.zar.kit.edu/DATA/veroeffentlichungen/237_237_Boehm_Cole-Data_Retention_Study-June_2014_1a1c2f6_9906a8c.pdf

Cole MD and Quintel T, 'Transborder Access to E-Evidence by Law Enforcement Agencies' [2018] SSRN Electronic Journal

——, 'Data Retention under the Proposal for an EU Entry/Exit System (EES) Analysis of the Impact on and Limitations for the EES by Opinion 1/15 on the EU/Canada PNR Agreement of the Court of Justice of the European Union' (October 2017), https://www.greens-efa.eu/files/assets/docs/data_retention_under_the_proposal_for_an_eu_entry_exit_system__ees_.PDF

Cole MD and Vandendriessche A, 'Case Note: From Digital Rights Ireland and Schrems in Luxembourg to Zakharov and Szabó/Vissy in Strasbourg: What the ECtHR Made of the Deep Pass by the CJEU in the Recent Cases on Mass Surveillance Roman Zakharov v Russia (App No 47143/06) and Szabó and Vissy v Hungary (App No 37138/14)' (2016) 2(1) *European Data Protection Law Review* 121

Colombo E, 'EU Databases and the Exchange of Information to Combat Illegal Immigration' (2014) 4 *European Criminal Law Review* 236

Coman-Kund F, 'Europol's International Exchanges of Data and Interoperability of AFSJ Databases' (2020) 26 *European Public Law* 181

Convey A and Kupiszewski M, 'Keeping up with Schengen: Migration and Policy in the European Union' (1995) 29 *International Migration Review* 939

Corbett R, *The Treaty of Maastricht: From Conception to Ratification: A Comprehensive Reference Guide* (Cartermill International 1993)

Coudert F, 'The Europol Regulation and Purpose Limitation: From the "Silo-Based Approach" to … What Exactly?' (2017) 3(3) *European Data Protection Law Review* 313

Craig P and de Búrca G, *EU Law: Text, Cases, and Materials*, 7th edn (Oxford University Press 2020)

Custers B, 'The Power of Knowledge Ethical, Legal and Technological Aspects of Data Mining and Group Profiling in Epidemiology', SSRN Scholarly Paper ID 3186639, 2004

——, 'Profiling as Inferred Data: Amplifier Effects and Positive Feedback Loops' in E Bayamlioglu et al (eds), *Cogitas Ergo Sum: 10 Years of Profiling the European Citizen* (Amsterdam University Press 2018)

Davis K, 'The European Union's Dublin Regulation and the Migrant Crisis Notes' (2020) 19 *Washington University Global Studies Law Review* 261

De Bruycker P, 'The European Border and Coast Guard: A New Model Built on an Old Logic' (2016) 2016 1 *European Papers: A Journal on Law and Integration* 559

De Carvalho SLD, 'Key GDPR Elements in Adequacy Findings of Countries That Have Ratified Convention 108' (2019) 5 *European Data Protection Law Review* 54

De Hert P, 'Trends in de Europese politiële en justitiële informatiesamenwerking' (2004) 25 *Panopticon* 26

De Hert P and Boehm F, 'The Right of Notification after Surveillance is over: Ready for Recognition?' (2012) 3(3) *Digital Enlightenment Yearbook* 1

De Hert P and Papakonstantinou V, 'The Data Protection Framework Decision of 27 November 2008 Regarding Police and Judicial Cooperation in Criminal Matters: A Modest Achievement However Not the Improvement Some Have Hoped for' (2009) 25 *Computer Law & Security Review* 403

——, 'The New Police and Criminal Justice Data Protection Directive: A First Analysis' (2016) 7 *New Journal of European Criminal Law* 7

——, 'Data Protection Policies in EU Justice and Home Affairs' [2019] *Routledge Handbook of Justice and Home Affairs Research* 169

De Hert P and Sajfert J, 'Police, Privacy and Data Protection from a Comparative Legal Perspective' in *Comparative Policing from a Legal Perspective* (Edward Elgar 2018)

——, 'Regulating Big Data in and out of the Data Protection Policy Field' (2019) 5 *European Data Protection Law Review* 338

De Hert P, Papakonstantinou V and Rielke C, 'Data Protection in the Third Pillar: Cautious Pessimism' in M Martin (ed), *Crime, Rights and the EU* (Justice, 2008)

De Zwaan JW and Goudappel F (eds), *Freedom, Security and Justice in the European Union: Implementation of the Hague Programme 2004* (TMC Asser Press 2006)

Demková S and Quintel T, 'Allocation of Responsibilities in Interoperable Information Exchanges: Effective Review Compromised?' (28 May 2020), https://ceec.ut-capitole.fr/cahiers-jean-monnet-n-6-actes-des-ateliers-doctoraux-2019-l-etat-de-droit-de-l-universite-degli-studi-di-milano-et-de-la-european-school-of-law-toulouse-centre-d-excellence-europe-capitole-862062.kjsp?RH=1572513344545

Den Boer M, 'Taming the Third Pillar: Management and Decision-Making in Justice and Home Affairs' (1998) Current European Issues, Maastricht, EIPA

——, 'The EU Counter-terrorism Wave: Window of Opportunity or Profound Policy Transformation?' in *Confronting Terrorism: European Experiences, Threat Perceptions and Policies* (Kluwer Law International 2003)

Den Boer M, '9/11 and the Europeanisation of Anti-terrorism Policy: A Critical Assessment' (2003) Policy Papers N°6, https://institutdelors.eu/wp-content/uploads/2018/01/policypaper6_01.pdf

Desoi M, *Intelligente Videoüberwachung: Rechtliche Bewertung Und Rechtsgemäße Gestaltung* (Springer Vieweg in Springer Fachmedien Wiesbaden GmbH 2018)

Dimitrova D, 'The Right to Explanation under the Right of Access to Personal Data' (2020) 6 *European Data Protection Law Review* 211

Dimitrova D and De Hert P, 'The Right of Access under the Police Directive: Small Steps Forward' in M Medina et al (eds), *Privacy Technologies and Policy* (Springer International Publishing 2018)

Drewer D and Ellermann J, 'Europol's Data Protection Framework as an Asset in the Fight against Cybercrime' (2012) 13 *ERA Forum* 381

——, 'May the (Well-Balanced) Force Be with Us! The Launch of the European Counter Terrorism Centre (ECTC)' (2016) 32 *Computer Law & Security Review* 195

Drewer D and Miladinova V, 'The BIG DATA Challenge: Impact and Opportunity of Large Quantities of Information under the Europol Regulation' (2017) 33 *Computer Law & Security Review* 298

Elfering S, *Unlocking the Right to Data Portability* (Nomos 2019)

Erne M, 'GDPR: A New Challenge for Personal Data Protection' (2017) 46 *Bankarstvo* 166

Fahey E, 'External Norm Primacy and EU Law: AFSJ Directives in the Post-Lisbon Legislative Cycle' in *The Global Reach of EU Law* (Taylor & Francis 2016)

Ferraro F et al, *Fundamental Rights in the European Union: The Role of the Charter after the Lisbon Treaty: In-depth Analysis* (Publications Office 2015)

Ferraro F and De Capitani E, 'The New European Border and Coast Guard: Yet Another "Half Way" EU Reform?' (2016) 17 *ERA Forum* 385

Fijnaut C, *A Peaceful Revolution: The Development of Police and Judicial Cooperation in the European Union* (Intersentia 2019)

Fijnaut C and Ouwerkerk J, *The Future of Police and Judicial Cooperation in the European Union* (Martinus Nijhoff 2010)

Fisher LE, 'Guilt by Expressive Association: Political Profiling, Surveillance and the Privacy of Groups' (2004) 46 *Arizona Law Review* 621

Fuster GG, 'Artificial Intelligence and Law Enforcement: Impact on Fundamental Rights', study requested by the LIBE Committee in the European Parliament (July 2020)

——, 'Fighting for Your Right to What Exactly: The Convoluted Case Law of the EU Court of Justice on Privacy and/or Personal Data Protection' (2014) 2 *Birkbeck Law Review* 263

——, *The Emergence of Personal Data Protection as a Fundamental Right of the EU* (Springer International Publishing 2014)

Fuster GG, Bellanova R and Gellert R, 'Nurturing Ob-scene Politics: Surveillance between In/Visibility and Dis-appearance' (2015) 13(3) *Surveillance & Society* 512

Fuster GG, de Hert P and Gutwirth S, 'Privacy and Data Protection in the EU Security Continuum' (*CEPS*, 14 June 2011)

Fuster GG and Gellert R, 'The Fundamental Right of Data Protection in the European Union: In Search of an Uncharted Right' (2012) 26 *International Review of Law, Computers & Technology* 73

Galli F, 'Legal Perspectives on Terrorism: Is Europe Unprepared? EU Counter-terrorism Policies to Address the Foreign Fighters and Returnees' in V Mitsilegas and S Hufnagel (eds), *Research Handbook on Transnational Crime* (Edward Elgar 2019)

——, 'Interoperable Databases: New Cooperation Dynamics in the EU AFSJ?' (2020) 26(1) *European Public Law* 109

Gans C, 'Nationalism and Immigration' (1998) 1 Ethical Theory and Moral Practice 159

Gellert R, 'Understanding the Notion of Risk in the General Data Protection Regulation' (2018) 34 *Computer Law & Security Review* 279

——, 'A Comparative Analysis of Anti-discrimination and Data Protection Legislations' in Bart Custers et al (eds), *Discrimination and Privacy in the Information Society: Data Mining and Profiling in Large Databases* (Springer 2013)

Giurgiu A and Lommel G, 'A New Approach to EU Data Protection' [2014] 97(1) *Kritische Vierteljahresschrift für Gesetzgebung und Rechtswissenschaft* 10

Gless S, 'Europol' in V Mitsilegas (ed), *Research Handbook on EU Criminal Law* (Edward Elgar 2016)

Gless S and Wahl T, 'A Comparison of the Evolution and Pace of Police and Judicial Cooperation in Criminal Matters: A Race between Europol and Eurojust?' in C Brière and A Weyembergh (eds), *The Needed Balances in EU Criminal Law* (Hart Publishing 2017)

Goel V and Perlroth N, 'Yahoo Says 1 Billion User Accounts were Hacked' *New York Times* (14 December 2016) https://www.nytimes.com/2016/12/14/technology/yahoo-hack.html

Gola and Heckmann, *Bundesdatenschutzgesetz: BDSG*, 13th edn (CH Beck 2019)

Gortázar Rotaeche C, Parra Cartagena MC and Segaert B, *European Migration and Asylum Policies: Coherence or Contradiction?: An Interdisciplinary Evaluation of the EU Programmes of Tampere (1999), the Hague (2004) and Stockholm (2009)* (Bruylant 2012)

Greenleaf G, '"Modernising" Data Protection Convention 108: A Safe Basis for a Global Privacy Treaty?' (2013) 29 *Computer Law & Security Review* 430

Groenendijk K, 'Reinstatement of Controls at the Internal Borders of Europe: Why and Against Whom' (2004) 10 *European Law Journal* 150

Guild E and Garlick M, 'Refugee Protection, Counter-terrorism, and Exclusion in the European Union' (2010) 29 *Refugee Survey Quarterly* 63

Guild E and Geyer, F (eds), *Security versus Justice? Police and Judicial Cooperation in the European Union* (Routledge 2008)

Guild E and Minderhoud P, *The First Decade of EU Migration and Asylum Law: First Decade of EU Migration and Asylum Law* (Brill 2011)

Guild E and Niessen J, *The Developing Immigration and Asylum Policies of the European Union: Adopted Conventions, Resolutions, Recommendations, Decisions and Conclusions* (Brill 1996)

Guild, E and Bigo D (eds), *Controlling Frontiers: Free Movement into and within Europe* (Routledge 2005)

Gutheil M et al, 'Interoperability of Justice and Home Affairs Information Systems', study for the LIBE Committee of the European Parliament (April 2018) 120

Guthrie Ferguson A, *The Rise of Big Data Policing* (NYU Press 2017)

Gutiérrez Zarza Á, 'Eurojust' in A Gutiérrez Zarza (ed), *Exchange of Information and Data Protection in Cross-border Criminal Proceedings in Europe* (Springer 2015)

Hailbronner K, 'The Right to Asylum and the Future of Asylum Procedures in the European Community' (1990) 2 *International Journal of Refugee Law* 341

——, *EU Immigration and Asylum Law: A Commentary*, 2nd edn (Beck 2016)

Hansen R and Papademetriou DG, 'Securing Borders: The Intended, Unintended, and Perverse Consequences (January 2014)' [2014] *Migration Policy Institute* 21

Hansson E and Jansson D, 'Who's Afraid of the "Beggar"? A Psychoanalytic Interpretation of the Crises Triggered by the Begging of "EU Migrants" in Sweden' (2021) 22 *Social & Cultural Geography* 339

Harris D et al, *Harris, O'Boyle, and Warbrick Law of the European Convention on Human Rights*, 3rd edn (Oxford University Press 2014)

Hayes B, 'Migration and Data Protection: Doing No Harm in an Age of Mass Displacement, Mass Surveillance and "Big Data"' (2017) 99 *International Review of the Red Cross* 179

Heinäluoma E, Lannoo K and Parlour R, 'CEPS-ECRIT Task Force Report: Anti-money Laundering in the EU – Time to Get Serious (Centre for European Policy Studies (CEPS), January 2021) https://www.ceps.eu/wp-content/uploads/2021/01/TFR_Anti-Money-Laundering-in-the-EU.pdf

Heinrich Amadeus W and Amadeus WH, 'Der EU-Richtlinienentwurf Zum Datenschutz in Polizei Und Justiz – Gehalt Und Auswirkungen Auf Das Strafprozess- Und Polizeirecht' in *Prävention und Repression im Raum der Freiheit, der Sicherheit und des Rechts* (Nomos Verlagsgesellschaft mbH & Co KG 2014)

Hendow M, Cibea A and Kraler A, 'Using Technology to Draw Borders: Fundamental Rights for the Smart Borders Initiative' 13 *Journal of Information, Communication and Ethics in Society* 39

Hijmans H, *The European Union as Guardian of Internet Privacy: The Story of Art 16 TFEU* (Springer 2016)

Hijmans H and Raab CD, 'Ethical Dimensions of the GDPR', SSRN Scholarly Paper ID 3222677, 2018

Hijmans H and Scirocco A, 'Shortcomings in EU Data Protection in the Third and the Second Pillars' (2009) 46 *Common Market Law Review* 1485

Hofmann R, 'Europäische Kriminalpolitik und die neue europäische Sicherheitsarchitektur' in R Hofmann (ed), *Flucht, Migration und die neue europäische Sicherheitsarchitektur: Herausforderungen für die EU-Kriminalpolitik* (Springer 2017)

Holiday Y, 'Legal Perspectives on Migration Crime' in V Mitsilegas and S Hufnagel (eds), *Research Handbook on Transnational Crime* (Edward Elgar 2019)

Hudobnik MM, 'Data Protection and the Law Enforcement Directive: A Procrustean Bed across Europe?' (2020) 21 *ERA Forum* 485

Hufnagel S, 'Policing and Intelligence Flows in Counter-Terrorism: Current Challenges for European Policing' in S Hufnagel (ed), *Policing Transnational Crime: Law Enforcement of Criminal Flows* (Routledge 2020)

Huysmans J, 'International Politics of Insecurity: Normativity, Inwardness and the Exception' (2006) 37 *Security Dialogue* 11

Jasserand-Breeman C, 'Reprocessing of Biometric Data for Law Enforcement Purposes: Individuals' Safeguards Caught at the Interface between the GDPR and the "Police" Directive?' (doctoral thesis, University of Groningen, 2019)

——, 'Law Enforcement Access to Personal Data Originally Collected by Private Parties: Missing Data Subjects' Safeguards in Directive 2016/680?' (2018) 34(1) *Computer Law & Security Review* 154

Jeandesboz J, 'Reinforcing the Surveillance of EU Borders: The Future Development of FRONTEX and EUROSUR' (CEPS Research Paper, 2009)

Jeroen J, 'Profiling of Asylum Seekers' (Federale Overheitsdienst Binnenlandse Zaken, August 2010)

Jones C, 'Monitoring "Secondary Movements" and "Hotspots": Frontex is Now an Internal Surveillance Agency' (*Statewatch*, December 2019), https://www.statewatch.org/media/documents/analyses/no-348-frontex-internal-surveillance.pdf

Joubert C and Bevers H, *Schengen Investigated: A Comparative Interpretation of the Schengen Provisions on International Police Cooperation in the Light of the European Convention on Human Rights* (Martinus Nijhoff 1996)

Jünemann A, Scherer N and Fromm N (eds), *Fortress Europe? Challenges and Failures of Migration and Asylum Policies* (VS Verlag für Sozialwissenschaften 2017)

Karanja SK, *Transparency and Proportionality in the Schengen Information System and Border Control Co-operation* (Martinus Nijhoff 2008)

Karbe D, Jawurek C and Sarder P, 'Legendierte Polizeikontrollen: Judgment from the German Federal Court of Justice (Bundesgerichtshof) of April 26, 2017, 2 StR 247/16' (2020) 21 *German Law Journal* 756

Katulic T and Protrka N, 'Information Security in Principles and Provisions of the EU Data Protection Law' [2019] *42nd International Convention on Information and Communication Technology, Electronics and Microelectronics (MIPRO)* 1420

Kaunert C and Léonard S, 'The European Union Asylum Policy after the Treaty of Lisbon and the Stockholm Programme: Towards Supranational Governance in a Common Area of Protection?' (2012) 31 *Refugee Survey Quarterly* 1

Kędzior M, 'GDPR and beyond: A Year of Changes in the Data Protection Landscape of the European Union' (2019) 19 *ERA Forum* 505

Kilpatrick J, 'Analysis: Frontex Launches "Game-Changing" Recruitment Drive for Standing Corps of Border Guards' (*Statewatch*, 2 March 2020), https://www.statewatch.org/analyses/2020/frontex-launches-game-changing-recruitment-drive-for-standing-corps-of-border-guards/

Kindt EJ, 'Having Yes, Using No? About the New Legal Regime for Biometric Data' (2018) 34 *Computer Law & Security Review* 523

Kipker D-K, '2. DSAnpUG-EU und die Talfahrt des deutschen Datenschutzrechts' (2019) 43 *Datenschutz und Datensicherheit* 371

Kirby M, 'The History, Achievement and Future of the 1980 OECD Guidelines on Privacy' (2011) 1 *International Data Privacy Law* 6

Kokott J and Sobotta C, 'The Distinction between Privacy and Data Protection in the Jurisprudence of the CJEU and the ECtHR' (2013) 3 *International Data Privacy Law* 222

Korff D, 'New Challenges to Data Protection Study-Working Paper No. 2: Data Protection Laws in the EU: The Difficulties in Meeting the Challenges Posed by Global Social and Technical Developments' (2010), https://ssrn.com/abstract=1638949

Kosta E, *Consent in European Data Protection Law* (Brill Nijhoff 2013)

——, 'The Retention of Communications Data in Europe and the UK' in L Edwards (ed), *Law, Policy and the Internet* (Hart Publishing 2018)

Koudelkova N, 'Internal Security Strategy' (*Migration and Home Affairs – European Commission*, 14 March 2017) https://ec.europa.eu/home-affairs/e-library/glossary/internal-security-strategy_en

Kugelmann D, 'Datenschutz bei Polizei und Justiz: Der Richtlinienvorschlag der Kommission' (2012) 36 *Datenschutz und Datensicherheit* 581

Kühling J and Buchner B, *DS-GVO Datenschutz-Grundverordnung: Kommentar* (Beck 2017)

Kuner C, Bygrave LA and Christopher Docksey C (eds), *The EU General Data Protection Regulation (GDPR): A Commentary Digital Pack* (Oxford University Press 2020)

Lambert P, *The Right to Be Forgotten: Interpretation and Practice* (Bloomsbury Professional 2019)

Lange H-J and Schenck J-C, *Polizei im kooperativen Staat: Verwaltungsreform und Neue Steuerung in der Sicherheitsverwaltung* (VS Verlag für Sozialwissenschaften 2004)

Lassalle M, *L'accès transnational aux données bancaires dans le cadre de l'enquête pénale* (Larcier 2021)

Lazaridis G, Campani G and Benveniste A, *The Rise of the Far Right in Europe Populist Shifts and 'Othering'* (Palgrave Macmillan 2016)

Lees C, 'The "Alternative for Germany": The Rise of Right-Wing Populism at the Heart of Europe' (2018) 38 *Politics* 295

Leiser M and Custers B, 'The Law Enforcement Directive' (2019) 5 *European Data Protection Law Review* 367

Lenaerts K, 'Exploring the Limits of the EU Charter of Fundamental Rights' (2012) 8 *European Constitutional Law Review* 375

Léonard S, 'EU Border Security and Migration into the European Union: FRONTEX and Securitisation through Practices' (2010) 19 *European Security* 231

Léonard S and Kaunert C, 'The Securitisation of Migration in the European Union: Frontex and its Evolving Security Practices' (2020) 48(6) *Journal of Ethnic and Migration Studies* 1417

Levade A, Picod F and Burgorgue-Larsen L, *Traité établissant une Constitution pour l'Europe. L'architecture constitutionnelle, Partie II – La Charte des droits fondamentaux de l'Union, Commentaire article par article* (Bruylant 2005)

Ljubanovic B and Sajfert J, 'Problematika Drzavljanstva Europske Unije: The European Union Citizenship Issue' (2009) 25 *Pravni Vjesnik* 27

Longo F, 'Justice and Home Affairs as a New Dimension of the European Security Concept' (2013) 18 *European Foreign Affairs Review* 5

Majcher I, 'The Schengen-Wide Entry Ban: How are Non-citizens' Personal Data Protected?' (2020) 48(8) Journal of Ethnic and Migration Studies 1944

Marquenie T, 'The Police and Criminal Justice Authorities Directive: Data Protection Standards and Impact on the Legal Framework' (2017) 33 Computer Law & Security Review 324

Martini M, 'Art. 22 DSGVO – Automatisierte Entscheidungen Im Einzelfall Einschließlich Profiling' in Boris P Paal and Daniel Pauly (eds), *Datenschutz-Grundverordnung* (Beck 2017)

Meijers H and Curtin D, 'The Principle of Open Government in Schengen and the European' (1995) 32 *Common Market Law Review* 391

Milt K, 'Counter Terrorism and External Border Management in Italy – in Depth Analysis, Requested by the Special Committee on Terrorism, PE 604.968 – May 2018' 27

Mitchell K and Sparke M, 'Hotspot Geopolitics versus Geosocial Solidarity: Contending Constructions of Safe Space for Migrants in Europe' (2020) 38 Environment and Planning D: Society and Space 1046

Mitsilegas V, 'The Implementation of the EU Acquis on Illegal Immigration by the Candidate Countries of Central and Eastern Europe: Challenges and Contradictions' (2002) 28 *Journal of Ethnic and Migration Studies* 665

——, 'Contrôle des étrangers, des passagers, des citoyens : surveillance et anti-terrorisme' [2005] *Cultures & conflits* 185

——, 'Databases in the Area of Freedom, Security and Justice: Lessons for the Centralisation of Records and Their Maximum Exchange' in C Stefanou and H Xanthaki (eds), *Towards a European Criminal Record* (Cambridge University Press 2008)

——, 'Immigration Control in an Era of Globalization: Deflecting Foreigners, Weakening Citizens, and Strengthening the State' (2012) 19 *Indiana Journal of Global Legal Studies* 3

——, 'The Value of Privacy in an Era of Security: Embedding Constitutional Limits on Preemptive Surveillance' [2014] 8(1) *International Political Sociology*, DOI:10.1111/ips.12043

——, 'Before Entry: Criminalisation as Prevention' in Valsamis Mitsilegas (ed), *The Criminalisation of Migration in Europe: Challenges for Human Rights and the Rule of Law* (Springer International Publishing 2015)

——, 'Conceptualising the Criminalisation of Migration' in Valsamis Mitsilegas (ed), *The Criminalisation of Migration in Europe: Challenges for Human Rights and the Rule of Law* (Springer International Publishing 2015)

——, *The Criminalisation of Migration in Europe: Challenges for Human Rights and the Rule of Law* (Springer International Publishing 2015)

——, 'Immigration Detention, Risk and Human Rights in the Law of the European Union. Lessons from the Returns Directive' in MJ Guia, R Koulish and V Mitsilegas (eds), *Immigration Detention, Risk and Human Rights: Studies on Immigration and Crime* (Springer International Publishing 2016)

——, 'Humanizing Solidarity in European Refugee Law: The Promise of Mutual Recognition' (2017) 24 *Maastricht Journal of European and Comparative Law* 721

——, *A 'Common' EU Immigration and Asylum Policy: National and Institutional Constraints* (Routledge-Cavendish 2020)

——, 'Measuring Irregular Migration: Implications for Law, Policy and Human Rights' in E Szyszczak et al (eds), *Irregular Migration and Human Rights* (Martinus Nijhoff 2004)

Mitsilegas V, Bergström M and Konstadinides T, *Research Handbook on EU Criminal Law* (Edward Elgar 2016)

Mitsilegas V and Ryan B, *Extraterritorial Immigration Control: Legal Challenges* (Martinus Nijhoff 2010)

Monaco F, 'Europol: The Culmination of the European Union's International Police Cooperation Efforts' (1995) 19 *Fordham International Law Journal* 247

Monar J, 'Cooperation in the Justice and Home Affairs Domain: Characteristics, Constraints and Progress' (2006) 28 *Journal of European Integration* 495

——, 'Justice and Home Affairs: The Treaty of Maastricht as a Decisive Intergovernmental Gate Opener' (2012) 34 *Journal of European Integration* 717

——, 'Eurojust's Present and Future Role at the Frontline of European Union Criminal Justice Cooperation' (2013) 14 *ERA Forum* 187

Moreno Lax V et al, 'Border-Induced Displacement: The Ethical and Legal Implications of Distance-Creation through Externalization' (*QIL QDI*, 28 February 2019)

Müller T, 'Die Europäische Union auf dem Weg zu einer Europäischen Innenpolitik?' in Thorsten Müller (ed), *Die Innen- und Justizpolitik der Europäischen Union: Eine Analyse der Integrationsentwicklung* (VS Verlag für Sozialwissenschaften 2003)

Nascimbene B and Pascale AD, 'The "Arab Spring" and the Extraordinary Influx of People Who Arrived in Italy from North Africa' (2011) 13 *European Journal of Migration and Law* 341

Niculescu-Dinca V, 'Managing Suspicion and Privacy in Police Information Systems' in S Gutwirth et al (eds), *European Data Protection: In Good Health?* (Springer Netherlands 2012)

Niedermayer O, 'Der Aufstieg der Alternative für Deutschland' (2014) 46 *Revue d'Allemagne et des pays de langue allemande* 231

Niemann A and Speyer J, 'A Neofunctionalist Perspective on the "European Refugee Crisis": The Case of the European Border and Coast Guard' (2018) 56 *Journal of Common Market Studies* 23

Niemeier M and Zerbst P, 'The Prüm Treaty: Stepping up of Cross-border Cooperation in Combating Crime in the EU' (2007) 8 *ERA Forum* 535

Oerlemans J-J, 'Investigating Cybercrime' (doctoral thesis, Meijers Research Institute and Graduate School of the Leiden Law School of Leiden University 2017)

Ojanen T, 'Making the Essence of Fundamental Rights Real: The Court of Justice of the European Union Clarifies the Structure of Fundamental Rights under the Charter' (2016) 12 *European Constitutional Law Review* 318

Olsson C, Bigo D and Bonelli L, The Field of the EU Internal Security Agencies [2008] *Centre d'études sur les conflits/l'Harmattan* 5

Paoli S, 'Migration in European Integration: Themes and Debates' (2016) 22 *Journal of European Integration History* 279

Papakonstantinou V and de Hert P, 'The PNR Agreement and Transatlantic Anti-terrorism Cooperation: No Firm Human Rights Framework on Either Side of the Atlantic' (2009) 46 *Common Market Law Review* 885

Parkin J, 'The Difficult Road to the Schengen Information System II: The Legacy of "Laboratories" and the Cost for Fundamental Rights and the Rule of Law' (CEPS, 2011)

Peers S, 'Key Legislative Developments on Migration in the European Union: SIS II' (2008) 10 *European Journal of Migration and Law* 77

——, 'Legislative Update: EU Immigration and Asylum Competence and Decision-Making in the Treaty of Lisbon' (2008) 10 *European Journal of Migration and Law* 219

——, 'Legislative Update, EC Immigration and Asylum Law: The New Visa Code' (2010) 12 *European Journal of Migration and Law* 105

——, 'An EU Immigration Code: Towards a Common Immigration Policy' (2012) 14 *European Journal of Migration and Law* 33

——, 'Reconciling the Dublin System with European Fundamental Rights and the Charter' (2014) 15 *ERA Forum* 485

——, 'Irregular Migrants: Can Humane Treatment Be Balanced against Efficient Removal?' (2015) 17 *European Journal of Migration and Law* 289

——, *EU Justice and Home Affairs Law: EU Immigration and Asylum Law* (Oxford University Press 2016)

——, 'Migration, Internal Security and the UK's EU Membership' (2016) 87 *Political Quarterly* 247

——, 'Immigration, Asylum and Human Rights in the European Union' in S Douglas-Scott et al, *Research Handbook on EU Law and Human Rights* (Edward Elgar Publishing 2017)

Perry WL et al, *Predictive Policing: The Role of Crime Forecasting in Law Enforcement Operations* (RAND Corporation, 2013)

Phull KK, 'Crossroads of Integration? The Future of Schengen in the Wake of the Arab Spring' in F Laursen (ed), *The EU and the Eurozone Crisis: Policy Challenges and Strategic Choices* (Ashgate 2013)

Piquet A, 'Supranational Activism as an Assertion Process? The Case of Europol' (2017) 13(1) *Journal of Contemporary European Research* 1185

Purtova N, 'Between the GDPR and the Police Directive: Navigating through the Maze of Information Sharing in Public–Private Partnerships' (2018) 8 *International Data Privacy Law* 52

Quelle C, 'Enhancing Compliance under the General Data Protection Regulation: The Risky Upshot of the Accountability- and Risk-Based Approach' (2018) 9 *European Journal of Risk Regulation* 502

Quintel T, 'United Kingdom Investigatory Powers Tribunal: *Privacy International v Secretary of State for Foreign and Commonwealth Affairs and Ors* Part II' (2017) 3 *European Data Protection Law Review* 387

——, 'Article 29 Data Protection Working Party Opinion on the Law Enforcement Directive' (2018) 4 *European Data Protection Law Review* 104

——, 'Connecting Personal Data of Third Country Nationals: Interoperability of EU Databases in the Light of the CJEU's Case Law on Data Retention. Available at SSRN Journal' (2018) https://papers.ssrn.com/sol3/papers.cfm?abstract_id=3132506

——, 'EDPS and Article 29 Working Party Opinions about the Commission Proposals on the Interoperability of Databases' (2018) 4 *European Data Protection Law Review* 217

——, 'The Impact of Interoperability on the Processing of (Biometric) Data of Third Country Nationals by Europol' (2018) 101 *Kritische Vierteljahresschrift für Gesetzgebung und Rechtswissenschaft* 332

——, 'Interoperability of EU Databases and Access to Personal Data by National Police Authorities under Article 20 of the Commission Proposals' (2018) 4 *European Data Protection Law Review* 470

——, 'Follow the Money, If You Can: Possible Solutions for Enhanced FIU Cooperation under Improved Data Protection Rules' (2019), https://ssrn.com/abstract=3318299 or http://dx.doi.org/10.2139/ssrn.3318299

——, 'From Tampere over Stockholm to Luxembourg and Brussels: Where are We Now? The Evolution of AFSJ Databases – Meandering between Security and Data Protection' (European University Institute, 2020)

——, 'Interoperable Data Exchanges within Different Data Protection Regimes: The Case of Europol and the European Border and Coast Guard Agency' (2020) 26 *European Public Law* 205

——, 'The EDPS on Europol's Big Data Challenge in Light of the Recast Europol Regulation' (2022) 8 *European Data Protection Law Review* 90

QUINTEL T and DIMITROVA D, 'Technological Experimentation without Adequate Safeguards? Interoperable EU Databases and Access to the Multiple Identity Detector by SIRENE Bureaux' in P de Hert et al (eds), *Data Protection and Privacy Data Protection and Artificial Intelligence* (Bloomsbury 2020)

RADJENOVIC A, 'EPRS Briefing: EU Legislation in Progress – European Travel Information and Authorisation System (ETIAS)' PE 599.298 (2018)

——, 'Reform of the Dublin System, European Parliamentary Research Service', PE 586.639 (*EPRS*, 1 March 2019)

——, 'Protection of EU External Borders, European Parliamentary Research Service', PE 630.316 (*EPRS*, June 2019)

RADJENOVIC A and ATANASSOV N, *EU Asylum, Borders and External Cooperation on Migration: Recent Developments: In-depth Analysis* (Publications Office 2018)

RIJPMA J, 'The Proposal for a European Border and Coast Guard: Evolution or Revolution in External Border Management? Study for the LIBE Committee' (European Parliament, Directorate-General for Internal Policies, March 2016)

——, 'External Migration and Asylum Management: Accountability for Executive Action outside EU Territory' (2017) 2(2) *European Papers* 571

RIJPMA J and VERMEULEN M, 'EUROSUR: Saving Lives or Building Borders?' (2015) 24 *European Security: Uncertainties at the European Union's Southern Borders* 454

RIJPMA J et al, *The New EU Data Protection Regime: Setting Global Standards for the Right to Personal Data Protection. The XXIX Fide Congress in the Hague, 2020 Congress Publications, Vol 2* (Eleven International Publishing 2020)

RITSERT R and PEKAR M, 'New Public Management Reforms in German Police Services' (2009) 5(2) German Policy Studies 17

RIVERS J, 'Proportionality and Variable Intensity of Review' (2006) 65 *Cambridge Law Journal* 174

ROGGENKAMP JD, '§ 21 Datenschutz und präventive Tätigkeit der Polizei' in L Specht and R Mantz (eds), *Handbuch Europäisches und deutsches Datenschutzrecht* (CH Beck 2019)

RUGANI G, 'La protezione dei dati nel settore della cooperazione giudiziaria e di polizia in materia penale alla luce della direttiva (UE) 2016/680: frammentazione ed incertezze applicative' [2019] *Freedom, Security & Justice: European Legal Studies* 75

SAFJAŃSKI T and JAMES A, 'Europol's Crime Analysis System: Practical Determinants of its Success' (2020) 14 *Policing: A Journal of Policy and Practice* 469

SAJFERT J, 'New Data Protection Regulation for EU Bodies: Another Piece of the Puzzle Completed' (2018) 4 *European Data Protection Law Review* 213

SAJFERT J and DE HERT P, 'The Role of the Data Protection Authorities in Supervising Police and Criminal Justice Authorities Processing Personal Data' in *The Needed Balances in EU Criminal Law: Past, Present and Future* (Bloomsbury 2017)

——, 'Variety, Velocity, and Volume of Personal Data in Criminal Investigations and Proceedings: The Limits Drawn by the Purpose Limitation and Data Minimization Principles in Directive (EU) 2016/680' in V Mitsilegas and M Bergström (eds), *Research Handbook on EU Criminal Law* (Edward Elgar 2022)

SAJFERT J and QUINTEL T, 'Data Protection Directive (EU) 2016/680 for Police and Criminal Justice Authorities (1 December 2017), https://ssrn.com/abstract=3285873

SAMATAS M, 'Greece in "Schengenland": Blessing or Anathema for Citizens' and Foreigners' Rights?' (2003) 29 *Journal of Ethnic and Migration Studies* 141

ŞANDRU Ş, 'Le Contrôle des Règles sur la Protection des Données à Caractère Personnel par l'intermédiaire des Autorités Administratives Indépendantes' [2015] *Revista Română de Drept Comparat* 165

SCHLEHAHN E, 'Die Methodik des Standard-Datenschutzmodells im Bereich der öffentlichen Sicherheit und Justiz' (2018) 42 *Datenschutz und Datensicherheit* 32

SCHREURS W et al, 'Cogitas, Ergo Sum. The Role of Data Protection Law and Non-Discrimination Law in Group Profiling in the Private Sector' in M Hildebrandt and S Gutwirth (eds), *Profiling the European Citizen: Cross-Disciplinary Perspectives* (Springer Netherlands 2008)

SIEGEL E, *Predictive Analytics: The Power to Predict Who Will Click, Buy, Lie, or Die* (Wiley 2016)

SNOWDEN E, *Permanent Record* (Macmillan 2019)

SPECHT L and MANTZ R (eds), *Handbuch Europäisches und deutsches Datenschutzrecht* (CH Beck 2019)

STERN R, 'At a Crossroads? Reflections on the Right to Asylum for European Union Citizens' (2014) 33 *Refugee Survey Quarterly* 54

SVANTESSON DJB, 'Extraterritoriality and Targeting in EU Data Privacy Law: The Weak Spot Undermining the Regulation' (2015) 5 *International Data Privacy Law* 226

SWAIN A, 'Increasing Migration Pressure and Rising Nationalism: Implications for Multilateralism and SDG Implementation', paper prepared for the Development Policy Analysis Division of the United Nations, Department of Economics and Social Affairs (June 2019)

TAKLE M, 'The Treaty of Lisbon and the European Border Control Regime' (2012) 8 *Journal of Contemporary European Research* 280

TRACOL X, 'EU–U.S. Privacy Shield: The Saga Continues' (2016) 32 *Computer Law & Security Review* 775

TRAUNER F and RIPOLL SERVENT A, 'The Communitarization of the Area of Freedom, Security and Justice: Why Institutional Change Does Not Translate into Policy Change' (2016) 54 *Journal of Common Market Studies* 1417

TRIMIKLINIOTIS N, *Migration and the Refugee Dissensus in Europe: Borders, Security and Austerity* (Routledge 2020)

TSOURDI E, 'Holding the European Asylum Support Office Accountable for its Role in Asylum Decision-Making: Mission Impossible? Border Justice: Migration and Accountability for Human Rights Violations' (2020) 21 *German Law Journal* 506

UKROW J, 'Data Protection without Frontiers? On the Relationship between EU GDPR and Amended CoE Convention 108' (2018) 4 *European Data Protection Law Review* 239

URQUHART L, SAILAJA N and MCAULEY D, 'Realising the Right to Data Portability for the Domestic Internet of Things' (2018) 22 *Personal and Ubiquitous Computing* 317

VAN ALSENOY B, 'Reconciling the (Extra) Territorial Reach of the GDPR with Public International Law' in G Vermeulen and E Lievens (eds), *Data Protection and Privacy under Pressure: Transatlantic Tensions, EU Surveillance, and Big Data* (Maklu 2021)

VAN BRAKEL R, MOLINER L and CLAVELL G, 'Surveillance: Ambiguities and Asymmetries' (2015) 13 *Surveillance & Society* 324

VAN BRAKEL R and VAN DER SLOOT B, 'Pre-emptive Big Data Surveillance and its (Dis)Empowering Consequences: The Case of Predictive Policing' (2016) DOI:10.2139/ssrn.2772469

VAN DEN BULCK P, 'Transfers of Personal Data to Third Countries' (2017) 18 *ERA Forum* 229

VAN DER SLOOT B, 'Privacy in the Post-NSA Era: Time for a Fundamental Revision?' (2014) 5 *Journal of Intellectual Property, Information Technology and E-Commerce Law* 1

——, 'Legal Consistency after the General Data Protection Regulation and the Police Directive' (2018) 9 *European Journal of Law and Technology* 1

VAN HOUTUM H and LACY RB, 'The Migration Map Trap: On the Invasion Arrows in the Cartography of Migration' (2020) 15 *Mobilities* 196

VAVOULA N, *The European Commission Package of ETIAS Consequential Amendments: Substitute Impact Assessment, PE 642.808 – December 2019* (Publications Office 2019)

——, 'Databases for Non-EU Nationals and the Right to Private Life' in F Bignami (ed), *EU Law in Populist Times: Crises and Prospects* (Cambridge University Press 2020)

——, 'Interoperability of EU Information Systems: The Deathblow to the Rights to Privacy and Personal Data Protection of Third-Country Nationals?' (2020) 26 *European Public Law* 131

——, *Immigration and Privacy in the Law of the European Union: The Case of Information Systems* (Brill Nijhoff 2022)

VAVOULA N and MITSILEGAS V, 'Strengthening Europol's Mandate: A Legal Assessment of the Commission's Proposal to Amend the Europol Regulation', PE 694.200, May 2021

Vermeulen G and Lievens E, *Data Protection and Privacy under Pressure: Transatlantic Tensions, EU Surveillance, and Big Data* (Maklu 2017)

Vermeulen M and Bellanova R, 'European "Smart" Surveillance: What's at Stake for Data Protection, Privacy and Non-discrimination?' (2013) 23 *Security & Human Rights* 297

Vogiatzoglou P et al, 'From Theory to Practice: Exercising the Right of Access under the Law Enforcement and PNR Directives' (2020) 11(3) *Journal of Intellectual Property, Information Technology and E-Commerce Law* 274

Voigt P and von dem Bussche A, *The EU General Data Protection Regulation (GDPR): A Practical Guide* (Springer 2017)

Völkel JC, 'Money for Nothing, the Cricks for Free: Five Paradoxes in EU Migration Policy' (2014) 2 *Comparative Migration Studies* 151

——, 'When Interior Ministers Play Diplomats' in A Jünemann, N Scherer and N Fromm (eds), *Fortress Europe? Challenges and Failures of Migration and Asylum Policies* (Springer Fachmedien Wiesbaden 2017)

Votoupalová M, 'Schengen Cooperation: What Scholars Make of it' (2020) 35 *Journal of Borderlands Studies* 403

Vradis A et al, 'Governing Mobility in Times of Crisis: Practicing the Border and Embodying Resistance in and beyond the Hotspot Infrastructure' (2020) 38 *Environment and Planning D: Society and Space* 981

Wachter S, 'The GDPR and the Internet of Things: A Three-Step Transparency Model' (2018) 10 Law, *Innovation and Technology* 266

Wachter S, Mittelstadt B and Floridi L, 'Why a Right to Explanation of Automated Decision-Making Does Not Exist in the General Data Protection Regulation' (2017) 7 *International Data Privacy Law* 76

Weyembergh A, Armada I and Briere C, 'Competition or Cooperation: State of Play and Future Perspectives on the Relations between Europol, Eurojust and the European Judicial Network' (2015) 6 *New Journal of European Criminal Law* 258

Wilson D, 'Marginalizing Migrants: Illegality, Racialization, and Vulnerability' in E Goode (ed), *The Handbook of Deviance* (Wiley-Blackwell 2015)

Winter H and Joachim B, 'Verkennend Onderzoek De Verwerking van Politiegegevens in Vijf Europese Landen – Exploratory Study on the Processing of Police Data in Five EU Member States' (Pro Facto, University of Groningen, 20 November 2020)

Zarsky T, 'The Data Mining Balancing Act' in S Gutwirth et al (eds), *European Data Protection: In Good Health?* (Springer Netherlands 2012)

——, 'Transparent Predictions' (2013) 2013 *University of Illinois Law Review* 68

Zarsky T, 'Incompatible: The GDPR in the Age of Big Data' (2017) 47 *Seton Hall Law Review* 995

INDEX

Lightning Source UK Ltd.
Milton Keynes UK
UKHW030339251122
412821UK00005B/38

9 781509 959631